Second Edition

Endless Opportunities for Infant and Toddler Curriculum

A Relationship-Based Approach

Sandra H. Petersen
ZERO TO THREE: The National Center for Infants, Toddlers, and Families

Donna S. Wittmer
University of Colorado, Denver

PEARSON

Boston   Columbus   Indianapolis   New York   San Francisco   Upper Saddle River
Amsterdam   Cape Town   Dubai   London   Madrid   Milan   Munich   Paris   Montreal   Toronto
Delhi   Mexico City   São Paulo   Sydney   Hong Kong   Seoul   Singapore   Taipei   Tokyo

Vice President and Editorial Director: Jeffery W. Johnston
Senior Acquisitions Editor: Julie Peters
Editorial Assistant: Andrea Hall
Vice President, Director of Marketing: Margaret Waples
Senior Marketing Manager: Christopher D. Barry
Senior Managing Editor: Pamela D. Bennett
Project Manager: Sheryl Langner
Production Manager: Laura Messerly
Senior Art Director: Jayne Conte
Cover Designer: Bruce Kenselaar
Photo Coordinator: Carol Sykes
Cover Art: Shutterstock
Full-Service Project Management: Munesh Kumar/Aptara®, Inc.
Composition: Aptara®, Inc.
Printer/Binder: Edwards Brothers Malloy
Cover Printer: LeHigh Phoenix
Text Font: ITC Berkeley Oldstyle Std 11/13

Credits and acknowledgments for material borrowed from other sources and reproduced, with permission, in this textbook appear on the appropriate page within the text.

Every effort has been made to provide accurate and current Internet information in this book. However, the Internet and information posted on it are constantly changing, so it is inevitable that some of the Internet addresses listed in this textbook will change.

Photo Credits: Natalia Olejarnik, pp. 3, 31, 45, 54, 59, 74, 82, 84, 135, 142, 162, 169, 176; Dawn Brackpool, pp. 7, 9, 33, 68, 119, 128, 210, 213, 242, 278; Krista Greco/Merrill, pp. 14, 17, 20, 35, 40, 53, 55–58, 61, 84, 88, 99, 105, 113, 115, 123, 140, 149, 151, 158, 177, 183, 189, 199, 218, 224, 241, 255; Emily Adams, pp. 28, 33, 206, 268; Donna Wittmer, pp. 37, 48, 59, 64, 67, 103, 173, 200, 220, 234, 264

Library of Congress Cataloging-in-Publication Data

Petersen, Sandra H.
    Endless opportunities for infant and toddler curriculum : a relationship-based approach / Sandra H. Petersen, Donna S. Wittmer.—2nd ed.
        p. cm.
    ISBN-13: 978-0-13-261312-5
    ISBN-10: 0-13-261312-3
1. Education, Preschool—Curricula—United States—Handbooks, manuals, etc. 2. Child care—United States—Planning—Handbooks, manuals, etc. 3. Curriculum planning—United States—Handbooks, manuals, etc. 4. Child development—United States—Handbooks, manuals, etc. I. Wittmer, Donna Sasse. II. Title.
LB1140.4.P48 2013
372.19—dc23

                                                                                            2012020543

10 9 8 7 6 5 4 3 2 1

ISBN 10:   0-13-261312-3
ISBN 13: 978-0-13-261312-5

This book is dedicated to children close to our hearts and children we see in different moments throughout our days. We learn from each of you and thank you for the windows you give us into how you see the world.

Preface

Endless Opportunities for Infant and Toddler Curriculum is designed to help infant/toddler care teachers plan a responsive and relationship-based curriculum. This is a practical book. It connects information about development and learning to how you, the teacher, make decisions about what you do. It will help you to observe infants and toddlers and respond in ways that promote their learning and deepen their relationships with you, their parents, and others. This book will help you to translate knowledge of development into effective, individualized curriculum.

Endless Opportunities for Infant and Toddler Curriculum directs the care teacher to appreciate that learning for infants and toddlers occurs in spontaneous moments and through brief interactions. Each shared expression of surprise or joy is a moment of learning. Infants and toddlers need many experiences from which to learn. They need many moments with each other, and they need many moments of meaningful language. With a little encouragement and support, infants and toddlers will make good use of the world's endless opportunities for learning and relationships!

WHAT IS NEW TO THIS EDITION?

There are several new pieces in this edition that will deepen the care teacher's understanding of development and inclusive programming.

- Each chapter now begins with Learning Outcomes developed around the "Respect, Reflect, and Relate" process.

- The vignettes of teachers and children in each group include a child with a significant disability and are also served by either an early mental health specialist or an early intervention team. This gives the new care teacher an idea about working with consultants. They also discuss practices that are considered or implemented for cultural reasons.

- Each development chapter has a small chart of developmental possibilities, giving the care teacher an idea of what typical development looks like in this age group.

- New action-oriented boldface subheads in Opportunities sections clarify and highlight intentional teaching strategies.

- Each chapter ends with Reflections questions, Applications, and a list of additional Resources.

- Each development chapter now has a section on theories and current research to help ground practice—the "why"—in the "what."

- New photos.

Who Can Use This Book?

This book will help the care teacher answer the question, "How will I *make decisions on Monday* that truly come from the child's interests?" This is not an activity book that will tell the care teacher *what to do* on Monday.

This book should be useful to college instructors and students by delivering research-based information on development through the stories of three age-based, inclusive groups. Each group has one child with significant disabilities. The programs are relationship-based, and the infant care teachers' decisions are guided by providing foundations for programming, such as ways of working with families, maintaining a safe and relationship-based environment, an approach to guidance, and using ongoing assessment for program planning. The chapters on development illustrate infant care teachers using an observation, assessment, and planning cycle to guide their decision making.

Child development and early childhood education students will be introduced to how responsive relationships and the care teacher's decisions are based on observation of each child. Graduate students who have a developmental background but no training in developing infant/toddler curriculum also will find this book useful.

Care teachers and home family care providers who are new to infant/toddler care will learn how to plan curriculum. Early Head Start teachers and home visitors will find several options for producing individualized lesson plans that reflect the child's interests and meet the criteria of the Head Start Program Performance Standards.

THEORIES AND BELIEFS

This text is based on several beliefs derived from the major theories of development:

- Infants and toddlers need responsive relationships because emotional development is the foundation of all later learning—an extension of Bowlby and Ainsworth's attachment theory (Ainsworth, Blehar, Waters, & Wall, 1978; Bowlby, 1969).

- The primary work of infant/toddler care teachers is to support the parent-child relationship—an extension of Bronfenbrenner's bio-ecological model (Bronfenbrenner, 2004).

- Infants and toddlers construct their knowledge of their world through their experiences—an extension of Piaget's and Bruner's constructionist models of learning (Bruner, 1996; Piaget, 1954).

- The construction of knowledge evolves within each child because of inherent abilities to build mental representations of objects, people, places, and events—an extension of Spelke's core knowledge systems (Spelke, 2000; Spelke & Kinzler, 2007).

- Infant/toddler care teachers guide children's learning through their own interactions and by providing an engaging, responsive, developmentally appropriate environment—an extension of Vygotsky's sociocultural model and Hinde's relationship-based theory (Hinde, 1992; Vygotsky, 1962).

- Infant/toddler care teachers need age-specific knowledge about development and need the skills of relationship-based, reflective practice—an extension of Erikson's stages of development (Erikson, 1950).

THEMES OF THIS BOOK

- Importance of relationships and responsiveness to brain development and learning
- Importance of culture and individual needs in curriculum planning
- Importance of observation
- Importance of collaborating with families
- Importance of reflection on teaching practices
- Importance of inclusive classrooms
- Running case study vignettes to illustrate high-quality practices
- Importance of continuity of care, primary caregiving, and low ratios

ORGANIZATION OF THIS BOOK

This book is different from other curriculum books in many ways. It is designed to help care teachers focus on their own decision-making process.

Part One: A Responsive, Relationship-Based Approach

The first section addresses how to bring relationship-based practices to larger program issues, including:

- Engaging families
- Responsive, safe, and healthy care-giving routines
- Creating environments
- Guidance and relationship realignments
- Using observation and documentation for responsive planning and ongoing assessment

Part Two: Opportunities for Relationships and Learning

This section provides curricular suggestions based on infant/toddler development and interests in the following areas:

- Attachment and emotional development
- Social development
- Learning
- Language, literacy, and music
- Creativity, symbolic play, and sensory development
- Fine motor development
- Movement development
- Learning about the outdoors

RESPECT, REFLECT, AND RELATE

This book describes a three-step process for care teachers to use in making decisions, planning for children, guidance, and working with families. The steps are:

- *Respect:* Using inquiring observation
- *Reflect:* Thinking about one's own experience and the experience of others
- *Relate:* Choosing a response that supports learning and the relationship

Using the "Respect, Reflect, and Relate" process, each chapter on the developmental domains begins with Respect, briefly introducing the major concepts theories, and current research for infants and toddlers in that domain. The next section, Reflect, offers a set of questions for thinking about development in that domain. The third section, Relate, is divided into the three age groups we use in this book: young infants, mobile infants, and toddlers and twos. The age groups derive from the major developmental themes of infancy:

- Young infants are motivated by a need for security.
- Mobile infants are driven to explore.
- Toddlers and twos work on issues of identity formation (Lally et al., 2003)

Each Relate section begins with a short statement about the age group and the effect of developmental themes. A scenario describing an infant care teacher and the four children for whom he or she is providing primary care follows. These are titled "A Glimpse of …" in the chapters.

- The young infant care teacher is a young woman named Miriam. She cares for:
  - Adara, 3 months, whose parents are immigrants from Jordan
  - Paulo, 4 months, whose family is Latino
  - Jack, 6 months, whose adoptive family is Euro-American but who spent his first four months in an East European orphanage and shows concerning signs of attachment difficulties
  - Takala, 7 months, whose family is Native American

- The mobile infant care teacher is Albert. He cares for:
  - Gemma, 9 months, whose family is Euro-American
  - Lily, 12 months, whose family is Euro-American and who has severe cerebral palsy
  - Radwan, 15 months, whose family is of Arab descent
  - Goro, 16 months, whose family is Japanese

- The toddlers' and twos' care teacher is Selena. She cares for:
  - Chita, 19 months, whose family is Latino
  - Bessie, 2 years, whose family is Euro-American and who has Down syndrome
  - Lan, 21 months, who has immigrated from Vietnam with his family
  - Sam, 30 months, whose family is Euro-American

These children are captured in the scenarios at a moment in time. They are the same age in each scenario, but each scenario concentrates on a different developmental domain. The children demonstrate a greater diversity than is likely to be found in any one program, but they help demonstrate how an infant care teacher needs to address both culture and disability in making decisions. It is assumed that each of these groups is in a program that practices continuity of care so the children are with the same care teacher from early infancy until preschool. Although many programs do not offer any version of continuity of care, the authors feel it is of great importance to quality and relationship-based care and have chosen to illustrate it here.

Emphasizes Decision Making Following the scenario, there is a discussion of decisions made by the care teacher, giving his or her observations of the children, adaptations he or she made because of disability or simply because of varying abilities, and issues that arose because of diversity or culture.

Next, suggestions for providing endless opportunities for learning and relationships are offered. For each age group in each developmental domain, there is a series of statements about development followed by suggested interactions, materials, or activities that would support learning. The following example comes from the chapter on attachment and emotional development:

Calm young infants quickly so they feel safe.
Young infants are having experiences with adults that provide the foundation for their attachment relationships. They are learning which adults are able to help soothe them when they are upset and help them to feel safe.

- Become a sensitive and accurate reader of each young infant's cues. Learn how each baby likes to be soothed and comforted. Quickly respond to a baby's cries and other signals of distress and help him to regulate his reactions and become calm (Siegel, 1999).
- Keep the environment calm and safe. A calm environment is tidy, does not have too many bright colors, and is checked continuously for safety.
- Spend time reflecting on your own early relationships. The research on attachment says that the strongest predictor of a child's attachment to his parents is how the parents have made sense of their own lives (Siegel, 1999, p. 6). This certainly applies to infant care teachers, as well.

Other Special Features

In the toddlers' and twos' section, there are also lists of suggested "Books for Babies." These are books that babies will enjoy and that reflect the chapter topic.

The last item in each age grouping is an opportunity to practice planning for the individual or the group for that developmental domain. Several planning guides are provided with directions for use.

The sections on adaptations for special needs include examples of working with a mental health consultant and members of an early intervention team.

Each chapter has a short table giving examples of typical development within expected age ranges.

Some information on current theories about that domain provide background in each chapter.

At the end of each chapter are three more special features: an inventory of teacher practices, reflection and application questions, and a resources list. The inventory encourages care teachers to self-observe and reflect on their practices in that area of learning. The questions can be used by an individual or for group discussion in a classroom. The additional resources provide information that may be of interest to the student.

TERMINOLOGY

Throughout the book, we use the term infant/toddler care teachers to refer to the adults who care for infants and toddlers in groups. The term is in increasingly popular use as a way to acknowledge that the work of the adult combines nurturance and providing learning opportunities.

ACKNOWLEDGMENTS

Developing a book that provides concrete steps to planning responsive teaching and caregiving has been a challenge. We would like to thank the many people who contributed to this effort.

This book would not have come to fruition without the guidance of Julie Peters, our Acquisitions Editor at Pearson. We thank her for her wisdom, her advice, and her knowledge of how to make a book accessible to all. We would like to thank the reviewers: Traci D. Delen, Pierce College; Irina Falls, University of North Carolina at Pembroke; Tracy L. Keyes, Kutztown University; Tara Mathien, Harper College; Amelia K. Moody, University of North Carolina at Wilmington; and Kimberly M. Ray, Borough of Manhattan Community College, who provided meticulous and immensely helpful reviews of the text as it was in process. We thank the infants, the toddlers, their teachers, and their families for their willingness to share their children with you and us.

We also thank our husbands, daughters, sons-in-law, and grandchildren who know how passionate we are about our relationships with them. They have supported us as we spent many hours trying to make responsive, relationship-based care real, visible, and attainable.

We hope that this book paints a picture of responsive, relationship-based care that readers will carry with them as they parent, care for, teach, and construct quality environments for infants and toddlers. We hope that infants and toddlers will experience the joy of love and learning forever.

REFERENCES

Ainsworth, M. D., Blehar, M. C., Waters, E., & Wall, S. (1978). *Patterns of attachment: A psychological study of the strange situation.* Hillsdale, NJ: Erlbaum.

Bowlby, J. (1969). *Attachment and loss: Vol. 1: Attachment.* New York: Basic Books.

Bronfenbrenner, U. (2004). *Making human beings human: Bioecological perspectives on human development.* Thousand Oaks, CA: Sage Publications.

Bruner, J. (1996). What we have learned about early learning. *European Early Childhood Education Research Journal, 4*(1), 5–16.

Erikson, E. (1950). *Childhood and society.* New York: Norton.

Hinde, R. (1992). Ethological and relationship approaches. In R. Vasta, *Six theories of child development: Revised formulations and current issues* (pp. 251–285). London: JKP Press.

Lally, J. R., Griffin, A., Fenichel, E., Segal, M., Szanton, E., & Weissbourd, B. (2003). *Caring for infants and toddlers in groups.* Washington, DC: ZERO TO THREE Press.

Piaget, J. (1954). *The construction of reality in the child.* New York: Basic Books.

Siegel, D. (1999). *The developing mind: How relationships and the brain interact to shape who we are.* New York: Guilford.

Spelke, E. (2000, November). Core knowledge. *American Psychologist,* 1233–1243.

Spelke, E., & Kinzler, K. (2007). Core knowledge. *Developmental Science, 10*(1), 89–96.

Vygotsky, L. S. (1962). *Thought and language.* Cambridge: MIT.

Brief Contents

Contents

Chapter 5   **Endless Opportunities for Guidance and Relationship Realignments   64**

Chapter 6   **Using Observation and Documentation for Responsive Planning and Ongoing Assessment   82**

Chapter 12   **Opportunities for Fine Motor Development and Learning   218**

A Responsive, Relationship-Based Approach

1

1

Relationships as the Basis for Curriculum

After reading this chapter, you will be able to:

- RESPECT
  - Explain what infants and toddlers are learning
  - Explain how infants and toddlers learn
  - Describe how relationships support brain development
  - Discuss the elements of a relationhip
  - Describe the "Respect, Reflect, and Relate" process

- REFLECT
  - Consider the many ways in which relationships are important for infants and toddlers
  - Review how the foundations of early learning are established
- RELATE
  - Understand the effect of early caregiving experiences
  - Know how to participate in responsive relationships

Often, directors cite the adage "the baby is the curriculum" or "the baby chooses his own curriculum" to describe their infant/toddler programs to visitors. But what exactly does this mean? What is curriculum for infants and toddlers? What is the infant care teacher's role in creating a learning environment and being a good relationship partner? What do you do if the child "chooses his own curriculum"? Are the children really learning—or are they "only" playing?

ARE INFANTS AND TODDLERS LEARNING?

In the first 3 years of life, infants and toddlers learn the following:

- What it is like to be in relationships and how to engage with others
- To express their own feelings and understand the feelings of others
- Who they are as individuals, members of a family, and members of a community and culture
- To use their bodies to move through space, to handle objects for exploration, and to meet their needs
- To use language, gestures, and facial expressions for meaningful communication
- To participate in friendships with peers
- To use pictures, written and spoken words, and pretend play in a beginning foundation of literacy
- To be enthusiastic, capable learners

HOW DO INFANTS AND TODDLERS LEARN?

Infants and toddlers learn through actively engaging with other people and with materials in their environment. They watch, touch, taste, and listen. They wonder what things are and how they work. Their curiosity is endless. You can watch them as they try to make things happen. For example, an infant may want to see what her feet do as she holds her own toes. A crawling infant may want to see how a friend reacts when he clutches her hair in his hand. A toddler may want to figure out how to get what appears to be out of reach. Your actions and reactions as a care teacher guide them as they learn.

When supported in their learning by adults who help just enough in responsive ways, infants and toddlers feel confident to pursue independent explorations. In doing so, they develop the following basic learning processes that cut across all domains, or areas, of development:

- Maintaining attention
- Curiosity
- Memory
- Gathering information
- Solving problems
- Persistence through frustration

These learning processes apply as much to an infant who is using his or her hands to balance her body while sitting as they do to the toddler who is using language to communicate needs and desires. Learning in any area depends on the ability to wonder, to pay attention, to remember experiences, and to use information to meet one's needs or interests. These processes are often referred to as "Approaches to Learning" in state early learning guidelines and the Head Start Child Development and Early Learning Framework.

A current theory of learning suggests that all of this learning is possible because human beings are born with "systems of core knowledge" that provide the foundation for learning skills and developing beliefs (Spelke, 2000; Spelke & Kinzler, 2007). The core knowledge systems are the "building blocks" of learning (Spelke, 2000, p. 1240). This theory suggests that infants are born with an ability to pay attention to the things that are important in their environment, which helps them learn from their early experiences.

WHAT IS INFANT/TODDLER CURRICULUM?

Infant/toddler curriculum, then, is every interaction and experience that supports the child's natural desire to explore and learn. Infant/toddler curriculum does not consist merely of infant care teachers doing activities with infants and toddlers. It is much broader, deeper, and more important than that. Curriculum for infants and toddlers emphasizes the social and physical environment of learning rather than the content of learning, which most people associate with elementary and secondary school.

> Responsive curriculum planning focuses on finding strategies to help infant/toddler teachers search for, support, and keep alive children's internal motivation to learn, and their spontaneous explorations of people and things of interest and importance to them. (Lally, 2000)

Ron Lally, a developmental psychologist and a leader in the infant/toddler care and education field, identifies the following 10 factors to consider when developing a curriculum for infants and toddlers. Each of these is addressed throughout this book:

1. Infancy has three stages.
2. Infants learn holistically.
3. Relationships are primary for development.
4. Infants develop their first sense of self through contact with others.
5. Home culture is an important part of a child's developing identity.
6. Infants are active, self-motivated learners.
7. Infants are not all alike—they are individuals with unique temperaments.
8. Language skills and habits develop early.
9. Environments are powerful.
10. Adults exhibit strong emotions and opinions when entrusted with the care of infants. (Lally, 2000, n.p.)

Curriculum planning begins with an understanding of the three stages of infancy and their dominant areas of interest: young infants (ages birth to 9 months)—security; mobile infants (ages 8 to 18 months)—exploration; and toddlers and twos (ages 16 to 36 months)—a growing sense of identity. Experiences and interactions are offered in ways that encourage learning in multiple domains. For example, a 7-month-old infant sits (large motor), playing with stacking cups (fine motor and cognitive), near another infant the same age (social) with the encouragement of the care teacher (emotional and language).

Infants and toddlers rely on their relationships with adults to feel secure, to focus their attention and learn from their experiences, and to have their routine bodily needs met. Through these relationships, the infant or toddler develops a sense of personal identity and of how people in his or her culture interact.

Infants and toddlers are curious, so they want to understand the elements of their environment. They approach the world in unique ways, and they are voracious learners. In the course of caring for and raising infants, parents and care teachers may differ in their ideas about what is the right thing to do. These differences, whenever they occur, need to be explored and resolved.

EARLY EXPERIENCES AND THE BRAIN

The infant's brain develops quickly in the womb, following the blueprint laid out by the child's genetic makeup. If the womb is free of toxins and the mother is in a physically and socially healthy environment, the brain will create its first neural circuits (or connections) correctly, producing the physical foundation for all later learning (National Scientific Council on the Developing Child, 2004). Both in the womb and after birth, the brain produces far more connections, called *synapses,* than will ever be used. Each synapse is formed as the senses take in and register information. If the child has repeated experiences, such as seeing his or her father day after day, the child's brain will strengthen the connections that have information and memories about these experiences. If the child has an isolated, unemotional experience, such as passing a stranger at a bus stop, the memory will be recorded; but after a while, that circuit will be "pruned," or lost from lack of use.

The development of the brain, which provides the physical circuitry for learning, is determined by genetics, the presence or absence of toxins, and the child's earliest experiences (2004). One of the most well known, prevalent, and dangerous toxins is lead, which, through intrauterine exposure or ingestion of lead paint, can significantly reduce the fetus's, infant's, or toddler's Mental Development Index (Hu et al., 2006). The external environment is not the only source of toxins, however. Brain researchers have found that hormones produced by the mother's emotions during pregnancy can be extremely damaging to the formation of the child's brain. The bodies of women who live in dangerous or chaotic situations produce high amounts of cortisone and adrenaline. These hormones change the developing infant's brain structure, making the child hypervigilant to danger and damaging the capacity to learn (National Scientific Council on the Developing Child, 2007). If the infant or toddler then lives in a violent or chaotic environment, the child's body will produce those same hormones, which will inflict more damage on the developing brain.

Our current understanding of learning and brain development has important implications for teachers. Infants and toddlers need to be in safe environments, receiving appropriate nutrition, with affectionate, responsive adults. The child needs to feel safe in order to keep his or her brain's "hormonal bath" healthy. The adults need to help the young infant be calm and alert during his waking moments.

In order to pay attention to and learn from toys and objects or interactions, infants and toddlers need to manage—or regulate—their reactions to events, feelings, or their own bodily experiences. As they gain control of their bodies, with the help of adults, they then can spend more time paying attention to the things around them (LeDoux, 2000; Panksepp, 2000). Research is showing strong connections between the parts of the brain that regulate emotion and those that are involved with aspects of cognitive development such as planning, problem solving, and decision making. Emotions, when well regulated, support early learning processes; however, emotions also can "interfere with attention and decision making when they are poorly controlled" (National Scientific Council on the Developing Child, 2004, p. 6).

ADULTS' ROLES IN INFANT/ TODDLER LEARNING

Nurturing, caring, safe relationships with adults provide the context that infants and toddlers need in order to learn. When we talk about adults, we mean care teachers, home visitors, parents, center directors, and others who interact

Sometimes a care teacher supports learning by joining a game devised by a toddler.

with the infant or toddler. Adults provide information about the emotional tone and safety of a situation, about cultural values and roles, about how people behave toward one another, and about how things work. Sensitive adults provide environments that are engaging and responsive without being excessively stimulating. For infants and toddlers, the adults provide the space for learning.

Adults support learning by making good decisions when they consider *what* a child is trying to do or learn and *how* the child is going about the task. Adults need to be able to see and appreciate the strategies that infants and toddlers use in their learning. Infants and toddlers bring their own questions or ideas of problems that they want to solve in their learning. Adults, by being an interested, encouraging presence, support the infant's natural abilities as an active learner who constructs knowledge.

HOW ARE RELATIONSHIPS IMPORTANT TO CURRICULUM AND LEARNING?

Relationships are often discussed as being vital for infants and toddlers. In a *relationship,* two people care about each other's well-being, respond to the other's needs, and have mutual feelings of trust. The qualities of the relationship change and grow with deeper understanding and acceptance of each other's ways.

For infants and toddlers, relationships ideally include consistent experiences of being understood and cared for. The experience of being truly known by another person provides the basic security needed for a healthy sense of identity and the ability to attend to others and learn about the world.

Secure Relationships Encourage Learning

Infants and toddlers need ongoing, responsive, and warm relationships as they work to achieve the basic developmental themes of this age period: security, exploration, and the formation of identity (Lally et al., 2003). Young infants grow to trust adults with whom they have relationships over time. If an adult is able to understand the infant, consistently help him or her feel comfortable, and keep her or him safe, the infant develops a sense of security in the relationship and trust in his or her ability to summon help. This sense of security helps the infant feel safe enough to explore while becoming mobile. The ability and permission to explore, in turn, encourage cognitive development. As the infant becomes a toddler, she or he develops a sense of being a competent person who knows how to behave with people in a culturally acceptable way, how to learn about the immediate environment, and how to use language to communicate with others. The developing toddler continues to use his or her secure relationships as a personal sense of identity forms.

Relationships Matter in Group Care

Studies have found that a higher quality of care is consistently related to better child outcomes. Researchers studying the central features of quality care have identified the following factors as critical: the relationship between the child and the care provider, and the amount of cognitive and language stimulation provided over the course of the day (Shonkoff & Phillips, 2000). In fact, one of the core concepts of development that came from a rigorous review of all current child development research was the following: "Human relationships, and the effects of relationships on relationships, are the building blocks of healthy development" (Shonkoff & Phillips, 2000, p. 314). Children need *continuity of care* for meaningful relationships to develop. Continuity of care means that a child is with the same home provider or care teacher for long periods of time, ideally the entire first 3 years of life. In one study, 91 percent of children who had been with their teacher for more than a year had secure attachments, compared to 67 percent who had been with their teacher for 9–12 months and 50 percent who had been with their teacher for 5–8 months (Raikes, 1993). Each child can focus and learn because he or she experiences caregiving that includes holding or hugging the child to provide comfort, engaging the child in prolonged conversation, or playing interactively with the child. Each child feels secure when caregivers are sensitive (warm, attentive, and engaged) rather than harsh (critical, threatens children, and punitive) or detached (exhibiting low levels of interaction) (Howes & Hamilton, 1992).

Dimensions of Relationships

Relationships develop over long periods of time, involve mutual caring and trust, and have a wide variety of kinds and qualities of interactions. Hinde's relationship-based theory defines relationships according to the following dimensions:

- *Content of the interactions:* You establish routines, show affection, play, provide guidance, and share interests and experiences . . . with a pleasant emotional tone.
- *Diversity of the interactions:* You share a wide range of interactions—conversation, walks, singing, routines—using each to achieve moments of closeness.

- *Qualities of the interactions:* You are sensitive to the infants' and toddlers' cues. You perceive their signals, correctly interpret them, select an appropriate response, and deliver the response in a timely, contingent manner.

- *Meanings of interactions:* There are different meanings to the infant or toddler if you touch him when you understand from his signals that he wants close contact rather than because you feel like holding a baby.

- *Usefulness of interactions:* You are able to coordinate with and build on the child's behavior to achieve mutual goals such as feeding, comforting, or making each other laugh.

- *Intimacy:* You maintain a warm emotional tone, a desire for closeness, a sense of security in the presence of the other, and a willingness to act on behalf of the well-being of the other.

- *Interpersonal perception:* You support how each partner feels the relationship affects him or herself.

- *Commitment:* You act on the other's behalf and work for the other's well-being in a relationship that endures over time. (Hinde, 1992)

This care teacher is supporting this toddler's arrival at child care. Later in the day, she will nurture, comfort, play with, and read to the child, and help negotiate conflicts. Their relationship has many dimensions.

RESPECT, REFLECT, AND RELATE

This book offers a relationship-based process of "Respect, Reflect, and Relate" to help you, the infant/toddler care teacher, develop reflective and responsive practices. You can use this process both in the moment and over time in your planning to support children in all the developmental domains as you observe and document their activities and provide guidance.

Respect involves observing infants and toddlers with a desire to understand their interests, feelings, and intentions.

Reflect describes your thought process as you wonder about the infant's or toddler's intentions, examine your own internal responses, and determine how you might best respond to the child.

Relate explains the actions that the infant/toddler care teacher takes (or chooses not to take) to best serve the relationship and the infant's or toddler's intention.

An example of how a care teacher used the "Respect, Reflect, and Relate" process *in the moment* involves a 2-year-old who was building an elaborate structure in the block area. An 18-month-old moved into the area with the clear intention of knocking down the structure. The care teacher moved between the two children and asked the younger one if she would like to build a tower and knock it down. The child accepted gladly, happy to build and to have the adult's attention. This teacher *respected* the intentions of both children, the one who was creating the intricate block structure and the child who wanted to knock down blocks. She *reflected*, in the moment, on what each child wanted to accomplish and how she might best support those efforts. She then *related* to each child by supporting them in completing their intended actions, using language to enrich the experience, and being emotionally attuned to their experiences. She shared the excitement of knocking down blocks with the younger child and the pride of accomplishment with the older child. She also supported the peer relationship by diverting the younger child and helping the children to work near each other without one destroying the other's structure.

Care teachers can also use the "Respect, Reflect, and Relate" model to plan for infants and toddlers *over time*. They observe the children's interests, goals, needs, and strategies for learning and relate by adapting their interactions and the environment to the children. When care teachers plan in this way, they are creating a responsive, relationship-based program.

THE CARE TEACHER AS A PROFESSIONAL

For many years, caring for children was not seen as a profession, and caring for infants and toddlers in groups was often seen as bad practice. Women increasingly expect to be in the workforce as well as to raise families; so, as scientists continue to learn about the fundamental importance of the first 3 years of life, the infant-toddler care teacher's role increasingly is becoming a professional one. In the spring of 2011, Great Start DC (2011) published a report titled "Preparing Our Infant and Toddler Professional Workforce for the 21st Century." In it, they list the following research-based core knowledge and competencies needed to do this unique work:

- A disposition toward working with very young children
- Knowledge of child development and learning
- The ability to create a stimulating, nurturing, and language-rich early learning environment
- An understanding of relationships and interactions with infants and toddlers
- Skills in child observation and documentation
- An understanding of special needs and how to promote inclusion
- Knowledge of health, nutrition, and safety
- An understanding of partnership with families
- Cultural competence
- Professionalism
- Administration and supervision skills

Taken together, these qualities describe a well-trained person whose profession has a large body of skills and knowledge to be mastered and who also possesses the personal qualities needed to provide intimate, responsive care to highly vulnerable young children. At this point in history, care teachers are expected to use observation and assessment, as well as their own knowledge of child development, to plan for individualized learning experiences. Care teachers are required to successfully include children with special needs and keep all children safe and healthy. Care teachers also must be capable of engaging in and valuing relationships with infants, toddlers, and their families—all the while supporting the relationship between the young child and his or her family above all else.

A body of knowledge and skills is an important part of any profession; so, too, is a code of ethics. In 2011, the National Association for the Education of Young Children (NAEYC) updated their Code of Ethical Conduct for the early childhood care and education profession. The Code of Ethical Conduct is based on the following core values:

- Appreciate childhood as a unique and valuable stage of the human life cycle
- Base our work on knowledge of how children develop and learn
- Appreciate and support the bond between the child and family
- Recognize that children are best understood and supported in the context of family, culture, community, and society
- Respect the dignity, worth, and uniqueness of each individual (child, family member, and colleague)
- Respect diversity in children, families, and colleagues
- Recognize that children and adults achieve their full potential in the context of relationships that are based on trust and respect (NAEYC, 2011, p. 1)

These values display many of the qualities listed earlier in the core knowledge and competencies. The Code of Ethical Conduct is a guide to resolving moral or ethical dilemmas that care teachers may encounter in the field. Reading the entire Code will help you understand and appreciate the depth of professionalism that now enriches our work. The Code is organized into four areas of professional relationships: children, families, colleagues, and communities and society. Care teachers now serve a majority of children under the age of 3 in nonparental care and even more in programs that serve young children and their families together. We are having an effect, for good or ill, on future generations, so we must take our work seriously and honor its effect. We must always attend to the first principle under "Ethical Responsibilities to Children" in the Code of Ethical Conduct:

> *Above all, we shall not harm children. We shall not participate in practices that are emotionally damaging, physically harmful, disrespectful, degrading, dangerous, exploitative, or intimidating to children.*
>
> *This principle has precedence over all others in this Code. (p. 3)*

SUMMARY

Infants actively seek information about themselves, others, and their world. In the first 3 years of life, they learn a great deal about these topics and they establish the basic processes for learning across domains. These include attention, curiosity, memory, gathering information, solving problems, and a desire for mastery. The desire and ability to learn come from a combination of inborn abilities to learn and environmental supports for learning.

Curriculum for infants and toddlers depends on the care teacher's ability to make decisions, both during planning and in the moment, that provide interactions, materials, and activities that support the child's natural interest in learning and exploration. Making good decisions requires that the care teacher have a good understanding of the stages of infancy, what infants are learning, and how infants learn. Care teachers also need to understand the importance of a responsive, ongoing relationship as a context for learning and development in infancy.

"Respect, Reflect, and Relate" is the relationship-based process that guides care teachers' decision making to assure that curriculum decisions are reflective and responsive.

INVENTORY OF TEACHER PRACTICES

Relationships as the Basis for Curriculum

Each chapter in this book includes an inventory of care teacher practices. This inventory is a tool for focusing your own reflections or having your work observed by a coach or mentor. It lists the main concepts of the chapter and asks the care teacher or observer to rate how frequently the care teacher demonstrates these specific practices. The right-most column provides space to make notes on the observed events.

Basic Concepts	A	S	R	Observation/ Reflection
I am aware of the many things infants and toddlers are learning. I watch them, expecting to see learning happening.				
I look for the underlying processes of learning such as curiosity, attention, and a desire for mastery.				
I find ways to support the infant's or toddler's natural desire to explore and learn.				
I use my relationship with each child to encourage their learning by smiling, using words, and celebrating their accomplishments.				
I support each child's ability to pay attention by helping them manage their reactions and feelings.				
I plan for each child with regard to their family's beliefs and values.				
I reflect on the quality of my relationship with each child.				
I use the steps of Respect, Reflect, and Relate in planning curriculum.				

A = Always, S = Sometimes, R = Rarely

REFLECTIONS

1. How does emotional state affect the ability to learn? How would feeling secure help an infant pay attention?
2. Consider the list of dimensions of relationships. Do you have relationships that include all of these dimensions? What is important to you in a relationship?
3. Do you see skills such as attention, memory, information gathering, persistence through frustration, and problem solving as basic to all learning? Describe the connections.

APPLICATIONS

1. Create a list of ways in which a care teacher could/should communicate to an infant or toddler that the teacher was interested in and appreciative of that child's learning?
2. Observe an infant or toddler for 15 to 20 minutes. Use the "Respect, Reflect, and Relate" process as you observe and relate.
3. Create a newsletter for parents explaining the importance of relationships as the basis of learning.

RESOURCES

- Center on the Developing Child at Harvard University.
  The Center's website has several multimedia features (at http://developingchild.harvard.edu/resources/multimedia), including the following:
    Brain Hero
    How Early Experiences Get Into the Body: A Biodevelopmental Framework
    InBrief: Early Childhood Program Effectiveness
    InBrief: The Foundations of Lifelong Health
    InBrief: The Impact of Early Adversity on Children's Development
    InBrief: The Science of Early Childhood Development
  The following two papers are also available on this website:
    National Scientific Council on the Developing Child. (2004). *Young children develop in an environment of relationships: Working Paper No. 1.* Retrieved from http://www.developingchild.harvard.edu
    National Scientific Council on the Developing Child. (2010). *Persistent fear and anxiety can affect young children's learning and development: Working Paper No. 9.* Retrieved from http://www.developingchild.harvard.edu
- NAEYC Code of Ethical Conduct and Statement of Commitment. (2011). Retrieved from http://www.naeyc.org/files/naeyc/file/positions/Ethics%20Position%20Statement2011.pdf
- ZERO TO THREE: Brain Development. Tips and Tools on Brain Development. Retrieved from http://www.naeyc.org/positionstatements/ethical_conduct

2 Opportunities for Engaging Families

After reading this chapter, you will be able to:

- RESPECT
    - Know many alternative ways to communicate with families
    - Identify families who may require your initiative for engagement

- REFLECT
    - Understand the importance of partnership with families
    - Consider specific issues concerning diverse families

- RELATE
    - Have strategies for communicating with families
    - Effectively work with diverse families

Sam's parents were beginning to plan for the transition to preschool. Selena had been his infant care teacher since he was 8 weeks old. It was hard to even imagine raising Sam without her input. Selena had become as important in their lives as she was in Sam's.

Infant/toddler care teachers often have a very close relationship with the families in their programs. They share a genuine concern and affection for the infants and toddlers, and in the best of circumstances, teachers and families develop a strong, mutual partnership.

This partnership can serve the child, the family, the infant care teacher, and the program. These important relationships require ongoing communication, mutual contributions, and, sometimes, concerted efforts to connect with one another. Frequent, open communication between the family and the infant care teacher can take many forms, and it creates the foundation of the relationship among the adults. Creating a reciprocal relationship in which families and infant care teachers both make contributions makes these partnerships more meaningful. Finally, there are several circumstances in which the early care and education program may need to make special efforts to reach out to families. With a good variety of skills and strategies in these areas, infant care teachers and families may create meaningful, valued partnerships.

OPPORTUNITIES FOR COMMUNICATION

The relationship between an infant/toddler care teacher and the child's family can be a complicated one. On one level, the relationship is between a consumer and a service industry; however, it rarely feels like that to the people involved. Infant care teachers develop deep feelings for the babies in their care. Families may be comfortable with, be ambivalent about, or feel very badly about leaving a baby in someone else's care. Programs should utilize every possible means of communication to assure that babies are being handled in ways that are comfortable for families and to assure an ongoing exchange of information.

Daily Exchanges of Information

Most early childhood learning and development programs require parents to sign an attendance sheet, once when they bring their child in and again when they pick their child up at the end of the day. Attendance sheets are useful for tracking attendance, for evacuating children in an emergency, and for assuring that the program can contact a parent on a day when the parent won't be at the regular phone number.

For infants and toddlers, who often do not have words to let their care teacher know that they missed breakfast or were up teething much of the night, a more thorough communication system is needed. Some programs use a "back-and-forth notebook" in which the care teacher notes feedings, diaper changes, nap times, and highlights of the child's day; the family, in turn, notes their current observations of the child and any particular needs of the child for that day. The notebook makes it easy to maintain the confidentiality of any information, but it can be cumbersome and accidentally left behind.

Some programs use a folder for each child, with the care teacher leaving a copy of her notes for the family to take home and providing a place for the family to leave

Box 2.1

Daily Information Exchanges

Infant Care Teacher Notes	Parent Notes

Name: *Jack*   **Date:** *10/1/12*

Feedings: *9:30 – 1/2 banana, 6 oz formula*
          12:00 – rice cereal, 8 oz formula
          2:30 – cereal, 6 oz formula

Diapers: *9:00 – wet*
          10:30 – bm
          12:45 – wet
          3:00 – wet

Napping: *1 – 3 pm*

Highlights: *Trying so hard to crawl! Very interested in toys and other children today.*

Child: *Jack*

Date: *10/1/12*

Breakfast __*x*__ yes _____ no

Regular night's sleep __*x*__ yes _____ no

I want you to know: *Jack bumped his head last night and we could not console him. He fought us off if we held him but then reached for us. He cried for almost 40 minutes. This just doesn't seem natural.*

notes for the teacher (see Box 2.1). The folder helps the program keep any information the family chooses not to share private. This confidentiality may allow families to share information on situations, such as stress or changes at home, that could be causing behavioral issues in an infant or toddler. It also allows the program to leave notes concerning tuition payments that are due or forms that need to be filled out.

Information that doesn't need to be kept confidential may be posted on a bulletin board, making it easy for families to see when they bring in their children. This information might include the general plan for the day, a request for families to contribute some materials for a special project, or documentation of a recent event. This kind of information helps families talk with babies about what they did that day.

Information About Policies

An important aspect of any partnership is having the partners be clear about their expectations of each other. The program should have a Family Handbook or Welcome Packet that clearly explains to families the program policies concerning the following:

- Arrival and departure times
- Payment
- Family participation requirements
- Illness and absence
- People authorized to pick up the child
- Consent forms
- Days the program is closed

Occasional Opportunities for Communication

In addition to established enrollment and daily communications, various effective methods for communicating with families exist. Some programs schedule family–teacher conferences several times a year. These may take the form of a home visit or may be scheduled at the program. Family meetings to discuss the program itself or a special topic provide good opportunities to hear the concerns and interests of family members and provide information. Providing child care, meals, and transportation, if needed, can help make meetings accessible to families. A welcoming attitude will promote a genuine give and take, with everyone's life experience being valued in the group discussion.

The exchange of information between families and programs is essential for children's well-being.

Family–child events, such as an annual picnic or a monthly dinner at the program, give families a chance to meet and socialize. Newsletters (see Box 2.2) can be a very effective method of sharing information.

Another effective way of communicating with families is by offering a *lending library*. This could include books on parenting, books to read with the baby, or developmentally appropriate toys with some ideas about how to play with the infant or toddler.

OPPORTUNITIES FOR PARENT CONTRIBUTIONS

The exchange of information between the families and the program is a fundamental level of partnership, but it doesn't begin to draw on all that families may be willing to contribute to their child's program. Programs vary considerably in how they are run, from the one-person home family provider taking care of two or three infants and toddlers, to corporate chains run by a central administration that could be located in another state. There are ways for all programs, however, to utilize the skills of families and welcome their contributions. These range from reliably providing diapers and breast milk or formula, to serving on a board of directors.

Holding an Image of Family Members

One way in which families may contribute to a program is by providing photographs of themselves for the children to look at during the day. Infants and toddlers may have difficulty remembering what their loved family members look and sound like as the hours in a group setting go by. Babies as young as 4 or 5 months old can enjoy looking at a photo album filled with pictures of their family. The program may be able to laminate family photos for babies to hold, or the photos can be securely taped to the floor or wall. Tape recordings of family members telling stories or singing lullabies may be very comforting, especially if the family's primary language is different from the one used in the program.

Box 2.2

Our Place Child Care Center Newsletter

Infant Room News and Views

Director's note: Our infant room team recently attended a class on infant/toddler care and decided to start their own study group. The first topic selected is brain development. The staff asked if they could share what they are learning in the newsletter and invite any parent who is interested to share their thoughts, information, and responses in the "Learning Journal" on the Parents' Counter. You will also find copies of some of the articles they have chosen to read and Web site addresses where they found some of their favorite information.

—Mary

P.S. They are doing this research on their own time and have discussions over coffee or pizza once a month on Saturdays. They say you are invited to join them if you wish!

Miriam's thoughts —Primary infant care teacher for Adara, Paulo, Jack, and Takala

I have been excited to learn about brain development. In class we learned how important the first three years of life are. The brain is growing fastest from prenatal time to age 3 . . . more than in any other period of our life. It makes my job feel very important. I learned that in the first year of life babies have more connections in their brains to be ready for any experience. Then they are able to prune out some of the extra connections to fit the environment they are growing in. I am amazed at this information.

I also learned about vision from the PBS "Secret Life of the Brain" Web site. Shela and I were both surprised to learn how blurry vision is for infants in the first six months. It changed our way of thinking about how our room is set up. It seems to be a natural way that vision improves as infants learn to change positions by themselves. We are excited to have this information to help us support your children's play and learning experiences.

Want more information on baby vision? Well, go to the Web site yourself: (You can use our office computer if you wish. It's listed in our favorites so it's fast to get to http://www.pbs.org/wnet/brain.) We loved the animation and examples of how the baby's world appears from their point of view. You will too!

We have changed some things in our room. You may have noticed that we have "baby centers" with mirrors and things hanging from the ceiling, different kinds of lighting in areas, some soft, some bright. We are trying to create a place for babies to learn and be interested in things even when we can't be holding them. I have noticed our little **Adara** seems to love the mirror. She will turn her head to look for a long time. I have to put her in another position so her neck won't get hurt from staring too long. She seems to like the books with the black and white pictures in them, too, so we prop those close by.

Paulo is enjoying his new ability to reach and sometimes roll. He is really interested in reaching **Adara** Rolling sometimes seems to be on purpose, but sometimes he rolls and then looks very surprised.

Jack spends lots of time on his knees, rocking back and forth. He likes to look in the mirror and seems surprised to see himself in this new position!

Takala is really mobile—crawling and climbing. We have to change toys quickly because she thoroughly explores and is ready to move on to new adventures!

Please give me your comments about the newsletter. I'll be sharing more as the learning group goes along. Thanks for reading!

—Miriam

Source: Adapted from a class assignment by Melode Mariner with permission from the author.

Being Present

Some programs welcome family members to volunteer and spend time with the children. Simply holding and rocking babies or sitting on the floor reading books or playing can be a wonderful contribution. Families may introduce languages, songs, and baby games from another culture. Some family members may even be able to bring in instruments and play music for the babies.

Family cooperative programs require parents or other family members to spend time in the classroom, and then they count those parents as staff. This has benefits in bringing parents into the classroom but can be problematic in providing a primary, consistent care teacher for each child every day.

Community Advocates

Every family becomes a representative of their early care and education program in the community. Consequently, people will know whether they are happy or not with their program. Programs often fill and create waiting lists just through word-of-mouth endorsements.

Sometimes families go further by using their connections to ask businesses to donate food for parent meetings or gifts of appreciation for program staff. Some families begin to learn about the wider early childhood system and participate in letter writing, visits, or demonstrations to influence the city council or state legislature on issues affecting children.

Participation in Maintaining Quality

Many programs call on parents to help make decisions affecting the quality of the program. Early Head Start and many nonprofit early care and education programs have policy or advisory boards that include parent representation. Some act as a board of directors with decision-making authority. Others have more of an advisory role, leaving decisions to the owner, director, or management team.

Leadership training may help families take meaningful roles as advocates or as members of an advisory board. For many parents, this will be their first experience in being heard in a decision-making process.

Some programs conduct periodic program evaluations, asking all the parents to provide feedback on their satisfaction with their experience. Programs use the information to refine and improve their services.

OPPORTUNITIES FOR REACHING OUT

Some groups of parents may require special knowledge from infant care teachers and special efforts at reaching out to them. Groups that are recognized as needing particular consideration include the following:

- Families whose cultural background, race, or religion is different from those of the care teacher or the majority of the families being served
- Military families with a deployed parent

- Families whose children have disabilities or other special needs
- Families where the adults have mental illness, including maternal depression
- Teen parents
- Same-sex couples
- Parents who are separated or divorced
- Fathers or other significant males

Cultural Differences

Infants and toddlers are constantly integrating their experiences into their sense of who they are, their developing identity. Some of the most important lessons for children in these early years concern their own culture: Children begin to understand that in their culture "this is how we treat other people, how we share food, how we talk to each other, what is encouraged and what is not allowed." Put another way: "The particular integrated ways of using language, thinking, and seeing the world and themselves can only be given to young children by their community" (Sanchez, 1999).

The United States is a country that is becoming increasingly diverse and that is both historically and currently ambivalent about this diversity (Phillips & Crowell, 1994). Infant/toddler programs often are unsure about how to serve children or engage families who have distinctly different cultures, who are not English-speaking, or who differ by race or religion. Sometimes when tension or conflicts arise between care teachers and families, it is because each side comes to the issue with assumptions from their own culture. These assumptions often are so deeply rooted that a person holds them as universal truths while they are, in fact, culturally bound. These ideas may have to do with gender roles, how children address adults or vice versa, or how routine care such as feeding, diapering, or napping should be performed.

Research is showing the importance of the first years of life in identity formation, the importance of cultural belonging to identity, and the cognitive benefits of growing up bilingual, so infant/toddler care teachers need to learn how to reach out to families.

Infant care teachers and families often come across culturally based differences in their beliefs about caring for infants.

The families can show the care teachers how to demonstrate the value of family cultures in the classroom. Reaching out to families may take two different paths. First, the teacher should personally acknowledge differences and demonstrate interest in the family. Second, the group space should be used to show genuine interest in the families by reflecting positive images of the children's cultures throughout the room, materials, and activities.

Ideas for Reaching Out to Families. The following ideas may be useful even when infant/toddler care teachers think they are working with a homogeneous group of families. These ideas open a dialogue on important personal beliefs about infancy and help the care teacher meet the child's expectations of how people behave.

- Ask the family if they use a language other than English at home. Ask them to teach you simple words of affection in their home language. Perhaps they could teach you words of relevance to an infant or toddler, such as *bottle*, *eat*, *hungry*, *diaper*, or *nap*. Feeling words such as *happy* or *sad* would be helpful.

- If the family uses a language other than English in their home and wants the child to learn only English, talk with them about the importance of their child being able to speak comfortably with grandparents and other relatives. Remind them of all they have to teach the child about the world and how important language is in capturing and sharing a worldview.

- Ask families about their child-rearing practices with infants and toddlers. Do they swaddle babies? Do they carry them much of the day or let them play on the floor? Where does the child sleep? In what circumstances do they say "no" and set boundaries for infants or toddlers? How does their child eat? What does their child like to eat?

- Discuss with the family which practices you will be able to integrate into your work, and which you cannot. For example, if a family member tells you to spank a child, you need to be very clear that you will not and that you are forbidden by law to do so.

- Invite family members to visit the program and sing songs, tell stories, or show books or pictures that demonstrate their culture, and, for toddlers, introduce culturally specific foods.

- Talk about the program's goals for children in the first 3 years, discuss differences, and find commonalities. For example, does the program support autonomy while the family values interdependence? Through discussion, the program and the family may realize that they have similar goals about being competent but different ways to achieve them. Some examples include:
  - Does the program want the children toileting by age 3 whereas the family wants them using the toilet by 9 months? Well, they share the common goal of children using the toilet.
  - Is the program comfortable with boys and girls learning to use the toilet together while the family is uncomfortable with different genders being naked together? Here, there are probably common goals about teaching children that parts of their body are private.
  - Does the program encourage floor time and messy play while the family values a clean and tidy appearance? Both probably share a goal about children growing up to be productive and creative.

- Ask the family how they know what the child wants. When a young child uses verbal and nonverbal communication that works within his family and then finds he is not understood by the infant or toddler care teacher, it can be very frustrating. Sanchez warns that this experience offers two distressing messages. The first is, "I am a person who cannot communicate effectively." The second is, "My family's home language and/or home culture is inappropriate or not of value" (Sanchez, 1999, p. 3).

- Learn more about the family's culture, race, language, or religion by visiting their community or home, reading, or talking with others.

Creating a Welcoming Space. If a family enters an infant/toddler program and sees no one among the staff or families of their race or culture, they may feel uncomfortable. Displaying posters, dolls, and books that present their culture in a positive light delivers a message of welcome. So does the staff's willingness to learn words for *hello* and *good-bye* from the family's home language.

All parents will feel welcome if:

- The infant/toddler care teachers greet the child and each family member by name when they enter the child care space.

- There are comfortable, adult-size chairs or sofas for adults to use in the program space.

- Sign-in sheets and other exchanges of information are in a language the parents understand.

- Bulletin boards and newsletters provide information to families in a timely manner.

- There are books for babies that represent different cultures and types of families (see Box 2.3)

Military Families

At a time when so many American soldiers are being deployed overseas, infant/toddler care teachers are finding new ways to support infants and toddlers and the family members remaining at home. Some suggestions for supporting families include:

- Help an infant or toddler prepare for deployment, even if you think he or she cannot understand the language you use. The remaining parent can be encouraged to talk over difficult feelings with an infant or toddler care teacher and then learn how to describe these difficult feelings to the child with simple words: "I'm feeling sad today because Mommy is leaving soon." Maybe the baby won't understand the words, but the parent's emotional tone and expressions will match in a genuine way.

- Help prepare tape recordings of the deploying parent telling stories or singing songs to the baby. Laminate photos of the parent with the infant or toddler and of the family together.

- Take time every day to look at these photos with the child and talk about the deployed parent.

Box 2.3

Books for Babies: Different Cultures

Amy Wilson Sanger's *First Book of World Snacks* series (Tricycle Press):

Sushi	Mangia, mangia
Yum yum dim sum	Let's nosh
Hola jalapeno	A little bit of soul food

Debbie Bailey's *Talk About* books (Annick Press):

Toys	Grandpa
Hats	Good night
Shoes	My mom
Clothes	My dad
The playground	Grandma

Military Families

A Paper Hug. (2006). Stephanie Skolmoski. Self-published.

Daddy Is a Soldier. (2004). Kirsten Hallowell. Trafford.

Special Needs

Kids Like Me . . . Learn Colors. (2009). Laura Ronay and Jon Wayne Kishimoto. Woodbine House.

Susan Laughs. (2000). Jeanne Willis and Tony Ross. Henry Holt and Co.

Same-Sex Parents

Mommy, Mama, and Me! Leslea Newman. (2009). Tricycle Press.

Daddy, Papa, and Me! Leslea Newman. (2009). Tricycle Press.

Oh the Things Mommies Do! What Could be Better than Having Two? Crystal Tomkins. (2009). Oh the Things Mommies Do Press.

Divorce

Raising You Alone. (2005). Warren Hanson. Tristan Publishing.

Two Homes. (2003). Claire Masurel and Kady MacDonald Denton. Candlewick.

Fathers

Daddy Hugs. (2007). Karen Katz. Little Simon.

My Daddy and Me. (2008). Tina Macnaughton. Good Books.

Daddy Kisses. (2003). Anne Gutman and Georg Hallensleben. Chronicle Books.

I Love My Daddy. (2004). Sebastien Braun. HarperCollins.

- Help the remaining parent anticipate that the child may regress or have unexpected outbursts. If the child does begin having tantrums, use words such as "I'm sorry you're so upset. I know it's hard having Mommy be away."

- Help the deployed parent by sending notes on the child's interests and accomplishments. Add photos of the child involved in activities.

- Suggest that the deployed parent read about the stage of the child's development. This will also help the parent have realistic expectations of the child when the parent returns.

- Help the family anticipate that the deployed parent's return may be upsetting to the child. It's another change, and a very young child's memory of the real parent, mixed with the experiences of photos and voice tapes, may leave the baby with an internal image of the parent that is quite different from reality.

Families of Children with Disabilities

Infant/toddler care teachers sometimes feel challenged when including infants or toddlers with disabilities. Along with concerns about being able to care for the child's special needs, they may also be worried about how to talk to the child's family. Here are some suggestions for reaching out to the family of a child with disabilities:

- Ask the family what they feel you should know about the child including likes and dislikes, expectations of routines, and anything that relates in particular to the child's disability.

- Be willing to talk about similarities and differences this child has in relation to the other children. Families want to hear about their child's accomplishments and want to know that the infant care teacher is comfortable with the effects of a disability. They also want to know that the real impact of the disability on the child and his family is respected.

- Use "people first" language. You might say, "Bessie [the name of the child] has Down syndrome" or "I've worked for years with children with Down syndrome" rather than "I've worked for years with Downs kids." You would never use the name of the disability as a reference for the child, as in "I have a Downs in my group." Put the person before the disability.

- Ask to be included in information exchanges between the family and the early intervention team. Ask to be included in Individualized Family Service Plan (IFSP) meetings. Talk with the early interventionist about how you can support the child in achieving the goals of the IFSP.

- If the child would benefit from specialized equipment, ask the early intervention team how to acquire it, pay for it, and use it.

- Trust your observation skills and knowledge of development to guide your trial-and-error presentations of materials.

- Accept that you and family members each may have the full range of feelings about the child. You, however, are in the unique position of holding an image of hope for the future for the family.

Early Intervention Services. The Individuals with Disabilities Education Act, the federal law regarding special education services, has a section devoted to early intervention services for infants and toddlers. Every state participates in Part C: The Program for Infants and Toddlers. Under Part C, a family that has concerns about an infant's or toddler's development has a right to a multidisciplinary evaluation to see if the child is eligible for services. Each state creates its own definition of eligibility, so a child may qualify for services in one state but not in another. Certain conditions automatically qualify a child if those conditions are known to cause developmental delays without intervention. These include biological conditions such as sensory impairment, Down syndrome, and cerebral palsy. Services may include early child-hood special education; physical, occupational, or speech therapy; and other related services. Part C services must be driven by the family's preferences for services outlined in an individualized family service plan and must be provided in "the most natural environment," including the home or child care program.

Referrals to Early Intervention. One of the most difficult conversations that a director or care teacher may have with a family is one that expresses concerns about a child's development. The program may feel strongly that the child should be referred for an evaluation and receive services, but that is a hard message for some families to hear. For most early childhood care and education programs, however, the infant care teacher is often the first to recognize delays in development. Following are some ideas adapted from a program at Purdue University called Provider-Parent Partnerships (Ramamoorthy & Myers-Walls, 2006).

- Keep a record of the child's behavior. An accurate written record of behaviors you observed that caused concern will help families understand your concerns. Ongoing assessment of development, shared with families, will keep the topic of development between you in an ongoing way.

- Ask parents to invite all important caregivers to the meeting, if they choose to.

- Put yourself in the parents' position and *find out how ready they are to hear the information*. Listen to parents and accept any reactions. Some parents will be relieved to know that someone else is seeing what they have seen. Others may feel criticized, blamed, or believe that you don't like their child. Some will just need time to think about it and observe the child themselves.

- *Be honest without being unkind* and *talk positively*. You are not in a position to diagnose children. Use language such as "He struggles with . . ." rather than "He'll never . . .".

- *Use common words and be calm but concerned*. Limit yourself to simple, clear descriptions of behavior. Be emotionally present but stay calm. If the family is upset, try to open the conversation to their feelings.

- *Know what resources may be available and how to have the child evaluated*. Have contact information for your local Part C early intervention services. They are required to perform an evaluation if the family has concerns about the child's development.

Directors and teachers may want to role play and practice these conversations to prepare themselves for these difficult topics. It is important to remember that a small delay in development is not a life-or-death situation. Not every child who elicits concern will need or qualify for early intervention services. Families may need time to absorb the information. Presenting your concerns as questions and requesting that a professional evaluation be done to help you understand what is going on may make it easier for the family to agree to an evaluation.

Families with Mental Illness or Maternal Depression

Maternal depression is often unrecognized and untreated, but its effect on an infant or toddler can be devastating. Mothers struggling with depression may be unable to provide the nurturance, protection, and responsiveness that infants need. The baby, in turn, also may suffer from depression, and cognitive, language, and social development may be compromised (NICHD Early Child Care Research Network, 1999; Onunaku, 2005).

Research on Early Head Start's effectiveness has found that although 48 percent of mothers with infants and toddlers enrolled in an EHS program were depressed, they were able to learn to respond sensitively to their children. This ability to respond helped the children's overall development even if the depression continued (Bennett, 2002).

Early childhood care and education programs are not in a position to diagnose depression or other mental illnesses, but they should be aware of them. The infant/toddler care teacher may help families become aware of maternal depression and its effects on infants and toddlers, and the teacher may make small interventions that help the child receive needed attention despite the parent's depression.

Here are some ways in which programs can reach out to parents with depression or other mental illnesses.

- Provide as warm and accepting a relationship as possible with each parent. If you are a good listener, you are more likely to pick up on issues of concern.
- Make pamphlets on maternal depression and mental health issues available in your parent information area. Pamphlets should be available from your local mental health clinics.
- Invite a mental health professional to present to staff at a professional development opportunity or at a family meeting.
- Your own active involvement can help protect the infant or toddler from some of the negative effects of maternal depression (Hossain, Field, Pickens, & Gonzalez, 1995; Sheppard, 1994).
- Look for a moment of positive interaction between the depressed parent and the child. Reflect on this moment with the parent, pointing out how well the parent is doing and what it means to the child.
- Point out to the parent when the child looks at her or tries to get her attention.
- Reassure the parent of her importance to the infant or toddler.

Teen Parents

Over 300,000 girls under the age of 20 give birth in the United States each year (National Center for Health Statistics, 2012). Child care often is vital if adolescent parents are to continue attending school and graduate. Many school districts offer childcare programs that include parenting education and other supports, but many teens rely on community center–based or home family child care programs.

Issues that may arise in offering care for teen parents may include funding for the child's tuition, the teen parent's unrealistic expectations of her child (Mann, Pearl, & Behle, 2004), the teen's own developmental needs, and boundaries and limits within the relationship (University of Illinois Extension, 2008).

Ideas for successfully reaching out to teen parents include:

- Listen. Teens may not have people in their lives who can just listen without giving unasked-for advice. Listening to the teen's story of her life and encouraging her to come up with solutions to challenges can demonstrate your faith in her.

- Determine who is involved in the child's daily life and what role they might play in your program. Who will be bringing the child to the program? Who spends time with the child at home?

- Help the teen parent understand the need to balance his or her own needs with the needs of the infant or toddler.

- Help the teen parent find community resources including public funding for child care, support groups, and programs such as food stamps or WIC (University of Illinois Extension, 2008).

Same-Sex Couples

Increasingly, same-sex couples are raising children. Some of these are biological children from a previous marriage or relationship, some are adopted, some are biological to one partner, and some are born through surrogates. Both the American Psychological Association (APA) and the American Academy of Pediatrics (AAP) have endorsed this family structure as being as good for children as are families with heterosexual parents (American Psychological Association, 2004; American Academy of Pediatrics, 2009a, 2009b). The AAP Policy Statement reads, in part, "A growing body of scientific literature demonstrates that children who grow up with 1 or 2 gay and/or lesbian parents fare as well in emotional, cognitive, social, and sexual functioning as do children whose parents are heterosexual. Children's optimal development seems to be influenced more by the nature of the relationships and interactions within a family than by the particular structural form it takes" (AAP, 2009b, p. 341).

Nonetheless, same-sex couples face both overt and covert discrimination within the general community. When early care and education programs serve the infants or toddlers of same-sex couples, care teachers may need to reflect on their own feelings and to explore or confront the feelings of other families. Care teachers may need to make an extra effort in making the same-sex couple feel welcome and comfortable within the program.

Divorce and Separation

When families with very young children go through separation or divorce, they may or may not talk to their child's care teacher about it. It is important for the teacher to reach out to families going through divorce. Divorcing parents may feel shame, anger, anxiety, fear, and embarrassment. In some ways, the care teacher may become the child's advocate as the parents become preoccupied with their own life adjustments. The care teacher can reach out to families going through divorce in the following ways:

- Help parents understand that even the youngest child is also a participant in the divorce.

- Maintain contact with both parents, be empathetic, and do not take sides.

- Pay attention to the child's behavior and discuss your concerns with both parents.

Care teachers can help fathers feel welcome and engaged in their children's care and education.

- Help parents think about how to keep problems away from the child, how to be pleasant to each other at transfer times, or how to use the child care program for transfers.

- Make sure that families keep you aware of any changes in contact information.

- Be sure you understand the custody arrangements and any restraining orders.

- There is some confusion over whether overnight visits are all right for young infants. Researchers recommend that the infant sleep in only one home to preserve the ability of the child to form a strong attachment. In the second year, a couple can begin some trial overnights (Bretherton, Seligman, Solomon, Crowell, & McIntosh, 2011).

Engaging Fathers and Other Significant Males

Child care centers are often relatively feminine environments. Most infant/toddler care teachers and program directors are women. Many men perceive program events as intended for the mothers.

Beginning in 1995, Early Head Start began a Fatherhood Initiative in an effort to get fathers more involved in their children's lives. Knowing that children's outcomes are better in most areas if they have a strong male influence in their lives, the EHS programs developed several effective strategies for reaching out to and engaging fathers. These included the following:

- Creating a welcoming environment that included posters of dads with infants and toddlers; sports, car and mechanics magazines if they had a parent waiting area; and more neutral and less feminine décor.

- Training to educate the staff on the importance of fathers in children's lives and to examine some of the staff's own feelings about men.

- Infant/toddler care teachers would engage fathers personally in conversations, including offering personal invitations to parent education or family events. Participation by fathers was much greater when the teacher invited them directly than if teachers just posted notices or sent invitations to the home.

- Sharing information with both mothers and fathers about the importance of males in the lives of children. (Burwick & Berlotti, 2005)

SUMMARY

Programs, families, and infants and toddlers benefit when there is an ongoing partnership between parents and teachers. The partnership may be as simple as daily information sharing, or it may involve family members as members of an advisory board.

Every level of parent participation takes effort on the part of the program staff. The invitation to participate must be genuine to be effective. Some groups of families face exceptional challenges and may need particular support or outreach from infant/toddler care teachers. These include families whose culture or race is different from that of the majority of program staff and families, military families in deployment, families of children with disabilities, families with mental illness or maternal depression, same sex parents, families going through separation or divorce, and fathers.

INVENTORY OF TEACHER PRACTICES

Engaging Families

Basic Concepts	A	S	R	Observation/ Reflection
I communicate daily with the family of each of the children for whom I provide primary care.				
Our program clearly communicates policies to parents.				
I am welcoming and friendly with all family members.				
I ask family members for information about the child's interests, development, routines, and needs.				
I provide some general information and education to families.				
I welcome families to spend time in the classroom.				
I ask families to provide photographs and tape recordings of themselves for their child to enjoy.				
I reach out to families whose language, culture, or race is different from mine.				
I provide information in families' primary languages.				
I reach out to military families on deployment.				
I reach out to families with infants and toddlers with disabilities.				
I reach out to families with mental illness or maternal depression.				
I reach out to families going through divorce and separation.				
I reach out to fathers and important males in the children's lives.				

A = Always, S = Sometimes, R = Rarely

REFLECTIONS

1. How are you most comfortable communicating with families? Is that method generally a good match for the families with whom you work?
2. How do you feel about out-of-home care for infants and toddlers? How does that affect your work?
3. Are there groups of parents with whom you might it find especially challenging to form a partnership? What skills do you bring to finding common ground with people who are different from you?

APPLICATIONS

1. Create a document that care teachers could use to maintain daily communication with the family of an infant or toddler in your care. Is it an *exchange* of information? Why did you choose this method?
2. Suppose that you have learned that a parent in your primary care group is about to be deployed overseas. What suggestions would you make to the family to help the infant or toddler through the transition?
3. Write down the steps you would take to assure that the cultural background of each child in your group is respected and represented in your space.

RESOURCES

- ZERO TO THREE. Parenting resources, brochures, articles. Available at http://www.zerotothree.org
- Early intervention program for infants and toddlers with disabilities (Part C of IDEA). Available at http://www.nectac.org/partc/partc.asp
- Grandparents raising grandchildren. Available at http://www.usa.gov/Topics/Grandparents.shtml

3

Responsive, Safe, and Healthy Caregiving Routines

After reading this chapter, you will be able to:

- RESPECT
    - Responsive, on-demand, predictable caregiving
    - Scrupulous attention to safe and healthy practices
- REFLECT
    - Promoting health
    - Maintaining a safe environment

- RELATE
    - Relationship-based caregiving

Miriam loved taking care of her young infants, but feeding, diapering, and napping seemed to take the whole day. She felt frustrated about when she would have time to be the teacher she was trained to be. Her supervisor observed and said, "Miriam, you're doing a great job. You're doing everything right!"

Much of a young infant's day is filled with urgent bodily sensations of hunger, elimination, fatigue, or need for comfort. Even to people taking care of only one baby, the day seems full of routine care. What did Miriam's supervisor see that was so impressive? Miriam quickly and respectfully responded to every communication from each of her four young infants, actively trying to understand what was wanted or needed. She stayed physically and emotionally available to them. She and her co-teacher kept a homelike, well-organized, clean, and safe environment. Her interactions with the babies and the homelike routines of her classroom provided numerous learning opportunities; every moment could be filled with language, the sharing of quiet attention, or the practice of new physical skills. Miriam uses documentation of her observations for individualized planning and for maintaining daily communication with parents. She understands that each baby needs to learn how to live in his or her own culture, and when she feels the need to correct behavior and offer guidance, she knows that this is a social part of learning. All of this wonderful, responsive caregiving was occurring while Miriam attended to the babies' routine needs.

RELATIONSHIP-BASED CAREGIVING: RESPONSIVE, ON-DEMAND, AND PREDICTABLE

Shela, as Miriam's co-teacher, also provided primary care to four babies. That meant that one teacher was almost always available to respond quickly to any baby in real distress while the other teacher divided her attention among the rest of the babies who were awake. For example, if Miriam was in the middle of a diaper change and one of her babies awoke crying, Shela would go to comfort the crying baby.

Very young babies are easily overwhelmed by the pain of hunger or of gas moving through their bowels. They may become tired but unable to relax into sleep. Left to these experiences, they may see the world as a chaotic place. But when the young infant's day is filled with caregiving experiences characterized by quick responses to cries, with accurate interpretations of the meaning of the infant's communication and in ways that let the baby count on being comforted, the infant begins to develop a sense of trust in the teacher and in his or her own ability to summon help. Through responsive, predictable, and on-demand caregiving, he begins to establish a sense of security.

Responsive Caregiving

Responsiveness refers to both how well the adult understands the baby's cues and how sensitively and accurately the adult responds. "A responsive adult is 'tuned-in' to the child and is sensitive and caring in response to the child" (Wittmer & Petersen, 2006, p. 3). A relationship-based model requires that over time, two people have repeated opportunities to get to know each other, develop affection, and deepen their understanding of each other. Moments of responsiveness provide a foundation for a deep and meaningful relationship.

Relationship-based care has benefits for both the baby and the teacher. The baby feels understood and able to affect the world around him- or herself. The teacher in turn feels competent and effective in reading the baby's communication, understanding it, and responding in ways that are helpful.

An important element of responsiveness is meeting the young infant's emotional tone. Babies don't understand words, but they recognize when an adult's face mirrors the feelings they themselves are experiencing. When a teacher communicates understanding of the baby's distress *and* remains calm and capable, the baby feels very comforted.

Responsive caregiving includes the adult understanding the young child's communication cues and positively relating to build strong relationships.

The teacher adds words to describe the feelings, "You're sooo hungry. Your tummy wants some food. You want that bottle!"; more words to describe what is happening, "I need to warm up this good milk mommy left for you. Mmmmm. This will taste so good."; and even words about what is about to happen, "We'll sit right over here by the window and have a nice, quiet snack. That will feel so good." The teacher is responding to physical needs and to emotional states while providing a wide, rich, and relevant set of words for the baby's "in-the-moment" experience.

On-Demand Caregiving

Albert and his co-teacher Marva were constantly aware of each of the children. So, when babies were napping, at least one of them was listening for sounds of babies waking. For example, when 9-month-old Gemma woke from her nap, Albert was quickly at her side. "Hello, Gemma. We've been waiting for you to wake up. What a nice smile. [He smiles in return.] Look, Bessie's sleeping right here. We'll be quiet. Let's get you a clean diaper while Marva gets your bottle ready."

Most elements of caregiving for young and mobile infants cannot be scheduled but need to be offered in response to the infant's communication of need. Feeding, diapering, and napping all should occur "on demand."

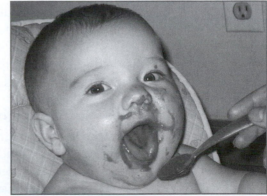

Feeding. It takes young babies months to develop a reliable feeding schedule. No sooner do they seem to have a pattern of eating a certain amount at a certain time than the pattern changes. This occurs because growth spurts generally occur at about 2 weeks, 6 weeks, and 3 months. These can cause a sudden increase in a baby's appetite. Breastfed babies may just seem to have settled into a schedule when a sudden growth spurt causes the need to eat very frequently. The additional sucking stimulates the mother's milk production. For children in group care, it is helpful if mothers can anticipate growth spurts so they can have additional milk available.

Mealtime is pleasurable when the care teacher is responsive to the infant's cues.

When a baby is fed because the teacher recognizes communication signals about being hungry, it helps the child to recognize the feeling in his tummy as hunger. It helps the child learn to summon help and increases his sense of effectiveness. Over the next several months, as the relationship becomes well established, it also helps the baby wait briefly and calmly for a bottle out of an assurance that his or her hunger will be satisfied.

Diapering and Toileting. Diaper changing is another routine that should take place on demand. Unfortunately, it is not unusual to find one teacher changing all the children in a row, marking off a chart for 8 A.M., 10 A.M., and so on. The process often feels mechanized, with a caregiver lifting the next baby up from what she was doing, silently changing her, and placing her back. Highly absorbent disposable diapers have added to this problem by making it hard for babies to feel the moisture against their skin. Still, diaper changing should occur in response to a realization that the diaper is wet or dirty. It is yet another way of helping a baby become aware of bodily sensations and develop a sense that adults will help him or her become more comfortable.

Toilet learning is likely to occur during the toddler years and needs to be coordinated between the family and the toddler care teacher. Different cultures vary in when and how to begin toilet learning. Expectations between parents and toddler care teachers may require some negotiation. There are also differences between a family helping their one toddler learn to use the potty and a toddler care teacher managing toilet learning for a group of three to five toddlers.

As a general rule, toddlers or preschoolers signal their readiness for toilet training when they prefer clean diapers, understand or use words such as "pee" or "poo" for eliminations, and move off to a corner to have privacy while filling a diaper (National Association for the Education of Young Children, n.d.). Toilet learning should be a positive experience, with parents and teachers together planning how to encourage and praise the child's attempts and successes and to manage disappointment over accidents.

Napping. Napping is the third caregiving routine that is really impossible to schedule for a group of young or mobile infants. In the first 6 months, babies usually take two or three short naps during the day and may awaken several times at night. Many babies have difficulty distinguishing day from night for some time. Some babies need help to fall asleep—cuddling or rocking; others comfort themselves and drift into a deep sleep minutes after their care teacher places them on their back in their crib. Timing and length of naps may vary. It is reassuring and pleasant for babies to have someone nearby to greet them as they waken.

Predictable Caregiving

Predictability refers to the "routines within routines." Even at a very young age, babies are trying to understand and make sense of the patterns of the activities around them. A baby begins to understand that crying will be followed by being picked up and comforted, being carried toward the refrigerator, watching the infant care teacher pull out the bottle and warm it—and then, being fed! The entire process becomes a recognizable—and predictable—sequence for the baby.

Seeing these predictable sequences over and over again throughout the day helps babies understand that certain actions usually follow others. The child learns that his or her actions and communications set predictable responses in motion, a very early notion of cause and effect. The baby's own sense of efficacy begins to take hold, as does his or her trust in the infant care teacher.

Routines help babies establish good sleep patterns. Rocking, swaddling in a blanket, and a quiet little sleeping song can be signals to the baby to relax into sleep. Within a few months, the routines may include a cuddle while reading a picture book. If a baby's family at home speaks a language different from the teacher's language, a song or words of affection in the home language might be especially comforting as the baby relaxes into sleep.

Routines can be helpful for the teacher as well. Following established protocols for diapering and food preparation creates a habit of safe and healthy practices. Documenting each feeding, nap, and diaper change can become a habit, providing good information for the teacher's files and keeping parents informed of the baby's routine care that day.

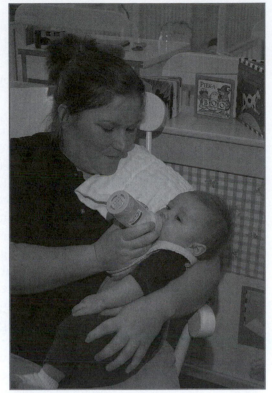

Rocking and humming a lullaby are age-old methods for helping infants fall asleep.

SCRUPULOUS ATTENTION TO SAFE AND HEALTHY PRACTICES DURING ROUTINE CARE

Some early childhood program directors recently were asked, "If you had to put one aspect of quality above all others, what would it be?" Although they answered the question independently, each said "Health and safety." But then almost everyone added, "But that has to be paired with responsive, relationship-based care."

The directors reasoned that young babies have immature immune systems and are highly vulnerable to the many germs present in group care. Keeping babies healthy can be a complicated matter involving good food handling, preventing the spread of disease, promoting healthy practices, and being vigilant about safety issues. If babies are not kept safe and healthy, group care would be detrimental. The directors cautioned, however, that *without caring relationships, group care would be equally detrimental.* So, another aspect of high-quality care is maintaining safe and healthy practices within a relationship-based model. The following recommendations come from the American Academy of Pediatrics and the National Resource Center on Health and Safety for Child Care's *National Standards for Health and Safety in Child Care* (American Academy of Pediatrics, 2002).

Food Handling for Young Infants

Young infants need feeding on demand by a consistent caregiver (Standard 4.013; AAP, 2002). A consistent teacher learns the unique hunger cues of her babies so that she can feed them before they cry. Babies may suck on their fingers, open and close their mouths, or seem to be reaching around in space. As the teacher learns to recognize hunger cues and prepare for feeding in a timely way, the baby learns about her own bodily experiences and builds a sense of security in their relationship.

Human Milk. Although the choice to breastfeed will be made by the parents, the American Academy of Pediatrics recommends that babies have only breast milk for the first 6 months, if possible. Human milk supports growth in weight and length. It also provides some protection from diarrhea and lowers respiratory disease and ear infections. Research suggests that human milk also results in fewer allergies and higher cognitive performance (American Academy of Pediatrics, 1997). Breast milk begins as colostrum, a thick, yellow milk made during pregnancy and right after birth. It is rich in nutrients and antibodies. In a few days, mature, whitish milk comes in. This milk has just the right amount of fat, sugar, water, and protein that the infant needs. The composition of the milk changes to meet the growing infant's changing nutritional needs (womenshealth.gov, 2011). Infants digest breast milk more easily than formula, and breastfed infants are healthier (American College of Nurse-Midwives, n.d.).

Mothers also benefit from breastfeeding. Breastfeeding supports the mother's experience of bonding through the skin-to-skin contact and the production of oxytocin, a hormone that produces feelings of affection. Breastfeeding tightens the uterus and uses up the fat stored during pregnancy. Women who breastfeed are less likely to get breast cancer, overian cancer, and possibly type 2 diabetes (American College of Nurse-Midwives, n.d.).

Programs should support whatever choice the family makes about breast milk or formula feeding. For mothers who are breastfeeding, however, the program should provide a private, comfortable space to come in and nurse their baby. Teachers should know how to safely handle human milk that mothers have expressed for their baby. The milk should be:

- Brought from home in a bottle labeled with the child's name.
- Refrigerated.
- Warmed in a bowl of warm water or under warm, running water. Heating with a stove or microwave can cause the milk to become too hot or heat unevenly. Excess heat may destroy some nutrients.
- Discarded if left in the bottle after feeding.

Families who choose not to breastfeed or are unable to breastfeed also should be supported in their choice. They should be equally encouraged to visit and feed their baby during the day.

Solid Foods. The decision about when to introduce semisolid foods should be made by the family and pediatrician, but the American Academy of Pediatrics recommends exclusively feeding with human milk for the first 6 months. Babies signal their readiness for solid foods in these ways:

- *Head control.* The baby needs to hold her head up steadily to swallow.
- *Supported sitting.* Swallowing solid foods requires an upright posture. Supported sitting on an adult's lap or in a seat works well.

- *Showing interest in or curiosity about the food that adults are eating.*
- *Hunger that is not satisfied by breast or bottle feeding.*

If these signals are clear, ask the family whether they are planning to offer semisolid foods to the baby. The care teacher should follow the plan of the family and their health provider. However, there are some general guidelines to consider in introducing foods to infants:

- Begin by introducing rice cereal. Rice is easily digested and less likely to cause allergies than are other grains. Mix one teaspoon of cereal with enough breast milk or formula to just thicken the mixture.
- Hold the baby in a supported sitting position on your lap.
- Offer a tiny amount on a small, plastic-tipped spoon.
- Give the baby time to figure out how to use the tongue to move the cereal to the back of the mouth and swallow.
- If the baby is not interested, wait a few days and try again.
- Wait at least 5 days between introducing new foods so that you can recognize allergic reactions.

Box 3.1

Hand Washing

Care teachers should wash their hands frequently using the following steps:

- Rinse hands under warm, running water.
- Apply soap and rub hands together, spreading lather over hands, between fingers, on wrists, and under jewelry, cleaning hands thoroughly.
- Rinse well under warm, running water until all soap and dirt are rinsed away.
- Use a towel to dry hands and then use the towel to turn off the faucet to avoid contamination from germs on the faucet handle.

Preventing the Spread of Disease

Young infants do become ill easily, and the teacher plays an important role in keeping them healthy. Keeping the ratio of adults to children and the group sizes small is helpful in containing the number of germs in the environment, but nothing is more important than meticulous adherence to good hand-washing protocols (see Box 3.1). Sinks used for hand washing should not also be used for food preparation.

This sink area in a toddler room with steps allows toddlers to wash their own hands with the support of a care teacher.

Toys. Young infants can spread disease through toys by mouthing them, touching them after putting their fingers in their mouths, or touching their diapers without good hand washing. Each toy should be removed from the play area after one child has mouthed it. Toys should have smooth, nonporous surfaces and be dishwasher safe for cleaning. Cloth toys should be machine washable. Suggestions for choosing and using an appropriate sanitizer are available in Caring for Our Children (AAP, 2002), Appendix I, available online.

As a general rule, a dishwasher or washing machine provides the most thorough cleaning. If toys are sprayed, wiped, or immersed in a cleaning solution, at least 1 minute of contact with the germ-killing solution should be allowed before drying the surface. Air drying is best (National Resource Center for Health and Safety in Child Care and Early Education, n.d.).

Diapering. Diapering offers the opportunity for a few minutes of intimate, one-on-one time between the teacher and child. It can be a rich language experience, talking about what is happening, showing affection, and learning a predictable routine.

A safe diapering procedure is important in order to reduce the spread of germs and infection (American Academy of Pediatrics, 2002). Without good procedures, the child, the teacher, and the materials in the changing area all are subject to contamination by germs. In addition, the child must be protected from dangers, such as falling off the table. Routines such as diapering should always occur with responsive interactions and lots of language describing what is happening. Every program should have the diapering protocol posted at the changing area. It should include these steps:

- Wash your hands. Organize the materials you will need. These include a clean diaper and clothing, a paper liner to cover the diapering surface, wipes, plastic bags, gloves, and any diaper cream removed from the container and placed on a tissue ready to apply.
- Cover the diapering surface with the paper liner and put on gloves.
- Bring the child to the changing area. Remove soiled clothing and put it into a plastic bag to send home.
- Remove the soiled diaper, and clean the diapering area. Use a fresh wipe for each stroke, and always wipe from front to back.
- Put disposable diapers into a foot-operated trash can or cloth diapers into a plastic bag to be sent home, keeping one hand on the child at all times. Remove and throw away your gloves.
- Wipe your hands with a wipe. Put on a fresh diaper and dress the child.
- Wash the child's hands and return him to the play area.
- Clean and disinfect the diapering area.
- Wash your hands.

PROMOTING HEALTH AND MAINTAINING A SAFE ENVIRONMENT

Infant and toddler care and education programs need to go beyond preventing the spread of disease to actively promoting health and keeping the environment safe. Teachers who promote healthy habits for young infants and toddlers are knowledgeable about immunizations and well-child care, oral health, nutrition (as described above), and physical fitness; reducing the risk of sudden infant death syndrome (SIDS) and shaken baby syndrome; and reporting child abuse and neglect.

Immunizations and Well-Child Care

The Centers for Disease Control and Prevention and the American Academy of Pediatrics recommend a schedule of immunizations and visits to the pediatrician or health clinic for well-baby care. Immunizations save lives by preventing children from becoming ill with common diseases. Many of these diseases were deadly or caused serious, permanent side effects before the vaccines were developed. Immunizations, however, are only a part of well-baby visits. Babies should have consistent care from a health professional who is regularly weighing and measuring the baby's growth, advising parents on nutrition, and keeping an eye on the baby's development. Programs may help a family find child health insurance and a medical home for their baby, if the family doesn't already have those. The Center for Disease Control and Prevention (CDC) provides schedules for teachers and parents concerning the most recent recommended immunizations for infants and toddlers at http://www.cdc.gov

Oral Health

Oral health for infants and toddlers is an area of increasing interest in early childhood and dentistry. Exposure to bacteria from the mother's mouth may result in dental caries, which causes tooth decay even as teeth are first erupting. The bacteria *Streptococcus mutans (S. mutans)* is present in as many as 40 percent of pregnant women, usually mothers with little education and from low socio-economic backgrounds. *S. mutans* interacts with sugary substances to break down the enamel on the tooth and cause decay. It may be transmitted during pregnancy or through sharing of saliva by kissing on the mouth, cleaning a pacifier in the mother's mouth before putting into the baby's mouth, or sharing spoons or cups. Fluoride varnishes applied as soon as the teeth erupt are helpful. Giving mothers of preschool-age children chewing gum with the sugar substitute Xylitol has been shown to substantially reduce the presence of *S. mutans* bacteria. Education and dental care during pregnancy are very important in combatting early-childhood dental caries (Marrs, Trumbley, & Malik, 2011).

For very young infants, the Office of Head Start suggests that every child have a dental home, a dental health professional that the child sees regularly, as soon as

When encouraging care teachers sit with toddlers during meals and snacks, everyone enjoys eating.

the first teeth appear. For infants under the age of 1, at least once during the program day, staff or volunteers must wash their hands and then cover a finger with a gauze pad or soft cloth and gently wipe infants' gums (Office of Head Start, 2005).

Nutrition and Physical Fitness

Families and teachers must be partners in following the nutritional recommendations of the pediatricians and health care professionals and providing opportunities to increase physical fitness. It may seem funny to think about the physical fitness of infants who are so young they need to be carried everywhere. However, programs exist that provide lots of opportunities for young babies to play on their tummies and practice rolling; and for older babies to pull themselves up into a sitting position and play using both hands, and then to crawl or scoot across a safe, inviting space. These activities help babies build muscles. The babies also are developing the habit of being active, which may prove valuable in preventing obesity.

Time outdoors every day also helps babies be more active. Many programs include both a daily walk in a group stroller and times to play in the play yard. Adults should also model good eating habits and an interest in movement and exercise.

Reducing the Risk of Sudden Unexpected Infant Death Syndrome

Sudden Unexpected Infant Death Syndrome (SUIDS) is defined as the death of an infant under one year of age where the cause of death is not immediately explainable before an investigation. SUIDS is the leading cause of death among infants from 1 to 12 months old and the third leading cause of overall infant mortality. Before the death, which usually occurs during sleep, the infant appears to be healthy. The occurrence of SUIDS is twice as high in Latino and American Indian/Alaska Native populations as in the general population (Center for Disease Control, 2011).

Thoughtful decisions require keeping knowledge current. Health care providers used to recommend that babies sleep on their stomachs out of concern for possible choking if the baby spits up in sleep. But since 1994, the National Institute of Child Health and Development (NICHD) has led a public relations campaign aimed at getting parents and caregivers to put babies on their backs when they go to sleep. The "BACK to SLEEP" campaign used current research on sudden infant death syndrome (SIDS) to reverse commonly held beliefs about choking dangers. During that time, SUIDS deaths have dropped by 50 percent.

Information from the campaign includes:

- *Babies sleep more safely on their backs.* Babies who sleep on their stomachs are much more likely to die of SIDS than babies who sleep on their backs.

- *Sleep surface matters.* Babies who sleep on or under soft bedding are more likely to die of SIDS.

- *Every sleep time counts.* Babies who usually sleep on their backs but are then placed on their stomachs, perhaps for a nap, are at very high risk for SIDS. So it is important that *everyone* who cares for a baby use the back sleeping position for naps and at night.

- *Young infants should sleep in the same room but not the same bed as other family members.* Adults may roll over onto an infant, or the loose bedding of an adult bed may smother him. (NICHD, 2006)

Further information is available online from NICHD.

Reducing the Risk of Shaken Baby Syndrome

Shaken baby syndrome (SBS) describes the signs and symptoms that result from nonaccidental injury such as violent shaking or impact of the head of an infant or small child. The brain damage that ensues depends on the amount and duration of shaking or the force of impact. Approximately 20 percent of the victims die within the first few days, and the survivors usually suffer lifelong brain damage, resulting in a range of disorders from learning disabilities to a vegetative state.

SBS is generally caused by a parent or caregiver having an aggressive reaction to infant crying that does not stop. Infant/toddler care teachers need to have a plan in place for how to handle inconsolable babies. This should include laying them in a crib when their needs have been met and stepping away to regain self-control. Having a co-worker available to step in is very helpful in group care (National Center on Shaken Baby Syndrome, n.d.).

Swimming

Some child care programs promote swimming lessons for infants and toddlers. Lately, many videos of very young infants swimming by themselves have appeared on the Internet. The American Academy of Pediatrics does not recommend swimming lessons for anyone under the age of 4. The reason given is that swimming lessons may give the child, parent, or care teacher a false sense of security concerning the child's safety in the water. The Academy's policy statement and technical report assert that young children must always be within reach of an adult when in the water, under constant supervision, and should never rely on inflatable water wings or rings to keep afloat. All pools, including free-standing aboveground pools, must always be protected by a four-sided wall with a secure gate and lock.

Safe Practices

Infant and toddler care teachers and home family providers need to be familiar with their program's procedures for keeping children safe. Each program should have written policies and procedures for:

- Daily safety checks of the environment

- Emergency procedures in the event of child illness, fire, earthquakes, hurricanes, or tornadoes

- Evacuation or lock-down plans
- Reporting child abuse and neglect

Parent contact numbers should be easily accessible and carried along during walks or other outings. Safety policies and procedures should be posted in places that are easily visible and available to staff, parents, and substitutes.

Reporting Child Abuse and Neglect

A particularly difficult and sensitive area of child safety is child abuse and neglect. Every state has a plan for addressing child abuse and neglect through the federal law known as the Child Abuse Prevention and Treatment Act (CAPTA) (Administration of Children and Families, 2003). Each state determines what groups of people are required to report suspected child abuse or neglect and at what point of concern or evidence they need to report.

Child care teachers are usually required by the state to report suspicion of child abuse or neglect. This is of particular concern to infant care teachers because as of 2001, the federal government found that "children younger than 1 year old comprised 41 percent of child abuse fatalities and 85 percent of child abuse fatalities were younger than 6 years of age" (Administration of Children and Families, 2003, p. 8). Box 3.2 identifies some of the most common signs of child abuse and neglect. Infant/toddler care teachers should bring their concerns to the attention of the program director but need to be aware that ultimately the responsibility of identifying and reporting is theirs alone. A complete list of phone numbers for reporting abuse is available on the government website Child Abuse Information Gateway at http://www.childwelfare.gov/responding/reporting.cfm.

Box 3.2

Identifying Child Abuse and Neglect

Some of the most common signs of child abuse or neglect are the following:

- Unexplained burns, cuts, bruises, or welts in the shape of an object
- Apathy or depression
- Inappropriate interest in or knowledge of sexual acts
- Unsuitable clothing for the weather
- Extreme hunger

Information on recognizing and reporting child abuse and neglect is available through the Childhelp National Child Abuse Hotline, 1–800–4-A-CHILD® (1–800–422-4453).

SUMMARY

Much of an infant's or toddler's day is busy with repeated routines of care such as eating, napping, and diapering or toileting. Each of these moments of care can be filled with rich and affectionate interactions between the baby and the infant care teacher. Relationship-based care is responsive, predictable, and given on demand. The infant care teacher takes every opportunity to build a relationship with each baby in her care.

Infant/toddler care teachers need to know and practice safe and healthy procedures when caring for young children. These include practices that promote health, such as good nutrition and physical activity; that prevent the spread of disease, such as hand washing and sanitizing the environment; and that keep children safe through established procedures and knowledge of issues such as child abuse and neglect, sudden infant death syndrome, and shaken baby syndrome.

INVENTORY OF TEACHER PRACTICES

Responsive, Safe, and Healthy Caregiving Routines

Basic Concepts	A	S	R	Observation/ Reflection
I provide routine care in ways that are responsive to each child's cues and needs.				
I provide routine care in ways that are predictable.				
I provide routine care on demand.				
I maintain a safe environment with daily checks of the space.				
I follow protocols for safe food handling.				
I follow protocols to prevent the spread of disease.				
I actively promote the health of the children by attending to: Well-child care Oral health Nutrition and physical fitness Reducing the risk of SIDS Reducing the risk of shaken baby syndrome				
A = Always, S = Sometimes, R = Rarely				

REFLECTIONS

1. Feeding, holding, diapering, comforting, and cleaning an infant are very intimate experiences. How do those aspects of the work make infant and toddler care different from working with other ages of children?
2. At the end of a day of routine care, do you feel any closer to the children? Are you satisfied with your work?
3. Are you comfortable with the level of health care that the infants and toddlers get from their families? Do you have ways to work with families around these issues?

APPLICATIONS

1. Identify ways in which a care teacher could organize space or materials to make routine times go more smoothly with infants, mobile infants, toddlers, and twos.
3. One of the most common mistakes made by infant/toddler care teachers is not washing their hands frequently enough during the day. Create a handwashing protocol that a teacher could post above the sink.
3. Develop an accurate and up-to-date written protocol for one aspect of health and safety listed in this chapter.

RESOURCES

• *A childcare provider's guide to safe sleep.* Retrieved from http://www.healthychildcare.org/pdf/SIDSchildcaresafesleep.pdf

A Responsive, Relationship-Based Environment

After reading this chapter, you will be able to:

- RESPECT
  - Understand the dimensions of the environment
  - Identify learning and playing areas
- REFLECT
  - Understand the effect of the environment on behavior and learning
  - Contemplate possible spaces and materials for infants and toddlers
- RELATE
  - Design interesting, appropriate environments for infants and toddlers

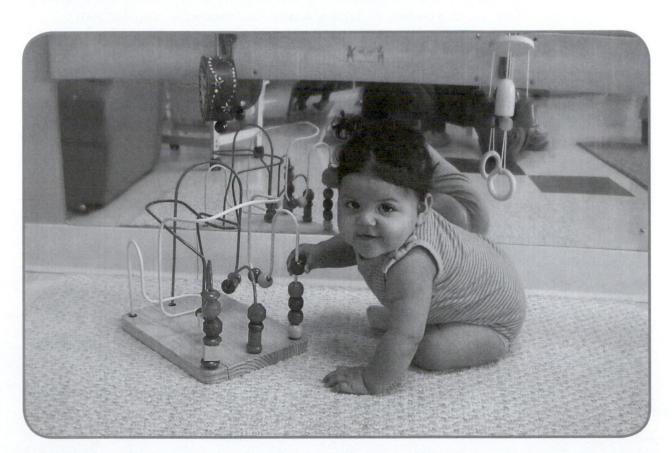

An environment is more than a setting or a place: It is an atmosphere. Infant/toddler care teachers create an ambiance—a feeling, a mood, a frame of mind—in a center, a room in a center, or a family child care home. This environment influences how children and teachers feel about others and themselves. As infant/toddler care teachers develop their environments, they should think about what they hope infants, toddlers, and families will experience in this setting.

Infant/toddler care teachers may find it difficult to create the kind of room that they envision for children. For example, the rooms in a center might be too small or large; or the center program may be located in community buildings where all of the equipment must be stored on Friday afternoon and set up again on Monday morning. In home family childcare, the materials may need to be stored every evening. Budgets may not allow infant/toddler care teachers to purchase all the beautiful equipment and toys that they see in catalogs. Within these parameters, how can teachers create an environment that engenders engagement and feelings of security and well-being?

Care teachers may have heard the saying that the environment is the third teacher. When educators say this, they mean that a well-designed environment supports child learning; creates opportunities for relationships to flourish; and builds on children's intrinsic motivation and enthusiasm to figure out, create, and discover. An environment, just like a teacher, can say to children, "I believe that you are capable, competent, and caring. I value you as an individual and as a member of this group." Each aspect of an environment, beginning with the entry, communicates the image that care teachers have of children, families, and themselves (Gandini, 2001).

Each state creates licensing rules and regulations that child care and education programs must meet. Check your state's regulations at http://nrckids.org/STATES/states.htm. The Colorado regulations that pertain to infants and toddlers are shown in Figure 4.1. State regulations are usually considered to be minimal standards created for the health, safety, and well-being of children in childcare. The following description of the dimensions of the environment expands on licensing requirements and describes additional quality aspects of environments that affect the care and learning opportunities available to infants and toddlers. This is an elaboration of a six-point environment observation guide developed by Wittmer and Petersen (2009, p. 283). The last section of the chapter describes the equipment and materials that create quality environments. These ideas will support care teachers in using the power of the environment to promote learning and relationships.

DIMENSIONS OF AN ENVIRONMENT

Takala's parents came from a culture in which relatives care for children if the mother must be away. When she was first born and the family came to visit the program, Takala's mother was very relieved when she walked into the infant room. It could almost have been a home! It had the toys and little tables of a childcare program and it was really just one room, but it felt like a home!

Rooms in center programs and family child care homes tell a story about who lives there every day. Not all environments should look the same because not all infants, toddlers, families, and teachers are the same. Children have different personalities,

7.702.71 General Requirements

A. Indoor and outdoor play equipment and materials must be appropriate for children's ages, size, and activities.

B. Indoor and outdoor materials and equipment must be sufficiently varied and appropriate for the developmental needs of the children and the number attending.

C. Indoor and outdoor equipment, materials, and furnishings must be sturdy, safe, and free of hazards.

D. Durable furniture such as tables and chairs must be child-sized or appropriately adapted for children's use.

F. In infant nurseries, an adequate number of high chairs or other suitable pieces of equipment that meet federal Consumer Product Safety Commission standards must be provided for infant feeding.

G. The infant nursery must have an adult rocking chair.

H. Each infant nursery must have a piece of sturdy equipment that is easily mobile and will hold a minimum of 5 infants for use in emergency exiting.

7.702.72 Play-Equipment and Materials

E. An appropriate supply of play materials must be readily accessible to children and must be arranged in an orderly manner so that children can select, remove, and replace the play materials either independently or with minimum assistance.

F. Toys and toy parts accessible to children under 3 years of age must be large enough that they cannot be swallowed or inhaled.

G. Toys made of brittle, easily breakable plastic are not permitted for children under 5.

H. In the infant nursery, some play equipment from the following list must be provided: mobiles, rubber washable toys, rattles, blocks, balls, record player, radio, tape player.

I. In the toddler nursery, some play materials easily accessible to children must be provided from each of the following categories:
   1. Gross Motor Development
   2. Fine Motor Development
   3. Language Development
   4. Social Interaction

Figure 4.1   Colorado Licensure Requirements for Child Care Equipment and Materials
Source: http://nrc.uchsc.edu/STATES/CO/colorado.htm

needs, and interests, and they are from diverse families and cultures. Families have different goals for their children, and each culture has unique values and beliefs. Consequently, environments change daily, weekly, and monthly to reflect the individuals who live there.

All infant and toddler environments will have some aspects in common, however, because all children have basic needs. Many elements combine to make a childcare space not only clean and safe, but also homelike and engaging. These include the basic equipment and furniture, the layout of the room, light, windows, the colors used on floors and walls, play materials—and all the procedures developed for keeping the space clean and safe. Many of these elements are articulated in state childcare licensing regulations, and many states and programs use the Infant Toddler Environment Rating Scale (Harms, Cryer, & Clifford, 2006) as an evaluation tool.

The following list describes the major elements of design for quality programs in a group care environment (Wittmer & Petersen, 2006).

1. *Environments for children are clean, safe, properly lighted, ventilated, and provide appropriate temperature regulation.* Every child should be safe and healthy while in group care. Daily routines for maintaining a clean environment, from wiping surfaces to cleaning toys that have been mouthed, must be in place and then monitored to

ensure that they are being performed. A safety check should be done daily to check for uncovered electric plugs, small materials that could cause choking, stacks of items that could fall, and furniture that could be pulled over.

Incandescent light, rather than fluorescent, provides softer, more focused areas of light that will also visually distinguish one area from another. Windows and skylights can be used to provide both natural light and ventilation in warm weather. Mechanical systems for heat and air cooling should be adjustable within each room. Heating sources should not be within reach of little fingers. Adequate storage allows teachers to keep necessary materials nearby without creating clutter.

2. *Environments contain design elements that reduce stimulation, create a sense of calm, and enable children to focus on each other, their teachers, and the materials they are exploring.* Some years ago, when most classrooms were splashed with primary colors, a teacher explained her cream-colored walls and floors this way: "In my room, the walls and floors are a calm surround. The color is from the children themselves and their play materials. That helps such little children to focus on each other and the materials and not be distracted by cartoons on the walls." This room was a remarkably calm setting, with children always engaged with each other or the play materials.

Flooring should be carpeted except in areas that are likely to get messy, such as where food is served, paints are used, or diapers are changed. Furniture arrangement helps divide the space to make it clear to the crawling infant that his or her path is not to go over the younger infant having tummy time! Spaces within the room are planned to serve the varying movement skills of this age group while supporting their social interactions.

3. *The environment has furniture and equipment that is child size.* Infants, toddlers, and twos should be able to reach materials on low shelves. Small, sturdy chairs allow them to climb on and off on their own. Sturdy, easy-to-clean, upholstered rings keep young babies safe from trampling by their friends during tummy time. Mobile infants appreciate a few steps that let them climb to a platform overlooking a window, even if the window just peeks into the next room. Low sinks help even the babies who are first

Low shelves support young children's ability to make choices.

standing to wash their hands. In a program that keeps children in one space for over 3 years, even young infant rooms need child-size potties.

4. *The environment has comfortable spaces that are inviting to children.* Spaces can be identified by pools of light, differences in floor coverings, play rings, low shelves, or cloth hung from the ceiling. Very young infants need spaces that protect them from somewhat older infants but still allow them to watch those very busy learners at work. The environment can be maximized to provide safety and invite socialization, but the adults must be close to the infants, interacting and mediating the physical and social experiences for all the babies. Box 4.1 highlights the effect of the environment on children's behavior.

5. *Teachers provide indoor and outdoor environments that furnish a rich variety of activity choices, materials, and toys that respond to children's varying levels of development, individual interests, and cultures.* No toys are usually more interesting to an infant than is being placed near another infant. That is because each baby will almost always react to whatever the other baby does. We are always looking for play materials that react to a child's actions, providing contingent responses that show a child that he can make things happen. Very young infants want toys that are small and light enough to grab and shake and mouth—without any danger of choking. Babies from 5 to 9 months may begin to notice categories of toys such as animals, cars and trucks, or blocks. Their play may still include mouthing, but is also likely to include throwing, dropping, picking up, flinging, dumping, emptying, banging together, and turning over.

Infants and toddlers need outdoor play areas as well. Simply discovering a stick or watching a beetle can be exciting for young children because everything is new to them. Outdoor areas need to provide shade from direct sunlight, grassy areas, and safe areas for young infants to crawl and roll. Blankets can define a play area, and toys that are familiar indoors may be more interesting when taken outside.

6. *Environments support adults in interacting with, supervising, and observing children.* Teachers of very young infants lift and carry them much of the time. Consequently, cribs, changing tables, sinks, and countertops should be at comfortable levels. Gliding rocking chairs or sofas that support quiet cuddles during feeding or when looking at books. Private areas invite family members to come in and breast- or bottle-feed their babies. Teachers need back support while sitting on the floor and perhaps some sturdy shelves to lean on while rising. Adequate storage within the room limits the number of times that teachers need to leave to gather supplies. All the children should always be within sight of the teachers. Cameras, clipboards, or even sticky pads help teachers document their observations in the moment.

Box 4.1

The Effect of Environment on Behavior

The physical environment affects children's learning and development in many ways. Well-designed environments support exploration, give young children a sense of control, and enable children to engage in focused, self-directed play. Poorly designed environments, on the other hand, discourage these activities. Because well-designed environments are engaging, they minimize problematic behaviors such as aggressiveness and aimless wandering.

The physical environment also affects relationships. Well-designed spaces evoke a sense of security, which is a prerequisite in the formation of a healthy identity. In appropriately designed classrooms, the children are given an opportunity to play both independently and in small groups and the teachers are supported in their role as observers and facilitators of children's learning and development. (Torelli, 2002)

MATERIALS, TOYS, AND EQUIPMENT IN EACH LEARNING AREA

The infant/toddler environment is homelike, while meeting the developmental needs of each age group (Figure 4.2). However, care teachers usually establish separate areas for different kinds of activities. Descriptions of these areas follow. Recommended materials, toys, and equipment are listed for each age group.

Figure 4.2 This toddler room has comfortable spaces that are inviting to the children and teachers.

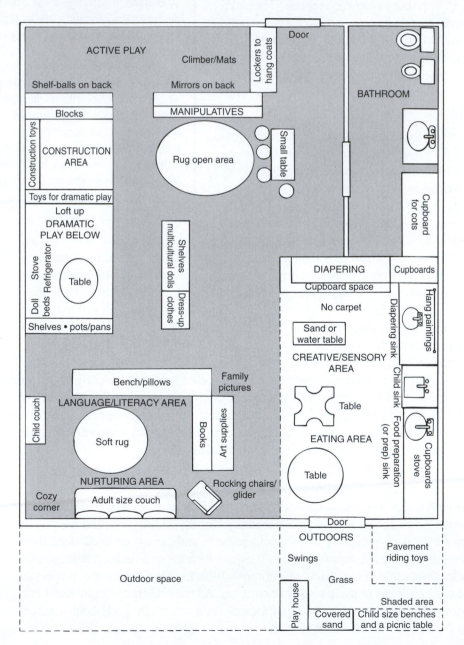

7.702.73 Rest Time Equipment [Rev. eff. 2/1/05]

E. In the infant nursery, individual cribs must be provided that allow sufficient space for the infant's length, size, and movement. Each crib must be sturdy, meet federal Consumer Product Safety Commission standards, and have a firm, comfortable mattress with safe, department-approved plastic sheeting or other type of waterproof material.

F. In the toddler nursery, a crib, sleeping cot, or 2-inch mat must be provided for each child, and there must be a minimum of 2 feet between each crib or cot. Aisles between cots or cribs must be kept free of all obstructions while cribs are occupied. No child under the age of 2 years should use a cot for sleeping without written permission of the parent or guardian.

   1. Individual cribs must provide each toddler with sufficient space for the toddler's length, size, and movement, and must meet federal Consumer Product Safety Commission standards. Each crib must be fitted with a firm, comfortable mattress and heavy plastic sheeting or other type of waterproof material. If individual cribs are used, they must be separated by a sturdy divider from the area used for activities.

   2. Sleeping cots and mats must be of firm construction and in good repair.

G. In the infant nursery, soft bedding materials that could pose a suffocation hazard are not permitted in cribs or playpens.

H. Infants who fall asleep in a swing or infant seat must be placed in their cribs for the remainder of their nap.

I. Infants must be placed on their backs for sleeping.

J. In the toddler nursery, a sheet and blanket or suitable covering must be provided for each child to be used only by that child.

Figure 4.3 Colorado Rules and Regulations Rest Time Equipment—Selected Items That Apply to Infants and Toddlers.
Source: http://nrc.uchsc.edu/STATES/CO/colorado.htm, p. 15.

Sleeping Area

A sleeping area invites infants and toddlers to nap tranquilly and peacefully—infants in their cribs, and mobile infants and toddlers on their cots placed in somewhat darkened, protected spaces. State licensing requirements specify additional requirements for this area in a program (see Figure 4.3). For example, to prevent suffocation, young infants sleep in cribs without blankets, pillows, or stuffed toys. As children develop, they begin to sleep on their own individual cots. Relationships flourish as care teachers rock infants to sleep; read stories to mobile infants, toddlers, and twos as they drift off to sleep; or pat a child's back and sing songs. Provide the following:

- Cribs with slats no more than 2 1/3 inches apart for infants
- Gliders for rocking infants to sleep
- A storage area for cots for toddlers and twos
- Bins to store each child's favorite blanket or stuffed animal

Feeding Area

Good eating habits begin in infancy. Environments that support healthy eating are quiet, social, and unhurried. Young infants drink their bottles of milk in the arms of caring teachers. When infants begin to eat solid food, teachers will need to add sturdy high chairs. Mobile infants, toddlers, and twos generally feed themselves while sitting at tables in short chairs with feet on the floor. They are learning about the pleasures of sharing a meal with friends. Provide the following:

- A high chair if a child can sit well
- Bibs
- Short tables and chairs
- Tablecloths or placemats
- Vases of flowers on the table

Diapering/Toileting Area

For all ages, a storage area with cubbies carefully labeled with each child's name makes diapering easier. The changing table must be near running water to wash both the teacher's and the child's hands. The sink used should not be the one used for food preparation. The changing table must face the room so that teachers can see other children while they are diapering one child. Neither infants nor toddlers need hanging mobiles over their heads. Rather, use diapering as an emotionally nurturing and language-rich opportunity by talking with infants and toddlers. A nearby bulletin board could display photos of the children and their families to spark conversations.

Young infants need frequent diaper changes throughout the day. This is one of the routines that makes up much of their experience. These moments should be used to build the relationship and offer affectionate and descriptive language. Provide the following:

- A changing table that can be easily disinfected
- Each child's clean diapers and wipes in separate containers

Figure 4.4   Use diapering time as an emotional and language learning opportunity with infants and toddlers.

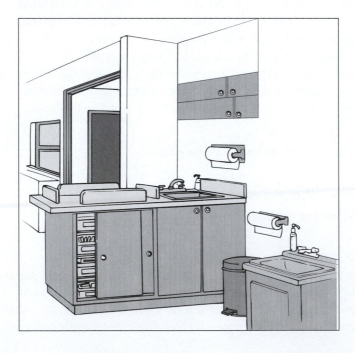

- Licensing-approved sanitation and disposal materials and equipment
- A place inaccessible to children for storing all diaper change supplies and disinfecting solutions and products

Mobile infants, toddlers, and twos understand the process of diapering and may come to expect it as a time during which they have your sole attention. As they get older, however, they may find it hard to stop what they are doing to take time for a diaper change.

- As children are able, add a wooden walk-up changing table that allows toddlers to climb up steps with railings on the side, with supervision.
- Some 2-year-olds will begin to use the toilet.

Cozy Corner

A cozy corner is just that—cozy and inviting. It may be situated in a corner, a tent, a box, or under a loft. Sometimes an infant or toddler wants to be alone for a while or to be with just one other person. A cozy corner provides a place where infants and toddlers can go for privacy, to relax, or to suck a thumb. Mobile infants, toddlers, and twos may pull a teacher to the cozy corner or climb in for some giggles with a peer. A child is never required to go to the cozy corner as a punishment; it is available as needed for comfort and nurturing.

This area meets children's needs in all domains. It meets children's emotional needs for comfort and safety. They may feel comfortable enough to express feelings to the teacher in this area that they do not in other areas. A quiet area can help infants and toddlers self-regulate (gain control of their body and emotions). Social skills and relationships blossom as a teacher and a child (or two children) relax together. Quiet cause-and-effect toys lead to thinking and fine motor development.

Young infants may want a cozy corner that is protected but not enclosed. Provide the following:

- A mirror
- Soft but firm toys
- Room for an adult and/or one or two infants
- A mat, a nest, or covered firm mattress (cover can be easily washed)

Mobile infants, toddlers, and twos may enjoy a cozy area into which they can climb and remove themselves from the activity of the room for a while. Add the following:

- Quiet cause-and-effect toys
- Firm pillows
- Pillows with a sleeve with a photo in it (Curtis & Carter, 2003)
- Music that a child can choose and control

A cozy corner in a center or family childcare home allows infants and toddlers to enjoy a quiet space.

Language and Literacy Area

A language and literacy area is a space where children explore books and other printed materials. In this area, teachers read books to children, and children look at books by themselves or with their peers. Toddlers and twos may use earphones to listen to stories.

A language and literacy space supports infants' and toddlers' love of books. Children grow emotionally, socially, cognitively, as well as in language and literacy. As children handle small books, their fine motor skills develop rapidly. Seven- to 9-month-olds who have been read many books will use their thumbs or fingers to try to turn the pages. They will scratch, stroke, and play with pages that provide different textures to explore.

Young infants may surprise you with their interest in books and pictures. Provide the following:

- A low bookshelf with covers of books showing
- A comfortable rug
- An adult-size couch
- Books, books, and more books
- All types of homemade books, for example, books created out of small photo albums with photos of children, families, and pets
- Flannel or Velcro boards to retell stories with props
- Puppets or stuffed animals that represent characters or objects in books and from different cultures

Mobile infants, toddlers, and twos will spend time looking at the pictures in books, practicing turning pages, and pointing to ask adults to supply the names of objects and pictures. They will need all the materials listed earlier. Add the following:

- A child-size couch
- Opportunities to write with crayons and safe markers (with the lids out of reach—they are a choking hazard)
- Meaningful words in this area (and others) written in English and in the children's other primary languages

Young infants may surprise you with their interest in books if there is a low bookshelf with the book covers showing.

In a book/reading area for toddlers, teachers and children can sit in a glider or on an adult-size couch. Children can sit on the floor, a child-size couch, or a child-size chair to look at books.

Creative Area

A creative area is one where children create with many different types of materials including paints, crayons, paper, glue, play dough, and clay. This area encourages children to invent, imagine, combine, mix, and create original works of art. Open-ended creativity is encouraged in this area, rather than products. Children express feelings and their self-worth grows when no products are required. Arrange the area so that there are opportunities for cooperation among peers.

Care teachers ask permission of infants and toddlers to print their names on the back of the work of art or on a separate card attached to the picture. Photographs of some of the artwork can be used for documentation of the activity or for a portfolio of the child's development.

Teachers can help children wash paint off fingers or cheeks when they locate this area near running water.

Young infants need to be supervised carefully with art materials. They may begin to show interest in this sort of activity at around 7 months as they are beginning to think about cause and effect. Every time a marker or paintbrush leaves color on a paper, it is an affirmation of cause and effect for the infant. Provide the following:

- Easy-to-clean floor space on which teachers can place large pieces of paper
- Nontoxic, washable tempera paint and finger paint
- Paintbrushes of various sizes and shapes
- Paint rollers
- Pieces of sponges, spools, or wands for painting
- Trays for individual children
- Smocks or long bibs to protect clothing
- A safe line or drying rack to allow wet pictures to dry

Mobile infants and toddlers/twos love to experiment with a variety of art materials. Over this age period, they will show increased interest in how the materials make

Toddlers enjoy painting at an easel.

marks or change their shapes. The materials listed earlier for infants continue to be important. Add the following:

- Short tables to stand beside and chairs, if needed
- Art materials such as crayons, both larger and smaller paintbrushes, play dough, and paper on a shelf at just the child's height
- Easels for both individual and cooperative opportunities
- No-spill paint cups with lids
- Rubbing plates, paper, and crayons
- Patterned, animal, and letter stamps for play dough
- Rolling pins and cookie cutters for play dough
- Collage materials and glue
- Smocks
- Displays of children's open-ended art creations

Sensory Area

This is a place to delight the senses—all of them. Teachers present ways to explore sounds, color, light, smells, and touch.

Young infants are fascinated, but some children can be easily overwhelmed by sensory information. Offer a limited number of choices or experiences to young infants to experience each day. Provide the following:

- Small bins of sand or water placed close together on the floor, under close supervision
- Feeling boxes with openings on each end to encourage two infants to interact with exciting objects to feel
- Large soda bottles with colored water and objects inside, hot-glued or taped tightly shut
- Sound cans
- Bubbles
- Musical toys

Mobile infants and toddlers/twos become more physically capable of sitting and standing as they use materials. Add the following:

- A light table or box with a light box accessory set and natural materials. A light table encourages children to experiment with how different objects and materials look. For example, the veins of leaves become visible on a light table.
- A larger sensory table. Experiment with adding water, sand, fabric pieces, balls, and unique materials to the tables.
- For the sensory table, funnels, waterwheels, sifters, cups, and household utensils
- Shallow pans of water holding beautiful pebbles. The pebbles must be large enough to prevent choking.

- Other materials, such as shaving cream, to use on safety mirrors, trays, and paper
- Consult with families before using food items on the sensory table. Some families may be sensitive to wasting food.

Dramatic Play Area

A dramatic play area invites mobile infants and toddlers to manipulate and pretend with child-size play household materials and appliances. Older toddlers imitate their families, pretending to cook, pour, feed babies, and rock babies to sleep. Social skills grow in this area as toddlers pretend together. When children use a pretend object, such as a plastic omelet, in their play they are learning about symbols, which is a literacy experience. Younger children manipulate clothing from their culture, pots and pans, and plastic dishes.

Young infants are not cognitively able to engage in dramatic play; however, they do enjoy exploring objects such as sturdy plastic cups and plates, hats, or play telephones and tools. Provide the following:

- Pegs on a wall to hang a few pieces of clothing
- Purses and other objects from home to explore

Mobile infants and toddlers/twos begin to enjoy more elaborate imitations of their real-life experiences. They may enjoy the following:

Sand and water provide important sensory opportunities.

- Child-size play appliances
- Child-size table and chairs
- Dolls, baby bed, blankets, bottles, baby stroller, baby car seat, doll high-chair, and other items to use with dolls
- Dress-up clothes—hats and clothing from their own culture and other cultures not represented in the group
- Replicas of kitchen items—play dishes, cooking pots, potholders, empty food boxes, food items from various cultures, and placemats
- Replicas of materials from familiar places—home; restaurant; grocery store, including cell phones, small grocery cart, safe tools
- Empty food boxes and other kitchen props
- Hats and props of community helpers
- Natural materials such as water, rocks, and grass (closely supervised)
- Children's books

Manipulative Area

A manipulative area has toys and materials that children can hold and explore with their hands and fingers.

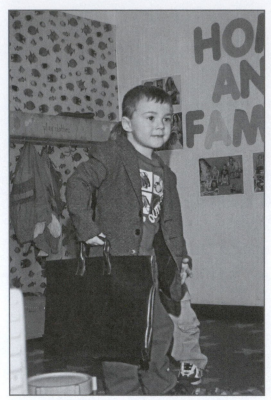

Mobile infants, toddlers, and twos pretend and develop friendships in a realistic dramatic play area.

Young infants enjoy looking at, handling, and sucking on pieces of manipulative toys. For the young infant, exploring different materials is closely associated with learning how to use her own body. Provide the following:

- Short shelves to attractively display toys
- Toys that infants can grasp with one hand, such as rattles of all shapes and sizes
- Toys that require both hands together (around 6 months)
- Rattles of all shapes and sizes
- Cloth or board books
- Stacking toys and rings
- Push and pop-up toys
- Musical toys
- Cars and trucks
- Containers and objects to put into and take out of containers
- Balls of all textures and sizes

Mobile infants and toddlers/twos will use manipulative toys to explore concepts such as parts of a whole, cause and effect, spatial relationships, matching, and sorting. Add the following:

- A short table and chairs
- Short shelves to display toys
- Toys that require a sequence of movements, such as a toy cash register
- More complicated cause-and-effect toys
- Large beads/strings
- Large building sets with multicultural people
- Puzzles with various numbers of pieces
- Shape sorters
- Rocks, shells, and other natural materials of various sizes and shapes
- Containers, boxes, and lids of various sizes and shapes
- Children's books

Construction Space

A construction space includes toys and blocks that children use to build, as well as props that children use to enhance their constructions. A hard surface, such as a low platform or a noncarpeted area, provides a stable foundation for building. Children learn about space, gravity, shapes, and color as they build alone or with others. Teachers provide rich language that describes children's actions and the materials, for example, the sizes and shapes of blocks.

Low shelves display a few manipulatives at a time so that young children can see each item.

Young infants may explore these materials by banging them together, sucking, throwing, turning them over, and looking at them. Some will begin to place one item inside another. Provide the following:

- Small blocks (large enough to prevent choking) of all textures, shapes, and sizes
- Wooden or plastic people, animals
- A short shelf
- Different sizes of containers

Mobile infants and toddlers/twos begin to explore how these materials might start as one unit and come apart, or how the pieces may be combined to become one object. They explore balance, gravity, and pretend play. Add the following:

- Unit blocks and other larger blocks
- Books on building
- Safe play cars and trucks

Children learn many concepts and use their fine motor skills as they play in the manipulative area of the room.

- Tape for making roads
- Other construction materials such as interlocking blocks, tubes, and cylinders
- Larger assortment of multicultural people and animals
- Material of various textures and sizes
- A storage shelf
- A large safety mirror

Active Area—Large Motor Activities

An active area encourages large motor activities such as crawling, climbing, throwing balls into containers, or jumping off strategically arranged low mats. Children use the large muscles in their arms and legs. They develop a sense of balance and stability.

Teachers and children use an open area for a variety of purposes. Infants lie on colorful quilts or mats on the floor and roll to their hearts' content. Mobile infants will bring toys, puzzles, puppets, and toy trucks to the area. Mobile infants and toddlers can gather while a teacher sits in the open area and begins to read a book, sing songs, and hold props such as puppets.

Young infants are working on the basic skills of supporting their heads, rolling over, and sitting. Primarily they need protected spaces and the support of an adult. Provide the following:

- Colorful mats set up in a variety of ways for creeping, crawling, climbing, cruising, and walking
- Swimming pool of safely sized balls of various textures

Mobile infants and toddlers/twos are all about movement—testing and refining their skills and trying new things. Add the following:

- Open area in which to be active
- A large ball hanging from the ceiling—high enough to reach, but not so high that the rope or string is a danger to children
- Laundry baskets and bean bags
- Balls of all shapes and sizes
- Large cube blocks
- A short climber
- Lofts with stairs to climb and a slide to come down
- A ladder in front of a safety mirror (Curtis & Carter, 2003)
- Boxes to climb into, sit in, or play peek-a-boo with windows cut out of the boxes

Walls and Bulletin Boards

Leave space open on walls. A cluttered wall, just as much as a cluttered floor, leads to stress for children and teachers.

Use walls to create the areas of the room. A window scene with curtains on the wall helps define a dramatic play area. Soothing wallpaper on the back side of a low shelf creates a cozy corner or part of the dramatic play area.

An active area for young infants includes mats and balls, and for older children, a climber and a ramp or slide.

Use the walls to enhance learning opportunities. A piece of contact paper attached to the wall with the sticky side out and a basket of natural materials invite children to stick items to their hearts' content.

Photos of children, families, and teachers help build relationships. Curtis and Carter (2003) recommend "bio boards"—posters with a photo(s) and information about a teacher, a child, or a family. These biographies help relationships deepen as teachers learn about families, and vice versa.

Mirrors on the wall expand a space and provide opportunities for infants and toddlers to see themselves and others.

Family and Teacher Space

Family and teacher space is separated from children's play areas by a divider, shelf, or curtain. Two comfortable chairs that recline or have footstools for putting feet up create an intimate space for mothers to breastfeed, for a chat with family members, or for teachers to relax with a cup of coffee or tea. Add magazines that teachers, mothers, and fathers might like to see as they relax. A small table with a colorful placemat and a vase with artificial or real flowers can enhance the ambiance of the space.

Adaptive Equipment

Adaptive equipment should be available to support the participation of any child with special needs. The purchase and use of this equipment should be planned with the family and early intervention team. Equipment may include special seating for positioning, adapted utensils for eating, or toys that become activated in response to sounds.

Display the children's work, children's and family photos, or painting in an attractive way for children to see. Windows also provide ever-changing views.

SUMMARY

Relationship-based, responsive environments promote children's relationships with their family, teachers, and peers. The environment is responsive to the infants' and toddlers' developmental levels, individual interests, and cultures. Care teachers should consider six dimensions of environments:

1. Environments for children are clean, safe, properly lighted, ventilated, and provide appropriate temperature regulation.

2. Environments contain design elements that reduce stimulation, create a sense of calm, and enable children to focus on each other, their teachers, and the materials they are exploring.

3. The environment has furniture and equipment that is child size.

4. The environment has comfortable spaces that are inviting to children.

5. Teachers provide indoor and outdoor environments that provide a rich variety of activity choices, materials, and toys that respond to children's varying levels of development, individual interests, and cultures.

6. Environments support adults in interacting, supervising, and observing children.

Different spaces in the center room or family childcare home invite infants and toddlers to engage in specific types of learning opportunities and to build relationships. These areas of the room include sleeping, feeding, diapering/toileting, cozy corner, language/literacy, creative, sensory, dramatic play, manipulative, construction, active play/large motor, and family/ teacher spaces. Infants and toddlers learn in all of the domains—emotional, social, motor, communication, and cognitive—in all of the spaces and moments in the program.

INVENTORY OF TEACHER PRACTICES

A Responsive, Relationship-Based Environment

Basic Concepts	A	S	R	Observation/ Reflection
I check each day to ensure the environment is clean, safe, properly lighted, ventilated, and has appropriate temperature regulation.				
I maintain design elements that reduce stimulation and create a sense of calm.				
The environment has furniture and equipment that is child size.				
I arrange for comfortable spaces that are inviting to children.				
I provide indoor and outdoor environments that provide a rich variety of activity choices, materials, and toys that respond to children's varying levels of development.				
I set up learning areas with developmentally appropriate materials.				
I maintain an environment that supports adults in interacting, supervising, and observing children.				
A = Always, S = Sometimes, R = Rarely				

REFLECTIONS

1. How can the environment be the third teacher?
2. What kinds of spaces did you most enjoy playing in as a child? Were they outdoors, full of sunshine, or have someone you loved nearby? Which of these qualities would you most want to recreate?
3. Think of an infant or toddler you know. What would need to be in a group environment to reflect that this child was a member of the group?

APPLICATIONS

1. In what ways could any one learning area support a child's emotional, social, language, literacy, cognitive, creative, sensory, and motor development?
2. In what ways could any one toy enhance a child's emotional, social, language, literacy, cognitive, creative, sensory, and motor development as the child enjoys playing with the toy?
3. How could a child explore concepts such as full/empty, in/out, up/down, light, gravity, and friendship in each area of the room?

RESOURCES

- The Program for Infant Toddler Care website has photographs of four model programs in California. Go to http://www.pitc.org/pub/pitc_docs/practice.html and click on California.
- Spaces for Children has photographs of beautiful child care programs, before and after pictures, and articles. Go to http://www.spacesforchildren.com.

5

Endless Opportunities for Guidance and Relationship Realignments

After reading this chapter, you will be able to:

- RESPECT
  - Understand the dimensions of the environment
  - Realize how hard it is to learn the rules of a culture from an infant's or toddler's point of view
- REFLECT
  - Recognize how infants and toddlers use behavior to communicate

- Know the difference between developmentally expected and concerning behaviors
- RELATE
  - Apply "Respect, Reflect, and Relate" to guidance
  - Think through the steps to realtigning relationships

Guidance is the adult's role in helping infants and toddlers learn how to be members of their culture and competent, lovable, sociable, and successful partners in relationships. Guidance is "a developmental, relationship-based, problem-solving approach to supporting young children's social and emotional development" (Wittmer & Petersen, 2006, p. 308).

GUIDANCE AS A RELATIONSHIP-BASED, INDIVIDUALIZED PROCESS

Throughout the first three years of life, when adults guide children they are supporting positive emotional and social development. They are helping children learn how to live harmoniously within their family, culture, and group program. This includes the formation of the infant's or toddler's own identity—a sense of who he or she is.

Infants and toddlers have much to learn about who they are and how they are supposed to behave on a particular day, in a particular situation, with particular people. To infants and toddlers, behavioral rules seem to change daily as they learn, for example, that they can laugh at home (except when Grandma is sleeping), but that they cannot laugh too loudly in church or synagogue (except when there is a social event). A child's culture may encourage behavior such as independence at school, but interdependence at home. Caring adults who guide children understand how challenging it is for infants and toddlers to learn how to act in different contexts. What does a care teacher need to know about guidance?

THE 3 Rs OF GUIDANCE: RESPECT, REFLECT, AND RELATE

Because becoming emotionally and socially competent involves learning, it is easy to understand that *"Respect, Reflect,* and *Relate"* is a process that is used for guidance as well as for planning learning opportunities and building strong relationships. Teachers can use this relationship-based approach to think about guidance with all children from birth to 3 years of age.

Respect

In each moment, a child learns about his own capabilities as well as how he or she will relate to others and the world. Infant/toddler care teachers view each *child,* each *experience,* and each *moment* as having value. With each experience infants and toddlers need to see through the eyes of family and teachers, that their feelings, goals, and physical needs are important and worthy of attention and response.

How do care teachers build children's sense of self-worth? First, they really listen to children. Second, they notice when the child is helpful and they appreciate the efforts of a child, for example, to sit at the table or not take a toy from another child. Third, they create opportunities for infants and toddlers to express their curiosity and desire to learn, experiment, set goals for themselves, and pursue their interests.

Fourth, they help each child learn ways to express his or her individuality while also becoming a member of a caring community. Fifth, they understand that infants and toddlers are capable and competent although with much still to learn about how to act in different situations with different people.

Teachers respect that each child is a member of a family and culture and develop guidance strategies in concert with families' beliefs and practices. In this way, guidance supports the family/child relationship as well as the teacher/child and peer relationships. For example, Mia (an 18-month-old) had increasingly out-of-control tantrums. The teachers and family assessed how much stress Mia was feeling with a new baby sister and decided to give her more positive attention. Her tantrums began to decrease. The relationships of the parent with the child and the teacher with the child improved. The respectful strategy that the teacher and parent chose in collaboration promoted Mia's positive relationships with her family and friends.

Care teachers also respect each child as a unique individual. A teacher who respects the shyness of a child does not push the child into social situations, but accompanies the child. Teachers who respect the uniqueness of a child also know that some children need to move frequently, other children share their feelings emphatically, and others quietly contain their anger and aggression. Teachers respect all of these styles.

Care teachers respect that each child is motivated to be socially and emotionally connected with others (Emde & Clyman, 1997). Care teachers build on infants' and toddlers' intrinsic desire to be with others.

Respectful care teachers understand that infants and toddlers communicate their feelings and intentions through their behavior. For infants and toddlers, all behaviors are a form of communication. An astute teacher "reads" the child's communication cues and responds with action or words. For example, when Luke, 9 months old, began to cry each day as he finished a bottle of milk, the teacher wisely knew that Luke was communicating distress, but did not know why. After consultation with the family, the teacher began feeding Luke more solid food. He then seemed happy and content after finishing a bottle, too. Instead of thinking that Luke was "just fussy," the care teachers listened to and respected his attempts to communicate his needs.

Knowledgeable adults also know that behaviors have different meanings at different stages of development. The developmental forces of security for the young infant, exploration for the mobile infant, and establishing a sense of self for toddlers and twos direct adults in how best to provide guidance.

Reflect

Reflection includes using knowledge of child development as a basis for thinking about what the infant or toddler is communicating through his behavior. The teacher reflects on how to help the child meet his or her needs while possibly encouraging different behavior. Reflection also provides an opportunity for the teacher to stop and think about her own reactions. Is the teacher's understanding of the situation accurate or is it influenced by other factors—the teacher's personal history, tension from other matters, or just not feeling well?

Wittmer and Petersen (2006) suggest using the following questions for reflection.

1. What is the child experiencing? What is the child's perspective on the situation?

2. What, when, where, and with whom does the behavior occur?

3. What is the child communicating that he or she wants or needs? What is the purpose of the child's behavior? What is the meaning of the child's behavior?

4. What do her family and I want the child to do/learn/feel?

As teachers and families answer these questions together, they find insight into how to relate to the child.

In warm, loving relationships, infants develop a sense of self-worth.

Relate

When teachers and families relate to young children, they use *relate guidance strategies*. These strategies are individualized and responsive to a child's unique temperament, needs, and strengths. Relate guidance strategies support children's healthy relationships with all of the important people in their lives, focusing on adult/child interactions that promote children's capabilities. In addition to changing the adult/child interactions, they may also change the environment to support infants' and toddlers' success in relationships and learning. Following are the relate guidance strategies (adapted from Wittmer & Petersen, 2009).

Relate Guidance Strategies

1. *Support Children's Healthy Relationships with All of the Important People in Their Lives.*
   • Support the children's healthy relationships with their families.
   • Build strong relationships between care teachers and families.
   • Build a strong, positive, trusting relationship with each care teacher and child— a truly caring relationship.
   • Use primary care and continuity of care systems to promote ongoing, secure teacher–child and peer relationships.
   • Have fun together.

2. *Focus on Adult–Child Responsive Interactions That Promote Children's Capacities.* Empathize with infants' and toddlers' goals, struggles, and feelings and ask the children what they need. Say what you think they are feeling or what you think they want.
   • Build emotional vocabulary—acknowledge and help children express strong feelings.
   • Patiently guide children toward controlling their impulses and behavior.
   • Recognize behavior as communication. Teach children to communicate.
   • Explain, teach, and show children *what to do* rather than *what not to do*. Make clear, positive statements to children.

- Notice and comment on children's positive behavior.
- Give short reasons and explanations to help young children begin to internalize the reasons for rules.
- Provide limits that keep the child, others, and materials safe and follow through when a child hurts himself, another child, or materials.
- Help children begin to take the perspective of others.
- Help children learn how to problem-solve and negotiate conflicts.
- Create loving rituals and routines that meet the needs of individual children.
- Use time-in (extra positive time with the teacher) and teach-in (help children learn what to do) rather than time-out (isolating children) with toddlers and twos.

3. *Create or Change the Environment to Support the Child's Relationships and Learning Depending on the Group of Children.*

- Provide toys, materials, and equipment that meet the interests and needs of children.
- Organize the environment to create less stress—less noise, less confusion, less running, softer lighting, and a private cozy corner for a child to relax.
- Add opportunities for children to learn to self-regulate—washable teething rings, a quilt on the floor, a mattress with a washable cover to lie on to rest, and nests to relax in.

As teachers *Respect, Reflect*, and *Relate* to children, they will think of more responsive guidance strategies to prevent children from feeling challenged and scaffold young children's emotional and social success. When care teachers use these strategies that focus on building children's relationships, infants and toddlers are more likely to be able to regulate and express feelings, learn how to cooperate and negotiate conflict, and develop a sense of self-worth within their family, culture, and childcare and education community.

Care teachers can use the process of "Respect, Reflect, and Relate" to figure out what children communicate with their facial expressions, body movements, and sounds.

"Respect, Reflect, and Relate" Scenario

Here is an example of how the 3 R process might look with a young infant.

A Glimpse of Guidance with Young Infants. With very young infants, the respect, reflect, and relate strategies deepen the teacher's understanding and help her respond in ways that increase the infant's sense of security and ability to regulate his reactions. Miriam's use of the 3 R's in working with Jack provides a good example:

At 6 months, Jack is not yet crawling, but he rolls or scoots wherever he wants to go. He is not very interested in the other children—but he wants their toys. He seems like a very self-contained little boy until Miriam needs to leave the room. At that point, he propels himself to the door and cries heartily. Shela, Miriam's co-teacher, cannot comfort him.

Both Shela and Miriam have observed this behavior for the last couple of weeks. They respect that this behavior has meaning for Jack and that he is communicating his feelings. But what are his feelings and his needs? Miriam reflects, asking herself the four reflection questions:

1. *What is the child experiencing? What is the child's perspective on the situation?* Miriam thinks that right now, Jack really feels secure only when she is in the room. Oddly, he is not that interested in her when she is in the room. However, he may be getting very frightened when she leaves. His crying is so loud that he seems unable to regulate his own reactions to the situation.

2. *What, when, where, and with whom does the behavior occur?* For the last two weeks or so, it has occurred whenever Miriam has left the room. Even if he is playing, Jack cries if he notices Miriam leaving. Jack does not mind other people coming in and out when Miriam is in the room.

3. *What wants or needs is the child communicating? What is the purpose of the child's behavior? What is the meaning of the child's behavior?* Miriam uses her knowledge of child development to think about the themes of security, regulation, and separation with Jack. She realizes that with primary caregiving, Jack really knows her better than he knows her co-teacher Shela—even though they are all together every day. Miriam feels that Jack is communicating fear and his goal is to feel secure again. Miriam asks Shela and Jack's parents whether her thoughts seem right to them. Jack's parents say that separation could be a challenge to Jack; they were warned that children from Eastern European orphanages have difficulty with attachment, but they adopted him so young, they thought he would be all right. Their apartment is so little that one of them is usually in his sight.

4. *What do I want the child to do/learn/feel?* Miriam hates the idea that she cannot leave the room without Jack being distressed. She wants him to feel okay whether she is there or not. It is tempting to just pick him up and take him along if she is running an errand in the building, but this wouldn't be helpful when stepping out to use the toilet or leaving for the day. Therefore, she wants Jack to feel secure and to be able to manage his feelings when she is out of the room.

Miriam and Shela made a plan for how they could relate to Jack and help him with his distress. They followed the relate strategies discussed earlier in this chapter:

1. Support children's healthy *relationships* with all of the important people in their lives.

2. Focus on adult–child *responsive interactions* that promote children's capacities.

3. Create or change the environment to support the child's relationships and learning.

Shela decided that she needed to make more of an effort to spend time with Jack when he is playing so that he might see her as a source of security. Miriam decided that she would use more words with Jack before she leaves the room, empathizing with his feelings, building his emotional vocabulary, and acknowledging his desire for her to stay. She will tell him that she is leaving, assure him that he will be fine with Shela, and inform him when she will be back. Then, when she reenters the room, she will go to Jack and show him that she has returned. Although Jack will not understand the words, Miriam hopes that he will feel understood.

Miriam and Shela had read that the game of peek-a-boo helps a child understand that people still exist even though they may be out of sight. They started to play peek-a-boo with Jack by holding a blanket over their faces for a few seconds and then peeking out with smiles on their faces to say "Peek-a-boo." They waited to see if Jack was interested in the game, and if he was, they continued the game until he lost interest.

Miriam talked with the family to support their relationship with Jack and to learn how they handled separation. Jack's parents discussed how his early experiences make separation difficult, and they only leave him when he is in child care. Miriam shared information on separation anxiety—what it is, when it occurs, and why a child might experience separation anxiety at a certain stage of development. She explained that Jack is beginning to understand object permanence because his eyes follow an object as it drops to the floor. He may also be experiencing person permanence—knowing that a person, although out of sight, still exists. She talked about the particular challenges Jack might have from lacking consistent, responsive caregiving for his first four months. Miriam and Jack's parents felt good about sharing information to understand the meaning of Jack's behavior and to support their relationships with Jack.

Miriam and Shela decided to laminate pictures of themselves for children to hold onto as well—especially hoping that it might help Jack to hold a picture of Miriam whenever she left the room.

Center for the Social-Emotional Foundations of Early Learning (CSFEL)

The Center for the Social-Emotional Foundations of Early Learning was created through funding from the federal Office of Head Start and the Office of Child Care. The CSFEL model begins with promoting healthy behavior and works through various meanings of behavior to the most challenging behaviors. The materials on the website include full training modules for infant toddler and preschool care teachers. Materials include lessons, activities, PowerPoint presentations, and video clips.

CSEFEL is based on a pyramid model. The pyramid represents using responsive caregiving to support attachment and self-regulation The materials are for care teachers, home visitors, and families of children from ages birth to 5. In many ways they echo the "Respect, Reflect, and Relate" process. The materials are free and available from http://csefel.vanderbilt.edu.

When Reflections Are Not Accurate

The tremendous vulnerability of young infants can stir all sorts of feelings in the adults around them. Adults who were not loved and cherished as infants can hear terrible reminders of loneliness in an infant's cries. They may find it much harder to understand the infant's needs for closeness and comfort as legitimate than does the adult who had loving, responsive relationships as an infant. Box 5.1 describes situations in which a teacher's thinking may not include accurate information on children's development.

Spoiling a Child

Sometimes adults worry about whether being responsive to infants will "spoil" a child, but what does it mean to "spoil" a child? Caregivers and parents might believe that picking up a baby when he or she cries or "giving in" to a child's demands will spoil the child. They legitimately want children to be kind, able to wait, and able to listen to adults. They are concerned that the child will become demanding, difficult, want to be carried around all the time, and become rude and uncaring.

However, children are more likely to exhibit demanding behaviors when no one is meeting their needs for protection, boundaries, love, kindness, and affection. Toddlers who exhibit daring or demanding behaviors may be also seeking limits. They want to know that they can count on someone to keep them safe from hurting themselves, others, and things.

Responsive care means meeting children's needs. If adults do not meet their emotional needs, the children may become defensive and angry (Gunnar & Cheatham, 2003). Table 5.1 highlights adults' beliefs about spoiling, the corresponding facts, and how adults can support children's emotional health. This information could be displayed on a poster placed in the room or family child care home or sent to parents in a brochure or a newsletter.

RELATIONSHIP REALIGNMENTS

In the development of infants and toddlers there are times when there is a shift in how they view the world (Brazelton & Sparrow, 2006; Gesell et al., 1940). These times occur because of the children's cognitive, emotional, social, language, and motor development. For example, an infant, when beginning to walk, sees the world differently. There is much more to explore and do when one is vertical rather than horizontal. There is a sense of freedom and separation from adults that the infant did not feel before. And not only does the infant view the world differently, but the world sees "the walker" differently. Relationships with family and teachers often must change as well—these relationships must be realigned. Several of these shifts in development and relationships occur when children experience separation anxiety, stranger anxiety, and the development of autonomy.

Box 5.1

When Reflects Are Not Accurate

What happens when your co-teacher "reflects" and then attributes reasons for an infant's behavior that are not developmentally possible? What do you do when your co-teacher says, "He's being manipulative" about a 6-month-old? Or "She just wants attention" about a 4-month-old? Or even, "He's so mean. I feel that he wants to hurt me."

Even though you know that young infants cannot have these motivations, it may be hard to think of a way to intervene that ensures that the infants in your care have their needs met and build a trusting relationship with a co-worker.

Consequently, you might say to your co-teacher, "In the class on infants I'm taking (or in the book I'm reading), they say:

- Young infants cannot really think about other people having their own thoughts and feelings about things. At this age, they are just trying to get their own needs met. The better they are at getting their needs met early, the more patient they will become in a few months—because they trust us to know what they want and to help them.
- It sometimes feels as if the infants wear you out, but they really do need to be held and they really do need our attention. They need you to help them feel safe and comfortable so they do not worry all the time."

If you are not sure whether your own reflections on the infant's behavior are accurate, check with the family, co-teachers, or others who know the infant well. Infants do not have ill intentions toward others—they are just using the communication skills they have to get the help they need.

Table 5.1   Spoiling

Belief	Fact	Support
Picking up a crying baby will cause the baby to cry more.	Infants under at least 1 year cannot be spoiled. Picking up a crying baby teaches the baby that he or she has self-worth, can trust adults, and can make things happen—increasing the child's motivation to learn and love. Infants who are responded to quickly actually cry less than do babies who are left to cry. Crying is a form of communication, and if adults talk with babies as they respond, the babies learn to communicate with sounds, words, and gestures as they develop and they cry less (reference).	There should be enough adult caregivers in the room to respond quickly to crying babies, comfort them, talk and sing to them, and help them become regulated.
If I pick up an infant or toddler who is fussing, distressed, or needing attention, the child will learn to demand attention all the time.	Infants or toddlers who are fussing or distressed may be bored, hurt, uncomfortable, sick, or they may want human companionship. They need affection. You can read their cues, figure out what they need, and then help them. A child who is bored can be picked up, or you can sit nearby and help the child get involved in an interesting activity while you stay near. Sometimes, though, children just need a hug, reassurance, or comforting. Of course, there may be days when they need to stay on a lap or be near a favorite adult all day. When caregivers respond to a distressed infant or toddler, they give the child hope that the world is a good place where their needs will be met. The children become confident and courageous. They can relate to others and they learn about cause and effect. Children whose needs are met are less likely to be demanding and are more likely to be able to love and learn.	A small group size allows caregivers to sit on the floor so that they are emotionally available to infants and toddlers. With primary care the child and caregiver form a secure attachment that helps the child feel safe.

Source: Adapted from *EQ Initiative,* 2007.

Separation Anxiety

One shift in relationships occurs around 7 months of age, when children begin to understand that the people they count on to keep them safe still exist when they are out of sight. Sometimes, this change occurs overnight. Suddenly one morning the infant cries vehemently when the parent says good-bye at the child care and education center or family child care home. The cries of an infant experiencing separation anxiety are often woeful and sorrowful—their cries are meant to bring their protector back into view. When this does not happen, the infant may sob, frequently look to the door where she last saw her parent, and have difficulty concentrating on play. It may be difficult for both the parent and the teacher to understand what happened, and both may feel confused about their relationship with the child. The parent may worry about leaving the child, and the teacher may wonder if the child likes him or her. Separation anxiety calls for relationship realignments. There are things that both the parent and teacher can do to support the child during this period of relationship realignment. Here are some ideas to help infants and toddlers with separation anxiety.

1. Teachers can assure the parent that separation anxiety occurs because of a change in how the infant thinks about people existing when out of sight. Infants "understand about people leaving before they learn about people returning. They can tell from your actions that you are about to leave. Anxiety begins to build even before you leave" (Greene, 2007).

2. Parents can begin preparing their child in the morning as they get dressed, ride in the car, and enter the child care and education setting. The parent might say, "First we are going to get dressed. Then we are going to ride in the car. Then you get to see Shela. She will be so excited to see you. Mommy will come back after you play and sleep." For parents inclined to sing, a routine song in the car helps prepare the child for separation. It can be a very simple song such as, "We are going to see Shela. Yea! You will get to stay and play." Or they can sing an adapted version of a Hap Palmer song: "Your mommy comes back, she always comes back. She always comes back and gets you." The young infant may not understand the words, but will become familiar with the routine and respond to the reassuring words and songs.

3. The parent can develop a ritual when saying good-bye—enter the room with the child, say "hi" to the teacher, make sure the child is with a teacher, give a kiss, and wave good-bye. A transitional object, a kiss in the hand to keep, or a special toy may help the mobile infant's separation anxiety.

4. It is important to say good-bye so that the infant does not always experience fear that her parent may sneak away. Over time, the infant will understand that when you say good-bye you will also be back. The parent can also create an "I'm back!" routine for when he or she picks up the child and says good-bye to the teacher.

5. The child's primary teacher can greet the child and family warmly, support the parent in carrying out the familiar routine, and be there for the child as the parent says good-bye. If the child cries, the teacher can say, "I know you are sad. Daddy will come back later." Have empathy for the child, comment on the child's feelings, and reassure him or her that Daddy will be back. During the day, a teacher can continue to build a strong positive relationship with the child, so that the child will feel secure. Primary caregiving and continuity of care ease children's separation anxiety.

Mobile infants, as well as infants and toddlers, experience times of disequilibrium. Their thinking changes as they develop an understanding of themselves as separate from the adults that take care of them, and that their favorite adults still exist even when they are out of sight. They may feel more powerful as they can move on their own, but they also feel more vulnerable (Lieberman, 1993). Stranger anxiety also may occur during this age period.

Stranger Anxiety

This can occur as early as 4 months of age and usually peaks between 12 and 15 months. An infant in a stroller may smile when a familiar caregiver peeks in at the infant, but suddenly look concerned and burst into tears when a stranger says "hello." A mobile infant or toddler may squeal and run to the safe arms of the teacher when a stranger enters the room or childcare home. This stage of development occurs because infants can recognize the special people in their lives and feel safest with them. At this age, children may feel safest with specific loved ones. Even grandparents, one of the parents, or a teacher may become a source of stranger anxiety. Some children feel this anxiety with very few people and others with many.

It is important to empathize with the child. The child who cries may be panicking at the thought of both leaving the loved one and being with a stranger or anyone other than the specific loved one. Introduce the child slowly to strangers. Encourage strangers, family members, and other teachers to approach slowly, show the child a toy, or sit and begin playing with toys while looking up at times and smiling at the child.

Tantrums

As infants grow into mobile infants, toddlers, and twos, they begin to realize that they are individuals who can express what they want to others—no bib, not eat, play longer, or no hand-holding as they cross the street with a family member. This stage is delightful, as infants, toddlers, and twos express their individuality and learn how to make decisions; however, relationship realignments often are required as adults realize that children can make choices while still needing protection. This stage can also result in children having tantrums.

Mobile infants and toddlers can become frustrated when they can't achieve what they set out to accomplish.

A toddler throws himself to the floor when the teacher says that it is time to put away toys and go to the table for lunch. Tantrums occur when the child wants to be independent, cannot regulate his or her behavior, and literally falls apart emotionally. One parent described a tantrum as "the emotional equivalent of a summer storm—sudden and sometimes fierce" (Tantrums, 2006).

Mobile infants and toddlers throw tantrums for a number of reasons. Infants or toddlers may be tired and feel stress and frustration from being rushed, feeling pressured, or from valiant efforts to feed themselves or put on socks. A mobile infant does not yet have the language to tell an adult that a particular bib is uncomfortable because it feels very scratchy on the chin. Mobile infants understand more than they can say. They want to accomplish tasks that they are not developmentally able to complete successfully. They may be able to control strong emotions at times but their attempts to self-regulate often fail them.

Prevention is sometimes possible. A child may give cues that a tantrum is coming, such as rubbing the eyes, looking very frustrated, or beginning to fall apart. The teacher can help the child express feelings, take a nap, or learn how to accomplish whatever task is frustrating the child. To prevent tantrums, give children choices. If they can decide whether to wear a coat or a sweater, they feel some control. You can read "You Are Not My Mother" or "Baby Animals on Parade," or sing "Thumbkin" or "There Once Was a Spider," where the characters develop autonomy, become decision makers, and begin to solve problems.

During a tantrum, stay close. Try to describe what the child is feeling and try to give him or her words to say instead of having a tantrum. Encourage children to say, "I'm angry" or "I'm sad." Parents report that when they teach their children sign language for "more," "eat," "drink," and "tired," mobile infants can express their needs and there are fewer tantrums. When a child is in the middle of the tantrum, stay calm—the child is out of control and becomes more frightened when the adult is out of control, too. They feel scared and need an adult to help them regulate and contain their strong emotions. The goal is self-regulation for the child and the teacher as well as relationship restoration.

If the child hurts self, others, or things in the environment, teachers can hold the child and go to a quiet place. The child's frustrated feelings should be acknowledged and the assurance given that the child will be brought back to play after calming down. Tantrums should peak at about 21 months and then begin to decrease. If tantrums continue throughout the toddler years and become more severe, then special support from a mental health consultant or referral for a complete health and developmental assessment is necessary to restore the child's emotional and social health.

RELATIONSHIP CHALLENGES

Infants, mobile infants, and toddlers may experience relationship challenges that interfere with learning, social relationships, and development. These challenges may include temperamental difficulties in coping with the environment, chaotic environments, or highly disruptive and distressing life events. Children who feel challenged need special support from caring adults who will try to figure out what is happening in the child's personal and physical environment. It is not helpful to label children as, for example, aggressive or destructive or to say that a child could behave if he or she just wanted to do so. Rather, think about the child's unique health, sensory processing and temperament, the child's experiences with relationships, and interactions and environment that may be influencing behavior.

Here are a few examples of relationship challenges that may occur with infants and toddlers and strategies for using the "Respect, Reflect, and Relate" approach to problem-solving. These children may need relationship restoration as their trust in adults may be diminished.

Child Who Bites People

When mobile infants, toddlers, and twos bite others, it is a serious matter. Biting hurts children and teachers. Family members, quite understandably, do not like it when they receive a call that their child has bite marks. Parents and teachers worry about health issues. Care teachers wonder, "What is happening in my room or child care home?"

Mobile infants actually are just learning that others have feelings that may be different from their own. If another child's arm interferes with attempts to play with a toy, a mobile infant might believe a bite on the other child's arm to be quite reasonable. Without adequate language, physical force may be a mobile infant's method of choice to move another child out of the way or express a strong opinion about keeping a particular toy that the other child wants too.

Here are useful strategies for dealing with biting:

- Respect that mobile infants do not have much language, but do have a sense of ownership and possession (Hay, 2006). Teach them how to communicate using facial expressions, words, and sign language.

- Respect that children often like to be with other children and have begun to play reciprocal games, but are still learning how to be social with peers (Eckerman & Didow, 1996; Eckerman & Didow, 2001; Eckerman & Peterman, 2001). Support them as they play and teach them social ways.

- Reflect on when the biting occurs and make a guess as to why it may be happening. Then try to prevent the biting.

- When a bite happens, relate to both the biter and the bitten. Both children will need support to repair their relationship. Help the children tell each other how they feel. Help them problem-solve. Show the biter other ways to relate to peers.

Child Who Feels Fearful, Cautious, and/or Withdraws from Others

Some infants and toddlers are temperamentally more cautious (Rothbart, 2007; Rubin & Coplan, 2004) and need teachers' and parents' support to enter a group or try out a new food or toy. Other children, however, seem fearful much of the time and constantly try to withdraw from teachers and/or peers. These children will need extra support from responsive, caring teachers to feel safe.

- Pair a mobile infant or toddler with a less fearful peer to play with sand or water.

- Prepare children for transitions with a calm, soothing voice.

- Do not scold the fearful child; rather, gently provide emotional support to the child to participate in the experiences offered in the room.

Child Who Hurts Adults, Other Children, or Materials in the Environment

Some researchers believe that most mobile infants and toddlers try to use aggressive behaviors and that adults need to help children learn alternative behaviors (Tremblay & Nagin, 2005). Some infants and toddlers who are aggressive may have observed violent behavior (Osofsky, 1995) in their homes. Other children who bite, hit, kick, spit, or pull hair are imitating behaviors that they have observed in their peers. Others become aggressive because they have little power in their lives, are overwhelmed, are stressed, or need attention. Some children receive attention when they are aggressive, while positive behaviors are ignored; or when hurtful behaviors are sometimes ignored and at other times reinforced.

- Observe carefully to determine what the child is trying to communicate and when, where, and how aggressive behaviors occur.
- Work closely with families to determine when aggressive behaviors began and to plan strategies for reducing aggressive behavior and teaching prosocial behavior.
- Build a positive, loving relationship with a child by giving one-on-one time often.
- Shadow a child who often uses aggression to teach him or her how to use signs, words, or gestures to communicate rather than use aggression.
- Give positive attention when the child is not using aggressive behavior.
- Change the environment to increase calm, engaged behavior.

Child Who Feels Rejected

Some mobile infants and toddlers are rejected by other children. They may be the object of toddlers' aggression and pushed out of a learning area. Rubin (2004) emphasizes that teachers must pay attention to these children because rejection by others can lead to future behavior problems.

- Observe carefully to chart when and why a child is rejected.
- Teach the rejected child how to be prosocial.
- If a rejected child is aggressive, meet the child's emotional needs for nurturance and teach alternative behaviors.

Child Who Experienced Trauma, Child Abuse, or Child Neglect

Children can suffer, experience traumatic events, and become angry, withdrawn, rejecting, and rejected. These children may be responding to a disorganized experience with relationships. They may be experiencing post-traumatic stress disorder, trauma, child abuse, and child neglect.

Post-Traumatic Stress Disorder. An infant or toddler may seem dazed, disoriented, fearful of the slightest sound, or afraid of being alone. Older toddlers may reenact the traumatic experience in play. They also may have witnessed violence or experienced maltreatment and abuse.

- Develop a system to report child abuse.
- Work with a mental health consultant in the community who can provide home visits and mental health intervention to the family.
- Work hard to develop a trusting relationship with the child.
- Always ask before hugging or holding a child.
- Provide many opportunities for sensory play with water, sand, and art materials (Malchiodi, 2008). These materials can help young children relax.

Witnessing Domestic Violence. Infants who witness domestic violence exhibit symptoms of trauma (Bogat, DeJonghe, Levendosky, Davidson, & von Eye, 2006). Mothers reported that 44 percent of infants exposed to severe domestic violence displayed at least one symptom of trauma—being on alert for danger, numbing or interference with development, or increased aggression. Infants were more likely to experience trauma symptoms when their mothers reported that *they* experienced trauma in response to severe violence.

- Observe for the symptoms of trauma.
- Develop a policy in the program for reporting child abuse and neglect.
- Work with a mental health consultant who can provide intervention services to the family and support to the teachers.

A Collaborative Approach to Supporting Children Who Feel Challenged

Care teachers and family members who observe that a child is feeling challenged can collaborate on figuring out what the child may need. The form in Figure 5.1 provides points for reflection for teachers, family members, and other professionals to use when a child feels challenged or adults feel challenged by a child's behavior.

---

1. **Respect the child: What is the child experiencing? What is the child's perspective on the situation?**
   Consider the following: What is the child feeling; what is the child is trying to communicate; is this a developmental stage; does the child know an alternative way to behave; what is the child's temperament; what are the child's expectations for relationships; is the child stressed; what has the child learned about how to interact with others; and what are the child's feelings of competence?

2. **Reflect on the following: What, when, where, and with whom does the behavior occur?**

3. **Reflect and Relate: What interactions and relationships does the child need going forward?**
   Does the child need (check one or more of the following):
   - more warm, loving, responsive relationships?
   - to feel regulated, safe, and secure?
   - to feel that she or he has some power/control in life?
   - his or her style of learning/playing is respected?
   - to receive more positive attention/admiration/love and caring?

Figure 5.1   Observation and Reflection of Children Who Feel Challenged
Note: Teachers and/or other professionals and family members complete the forms together.

- to develop self-worth as a lovable child?
- to feel that his or her communication cues and goals are respected?
- to learn how to communicate his or her needs and feelings (develop an emotion vocabulary)?
- to learn an alternative behavior?
- a fairly consistent but flexible schedule and loving routines?
- more/fewer/better organized choices and interesting learning opportunities in the environment?

Other:

4. Relate: What do you want the child to do instead of the challenging behavior?

5. Relate: How can adults and peers support this new behavior? Create an action plan.

Figure 5.1 (*continued*)

SUMMARY

Adults offer guidance to infants and toddlers by helping them learn the social rules of their culture and the skills needed for relationships. The process of "Respect, Reflect, and Relate" helps care teachers individualize the guidance offered. The adult respects and tries to understand the child's experience. She reflects on the causes and meanings of the behavior she observes. Finally, she chooses strategies that should help the child learn more-effective responses to the situation.

Relate guidance strategies include:

1. Support children's healthy relationships with their families.

2. Focus on adult-child responsive interactions that promote children's capacities.

3. Create or change the environment to support the child's relationships and learning.

Relationship realignments may be needed when the child goes through development shifts and experiences the world differently. These shifts may become visible as children demonstrate separation anxiety, stranger anxiety, and a growing sense of autonomy. Specific relationship challenges seen in the first 3 years of life include biting, fearfulness and withdrawal, aggression, rejection by peers, trauma, child abuse or neglect, and witnessing violence.

Each of these challenges can be best served by care teachers and family members working together to understand what the child may need. Observation, reflection, and planning protocols should be established within the program to support young children who are struggling with difficult issues.

INVENTORY OF TEACHER PRACTICES

Guidance

Basic Concepts	A	S	R	Observation/ Reflection
I support children's relationships with key family members and myself.				
I am responsive to individual children's uniqueness, temperament, and sensory needs.				
I show affection and comment on children's positive behavior.				
I teach and show children what to do instead of focusing on what not to do.				
I give short reasons when I ask children to do things.				
I build children's emotional vocabulary and ability to recognize and express feelings.				
I recognize that there are individual family and cultural differences in how to guide children and goals for children.				
I help children problem-solve and negotiate conflicts.				
I support children's peer relationships.				
I change the environment to respond to children's needs.				
I provide interesting and fun choices for children.				
I use "time-in" rather than "time-out."				
When children feel challenged I work collaboratively with the family to determine why and how to help the child.				
I consult with the family to refer them to community agencies for more support.				

A = Always, S = Sometimes, R = Rarely

REFLECTIONS

1. How can you use the "Respect, Reflect, and Relate" process in understanding an 18-month-old toddler's biting?
2. Why is it important that care teachers always collaborate with a child's family if that child is under stress?
3. In what ways could the manner of guidance (discipline, punishment) affect the developing sense of self?

APPLICATIONS

1. A 26-month-old is lashing out at other children all day long. She grabs toys, knocks down block structures, and does not want anyone sitting near her at the art table. Her father has been traveling frequently on business, and she has been bringing a small suitcase to school. Use the Relate guidance strategies to develop a plan to help this little girl manage her behavior.
2. Write a short parent newsletter article informing families about separation anxiety.
3. What steps could a care teacher take to support an infant or toddler who has suffered abuse, neglect, or other trauma?

RESOURCES

- Center for Evidence-based Practice: Young Children with Challenging Behavior. Available at http://www.challengingbehavior.org
- Center for Social Emotional Foundations of Learning. Available at http://www.csefel.vanderbilt.edu.
- *ZERO TO THREE*: This website has a section on challenging behaviors. Go to http://www.zerotothree.org and click on the "Find it fast" button.

6 Using Observation and Documentation for Responsive Planning and Ongoing Assessment

After reading this chapter, you will be able to:

- RESPECT
  - Observe infants and toddlers with understanding
  - Focus observation with tools
- REFLECT
  - Ways observation and assessment can enrich your experience
  - Ways observation and assessment can be used to engage families
- RELATE
  - Use observation and assessment for individualized planning

When Selena started caring for infants and toddlers, the work was called "babysitting" and no one thought much about special training. Her "plans" were just ideas she had, and "sitters" certainly didn't assess infants. No one did.

Now Selena takes notes and photos of the children, thinks about their interests and goals, and offers materials and activities she thinks will help them. She also tracks their development and discusses it regularly with the parents. She feels very attuned to the children in her care.

Selena is using the process of "Respect, Reflect, and Relate" to guide her planning for the children. "Respect, Reflect, and Relate" is a relationship-based approach to curriculum with these steps in planning:

Respect is the teacher's process of observing children's actions and assuming that they act in pursuit of their interests and questions about the world. Respect assumes that even very young infants have goals and try different strategies to meet their goals or figure out how things around them work. Respect includes creating documentation of the baby's actions, expressions, or vocalizations through photos, video, or anecdotal notes for later reflection.

Reflect is a two-part process for the teacher. On one level, the teacher thinks about the meaning of the baby's actions: What are the child's goals? What feelings is he or she trying to express? What is the infant trying to understand? On another level, the teacher is reflecting on her own feelings about the infant or toddler and on what could be done to deepen their relationship, keep the child comfortable, and help him or her achieve goals as best the teacher can understand them.

Relate describes the many actions that the teacher takes guided by understanding gained through respecting and reflecting. These actions should serve the relationship between the teacher and the child. The teacher lets the infants or toddlers know that he or she can recognize and respond to their feelings, can understand their interests and goals, and can support their efforts to feel safe and make sense of the world.

As more is learned about how very young children learn, appreciation for the discoveries they are constantly making grows. Selena *respects* children's learning by observing and taking notes and photographs. She *reflects* by studying her notes and pictures. She wonders about what the children are trying to do or understand. She thinks about what she might offer in interaction or changes in the environment that would further the child's exploration and knowledge. Finally, she *relates* to the child by taking some action.

For example, Selena has noticed that Bessie, a 2-year-old with Down syndrome, is most likely to attempt walking when she wants to join other children having fun at some distance from where she is. One day, when Selena noticed Sam and Chita laughing and playing at the sand table, she looked to see if Bessie had noticed them as well; she had not as of yet. Selena, in the first step of respect, started taking pictures of Bessie and was able to catch the moment she saw them. The pictures showed Bessie watching Sam and Chita and making up her mind to go to them. Other pictures showed Bessie's efforts to get up and walk and Bessie successfully joining her friends in play. Later that day, Selena reflected and examined the photographs and thought about what it might mean to Bessie to watch her friends from afar, get up to walk, and then join them. For the next few days, Selena related to Bessie's view of how things work and pointed to her friends playing across the room or the play yard, motivating Bessie to try walking without pressuring her.

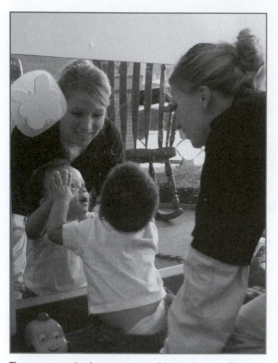

The care teacher's greatest tool in understanding each child is the ability to watch a child with the desire to understand the child's actions.

This chapter describes how infant/toddler care teachers use the process of "Respect, Reflect, and Relate" as they observe and document children's activities, plan for interactions and environments, and maintain an ongoing assessment of the children's development.

OBSERVATION

In many ways, observation is the cornerstone of early childhood education. Young children, especially infants and toddlers, approach the world with unique perspectives, their own brief history of experiences, and an endless succession of new discoveries. The infant/toddler care teacher's greatest tool in understanding each child is the ability to watch a child with the desire to understand the child's actions. Curtis and Carter write that "Listening, observing, and documenting is a pedagogy . . . (a way of thinking about learning and caregiving). . . . Caregivers who subscribe to a pedagogy of this nature come from a place of curiosity, believe in children's capabilities, and know they are engaging in a process that is unfolding, not static" (2000, p. xiii).

A care teacher documented Keenan's ability to focus even with other children playing near him.

Anecdotal Observation

Observer: *Selena*
Date: *9/26/11*
Place: *Play room*

Sequence	Inference
Bessie was playing with the toy cash register on the floor; pushing the buttons, smiling when the drawer popped out, and pushing it back in to start over.	Bessie was exploring the way the toy cash register worked. She seemed so interested that she wasn't aware of anything else in the room.
She heard Sam and Chita laughing at the sand table, watched them for about a minute, set the cash register aside, and pulled herself up on the shelving.	Then she noticed that Sam and Chita were laughing at the sand table.
	She seemed torn between staying with the toy she enjoyed and joining her friends.
She toddled over to them, stood and watched again for about a minute, and then joined them at the table.	After a moment, she dropped the toy and pulled herself up on the shelving to toddle over to her friends.
	She seemed very pleased to join them.

Figure 6.1 Anecdotal Observation

Observation is a process of respect because it assumes that each infant and toddler approaches the world with his or her own questions and is able to come up with strategies to answer those questions.

Observation Is More Than Watching

Observation is intentional. The infant/toddler care teacher watches the child with the intention of understanding. Observation may be objective, a notation or photograph that describes actions without attributing causes; or it may be interpretative, creating documentation that describes intentions.

For example, an intentional observation might be Selena paying attention to the moments that she thinks inspire Bessie to walk. It may also be simply watching Bessie with a sense of curiosity about what interests Bessie. An objective observation would record only what can be seen. An interpretative observation would include inferences. See Figure 6.1 to look at an anecdotal record.

Both observations represent intentional observation. Selena was certainly watching with the desire to understand Bessie. Both observations are probably true, and each would be useful. What teachers need to know is when they are adding interpretation to an observation. If they interpret too quickly, they may not be open to wondering about the child's experiences and intentions.

Observation Builds Relationships

Taking the time to look at children, to listen to them and wonder about them, slows us down. Moments of surprise or puzzlement or joy are seen that we could easily have missed otherwise. One teacher reported, "It is the act of observing—of giving someone my attention and trying to understand that child—that opens my heart. As I observe, I begin to know a child. A feeling bridge is built" (Jablon, Dombro, & Dichtelmiller, 1999, p. 10).

Sometimes in group care, an infant/toddler care teacher develops emotional connections with some children more readily than with others. These connections may arise from similarities in temperament, as, for example, when an energetic teacher enjoys the enthusiasm a feisty toddler brings into the room; or the care teacher may feel closer to children of his or her own race or culture. A teacher also may find one child charming and another sparkling and lively.

Observation can help promote close and caring relationships when they do not develop automatically. Focusing on how any child operates in the world is likely to help the teacher both understand and appreciate this child.

Guiding Observations with Questions

It can be helpful for the beginning observer to focus observation on a particular area. Here are some questions to guide observations of infants and toddlers:

- What does this child find interesting? How does he or she show interest?
- How does the child let me know what he wants or needs? What other strategies does he use to get what he needs? Is he persistent? Does he give up easily? Does he get frustrated?
- What is her physical condition? Does she eat well? Sleep well? Have energy?
- Should I expect the child's cultural expectations to be similar to or different from mine?
- What is the child's emotional range and reaction to the world? Is she generally mellow, shy, or intense? How is she comforted when she gets upset?
- How does he react to other infants and toddlers? To adults?
- Am I seeing anything that causes me concern for the child's development?

These questions may be a good place to begin practicing observation. After a while, studying the records of your observations will lead you to develop your own questions and guide further observations.

DOCUMENTATION: RECORDING OBSERVATIONS

Albert has cared for his mobile infants since they were very young. He knows them well, but their skills and interests change so quickly that he still records his observations. His notes and photos help him to understand the children's individual development and learning. His biggest challenge is finding time to take notes while caring for four mobile infants!

There are really two major skills in using documentation. The first is finding a way to record observations in the midst of the activity of infants and toddlers in group care. The second is learning to reflect on the information in ways that can inform planning for the child and the group.

Recording Observations

The most important thing about recording an observation is that the process be useful to the teachers and not a burden. Here are some ideas:

- Write on sticky notes that can be stuck in the child's file until you can study them.
- Plan to observe one child each day. Prepare your questions on a sheet of paper on a clipboard that you keep handy all day for note-taking. For example, Albert has been watching 16-month-old Goro following him and imitating much of what he does. Goro's mother calls Goro "little Albert." After studying his notes, Albert realized that Goro also imitated many of his father's actions in play: He used a block as a cell phone and said hello and good-bye to baby dolls in Japanese. Albert realized that Goro was practicing being like the men in his life. He decided to provide more props, such as a briefcase, play cell phones, and baseball caps, to promote that play.
- Have a prepared form with the child's name on the top and each developmental domain listed on the side, leaving space for observations in areas such as motor, cognitive, emotional, social, and language. Keep the sheets handy on a clipboard. (See Figure 6.2).
- Take photographs or videos of the children. A series of snapshots taken over the course of several minutes can be extremely revealing. Digital cameras allow you to take many photos without the cost of processing and developing, but they do require the use of a computer and printer.

Many infant/toddler care teachers reading this book will not have the luxury of using digital cameras to take a series of pictures. However, written notes are a fine place to start.

CHILD: *Lily*
OBSERVER: *Albert*
DATE: *10/5/11*

DOMAINS	OBSERVATION
MOTOR	*Lily used her Velcro mitt to play with the scarves and music. Sitting pretty well but chair needs some adjustment—still sliding down. Feet don't seem supported enough.*
LANGUAGE	*Lily is LISTENING! She wants me to both tell the names of pictures in books and sign them. Her signs are hard to read— but mine might not be much clearer. Talk to speech therapist.*
LEARNING	*It's hard to tell with our language limitations, but her attention tells the story. Is "reading" Hug over and over. Smiling. Velcroed corner of board books.*
EMOTIONAL	*What a sweet person. Goro tripped and cried. Lily reached out to touch him making little sounds. Comforting.*
SOCIAL	*Still not initiating much—only 1. Likes being near the others.*

Figure 6.2 Domain Chart

Documenting observations and studying the documentation has been the basis of the work at the infant schools of Reggio Emilia in Italy. In a description of documentation, Gandini writes:

> Documentation is an indispensable tool for educators in constructing positive experiences for children and in facilitating professional growth and communication for adults . . . In early childhood education, when we document, we make the deliberate choice to observe and record what happens in our environment in order to reflect and communicate the surprising discoveries in children's everyday lives and the extraordinary events and happenings in places where children are cared for. (Gandini & Goldhaber, 2001, pp. 123–124)

It is wonderful to have a second chance to think about and experience the infants and toddlers making "surprising discoveries": Where did that sound come from? Can I make these beads fit into this cup? Can I crawl up the slide? Can I do what my mommy does? The very act of trying to understand the infant's or toddler's actions is an act of respect. It naturally leads to possibilities of "constructing positive experiences for children" in planning processes that truly follow the lead of the baby.

Through photo documentation, care teachers can begin to understand how toddlers interact.

PLANNING FOR INFANTS AND TODDLERS

Miriam plans for her relationship with Paulo by sharing in his great joy when he manages to roll over. She is both physically and emotionally present for this repeated but still unreliable accomplishment. She laughs in attunement with his joyful face and sometimes claps her hands or uses words such as, "Look at you rolling, Paulo!" These very simple actions are the result of Miriam using the process of "Respect, Reflect, and Relate" in planning for supporting meaningful relationships.

The whole idea of planning for young infants can be a little challenging for teachers. When we think of planning, what comes to mind is lesson plans—something that we intend to teach and how we intend to teach it. When curriculum is a process of "Respect, Reflect, and Relate," however, "teaching" and "lesson plans" are no longer the primary part of the process. Planning becomes a process of observing babies, thinking about their interests and the purpose of their actions, and then planning for moments of interaction that have emotional meaning and support learning through exploration and discovery.

With young infants, teachers first plan for opportunities that will support their relationship with the infants, the baby's relationship with the family, and the babies' relationships with each other.

Teachers of young infants also recognize the importance of routines as they plan. A teacher will plan learning and relationship-building interactions during routines. These may include calming and murmuring to 3-month-old Adara as she hungrily sucks her first bottle of the day or singing the hand-washing song with 7-month-old Takala after diapering.

Early Learning Guidelines

As part of President George W. Bush's "Good Start, Grow Smart" early childhood initiative, the states were required to create Early Learning Guidelines in language, literacy, and mathematics for children from ages 3–5. The guidelines needed to align with the K–12 standards. The process of exploring what young children should know and be able to do proved so valuable to the early childhood communities in the states that many states chose to go through a similar process for children from birth to age 3. Some of these guidelines have been well researched and provide a good description of what infants and toddlers should be learning and doing. They can be very helpful in the planning process.

Early Learning Guidelines specific to infants and toddlers are currently developed by 19 states and 3 territories (AR, CA, CNMI, CT, DC, DE, FL, GA, GU, KY, LA, MD, ME, MI, MN, MS, NC, ND, NE, OH, PA, PR). Early Learning Guidelines are established in a birth through age 5 framework in 12 states (AK, AL, IA, ID, IN, KS, NH, OR, TN, VA, WA, WI) (National Infant Toddler Childcare Initiative, 2010).

The Infant Toddler Early Learning Guidelines (IT/ELG) usually include examples of how children might demonstrate the skill or knowledge and how adults can support their emergence. There are a variety of resources regarding IT/ELGs; some are listed at the end of this chapter. For an example of a well researched IT/ELG, see Figure 6.3.

Planning Forms

Plans for individuals and groups should be prepared every several days or weekly. The following individual and group planning forms provide examples of ways to use the "Respect, Reflect, and Relate" process for curriculum planning that includes relationships and routines.

The first individual child planning guide (Box 6.1) includes specific spaces for each developmental domain. The second version (Box 6.2) takes a more integrated approach to development. Each form asks the teacher to observe the infant or toddler and infer from the child's actions and expressions what interests, excites, or intrigues the child. Then the teacher reflects on his or her understanding of the infant or toddler and personal ideas on furthering the child's interests and development. In planning, the teacher will consider the needs of each individual and the group as well as the logistics of their situation. For example, Miriam would list Paulo's interest in cooing, in reaching, and in being with her, and then plan to spend time playing with him by offering toys he can reach for and grab while she makes the game more exciting by saying, "How about this one? Do you want this bear, Paulo? Ooooh! You got it!"

Box 6.3, the next planning guide, provides a way for care teachers to summarize the current interests of the group and to plan for the group in a way that is responsive

Foundation: Memory

California Infant/Toddler Learning & Development Foundations

The developing ability to store and later retrieve information about past experiences

8 months	18 months	36 months
At around 8 months of age, children recognize familiar people, objects, and routines in the environment and show awareness that familiar people still exist even when they are no longer physically present.	At around 18 months of age, children remember typical actions of people, the location of objects, and steps of routines.	At around 36 months of age, children anticipate the series of steps in familiar activities, events, or routines; remember characteristics of the environment or people in it; and may briefly describe recent past events or act them out. (24–36 mos.; Seigel, 1999, p. 33)
For example, the child may:	*For example, the child may:*	*For example, the child may:*
Turn toward the front door when hearing the doorbell ring or toward the phone when hearing the phone ring. (8 mos.; Meisels and others, 2003, p. 20)	Get a blanket from the doll cradle because that is where baby blankets are usually stored, after the infant care teacher says, "The baby is tired. Where's her blanket?" (15–18 mos.; Parks, 2004, p. 67)	Communicate, "Big slide" after a trip to neighborhood park. (24–36 mos.; Seigel, 1999, p. 33)
Look for the father after he briefly steps out of the child care room during drop-off in the morning. (8 mos.; Meisels and others, 2003, p. 20)	Anticipate and participate in the steps of a nap routine. (18 mos.; Fogel, 2001, p. 368)	Tell a parent, "Today we jumped in the puddles" when picked up from school. (Siegel, 1999, p. 34)
	Watch the infant care teacher placing a toy inside one of three pots with lids and reach for the correct lid when the teacher asks where the toy went. (8–18 mos.; Lally and others, 1995, pp. 78–79)	Recall an event in the past, such as the time a family member came to school and made a snack. (18–36 mos.; Siegel, 1999, p. 46)
	Continue to search for an object even though it is hidden under something distracting, such as a soft blanket or a crinkly piece of paper.	Identify which child is absent from school that day by looking around the snack table and figuring out who is missing. (18–36 mos.; Lally and others, 1995, pp. 78–79)
	See a photo of a close family member and say his name or hug the photo.	Act out a trip to the grocery store by getting a cart, putting food in it, and paying for the food. (24 mos.; Bauer & Mandler, 1989)
	Go to the cubby to get his blanket that is inside the diaper bag.	Get her pillow out of the cubby, in anticipation of naptime as soon as lunch is finished.
Behaviors leading up to the foundation (4 to 7 months)	**Behaviors leading up to the foundation (9 to 17 months)**	**Behaviors leading up to the foundation (19 to 35 months)**
During this period, the child may:	*During this period, the child may:*	*During this period, the child may:*
Explore toys with hands and mouth. (3–6 mos.; Parks, 2004, p. 10)	Ask for a parent after morning drop-off. (9–12 mos.; Lerner & Ciervo, 2003)	Say "meow" when the infant care teacher points to the picture of the cat and asks what the cat says. (12–24 mos.; Siegel, 1999, p. 32)
Find a rattle hidden under a blanket when only the handle is showing. (4–6 mos.; Parks, 2004, p. 42)	Reach in the infant care teacher's pocket after watching him hide a toy there. (11–13 mos.; Parks, 2004, p. 43)	Give another child an object that belongs to her. (12–24 mos.; Siegel, 1999, p. 32)
Look toward the floor when the bottle falls off table. (Scaled score of 10 for 5:06–5:15 mos.; Bayley, 2006, p. 55; 8 mos.; Meisels and others 2003, p. 20; birth–8 mos.; Lally and others, 1995, p. 72)	Look or reach inside a container of small toys after seeing the infant care teacher take the toys off the table and put them in the container. (Scaled score of 10 for 8:16–9:15 mos.; Bayley, 2006, p. 57; birth–8 mos.; Lally and others, 1995, pp. 78–79)	Remember where toys should be put away in the classroom. (21–24 mos.; Parks, 2004, p. 318)
	Lift a scarf to search for a toy after seeing the infant care teacher hide it under the scarf. (By 8 mos.; American Academy of Pediatrics, 2004, p. 244; 8 mos.; Kail, 1990, p. 112)	Find a hidden toy, even when it is hidden under two or three blankets. (By 24 mos.; American Academy of Pediatrics, 2004, p. 273)
		Express "mama" when the infant care teacher asks who packed the child's snack.

Figure 6.3   California Infant/Toddler Learning & Development Foundations

Box 6.1

Individual Child Planning Guide (1) for Paulo

Child's Name: _Paulo_   Plans for Week of (Date): _March 12, 2012_

Person Completing the Guide: _Miriam_

Respect: Child's Emotions, Effort, Goals, Learning, and Relationships

Write an observation or use a picture or other documentation here—date all notes

Paulo is very active and loves to play. Rolling. Reaching. Likes Adara. Sometimes needs a break from the action.

Respect and Reflect	Relate
What am I doing? _Turning away_ _Drooling_ **How am I feeling?** _I may be feeling overstimulated—need a break_ **What am I learning?** • **Emotional** _I can express my feelings_ • **Social** _Rolling to Adara_ • **Cognitive** _Reaching for what I want_ _Making noise with toys_ • **Language** _Cooing, taking turns_ • **Motor** _Rolling, reaching_	**What will you do to support my learning?** • **Responsive interactions** _Play with Paulo with rolling and reaching_ _Watch for signs of needing a break_ • **Environment: Toys, materials** _Offer reaching experiences_ _Lap time for hands together_ _Time with Adara_ • **Opportunities**

to the individuals. The fourth planning guide, Box 6.4, is organized around the typical routines that make up so much of infant care.

Each of these options centers on the interactions that the care teacher will provide and responsive changes that he or she will make to the environment. Each guide follows the process of "Respect, Reflect, and Relate." Blank copies of the forms are available in Appendix A at the end of this book.

Box 6.2

Individual Child Planning Guide (2) for Takala

Child's Name: *Takala*   Plans for Week of (Date): *March 12, 2012*

Person Completing the Guide: *Miriam*

Respect: Child's Emotions, Effort, Goals, Learning, and Relationships

Write an observation or use a picture or other documentation here—date all notes

3/11/12 Takala has been away for a week and did not want to leave her Dad this morning. She turned her head away from me and buried it in her Daddy's chest. She let me comfort her as Dad left and settled in with her friends after about 20 minutes.

3/13/12 Takala seems to have a whole new interest in babbling since her vacation. She plays with making sounds but also loves it when we imitate her sounds.

3/13/12 Takala is crawling with new control and purpose too. She only gets so far and then drops on her tummy but it almost seems as if she's doing it as much to amuse (or tease) Jack as from her own desire to move.

Reflect	Relate

Date all notes:
 	
What am I doing?
Crawling for fun and to get things
 	
What am I feeling?
Unhappy around strangers; miss mommy and daddy
 	
What am I learning?
Playing with sounds, talking
	What will you do to support my development and learning?
	
	• **Responsive interactions**
	   Support separation, concern around strangers
	
	• **Environment: Toys, materials**
	   Safe places to crawl; favorite toys on low shelves
	
	• **Opportunities**
	   More outdoor time

ONGOING ASSESSMENT

Selena has cared for children for many years, but only recently has the program begun to use formal assessment. At first, all the infant/toddler care teachers objected. They were already doing observations and documentation. How would they find time to do assessments? How would assessment make any difference in the care they offered?

Following the infant or toddler's lead is exactly the right principle in planning for materials, activities, and interactions. However, the infant/toddler care teacher also wants to keep an eye on whether each child is functioning within an expected developmental range. Programs use various kinds of assessments to track children's development.

Box 6.3

Individually Responsive Group Planning Guide

Name of Group: *Butterflies*   Week of: *March 12–16, 2012*

Person(s) completing this guide: *Miriam*

Respect and Reflect

The children in my group are . . .

(Summarize information from the individual planning guides)

Working on regulation/self-regulation around routines and separation

Exploring cause/effect

Enjoying using their bodies in different ways

Interested in each other

Trusting adults to respond to them and have fun with them

Learning to use sounds for communication

Relate: Plans for the Week to Meet Children's Interests and Needs

Songs/Fingerplays/Music

Keep singing—Twinkle, twinkle and Itsy, Bitsy Spider

Tapes of the families singing the songs of their cultures

Stories/Books

Look at a book with each child at least once a day.

Responsive Interactions

Follow children's lead in interactions.

Take advantage of diapering and feeding times for quiet, intimate one-on-one interactions.

Respond to children's language with imitation.

Use words to name the children's feelings and actions.

Environment: Toys, materials

Provide a cozy ring for Adara that keeps her safe while letting her watch everyone else moving around.

Provide lots of open space for the rolling and crawling that is so interesting to Paulo, Jack, and Takala.

Bring in additional soft plastic toys for "chewing" because we have several children teething and need to keep a big supply of clean toys on hand.

Opportunities

Family/Cultural Experiences

Other

Box 6.4

Group Planning for Routines

Name of Group: _Miriam's Group (Age Range—3 to 9 months)_   Week of: _March 12—16, 2012_

Person(s) Completing This Guide: _Miriam and Shela_

Developing a caring community: Think about what is happening and what could happen to develop a relationship-based program for children, families, and teachers.

Routine	What is going well for the children and teachers?	What could we do to improve the experience for children, families, and teachers?
Greeting Time or Good-bye Time	Morning greetings are going well. The babies are so young they are pretty comfortable. There are always a few minutes for parents to sign in and chat.	Takala needs extra support in separating. Adara arrives asleep and is placed right into her crib.
Feeding Infants and Toddler Eating Times/ Oral Health	Everyone eats on demand. Usually they stagger their feedings but if someone has to wait, the older babies do better waiting a few minutes. We clean children's gums with a damp gauze once a day.	An extra helper in the late morning would prevent any waiting. Maybe our director could come in for half an hour.
Infant Sleep and Toddler Nap Times	Everyone sleeps when they need to.	Takala and Paulo are rocked to sleep. Jack and Adara fall asleep in their cribs.
Diapering	Everyone is changed, as they need it. Notes made for parents; we use this time for talking with babies.	No change.
Toileting		
Play Times	The babies are interested in each other.	Much of the play is examining, mouthing, and tossing small toys. We need to increase the number of toys available because so many are being cleaned at any time.
Outdoor Times	We use the group stroller for a walk every day and use the play yard.	No change.
Transitions	No formal transitions because all care is "on demand."	No change
Other Routines		

What Is Assessment?

Assessment involves observing a child's performance compared to certain skills that usually appear in a predictable order or within a certain age range. Assessing development in infants and toddlers should involve several ways of collecting information and should occur over time. These methods include the teacher observing the infant or toddler, parents reporting what they observe, and the use of some sort of milestone-based test. Definitions will be helpful in understanding the sometimes-confusing array of assessment materials for infants and toddlers.

- *Screening* "is used to determine if developmental skills are progressing as expected or if there is cause for concern and further evaluation is necessary" (EHS NRC, 1996).

- *Assessment* is the ongoing process used to identify the child's strengths, interests, and developmental needs.

- *Evaluation* is the process used when there is concern about a possible developmental delay. An early intervention team, following concern expressed by the parents, generally conducts it.

Early childhood care and education programs generally use some instrument as part of their ongoing assessment of children. There are basically two kinds of instruments available: task oriented and functional.

- *Task-based assessment tools* usually involve an examiner presenting a specific material to an infant or toddler and asking him or her to copy an action (stack these blocks) or to answer a question (point to the doll's eyes). The tasks are matched to recognized milestones (Dichtelmiller & Ensler, 2004). Task-based assessments may be norm-referenced or criteria-referenced.

- *Norm-referenced assessments* compare how a child performs to how a large group of children that age perform on the same task. The child is not necessarily expected to have practiced and mastered the particular item being tested. Rather, the item should be achievable by a child at a certain developmental level.

- *Criteria-referenced assessments* measure what the child being tested knows and can do. The items being tested are skills or knowledge arranged in a predictable order of development (Bond, 1996).

- *Functional assessment* tools involve the caregiver looking "for each child's individual way of accomplishing certain functions or purposes. For example, a caregiver might observe a child at the center or during a home visit in order to discover how the child shows trust in others, communicates, or moves around his environment" (Dichtelmiller & Ensler, 2004).

How Is Assessment Helpful to Infant/Toddler Programs?

It is difficult for infant/toddler care teachers to find the time to complete assessments, but there are many benefits for the teacher, the child, and family. Assessment helps infant care teachers build relationships with infants and toddlers for the same reason that observation and documentation do. Taking time to really look at what infants and toddlers are trying to do and how they are going about the task increases the infant care teacher's understanding and feelings of closeness to the child (Jablon, Dombro, & Dichtelmiller, 1999).

Assessment also provides a developmental foundation for individualized planning. The process of "Respect, Reflect, and Relate" is a good guide to building on a child's strengths and interests. An assessment helps to remind the infant/toddler care teacher to consider areas in which the child is not showing interest. The teacher may want to offer more interesting opportunities in that area. For example, if the toddlers in a group are each playing alone but seldom play with one another, the toddler care teacher may want to offer activities that bring children together, such as putting stickers on a large sheet of butcher paper or using spray bottles with colored water to paint a sheet hanging outdoors.

A third, but extremely important, role for ongoing assessment is to track the development of each child to look for delays. If a child's development is not progressing over time, the infant/toddler care teacher will need to discuss these concerns with the family. A referral for an evaluation by early intervention may be in order. Many delays or disabling conditions may be identified and most effectively treated in infancy (Dichtelmiller & Ensler, 2004).

What Are Some Commonly Used Assessments?

Some testing instruments available today are to be used only for screening. They give a quick, simple look at whether developmental milestones are being met. Other tests provide an in-depth look at one or more specific areas of development. These are generally used for ongoing assessment or evaluations.

Group care programs need tools for ongoing assessment that inform planning and monitor development. Some of the most commonly used assessments are the Ounce Scale; the Child Observation Record (COR); the Teaching Strategies Gold assessment; the Assessment, Evaluation, and Programming System (AEPS); and the Hawaii Early Learning Profile (HELP). Use of these assessments may be required by federal or state agencies for programs that receive public financing. Some programs also use self-created milestone charts that employ a sort of ongoing screening rather than an assessment.

- *The Ounce Scale* (Meisels, Dombro, Marsden, Weston, & Jewkes, 2003) is an observational and functional assessment. It includes an observation record and developmental profile, standards for infant/toddler care teachers, and a family album for family members. The caregiver uses observations from the observation record and family album and compares them to the developmental profile to evaluate the child's development. The Ounce Scale is organized around six meaningful areas of development:

  Personal connections—how children show trust
  Feelings about self—how children express who they are
  Relationships with other children—how children act around other children
  Understanding and communicating—how children understand and communicate
  Exploration and problem-solving—how children explore and figure things out
  Movement and coordination—how children move their bodies and use their hands

- *The High/Scope Child Observation Record* (COR) *for Infants and Toddlers* (High/Scope, n.d.) is an observational assessment used by infant/toddler care teachers and families over months of observation. Using a method called authentic assessment, the COR looks at children's strengths, helps teachers to know children better, and supports individualized planning. It also provides a framework for discussing children's developmental needs with parents. COR covers the following developmental areas:

  Sense of self
  Social relations

Creative representation
Movement
Music
Communication and language
Exploring objects
Early quantity and number
Space
Time

- *Teaching Strategies Gold Birth through Five Assessment* (Berke, Bickart & Haroman, 2010) is a criterion-referenced tool that is part of an entire curriculum system. The developmental continuum for infants, toddlers, and twos describes the typical progression of development in four areas:

Social/emotional
Physical
Cognitive
Language

The system is designed to help teachers observe children intentionally; use that information to respond to each child's interests, strengths, and needs; and communicate with families. It identifies children's levels of development and links individualized curriculum to the assessment. It is also designed to help teachers support the inclusion of children with disabilities.

- *The Hawaii Early Learning Profile* (HELP) is also a curriculum-based assessment (VORT, 2004). It covers 685 skills in six domains:

Cognitive
Language
Gross motor
Fine motor
Social
Self-help

HELP is criterion-referenced, used for identifying needs, tracking growth and development, and planning for next steps. Play activities and early intervention strategies are provided for each skill. HELP is widely used in childcare and early intervention programs.

SUMMARY

The most important work of the infant/toddler care teacher is in developing relationships with the children for whom primary care is provided and their families. Using a system of observation, documentation, planning, and assessment helps the infant/toddler care teacher to deepen understanding of each child, individualize planning, and track development. Most importantly, it helps each teacher develop an appreciation of each child's view of the world, unspoken questions, and strategies he or she uses to answer those questions. The focus of the "Respect, Reflect, and Relate" process slows down the busy infant care teacher, providing more opportunities for developing a meaningful relationship with each child.

Respect involves intentional observation, including recording observations for later study. Reflect includes the study of the recorded observations, trying to understand the meaning of those moments for the child, and examining one's own reactions and feelings. Relate is the process of choosing interactions, materials, or experiences to offer the child to further his or her interests and learning. Ongoing assessment keeps a developmental perspective on each child, assuring that teachers offer activities to strengthen areas of development that are of less interest to the child and to identify developmental concerns.

INVENTORY OF TEACHER PRACTICES

Observation, Documentation, Planning, and Assessment

Basic Concepts	A	S	R	Observation/ Reflection
I take time to observe each child each week.				
I find that regular observations help build my relationship with each child.				
I sometimes create specific questions for my observation. (How is Sam building with blocks?)				
I keep records of each observation (anecdotal notes, photos).				
I review the observation documentation to deepen my understanding and use as a basis for planning.				
I create individual written plans for each child (or each child within the group).				
I use a system of ongoing assessment to track each child's development.				
I regularly discuss each child's development with his or her parents.				

A = Always, S = Sometimes, R = Rarely

REFLECTIONS

1. How do you find time to observe and record your observations while caring for infants and toddlers?
2. A documentation may be a series of photos. Look at these photos. What might this girl be trying to accomplish?

3. In what ways do assessments feel like testing young children?

APPLICATIONS

1. Some infant care teachers have never used assessments. Some complete them because they are required but then file them away without using them. Write a one-page document answering the following questions: What would you want an assessment to tell you? How could you use the results? Share your document with others for feedback.
2. Write an objective anecdotal record on an observation. Then write an inferential record of the same observation. Compare and contrast the records.
3. Have members of a group each review one of a variety of infant toddler assessments. In what ways would each assessment be useful?

RESOURCES

* Bagnato, S. J., Neisworth, J. T., & Pretti-Frontczak, K. (2010). *Linking authentic assessment & early childhood intervention: Best measures for best practices.* 2nd ed. Paul Brookes: Baltimore.
* ZERO TO THREE. *Tips for surviving child developmental assessment.* Retrieved from http://www.zerotothree.org/child-development/mental-health-screening-assessment/tips-for-surviving-child-developmental-assessment.html

Opportunities for Relationships and Learning

Opportunities for Attachment and Emotional Development and Learning

7

After reading this chapter, you will be able to:

- RESPECT attachment and emotional development by:
  - Describing these important aspects:
    - Security, trust, attachment
    - Self-regulation
    - Emotional expression
    - Sense of self, sense of self with others, separation anxiety, stranger anxiety, and social referencing
    - Temperament and goodness of fit
  - Knowing current theories of attachment and emotional development
  - Being familiar with the milestones of attachment and emotional development
  - Being aware of possible delays or disorders

- REFLECT ON:
  - The individual child's progression of attachment and emotional development
  - Recognition of atypical attachment and emotional development
  - Helpful responses and adaptations for atypical attachment and emotional development
- RELATE TO:
  - Planning interactions, materials, and envronments, for individual and small groups of children, to promote attachment and emotional development.

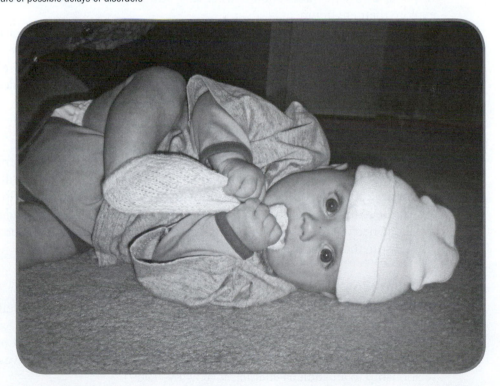

Every moment of life is experienced with feelings, bodily responses, thoughts, and memories. Throughout the first 3 years of life, infants and toddlers use these internal experiences to establish a sense of security, to develop close and meaningful relationships with others, and to develop a sense of who they are.

As infants go through their early months with sensitive family members and infant care teachers who respond to their distress and share their joy, the babies develop trust in their ability to summon help and trust in adults' ability to help them. In the first year, these feelings of trust become a bond of attachment to trusted adults. Over the first 3 years, infants and toddlers use their personal history of feelings to establish an idea of who they are: a sense of their own identity.

RESPECT ATTACHMENT AND EMOTIONAL DEVELOPMENT

Emotional development and attachment can grow only through ongoing, responsive relationships. Babies are born with some abilities to express feelings, and quickly develop skill at understanding the feelings of others with whom they spend time. Long before they can communicate with words, they use facial expressions, both their own and those of these trusted adults, to engage in animated exchanges.

These feeling-based communications are more than precursors to language. Many aspects of emotional development are recognized as the foundations of learning. As infants and toddlers begin to control their reactions to feelings within their bodies or events around them, they are able to pay more attention to the world, increasing their abilities to learn. If their families and care teachers are sensitive and responsive, infants and toddlers trust that adults will keep them safe while they explore their environment.

Over time and after repeated experiences with people, the infant or toddler comes to know whether he or she is liked, found interesting, and effective in relationships with others. This knowledge forms the base of a life-long sense of self.

Infants and toddlers are achieving certain milestones in emotional development and attachment, as we discuss next.

Self-Regulation

Self-regulation is the ability of an infant or toddler to manage his or her own reactions to feelings within his or her body or to surrounding events (Williamson & Anzalone, 2001). This ability evolves through the support of adults in helping infants and toddlers regulate or manage their reactions, sometimes called *co-regulation*. Children may need more or less support in regulating their reactions as they interact with and explore the world around them.

Attachment

Attachment describes the sense of safety a child feels with particular adults through established relationships. Infants and toddlers have a great desire to explore and learn about the world. They have an equally strong desire to feel safe. John Bowlby, an English psychiatrist, described the sense of security a baby derives from his relationship to an adult as *attachment* (Bowlby, 1969).

Trust. Trust refers to young children's growing sense that they can be effective in getting the attention, interest, and help of adults when they need it and that adults like and care for them. Erik Erikson introduced the idea that a child's first developmental crisis is to determine whether his or her world should be trusted or mistrusted, as well as whether he or she can trust him- or herself to function effectively in the world. It is a struggle that may continue throughout a lifetime (Erikson, 1950).

Security. "Security" is a key construct in attachment theory (Waters & Cummings, 2000). A secure infant is able to use one or more close adults as a secure base from which to explore and as a safe place to return. The adult may be a secure base if perceived by the infant as available, responsive, and competent (Waters, Hamilton, & Weinfield, 2000).

Emotional Expression

Emotional expression refers to the baby's ability to express feelings and be understood and to understand the emotional expressions of others. Some facial expressions of emotion appear to be rooted in evolution and are recognizable around the world as joy, anger, fear, surprise, disgust, sadness, interest, and contempt (Izard & Malateste, 1987). Early emotional expression is an important part of developing early relationships (Losonczy, 2004).

Sense of Self or Identity

The infant is in the process of becoming an individual—that is, his or her identity is forming (Lally, 1995). This sense of self or identity is an internal mental image of what it means to be oneself: Can I elicit help when I need it? Am I good, competent, loved? What does it mean to be male or female? Who am I in my family and culture?

Sense of Self with Others

One's sense of self with others is the internal mental image of what it is like to be oneself in relationships with others: Is it pleasant? Mutually satisfying? Do people accept my feelings? How do I become like the people I am with?

Separation Anxiety. Separation anxiety is the extreme distress that young or mobile infants sometimes experience when leaving a parent or other very close adult. It usually occurs between 5 and 9 months as the infant is developing an understanding that objects and people exist even when they are out of sight.

Stranger Anxiety. Stranger anxiety is the fearfulness that mobile infants or toddlers may show toward unfamiliar adults. The baby may stare at the stranger, cry, or hold tightly to the familiar adult. It is another sign of the development of object permanence.

Infants can experience stranger anxiety and separation anxiety from the middle of the first year of life to the middle of the second year.

Social Referencing. Social referencing describes the infant looking to a trusted adult for signals (facial expressions, gestures, or words) regarding the emotional tone or safety of a situation (Klinnert, Emde, Butterfield, & Campos, 1986).

Temperament

In addition to the growth of emotional development and attachment, basic elements of personality are seen early in infancy and appear to be fairly constant throughout life. These are biological elements that affect how a person responds to the environment. They are referred to as *temperament traits* (Thomas & Chess, 1977). They include the following:

Activity level. Some babies never seem to stop moving; others just quietly take in information.

Regularity or rhythmicity. The predictability of the cycles of waking and sleeping, times of hunger, and elimination.

Approach and withdrawal. A child's comfort and willingness to adapt to new, unfamiliar experiences.

Adaptability. A child's comfort in accepting new situations over time.

Sensitivity. The baby's reactions to sensory experiences such as bright lights, noise, flavors, and textures.

Intensity. How much energy is in the baby's response to events.

Mood. The general attitude of the baby, which could usually be pleasant and easygoing or perhaps more generally unhappy.

Distractibility. How easily a baby's attention may be shifted from an interesting activity by a noise or movement nearby.

Persistence. How long a child may spend on an activity despite interruptions or frustration.

These temperament traits are usually found in groupings referred to as *temperament types*. Thomas and Chess (1977) originally called these types *easy, difficult*, and *slow-to-warm*. Lally uses the same configurations of traits but calls them *flexible, feisty*, and *fearful* (WestEd, 1995). These groupings of traits are defined as follows:

Flexible: Regular biological rhythms, positive mood, adaptable, low intensity, low sensitivity

Feisty: Active, intense, distractible, irregular biological rhythms, sensitive, moody

Fearful: Slow to adapt, withdraws from new situations

Although these temperament traits determine how a child responds to the world, the child's reactions will also be influenced by the actions of the adults that are present. The feisty child can be supported with warnings of coming transitions, opportunities to use her energy in active play, and with redirection when feelings are getting out of control. The fearful child can be supported by slowly drawing the child into play with other children.

Goodness of Fit. Thomas and Chess were very clear that there is not a good or bad temperament—there is only a goodness of fit between one's temperament "and other characteristics such as motivation and levels of intellectual and other abilities" to meet the "successive demands, expectations, and opportunities of the environment" (1977, p. 15).

So, a young child whose temperament and other personality characteristics fit well into the family's expectations and values is likely to feel competent and positive about him- or herself. If not, a poor sense of self may begin to develop. Different cultures value the temperament types differently. In the United States, we tend to think most highly of flexible children. Countries like Israel, which has always been at war, value feisty children. Some Asian countries find that fearful or slow-to-warm children are more in line with the cultural norm of interdependence (Klein, 1991; Kohnstamm, 1989).

RESPECT: THEORIES OF ATTACHMENT AND EMOTIONAL DEVELOPMENT

The current theories of attachment and emotional development emerged during the 1970s but have been explored and expanded. These theories provide depth to the understanding of attachment and emotional development.

Regulation

Regulation may have more of a research base than a theoretical base; however, there is a theoretical connection between the ability to self-regulate and the increasing ability to purposefully pay attention during the first 18 months of life. As the 1-year-old increases control of intentionally attending to people, objects, or events for longer periods, he or she begins to process more of the available information (Courage & Richards, 2008). The ability to regulate, or manage, one's reactions to internal and external experiences is understood to be the basis of attention and executive function. "Executive function is a set of mental processes that helps connect past experience with present action. People use it to perform activities such as planning, organizing, strategizing, paying attention to and remembering details, and managing time and space" (National Center for Learning Disabilities, 2010). The process of being able to become quiet and alert as a newborn, with the calming help of an adult, provides the infant with opportunities for interaction and exploration. As the ability to regulate reactions increases, the child's ability to pay attention increases. This is the very foundation of learning and being a partner in a relationship.

For example, a recent study demonstrated that 6- and 7-month-old infants were able to anticipate the reappearance of an object passing behind an occlusion. This anticipatory looking was accompanied by self-regulatory behaviors. The conclusion is that anticipatory looking, which is an executive function, is related to self-regulatory skills (Sheese, Rothbart, Posner, White, & Fraundorf, 2008).

Attachment

Mary Ainsworth furthered our understanding of attachment with a series of real-life observations of the relationships between infants and their mothers (Ainsworth,

Blehar, Waters, & Wall, 1978). Ainsworth found that infants almost always find ways to use their mothers as a base of security and safety, whether or not their mothers are responsive and nurturing.

The quality of the infant's attachment, however, appeared to develop according to the mother's behavior. Infants with *secure* attachments were able to play and explore and use their mothers for comfort when they became distressed. These mothers were sensitive and responsive to their infants' cues. Babies with *anxious ambivalent* attachment found it difficult to concentrate on play and use their mothers for comfort. Their mothers tended to ignore or to attend to their infants according to the mother's own needs or interests rather than in response to the child's cues. The mothers could also be intrusive and negatively controlling, and the infants experienced higher separation anxiety (Scher & Mayseless, 2000). A third group of infants had *anxious avoidant* attachment. These mothers were often emotionally unavailable, or even unexpectedly enraged, often due to depression. These infants found a way to stay close enough to their mothers to feel safe without enraging her—sometimes by keeping their backs to her (Ainsworth, Blehar, Waters, & Wall, 1978). The infants learn to hold back their emotions of distress and anger with their mothers (NICHD Early Child Care Research Network, 2006), but may show their negative feelings with other adults and peers (Carlson & Sroufe, 1995).

Ainsworth developed an experimental protocol called the Strange Situation in which toddlers were separated from their mothers for a few minutes at a time in increasingly stressful situations. The reunions, when the mothers returned to the toddler, were the most telling. Securely attached infants, although stressed and crying, would go to their mothers and be comforted. Anxious ambivalently attached toddlers would go to their mothers and then arch away from the mothers' attempts to comfort them. Avoidant ambivalently attached toddlers might not even approach their mothers or might back up to them, avoiding eye contact but vigilantly keeping track of them (Ainsworth et al., 1978).

Bowlby (1979) and Bretherton (1985) both theorized that the attachment relationship becomes a mental template for all later relationships. However, Main (1983) believes that a person can change an unhealthy template through self-reflection and counseling.

Emotional Expression

In 1987, Izard and Malatesta published their seminal paper on infant facial expressions being universal expressions of emotions. Since then, facial expressions have been seen as universally recognized expressions of emotion. Today, new theories are encompassing a more comprehensive look at emotional expression. Hertenstein (2011) theorizes that emotional expression may not just reflect the internal state of the infant but also perform the function of having an impact on others; for example, frowning might bring the adult partner into closer proximity. In addition, he proposes that the understanding of emotional expression would need to go beyond facial expressions to include studies of postures, gestures, and movements. Third, he encourages thinking of emotional expression as being influenced by development and the social environment (pp. 130–131).

Sense of Self and Sense of Self with Others

In a recent book, Phinney and Baldelomar (2011) write about two important elements of the development of identity. First, identity development is a process of experiencing oneself *with* others *and* experiencing oneself *as separate* from others. Identity can only be formed within social relationships. Second, identity development, both as a self and as a self with others, occurs within relationships that are culturally bound. Identity is always interwoven with cultural practices, beliefs, and values.

Temperament

Current theories about temperament consider the roles of reactivity and self-regulation as the young child interacts with his or her world. Reactivity refers to physical and emotional responses to internal or external events. Temperament affects the strength of the reaction to events. The child who is able to bring self-regulation skills to his reponses will have more successful interactions with the world (Rothbart, Derryberry & Hershey, 2000). The interaction between temperament, reactivity, and self-regulation are of great interest in current studies and theories of temperament.

Table 7.1   Respect Possibilities in Attachment and Emotional Development

Young Infants	Mobile Infants	Toddlers	Twos
0–9 Months	9–18 Months	16–24 Months	24–36 Months
Infants can get overwhelmed and begin to yawn, look away, or fuss.	Mobile infants will look at a familiar adult to determine whether a situation is safe or dangerous.	Toddlers begin to control some impulses, saying, "no, no, no" as they begin to throw blocks.	Twos like to study pictures of themselves, their friends, and their families.
Infants begin to calm themselves by sucking on their hands or listening to an adult talk quietly to them.	Mobile infants will cling to a familiar adult when they are in a strange situation.	Toddlers may not want to stop playing when their parent comes to pick them up.	Twos listen to your words and the tone of your voice when you talk about them. They want you to be interested in them and proud of their accomplishments.
Infants use their faces and bodies to express many feelings: everything from frowning and crying to laughing out loud.	Mobile infants will use a favorite blanket or stuffed animal to help them calm themselves.	Toddlers may cry when they are unable to master what they are trying to do.	Twos need clear and consistent limits. They will forget rules, or test rules, but feel secure when you remind them and help them to follow the rules.
Infants express their feelings more clearly to familiar people and are more reserved with strangers.	Mobile infants will protest loudly when their parents leave them.	Toddlers know their own names and may use "me" and "mine."	Twos may use words to express their feelings, or they may hit or bite.

RESPECT SIGNS OF CONCERN IN ATTACHMENT AND EMOTIONAL DEVELOPMENT

Infants and toddlers who suffer abuse or neglect or live in unstable circumstances may exhibit symptoms of attachment disorders and emotional distress. These issues most commonly arise from infants and toddlers who are in living or group care situations where their needs are not met. Infant mental health consultants are increasingly available to Early Head Start, child care, and family child care programs. Common disorders and symptoms are listed below.

Reactive Attachment Disorder (RAD) RAD occurs when an infant's social, emotional, and/or physical needs are not met. The child "avoids the caregiver, avoids physical contact, is difficult to comfort, does not make distinctions when in social situations, resists social interaction, and wants to be alone" (MedLinePlus, 2011).

Regulatory Disorders. Infants who are unable to self-soothe and calm themselves may develop regulatory disorders. The infants and toddlers are not able to manage their emotional reactions or behavior in a way that meets social demands. These infants may have both temperamental and hypersensitive physiological behavior affecting the regulatory difficulties (Dale, O'Hara, Keen, Porges, 2011).

Depression. Infants may suffer from depression, especially if their mothers are depressed. Depression may appear as withdrawal, fussiness, or lack of interest in food or social interaction.

RELATE TO ATTACHMENT AND EMOTIONAL DEVELOPMENT

The infant/toddler care teacher has an important role to play as he or she *relates* to each child's emotional development. Infants, toddlers, and twos need intimate, loving care. They need holding, touching, feeding, diapering, washing, and comforting. Historically, this kind of close and personal care has occurred only within families or family-like tribes. Today, deep personal commitment is offered as part of a paid service, which can be very challenging.

Infants, toddlers, and twos depend on their care teachers to provide an emotional foundation of interest and affection. The motivational themes of security, exploration, and identity

---

Box 7.1

Reflect on Attachment and Emotional Development

Self-Regulation

- Does the infant allow a trusted adult to help him or her calm down when upset?
- Is the infant or toddler beginning to find ways to calm him- or herself?

Emotional Expression

- What emotions do the infants and toddlers express? How do they express the emotions?
- Are you able to understand most expressions of emotion?
- Are there infants or toddlers who are often fearful, angry, or sad?

Security/Trust/Attachment

- Does the infant or toddler go to a primary caregiver for comfort?
- Does the infant or toddler allow him or herself to be comforted?
- Does the child explore the environment with confidence that the care teacher is nearby?
- How is each child comforted?

Sense of Self/Sense of Self with Others

- Is each infant responding to his or her own name?
- Does the infant or toddler seem able to communicate likes and dislikes?

formation are clearly at play and require different actions from care teachers at different stages of the young child's development. The following sections describe attachment and emotional development experiences for young infants, mobile infants, and toddlers and twos.

THE YOUNG INFANT: BIRTH TO 9 MONTHS

Newborns are highly dependent on adults to help them regulate or manage their reactions to their own bodies and the environment. At first, babies struggle to manage breathing on their own, sucking and swallowing, digesting and eliminating, and maintaining their temperature. Sensitive adults use cuddling, quiet murmuring, swaddling, and other responses to help the babies eat, sleep, and stay quietly alert.

Through repeated experiences with responsive adults, babies begin to find ways to calm themselves, such as sucking on their fingers. They maintain attention a little longer and sort out their waking and sleeping cycles. This help with regulation from adults evolves into a sort of trust that others will be available to help and that the baby is able to summon help when needed.

From birth, young infants also show interest in the expression of emotions. These "relational" emotions are evident in babies' imitation of facial expressions and in their anticipation of an adult's interest and willingness to cooperate in achieving the baby's purpose (Trevarthen, 2001). Babies are active conversationalists through expression and gesture long before they have the use of language.

A Glimpse of the Young Infant's Attachment and Emotional Development

Miriam's training in child development has emphasized the importance of emotional development as a foundation for all later development. She has taken to heart the importance of supporting regulation, providing a sense of security, meeting the children's emotional needs, and building on their strengths.

Adara, the youngest child at 3 months, has been with Miriam from the age of 6 weeks. Adara is fascinated when Miriam imitates her facial expressions with slight exaggerations. Adara shares a little smile with Miriam. Miriam returns a smile just a little bit bigger and widens her eyes with a happy look. Adara grins back. Miriam finds that the use of facial expressions and her quiet voice are very effective in helping Adara calm down when she is upset or if something is making her uncomfortable.

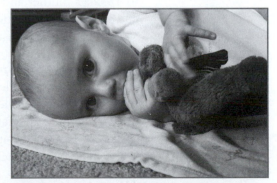

Paulo can both use and understand a greater variety of facial expressions than can Adara—and his smile is a heartbreaker. Paulo also has been with Miriam since the age of 6 weeks, and Miriam has seen enormous changes in his ability to manage his reactions to sudden sounds or surprises. At 4½ months, he seems more solid emotionally than Adara. However, Miriam feels that both children are still establishing a sense of trust. They are easily upset and, although both know her well, they seem to calm more readily with their parents than with her.

Kai finds a way to calm himself because he has experienced responsive adults who help him become calm when he is distressed.

At 6 months Jack greets Miriam excitedly in the morning and she feels that her relationship with him is well established. If he is happy or sad, he can communicate those feelings from a little distance away and accept her reassurance through words or a smile. He prefers Miriam's comforting to that of Shela, the co-teacher, but he also accepts Shela's help. Jack is able to suck his fingers to comfort himself as he goes to sleep and cries for help when he can't manage on his own.

Takala has always seemed like a pretty easygoing baby; but now, at 7 months, she has been acting very differently. She doesn't like leaving her mother's arms to go to Miriam in the morning, yet she speeds to hang on Miriam's leg if a stranger enters the classroom. She may burst into tears if the stranger (who is likely to be the director of the program) should speak to her.

The Young Infant Care Teacher's Decisions

Even with the small age range of the children under her primary care, Miriam is responding to very different levels of emotional development and attachment behavior.

With Adara, regulation of reactions is a high priority, and Miriam tries to help her make the transition from sleeping to waking or by calming her in times of distress. Adara is also very interested in human faces, and Miriam knows that she is learning about the expression of human emotions. When Adara seems ready for a "conversation," Miriam holds her where they are comfortably face to face and talks quietly to her. She uses slightly exaggerated expressions, sometimes taking both her own and Adara's side of the conversation.

With Paulo, Miriam is trying to encourage his growing interest in the world around him while assuring him that she is nearby and keeping him safe. She has observed that he plays far more comfortably when she is within touching distance. His special smiles for her, drawing her in, and his attempts to stay close to her suggest that he is developing a secure attachment with her.

Jack is beginning to concern Miriam. He seems equally willing to be with any adult and is not demonstrating the kinds of early attachment behaviors she expects to see. He is not particularly upset when his parents drop him off or happy when they pick him up. He makes no attempt to be close to Miriam or Shela during the day.

Takala is going through an almost classic period of stranger anxiety—and right on time. (Miriam thinks it is as if Takala has read the textbooks!) Miriam has talked to Takala's mother and together they spend time each morning talking with Takala and making the transition easier. When Takala is frightened by an unfamiliar person, Miriam accepts her feelings but also reassures her that she is always safe at school.

Adaptations for Special Needs. Because of Miriam's understanding of early attachment, she is a little concerned about Jack's lack of specific emotional connections. After consulting with her director, they decide to ask Jack's parents for permission to bring in an Infant Mental Health Consultant from the university clinic. As a care teacher, she doesn't want to jump to conclusions, but she is getting increasingly concerned. She is also nervous about talking to Jack's parents and asks her director to meet with them.

Diversity/Culture. Adara's parents grew up in Jordan but met in the United States as medical students. Although Adara's mother is dedicated to completing her medical training, the use of child care outside the family is not comfortable for her. She likes and trusts Miriam, but struggles with a strong cultural tradition of protecting young children within the extended family. She needs the child care service, but feels guilty about using it. Miriam accepts these feelings without taking them personally and reassures Adara's mother that she treasures this wonderful little girl. She is even learning a few words of affection in Adara's home language to murmur to her in comfort.

A young infant's sense of security begins with warm, responsive nurturing.

Opportunities for Young Infants' Attachment and Emotional Development

Support Young Infants' Growing Ability to Manage Their Reactions. Young infants react to all sorts of internal and external sensations—gas in their tummies, hunger, fatigue, as well as noises, bright lights, and changes in the environment. They learn to manage or regulate their reactions with the help of responsive infant care teachers.

- Watch young infants closely so that you can learn how they express their discomfort and needs.
- Try swaddling, talking or singing quietly, holding a baby face down over your knees while rubbing his back, or up over your shoulder near your heartbeat.
- Observe what the baby finds helpful in particular circumstances and learn from her family about how they help calm and comfort her.
- Try to anticipate when a baby will need to eat, and be ready to feed her before she becomes distressed.

Build Young Infants' Feelings of Security. Young infants develop a feeling of security—a sense that they are safe to observe, learn, and relax—through their relationships with others.

- Be consistent and predictable in how you respond to a baby.
- Use words to reassure the baby that you are nearby and will keep him safe.
- Stay close by and at eye-level as young infants play on the floor or eat meals.

Provide Responsive Relationship Experiences. Young infants begin to shape an idea of what it is like to be with other people: Will they understand me and try to care for me? As repeated experiences assure them that adults will understand and respond to their messages, they begin to trust their own ability to interest adults and elicit help and to trust adults to be available.

- Respond as quickly and accurately as possible to a baby's messages of distress or desire for attention.
- Talk to the baby about how well he told you what he needed: "You need some help, huh? I could tell when you cried you needed me."

- Appreciate that the baby wants your attention. She's following a healthy and natural desire to be with other people and develop relationships. Take time just to hold, play with, and talk to the baby.

Help Young Infants Learn about Emotional Expressions. Young infants respond to the expressions of emotions by others and are learning to express their own emotions. Through their facial expressions and bodily postures, newborn infants are able to feel and express interest, distress, and disgust. In the next few months, they quickly learn to smile and express a wider range of feelings including joy, anger, sadness, surprise, and fear (Izard & Malateste, 1987). Young infants will watch the emotional expressions of others with interest and often try to mimic the facial expressions.

- Understand that the facial and postural expressions of emotion seen in even the youngest babies are expressions of genuine feeling, seeking response from caring adults.

- You probably do this naturally, but mirror the infant's expressions back to him. If he is distressed, frowning and crying, offer your own sad frown as you pick him up and say, "You're so unhappy. I'm going to help you." Or, if the baby offers you a small smile, return a smile that is just a touch bigger and brighter.

- Play games with the baby as you take turns mimicking each other's facial expressions. This game will probably start naturally with the baby watching you and imitating your expressions, but it will quickly get very interesting to the baby if you mimic his or her expressions.

- Add words to facial expressions to help the baby build a vocabulary of emotional expression. For example, if the baby is in a really good mood, you might say, "You seem so happy today. Your smiles and laughter are making me feel good."

Calm Young Infants Quickly So They Feel Safe. Young infants are having experiences with adults that provide the foundation for their attachment relationships. They are learning which adults can help soothe them when they are upset and help them to feel safe.

- Become a sensitive and accurate reader of each young infant's cues. Learn how each baby likes to be soothed and comforted. Quickly respond to a baby's cries and other signals of distress and help him to regulate his reactions and become calm (Siegel, 1999).

- Keep the environment calm and safe. A calm environment is tidy, does not have too many bright colors, and is checked continuously for safety.

- Spend time reflecting on your own early relationships. Research on attachment says that the strongest predictor of a child's attachment to his parents is how the parents have made sense of their own lives (Siegel, 1999, p. 6). This certainly applies to infant care teachers, as well.

Show the Young Infant That You Enjoy Being with Her. Young infants are establishing ideas about who they are: a sense of self or identity: Do people like me?

Do they listen to me? Can I get help from others? Do they understand when I tell them what I need?

- Use the baby's name frequently.
- Use terms of affection in the baby's home language.
- Attend and respond quickly to the baby's cries, gestures, and facial expressions.
- Mirror the baby's facial expressions in quiet times of closeness.
- Smile in welcome when you greet the baby in the morning and when you greet him again after naps.
- Use words to tell the baby how much you like and enjoy him or her. Describe things the baby is doing well: "You're looking right at me!" "Oh, you're holding your head up and looking around." "I'm listening to you shaking that rattle, shake, shake, shake." Your sparkling eyes and smile tell the baby how much you appreciate what he or she does.

Demonstrate Care and Cooperation with the Young Infant. Young infants are developing ideas of who they are in relationships with others. If they have healthy adult partners, they are learning how people work together to accomplish things, how people show they care for each other, and how people try to understand each other.

- Demonstrate your affection for the baby and your pride in his or her accomplishments.
- Follow through on what you say you will do. When you say, "I'm changing Frannie's diaper but I'll be right there," make sure you go to the waiting baby as soon as possible.
- Make time for relationships. Work with co-teachers and directors to arrange group sizes and schedules that provide every child some quiet one-on-one time with his or her primary infant care teacher.

Respect the Real Distress of Separation. As young infants begin to develop meaningful relationships with their parents and infant care teachers, they may begin to show distress and anxiety at moments of parting. Separation anxiety, the crying and misery that infants show as their parents leave them, even with trusted and loved infant care teachers, may surface between 4 and 7 months. It is difficult for everyone involved, but a sign of good emotional development and attachment.

- Talk with families ahead of time about the positive developmental meaning of having strong feelings for people who are special in a baby's life. Assure families that you and the baby also have a good relationship, but it will never have the same meaning as the family's relationship with their baby.

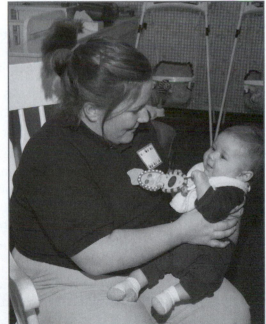

Young infants are developing ideas of who they are in relationships with others.

• Different strategies help different babies with separation. Help parents say good-bye to their baby and then leave, perhaps turning back to wave through a window. Some babies prefer a moment to get involved in play. Some will need to cry for a little while.

Reassure Young Infants When Strangers Worry Them. Stranger anxiety is similar to separation anxiety in that it is a good sign that young infants are making clear distinctions between people they know and strangers. This is both an emotional and a cognitive achievement. Even with the safety of being held by a trusted adult, the young infant may become wary or distressed near a stranger.

• Simply show the child that you will keep her safe, and reassure her if you know the stranger. Try to avoid ever having a complete stranger substitute in a child care setting.

Remember That the Babies Will Look to You for Signals on How to React to a Situation. Between 7 and 9 months, babies begin to watch the expressions of adults and older siblings to get signals about the safety of the social situation. This process is called *social referencing.*

• Remember that the babies in your care are watching your expressions and learning from you all the time. Be genuine and honest about your feelings.

• During this period, you can begin to encourage babies to continue what they are doing by smiling and nodding from a distance, or discourage them by frowning, shaking your head, and saying "no." They will not always have the control to stop themselves, but they are beginning to maintain their connection to you over a small distance.

Keep Temperament in Mind When Considering How Young Infants Interact with the World. For young infants, temperament can be a strong factor in how well they establish routines and relationships.

• Help feisty infants to establish routines for eating and sleeping. Comfort them when they are fussy.

• Support fearful or slow-to-warm infants as they establish routines and meet new situations.

• Remember to attend to the flexible infant. Even easygoing babies need the care teacher as a relationship partner.

Planning for Young Infants' Attachment and Emotional Development

The planning guide in the following feature (Box 7.2) will give you a chance to practice planning when you are following the infant's interests. A short description of an observation is provided, and you can add ideas for what you might do with this baby. In this planning guide, you would want to note how you keep him feeling secure while he is rolling away, how you add language to his actions, and how you provide space for him. What else might you include?

Box 7.2

Individual Child Planning Guide (1) for Jack

Child's Name: *Jack*   Plans for Week of (Date): *March 10, 2012*

Person Completing the Guide: *Miriam*

Respect: Child's Emotions, Effort, Goals, Learning, and Relationships

Write an observation or use a picture or other documentation here—date all notes.

Jack rolls or lies still sucking his thumb and touching his hair. He likes to watch the other children. He is easily upset but not easy to comfort.

Respect and Reflect	Relate
What am I doing?	**What will you do to support my learning?**
How am I feeling?	• **Responsive interactions**
What am I learning?	• **Environment: Toys, materials**
• **Emotional**	• **Opportunities**
• **Social**	
• **Cognitive**	
• **Language**	
• **Motor**	

THE MOBILE INFANT: 8–18 MONTHS

The mobile infant wants to move and explore. He still needs to feel safe in order to venture out, but now he is able to use adult support, such as a smile or encouraging words, as he moves a short distance. Mobile infants have some abilities for self-regulation and are very good at expressing and understanding emotions. They have clearly developed attachment relationships with one or more adults.

A Glimpse of the Mobile Infant in Attachment and Emotional Development

Gemma is the great, busy explorer in Albert's room. Her exploration is as intense when she is in Albert's arms as when she is on the move. She is fascinated by the faces of people she knows. She touches them, looks at them, and even imitates them in play. Gemma seems very aware, at 9 months, of how important facial expressions are in communication.

One-year-old Lily has a fearful or slow-to-warm temperament. Her cerebral palsy makes it difficult to read her expressions at times. It is hard for Albert to tell when she wants to be close to the other children, and when she wants to be alone. She shares her feelings only with people she knows. When she sees strangers, she gets a very serious look on her face and casts her eyes down. If a stranger approaches her, she buries her head in Albert's shoulder or cries.

Albert thinks of Radwan as the perfect example of secure attachment. At 15 months, Radwan is comfortable with most people, enjoys moving around and playing, and seems well liked by the other children. He seems to know he can count on the adults in his life to be nearby and to be helpful to him. If a situation feels uncertain, he finds Albert and uses him as a source of security. He is already demonstrating a certain confidence in himself as an explorer and as a person who is well liked.

Goro likes being close to Albert and follows him around, imitating his actions and his words. Sometimes it looks as if Goro knows he is the oldest child and is trying to be the teacher, but Albert believes that Goro is just practicing being like one of the men he knows best.

The Mobile Infant Care Teacher's Decisions

Albert enjoys providing a base of security as the children in his care begin to realize their ability to move into the world. Although Gemma is the most active explorer, she is most likely to suddenly notice that Albert is all the way across the room. She will stop in her tracks, sit down, and howl! Albert knows that it is hard for her to feel comforted from a distance, and he moves swiftly to reassure her when she needs him.

At 1 year, Lily has clear attachment relationships with her parents, but her relationships with her peers sometimes confuse Albert. He sometimes finds that the effects of the cerebral palsy on her facial expressions make it difficult to know what she wants. Albert does support her in new situations, which always seem hard for her.

Radwan and Goro seem able to feel and express a wide range of emotions—sheer joy being one of the most common. Both boys love their new abilities to run, climb, and jump. They show fierce faces and laughing faces to each other, but each turns back to Albert when they need the quiet of loving arms. Albert thinks about how important it is for him to be tender with these "little men."

Adaptations for Special Needs. Albert knows that a physical disability like Lily's can challenge the ability to communicate feelings through facial expressions, gestures, and postures. Albert often observes her with her parents and tries to learn from them how to interpret her emotional messages. He also discusses his challenges with the physical therapist who provides early intervention services for Lily. The therapist is helping him pick up on Lily's more subtle emotional communications.

Diversity/Culture. Albert's family valued traditional images of masculinity such as strength and athletics, but the men in his family were also fathers who deeply loved their children. Albert is uncertain as to whether his own values for male tenderness toward children would be shared by Goro's Japanese family or Radwan's Arab family. As these young boys develop an early sense of identity, gender is an important factor. Albert decides to hold a parent meeting on fathering and bring this question to the discussion.

Opportunities for Mobile Infants' Attachment and Emotional Development

Encourage Exploration. Mobile infants are balancing their desire to explore with their continuing need to feel safe and secure.

Be emotionally available when a mobile infant crawls away and then returns for "emotional refueling."

- Encourage exploration by assuring the mobile infant that you are watching him from a small distance. Use words and facial expressions to demonstrate your enthusiasm for whatever catches the infant's interest.

- Take fearfulness around strangers or in new situations seriously and assure the mobile infant that you are there and will always keep him or her safe.

- Check in as the mobile infant begins to crawl away, turning back to look at you. Say something like, "I see you! Look at you crawl!"

Admire Attempts at Self-Comforting. Mobile infants have a variety of strategies for self-regulation and for moderating their reactions to events in the world around them.

- Encourage the use of a favorite stuffed toy or blanket for calming. Thumb, finger, or pacifier sucking is also helpful for self-calming and does not cause damage to the teeth during this period (American Association of Pediatric Dentists, 2007).

- Provide open arms for cuddling when close contact will give comfort.

- Recognize when a mobile infant who has been crying hard is working to focus and bring himself under control.

Remember That the Mobile Infant Is Watching You. For the mobile infant, emotional expression becomes an important tool for maintaining contact with a trusted adult over small distances. In social referencing, the mobile infant looks at the adult to see how he or she is reacting to a situation.

- Remember that infants are watching you to determine the safety of a situation. Communicate over distances with assuring or encouraging looks and words.

- Use this new ability of the mobile infant to understand your communications. The infant may point to something (or watch you point to something) and understand that both of you are looking at the same thing. This is another way in which you support the infant's explorations.

Keep Contact over Small Distances. Mobile infants are beginning to demonstrate how they experience their attachment relationships. Secure infants will explore with interest but frequently check back for a moment of closeness.

- Continue to be emotionally available as mobile infants crawl away.
- Notice if a mobile infant lets you comfort him when he is frightened or tired. If not, think about how sensitively you have been responding to his cues. Do you feel that you understand what this child wants and needs?

Honor the Mobile Infant's Depth of Feelings. Mobile infants are establishing their sense of who they are and their sense of identity, and they are having very deep feelings for the important people in their lives.

- Use the child's name frequently. Talk about his or her likes and dislikes as you understand them.
- Provide photographs of each infant's family. Laminate photos so that the mobile infant can carry them around or post them on a wall as a destination for the young explorer.

Be Sensitive About Strangers. Stranger anxiety may peak and then subside during this period.

- Demonstrate to the mobile infant that you are comfortable when a new parent or the director comes into your classroom.
- Hold the child and be reassuring if she is extremely distressed. Respect the depth of the mobile infant's feelings while providing a sense of safety.

Factor in Temperament. Temperament continues to be evident in mobile infants. Flexible infants find ways to move into the world while maintaining contact with the infant care teacher. Fearful children may be equally interested in exploring, but find it difficult to leave the infant care teacher's side. Feisty children may begin to have some conflicts as they respond loudly to another child's taking their toy. In turn, their enthusiasm to move may provoke protests as they crawl over their friends.

- Keep temperament in mind as you plan for each child. The fearful child may need additional time and support from you before she moves away.
- The feisty child may need more support in focusing and play.

Planning for Mobile Infants' Attachment and Emotional Development

In the planning guide (Box 7.3), you have another opportunity to think about planning for one child using observation as the basis for your decision. What materials could Albert introduce now? Do you know of good picture books showing people's emotional expressions? What else would promote Radwan's learning about emotional expression?

Box 7.3

Individual Child Planning Guide (1) for Radwan

Child's Name: *Radwan*   Plans for Week of (Date): *March 10, 2012*

Person Completing the Guide: *Albert*

Respect: Child's Emotions, Effort, Goals, Learning, and Relationships

Write an observation or use a picture or other documentation here—date all notes.

Radwan is making faces all the time. Loves imitating faces with Goro. Really checking out how we express feelings.

Respect and Reflect	Relate
What am I doing?	**What will you do to support my learning?**
How am I feeling?	• **Responsive interactions**
What am I learning?	• **Environment: Toys, materials**
• **Emotional**	• **Opportunities**
• **Social**	
• **Cognitive**	
• **Language**	
• **Motor**	

TODDLERS AND TWOS: 16–36 MONTHS

The emotional life of toddlers and twos is far more complicated than that of younger infants. Their world is larger and they struggle to figure out how they fit into it. The ongoing questions of identity formation, "Who am I?" and "What is it like for me to be with other people?", are major ideas of this period of development. This means that toddlers can be very attuned to their own feelings and interested in the idea that other people have feelings that differ from their own.

People often associate this period of emotional development with resistant behavior and temper tantrums. In fact, tantrums are likely to reach a peak early in this period and then fade away. The resistance may, in part, be testing whether the adult really is thinking something different from what the toddler is thinking: "Does teacher mean it when she says, 'No! Don't pinch!'? It's so much fun when I pinch Charlie and he yells." This is also part of their figuring out the rules of their culture.

Tantrums may be an outlet for the frustration felt by toddlers, who have so many ideas of things to do and try and are so often limited by physical or language abilities. Toddlers are working to become proficient in movement, mastering language, developing symbolic thought, and solidifying a sense of who they are. No wonder they become easily frustrated.

A Glimpse of Toddlers' and Twos' Attachment and Emotional Development

Chita has always been a lovely, lively child. At 19 months, she has started reacting to being told "No" by throwing herself on the ground, crying and screaming. Sometimes Chita explodes into these tantrums when she can't get a doll into a crib or her block tower falls before she can knock it down.

Lan comes from a culture that values cooperation over independence. Some children are becoming fiercely independent by their second birthday, but Lan sometimes seems very passive as he continues to let Selena dress him and even feed him. He uses words and facial expressions to demonstrate his feelings. When he is frightened, he sometimes seems unable to let Selena help him.

Bessie is usually friendly to other people and generally maintains a pleasant, comfortable manner. When she does become distressed, however, it is very hard for her to become calm again. She also may become aggressive when someone else has something she wants. She does not seem able to regulate her impulses at all. She has a strong attachment to Selena. She doesn't use many words, but she can use signs for simple emotions, and she certainly communicates her feelings with her whole body, sometimes doing a little dance of sheer happiness.

Of all the children Selena cares for, Sam has the best use of words . He loves using words that describe emotions, declaring that he is "happy" or "mad."

The Toddler Care Teacher's Decisions

Selena has been watching and supporting children through tantrums for 30 years. She knows that tantrums can be an opportunity to let a toddler know that you understand her feelings. Chita usually has tantrums only when she is unable to accomplish a task. Selena lets her cry for a moment and then tells her, "It's okay. You were trying so hard to get that baby in the crib. Let's work on it together." Selena understands that Chita's ideas often are more sophisticated than her motor skills, and her ambitions lead to frustration.

Bessie is sometimes upset by Chita's outbursts. Selena knows that she has to keep an eye on Bessie even as she helps Chita regain control. Sam is very easy to relate to emotionally. Lan, however, is confusing to Selena. She understands his surrender to being cared for as being part of an interdependent culture, but she does not know why he seems to freeze when he is afraid. Selena decides to pay special attention to Lan's reactions to being comforted.

Adaptations for Special Needs. Selena has worked with several infants and toddlers with Down syndrome over the years. Although both learning and muscle tone can affect how often and vividly a toddler with Down syndrome expresses feelings, Selena knows that children with Down syndrome are well able to express and understand feelings (Carvajal & Iglesia, 2002). Selena does make a point of reading stories about feelings and playing imitation games about feelings with Bessie. Selena knows that Bessie's outbursts of frustration or aggression are, in part, a common problem for young children with Down syndrome. It is as though she cannot regulate her reactions at all. Selena seeks advice from the special education teacher who provides early intervention services to Bessie. Selena is working to keep directions to Bessie clear and rules firm.

Provide opportunities for toddlers and twos to participate in caring for dolls in a dramatic play area.

Diversity/Culture. Selena is struggling to understand whether Lan's reaction to fear is cultural or part of his own unique personality. Lan's mother tells Selena that such a young toddler should never be frightened, so Selena is wondering whether the normal experiences of loud noises or angry faces just are not part of his experience.

Opportunities for Toddlers' and Twos' Attachment and Emotional Development

Provide Continuity. Toddlers and twos should be benefiting from a sense of security within established relationships, especially if the child care program is set up to keep infant and toddler care teachers and a small group of children together for the first 3 years.

- Continue to support your secure relationships with the children. If your program does not use continuity of care, discuss the reasons why this is important with other care teachers, administrators, and families.

- If you have children moving in and out of your group, focus on developing a sense of security in the new children. This process can be upsetting for the children who are moving and those who remain. Be sensitive to their need to reestablish a secure relationship with you.

Treat Tantrums as an Opportunity to Learn Emotional Regulation. Self-regulation may appear to be more established in children as mobile infants than as toddlers. For the toddler, tantrums are a loss of control and can be frightening.

- Accept tantrums as a part of development. Stay calm, nearby, and reassuring. As one teacher recently said, "The middle of a tantrum is not a teachable moment."

- Think about tantrums in terms of self-regulation, and help the toddler regain focus and attention.

Play with Emotional Facial Expressions. As toddlers and twos come to understand gradations of emotion, they become interested in the words that describe emotions and the way faces communicate emotion.

- As you read stories that describe emotions, make the facial expressions with the toddlers: "The wolf is very angry. Let's make angry faces."
- Introduce the familiar songs about feelings, such as "If You're Happy and You Know It."
- Play imitation games with facial expressions.
- Let toddlers and twos spend time exploring their images in mirrors.

Continually Support the Formation of Identity. The big question is, "Who am I?" The work of toddlers and twos is to develop a sense of identity.

- Assign a primary caregiver to each toddler or 2-year-old. Maintain the relationship between the care teacher and the child throughout this age period. The main work of that care teacher is to truly know and understand each child within the context of the child's family and culture.
- Follow each child's interests and build on those rather than planning theme or activity-based lessons. Constantly provide the message that you find the toddler interesting, that you can know and share in his or her feelings, and that you really like him or her.
- Treat each family's culture and home language with respect.
- Do not promote gender stereotypes, but respect that toddlers are learning about what gender means in their own family and culture.

Value the Experience of Relationships. One aspect of identity formation for toddlers and twos is their understanding of being in relationships. They are learning how it feels to be "me" in a relationship and how it feels to be with others.

- Try to understand the toddler's or two's intentions and help put them into words.
- Respect that your responses to the toddler or two may be felt deeply.
- Demonstrate your affection and concern for the toddler's or two's feelings, but remember that he is also looking to you for clear information about the rules of being together.

Books for Babies: Feelings

These board books are filled with photographs of babies showing different emotions.

Hugs and Kisses (Baby Faces), R. G. Intrator and N. Bishop. Scholastic Books (2002).

If You're Happy and You Know It, A. Kubler. Baby Board Books (2001).

Everywhere Babies, S. Meyers. Harcourt Children's Books (2004).

Baby Faces, M. Miller. Look Baby! Books (1998).

Planning for Toddlers' and Twos' Attachment and Emotional Development

In the following planning guide (Box 7.4), you have another opportunity to think about planning for one child using observation as the basis for your decision. What materials could Selena introduce now? Do you know of good picture books showing people's emotional expressions? What else would promote Lan's learning about emotional expression?

Box 7.4

Individual Child Planning Guide (1) for Lan

Child's Name: *Lan*   Plans for Week of (Date): *March 10, 2012*

Person Completing the Guide: *Selena*

Respect: Child's Emotions, Effort, Goals, Learning, and Relationships

Write an observation or use a picture or other documentation here—date all notes.

Lan is clear in expressing his emotions. I think he is securely attached to me but doesn't come to me when he is afraid. Cultural differences around attachment?

Respect and Reflect	Relate
What am I doing?	**What will you do to support my learning?**
How am I feeling?	**• Responsive interactions**
What am I learning?	**• Environment: Toys, materials**
• Emotional	**• Opportunities**
• Social	
• Cognitive	
• Language	
• Motor	

SUMMARY

The infant/toddler care teacher has a vital role in supporting emotional development. In the first years of life, children are working on the following tasks:

- Self-regulation, trust, and security
- Expression and understanding of emotions
- Attachment relationships
- The formation of identity

Additional elements of emotional development include the following:

- Sense of self with others
- Separation anxiety
- Stranger anxiety
- Social referencing
- Temperament

These tasks of emotional development are mastered through the day-to-day interactions that occur within meaningful relationships over a period of time. Emotional development is recognized as the foundation of later learning and should be seen as the primary work of the infant/toddler care teacher. Responsive caregiving and teaching provide each infant and toddler with positive experiences of relationships, which contribute to the development of a strong sense of identity.

INVENTORY OF TEACHER PRACTICES
Emotional Development

Self-Regulation	A	S	R	Observation/ Reflection
I understand how young infants show me they need comfort (seek closeness, cry).				
I have many strategies to help calm a young infant (swaddling, holding upright, murmuring, rocking).				
I notice and support the ways a young or mobile infant begins to comfort himself (sucking fingers, lovey).				
I help toddlers recover from tantrums (stay nearby, say, "You were so upset!").				
I maintain a calm and pleasant attitude throughout the day.				

Emotional Expression	A	S	R	Observation/ Reflection
I understand what infants, toddlers, and twos are feeling (facial expressions, body language).				
I use my face and words to tell the children I understand their feelings.				
I use my facial expressions to stay in touch with mobile infants and toddlers over a distance.				
I play games with infants, toddlers, and twos—imitating each other's expressions or "making happy faces, making angry faces."				
I use many words to describe feelings, read books about feelings, and sing songs about feelings.				

Attachment	A	S	R	Observation/ Reflection
I respond quickly and sensitively to each young baby's cues.				
I show affection to each child.				
I encourage mobile infants to move and explore by letting them know I'm keeping them safe (smiling, using words, "I see you, I'm right here.").				
I have thought about my own childhood relationships and understand what made me feel safe and understood, and what did not.				

A = Always, S = Sometimes, R = Rarely

REFLECTIONS

1. How would it make you feel if you could not comfort an infant or toddler who was clearly distressed? Or frequently having tantrums?
2. Have there been people in your life whose temperament seems like a perfect match to yours? Or whose temperament seems like an exact opposite to yours? How does temperament affect your comfort with other people?
3. As you reflect on your own childhood, what sort of attachment pattern do you think you had with your primary caregiver?

APPLICATIONS

1. What materials and activities can an infant/toddler care teacher use to help children express and understand the expression of emotions?
2. What would you observe that tells you that an infant, mobile infant, toddler, or 2-year-old has a secure attachment to you? How might attachment look different as infants develop into toddlers and twos?
3. How can you support the self-regulation of a mobile infant who gets overly excited by her own, new mobility?

RESOURCES

- *Child of Rage*
  An HBO documentary about a child who was severely abused before the age of 19 months and the devastating effects it had on her life. Available at http://www.youtube.com/watch?v=g2-Re_Fl_L4&feature=related
- *The Strange Situation*
  A demonstration of the paradigm developed by Mary Ainsworth to determine the quality of attachment of 1-year-olds to their mothers. Available at http://www.youtube.com/watch?v=zWsyIVVvDdw&feature=related

8

Opportunities for Social Development and Learning with Peers

After reading this chapter, you will be able to:

- RESPECT
  - Understand the foundations of social development with peers
  - Describe what children learn as they have social experiences with peers
  - Learn the developmental possibilities of children
  - Learn the behaviors of children that may indicate possible delays or disorders
- REFLECT
  - Consider the individual child's and group's interests and goals and how to be responsive to them

- Reflect on your own comfort with creative and sensory play materials and activities
- Describe how culture may influence a child's, family's, and your own attitudes about creative, sensory, and symbolic/dramatic play
- RELATE
  - Plan interactions, materials, and environments for individual and small groups of children to promote social development and learning with peers.

An enjoyment of peers begins in infancy. "One of the benefits of group care, in fact, is the opportunity to experience peer relationships. The relatedness that children feel with their peers will enrich their lives and help set the stage for positive peer relationships throughout life" (Wittmer, 2008). However, infant/toddler care teachers will need to actively develop positive relationships with children and support peer interactions to ensure that they are enjoyable and meaningful. A goal for care teachers and family members is to develop the child's relational capacity—a desire to be with and enjoy other people, including peers.

RESPECT SOCIAL DEVELOPMENT

For infants and toddlers, social skills and attitudes include an interest in and enjoyment of peers, the ability to play well with others, and the ability to be prosocial—helping, being empathetic, and being kind. Mobile infants and toddlers also need to learn how to negotiate conflicts with peers and manage aggressive feelings. These aspects of social development grow with nurturing, caring teachers and families.

When care teachers value and notice peer relationships and work closely with families, they will find many creative ways of supporting infants' enjoyable interactions with other children. Thoughtful reflection on the collected information leads to planning for individuals and a caring community in the program. For example, one family home provider, Rose, noticed that a 2-year-old in her care could make a 7-month-old laugh with her silly antics. This helped Rose feel that her encouragement of social interactions in her multiage group was working well, and she used the information to plan responsively for more interactions. She shared photographs of the interactions with the children's parents, who delightedly described other ways in which their children enjoyed peers.

The following describes the components of social development.

Interest and Enjoyment of Peers and Play Skills with Peers

Babies seem to know that other babies are like them. Interest in and enjoyment of peers begins early and continues to develop during infancy (Wittmer, 2008). A child's secure attachment with his or her primary caregivers influences interest and enjoyment of peers. When infants are securely attached to several primary caregivers, they are also more likely to be successful in peer interactions (Fagot, 1997; McElwain, Cox, Burchinal, & Macfie, 2003).

Play skills refer to the ability to engage in activity with peers with toys, equipment, and materials. Play skills and interactive games and rituals emerge earlier than many people think. Two-year-olds are becoming true social partners (Brownell, Ramani, & Zerwas, 2006). They can cooperate to accomplish a task. By 3 years of age a majority of children play reciprocal, turn-taking games, and many play cooperative social pretend play (Howes, 1988). One child might pretend to be the mom, one the dad, and another, the dog. They are cooperating and pretending at the same time.

Infants show great interest in others who are just their size.

Prosocial Attitudes and Skills

Prosocial behaviors are those that are positive and helpful. The ability and desire to comfort, help, defend, and become friends with peers begins in infancy (Eisenberg & Fabes, 1998; Hay & Cook, 2007; Howes, 2009; Wittmer, 2008). Empathy for others is key to prosocial development (Hastings, Utendale, & Sullivan, 2007). The ability to think about others' feelings and perspectives begins to grow when children are mobile infants and flourishes when children are toddlers.

Friendships can occur as early as early as 1 year of age. Howes (1988) found that "fifty-one percent of children aged 16–33 months of age engaged in reciprocal friendships, and these friendships were maintained over the course of the year-long study" (p. 386).

Toddler friendships become even stronger (Whaley & Rubenstein, 1994). Friends help each other, express intimacy by excluding others, defend their friend's possessions, imitate each other, play games that they don't play with others, and grieve when a friend leaves the program (Whaley & Rubenstein, 1994). Mobile infants, toddlers, and twos can express "toddler glee"—laughing with abandon with each other (Lokken, 2000a, 2000b). Supporting prosocial behavior and attitudes among infants and toddlers is critically important.

Conflict Negotiation and Management of Aggressive Feelings

While there is a strong tendency for infants and toddlers to develop prosocial behaviors, there is also a tendency to use physical aggression such as hitting, biting, and kicking (Hay, Payne, & Chadwick, 2004). Recent research concluded that by 17 months of age, many children use physical aggression. In a study of 572 families, approximately 30 percent of 17-month-olds displayed little or no aggression, 58 percent demonstrated modest aggression, and 14 percent demonstrated high levels of physical aggression (Tremblay et al., 2004). The authors of the study stressed that it is important for adults to use positive guidance to help young children learn alternative strategies to express themselves in more socially acceptable ways. Infants and toddlers are capable of learning strategies for managing the aggressive and angry feelings that frequently occur during the early years. They also, with the help of kind and empathic adults, develop the ability to engage in healthy disagreements and use negotiation and problem-solving strategies in response to disagreements.

Children's development in each of these areas, as well as strategies that care teachers can use are discussed later in the chapter. Knowing which strategies to use begins with observing and reflecting on young children's interests, skills, and challenges.

RESPECT THEORIES CONCERNING SOCIAL DEVELOPMENT AND LEARNING

There are multiple theories that apply to social development with peers. Social cognitive/ learning theory (Bandura,) emphasizes the role of imitation in infants' and toddlers' social learning. Meltzoff and other cognitive scientists have expanded on Bandura's work by investigating social intention, imitation, empathy, and memory. For example, in a study of whether toddlers could imitate more than one behavior at a time, Ryalls, Gul, and Ryalls (2000) found that 14- to 18-month-olds could imitate a 3-step sequence modeled by a peer.

Constructivist theorists emphasize that infants and toddlers are constantly seeking to assimilate and accommodate to information they receive by making generalizations, testing hypotheses, and attempting to gain clarity when information is confusing.

According to the Core Systems Theory of human cognition (Kinzler & Spelke, 2007; Spelke & Kinzler, 2007), infants have a core system for "identifying and reasoning about potential social partners and social group members" (Kinzler & Spelke, 2007, p. 260). This means that these theorists think that infants have the brain capacity to distinguish between those who look like their social group and those who do not; to identify those who speak a familiar language versus those who do not; and to prefer food that is given to them by a person who speaks their language. The Core Systems Theory uses brain science to conclude that young children are social beings who early on distinguish who is in their social group.

Dynamic systems theory emphasizes the role of culture as influential in children's social development and learning. Each family and culture encourage social experiences in different ways. Bioecological systems theory (Bronfenbrenner, 2004) emphasizes that the microsystem that includes family and peers has the most influence on how young children interact socially with others. The young child is also influenced indirectly by the macrosystem that includes the child's culture and socioeconomic status. Some children in one culture may be encouraged to be less aggressive, while children in other cultures may be encouraged to be more aggressive (e.g., hit back).

In summary, all of these theories partially explain why social development with peers is important, what behaviors are developed, and how young children learn social behaviors and attitudes.

RESPECT DEVELOPMENTAL POSSIBILITIES IN SOCIAL DEVELOPMENT WITH PEERS

Table 8.1 identifies the developmental possibilities for young children as they develop and learn throughout the first 3 years of life. It is always important, though, to remember that children from different cultures may display knowledge, skills, and

Table 8.1   Respect Developmental Possibilities in Social Development with Peers

Young Infants	Mobile Infants	Toddlers	Twos
0–9 Months	9–18 Months	16–24 Months	24–36 Months

INTEREST IN PEERS AND PLAY WITH PEERS

Young Infants	Mobile Infants	Toddlers	Twos
Beginning early in this period, infants like to look at each other. Young infants may cry if they hear another infant cry. Later in this period, infants may show a peer an object and touch each other.	Mobile infants may play beside each other but also imitate and give and take toys. Mobile infants can often imitate each other's actions.	Children in this age group will have motor conversations—taking turns with a ball, taking turns going up and down a slide.	Peers may play turn-taking games, such as "run and chase," where they change roles. Some children will act out roles, e.g., one playing a dog and the other taking the dog on a walk.

PROSOCIAL ATTITUDES AND SKILLS

Young Infants	Mobile Infants	Toddlers	Twos
Starting around 3–4 months, infants may smile and laugh at each other.	Mobile infants will hug and give food to other children. They may look concerned when another child is upset. First friendships develop.	Toddlers comfort, help, and defend other children. Friendships increase and become stronger. The reciprocal play of friends indicates that they are more "in tune with each other" than nonfriends are.	Friends want to be close and show affection. Children at this age may think of a variety of ways to help a peer.

CONFLICT NEGOTIATION AND MANAGEMENT OF AGGRESSIVE FEELINGS

Young Infants	Mobile Infants	Toddlers	Twos
Later in this age group, infants may take another child's toy and grab tightly onto theirs to keep it.	These children are "on the move" and may climb over someone to get a toy. Mobile infants are constantly exploring cause and effect, so they may smile, poke, hit, take a toy to see what will happen. Children in this age group lack verbal skills, so they may hit or push another child away.	They are learning about self and other. May clutch a toy and say, "Mine." Conflicts arise over space and objects. Biting may occur, as toddlers often do not have the language to express themselves with words. Many toddlers, however, demonstrate few aggressive behaviors, while a small percentage may be quite aggressive. These latter children need positive guidance to learn alternative strategies to interact.	Conflicts continue to arise over objects and personal space. Many children, however, are able to play without conflict and aggression. Unfortunately, a few children may gain a reputation for aggressive behavior. These children need immediate positive support from parents and teachers. Dominance of one child over another may occur. If this happens, monitor the situation closely to determine if one child is a victim.

dispositions in unique ways. For example, children in extreme rural northern areas of the world may not have slides and balls, but have "motor conversations" as they take turns chasing after each other.

RESPECT SIGNS OF CONCERN IN SOCIAL DEVELOPMENT WITH PEERS

Autism in children has become a national and international concern. The Autism Society (2012) defines autism as follows:

> Autism is a complex developmental disability that typically appears during the first three years of life and affects a person's ability to communicate and interact with others. Autism is defined by a certain set of behaviors and is a "spectrum disorder" that affects individuals differently and to varying degrees. There is no known single cause for autism, but increased awareness and funding can help families today. (Autism Society, 2012)

More research is being conducted on early diagnosis of autism. For example, Zwaigenbaum et al. (2005) and Iverson and Wozniak (2007) are conducting longitudinal studies on the signs of autism in the first year of life. The hope is that these studies will soon tell us whether or not we can observe signs of autism in the first year of life. If autism could be diagnosed in the first year of life, treatment could begin early.

Signs of autism with toddlers include not pointing yet to communicate, not watching the gaze of others for information, and not engaging in symbolic play (e.g., using a play telephone to "talk" to someone) (Wong et al., 2004). The Autism Society (2012) also includes persistent fixation on parts of objects, lack or delay in spoken language, repetitive use of language or motor mannerisms (hand flapping/twirling objects), and a lack of interest in peers as signs. Teachers and parents should know, however, that children who are developing typically may exhibit one or more of these signs as they develop, so it is always crucial to refer children for a more complete diagnosis.

Early diagnosis of autism greatly improves outcomes for children. Treatments for children include behavior and development programs; education and learning programs; medications; and other treatments that include music therapy, speech and language therapy, and acupuncture (Warren et al., 2011). Parents may have a difficult time choosing from these types of therapies for children who have been diagnosed on the autism spectrum.

REFLECT ON CHILDREN'S DEVELOPMENT AND LEARNING

Observation of young children is the key to planning for them. If a team of teachers, for example, asked the first three questions under the following section, Interest in and Communication with Peers, they might find that young infants show great interest in their peers and communicate to them in a variety of ways. This information, together with photos, would make an interesting documentation panel for children, parents, and teachers. Once aware of how many ways young infants are communicating, teachers then could support peer interactions by placing infants next to each other on a blanket or some other place where they can see each other.

Box 8.1 provides questions that care teachers and parents may ask and try to answer together. As you reflect on these questions, add your own questions to the list.

Box 8.1

Reflect on Social Development with Peers

Interest in and Communication with Peers
- What interests each child about his or her peers?
- How do children show interest in each other at different stages of development?
- How does each child communicate with his or her peers? Is a child communicating through sounds, touch, eye contact, movement, or words?
- Are there individual differences in how each child communicates?
- How does each child communicate his or her pleasure or displeasure with other children?
- Do you see children begin to imitate their peers?
- What behaviors do children imitate?
- What do parents and teachers do to encourage children's interest in and communication with peers?

Prosocial Development
- How do infants, mobile infants, and toddlers demonstrate that they like each other?
- What prosocial behaviors, such as smiling, approaching, or offering something, does each child use?
- How does each mobile infant and toddler show empathy for other children?
- How does each mobile infant and toddler help his or her peers?
- How does each mobile infant and toddler show that he or she is a friend to another child?
- When do children laugh with each other?
- When and how do toddlers cooperate with each other?

Play with Peers
- In what stage of play development is each child? (See Howe's stages of play described later in the chapter.)
- Do you see any children beginning to play reciprocal games in which each child takes a turn in the interaction, such as peek-a-boo or run and chase?
- Do you see children beginning to pretend that they are someone else, such as a mom, when playing with others?
- Which children like to play together? Which children do not?

Conflict with Peers
- When you observe conflicts, can you tell what they are about? For example, are there conflicts over toys, control, possession, ownership, or attention?
- What feelings are expressed during conflicts?
- When are conflicts most likely to happen?
- What strategies do children use during conflicts?
- How do individual children express anger and handle conflict?
- What strategies do teachers use to support children's problem-solving and perspective taking?

RELATE TO SOCIAL DEVELOPMENT WITH PEERS

Opportunities to observe and reflect occur each day. A family child care provider observed how a 3-month-old stared intently at his active crawling peer and asked herself why this might be happening: Did the younger infant enjoy movement, or did he particularly enjoy watching another child move? Another care teacher documented with photographs how two infants, placed close to each other on the floor, each turned their heads to look at the adjacent peer. One looked very surprised when she rolled over and landed abruptly on the child next to her. The infant who was rolled upon wriggled her body in an attempt to move away, but did not cry. Through these and other observations, the teacher realized that if she stayed calm and observed the infants in these types of situations, they often needed emotional but not physical support.

Emotional support, such as words to describe what happened as well as how each child felt, gave the children a sense of safety and security. The observant, caring teacher used this documentation of the infants' interests and capabilities to plan age-appropriate, individually and culturally effective social opportunities for them.

Care teachers can also document individual children's social style. Some infants will creep quickly over to another infant, while others may just watch. If a child seems afraid of other children, sharing reflections with the child's family will guide the care teacher in gradually supporting the child to interact with peers. Cultural differences may be apparent, as some children are accustomed to being on the floor with other children nearby. Other infants may spend their hours at home in the arms of a parent or as a single child with few experiences with other children. When families are asked to share their impressions of children's social style and experiences, care teachers will then be able to relate to the children as individuals who live within their culture and family.

THE YOUNG INFANT: BIRTH TO 9 MONTHS

The infant's relationship with care teachers in group care is primary during the ages of 6 weeks to 8 months; however, peer interest emerges and provides young infants a different emotional and social experience than they have with adults.

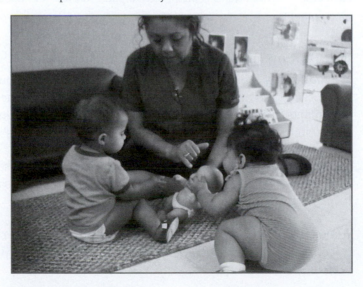

For young infants, the relationship with infant care teachers is primary; however, peers provide an important social experience.

A Glimpse of the Young Infant's Social Development with Peers

Miriam is fascinated with the interest that the children show for each other at such young ages. She knows that the quality of her relationship with the infants is of the utmost importance at this age and that the children need to feel safe and secure to feel comfortable with peers. She has also noticed, though, how she can support the beginnings of peer relationships.

Takala, who is displaying signs of stranger anxiety with unfamiliar adults, does not show these behaviors around her peers, with whom she has been since their early months. She sits and watches the other children with interest. At times, she crawls toward them and looks at Adara and Paulo, who are lying on the floor with a teacher close by. As Takala reaches out to touch them, Miriam shows her how to gently touch or pat the baby. Miriam uses words such as, "Nice babies, touch gently. Adara and Paulo like it when you pat them."

Miriam places Jack and Paulo near each other on boppy pillows. Paulo uses and understands a variety of facial features, and Miriam notices that Paulo watches Jack's face intently. Sometimes she places Jack and Paulo close enough to touch hands, and at other times she places them so that they can see each other. One time, when they were on the floor near each other, Paulo turned to his side and tried to grasp Jack's shirt to help him turn himself over. His screeches scared Jack, but when Shela, Miriam's co-teacher, calmly put one hand on Jack and the other on Paulo and said, "Jack, Paulo is trying to turn over," they both became calm.

Miriam and Shela set up the room so that two infants could lie on their stomachs, looking into a mirror placed horizontally low on the wall. In another corner, they placed a nest, and in another area a low shelf with toys placed strategically where crawling babies could reach them. A small book area, with cloth and cardboard books in a small, short bookrack, was big enough for a teacher to sit comfortably with at least two infants on her lap.

In the nest together, Miriam observes closely as Jack and Takala smile at each other. When Jack makes cooing noises, Takala makes noises back at him. They smile again at each other. Miriam takes some photos to place in their "All about Me" books to share with their families.

The Young Infant Care Teacher's Decisions

Miriam knows that she must provide opportunities for young infants to watch and touch each other. She sets up an environment in which the care teacher and one or two infants can lie on the floor together or sit in a nest. She knows that her presence is important as a calming influence and as a support to infants' enjoyment of each other.

Adaptations for Special Needs. Each of the children seems appropriately interested in the others at this time. Miriam does need to make safety adaptations because these young infants are able to move around to each other.

Diversity/Culture. The families in this group, and Miriam herself, are all from interdependent cultures. The families highly approve of Miriam's supporting these very early relationships.

Opportunities for Young Infants' Social Development with Peers

Care About Caring. Support young infants' secure, affectionate, caring relationships with family members and the care teachers in the program or family child care home.

- Support families to ensure a strong, positive relationship between family members and their child.
- Ensure that each child has a secure attachment with a care teacher.

Observe Children for Signs of Depression, Confusion, and Avoidance of Relationships. If infants are depressed, confused, or avoid relationships with adults, they are likely to have difficulty with peer relations.

- Pay attention to signs of a child's lack of interest in others. It may be a sign of emotional difficulties.

Support Prosocial Development Among Children. The roots of children's prosocial behavior begin to grow in their earliest experiences with others.

- Adults can help infants feel what it is like to be treated with kindness, touched gently, genuinely liked, receive affection, and engage in turn-taking conversations.

Support Young Infants' Interest in Each Other. Young infants show interest in each other. A 4-month-old will reach out to touch another infant. Six- to 7-month-olds sit and watch peers. Seven- to 9-month-olds can creep or crawl toward a peer and will laugh at a peer's antics. Infants begin to imitate each other by the end of this age period.

- Encourage social interactions during each day.
- Use each child's name often.
- Floor time together supports peer interest. Two infants placed next to each other on a blanket on the floor may touch hands.
- When feeding an infant, a care teacher can place another infant close by so that he or she can talk with both.
- To develop relationships and imitation, focus one child's attention on a peer and comment on what that peer is doing.

Create a Environment That Supports Social Development. The environment contributes to positive social interactions.

- Create cozy places for two infants and, of course, the care teacher.
- Place a safety mirror low on the wall so that infants can lie on their tummies and look into the mirror at themselves and each other.
- Place two crawling infants together in the active area.
- Provide nests for two infants to sit in together.
- Provide a variety of toys, including ones that lead to peer interactions such as balls and a rocking boat.

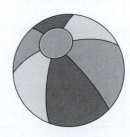

Understand That Young Infants Are Learning How to Interact with Others . . . Be Kind. When placed together, infants may touch each other, sometimes too hard, as they learn how the other little person is different from the objects that they touch and shake each day. One infant might crawl over another on the way to a care teacher. An older child in this age group might poke or push another child to see what will happen and then look surprised when the other child cries. An older child might also grab an object out of another child's hand.

- Rather than directing infants not to touch, encourage them to "touch gently" and show them how.
- If an infant grabs an object out of another infant's hand, as if not seeing that the other infant was holding the toy, understand that she is not being maliciously grabby; she is just learning the boundaries of her body and other children's. Your calm reaction and engaged observation of each child's reaction will guide your response.
  - Stay calm.
  - Describe what happened.
  - Empathize with the child.
- Comment on how a peer is feeling and encourage older infants in this age group to watch peers' faces.

Box 8.2

Individual Child Planning Guide (2) for Paulo

Child's Name: *Paulo* _____ Plans for Week of (Date): *March 12–16, 2012* _____

Person Completing the Guide: _____

Respect: Child's Emotions, Effort, Goals, Learning, and Relationships

Write an observation or use a picture or other documentation here—date all notes.

3/11/12 At 4 months, Paulo is becoming very social. He works very hard to get everyone's attention—lots of smiling and eye contact.

3/13/12 Paulo is rolling to get close to Adara. He loves touching her and grabbing her hair. In the nest together, they look at each other and smile. He babbles and she smiles.

3/13/12 Paulo couldn't take his eyes off Jack trying to crawl today. Is he already thinking about crawling? Or does he want to be closer to Jack?

Reflect	Relate
What am I doing?	**What will you do to support my development and learning?**
What am I feeling?	• **Responsive interactions**
What am I learning?	• **Environment: Toys, materials**
	• **Opportunities**

Planning for Young Infants' Social Development with Peers

In this chapter, the reader will have the opportunity to use an alternate planning guide. Using the "Respect, Reflect, and Relate" process, the following planning guide (Box 8.2) asks the care teacher to keep observation notes or photos of the child and then use them to reflect, from the child's perspective, on what he or she may be experiencing. In the Relate section, the care teacher is asked to plan for responsive interactions and changes in the environment that she could make to further the child's learning.

Each set of observations provided will focus on social development. Your reflections and relate ideas should support social development.

THE MOBILE INFANT: 8–18 MONTHS

Children's interactions with peers increase significantly in the period of 8 to 18 months of age. One child might pound a table, and another joins in. Soon, more children participate in the nonverbal "conversation" (Lokken, 2000a, 2000b). One child chases a fly, and soon several children fall in behind, imitating the fly chaser. They play reciprocal turn-taking games where one child runs through a curtain and then waits for the other child to run through. They begin to use words, too, in their interactions with their peers (Forman & Hall, 2005).

A Glimpse of the Mobile Infant's Social Development with Peers

Albert watched while Goro (16 months) and Radwan (15 months) played "running through the curtain." Goro ran through the see-through curtain hanging from the ceiling while Radwan watched and laughed. As Goro came back through the curtain, Radwan took off for his turn while Goro watched and laughed. After five turns each, Goro took off to play with the blocks, with Radwan following close behind. Albert was pleased that his placement of the curtain led to two children's reciprocal play.

Later, Radwan pushed Goro when he came too close as Radwan sat in the book corner. Goro pushed back, and both boys started to cry. Albert moved near them, while his co-teacher looked quickly to see how the other children were responding. As Albert approached, Goro pushed Radwan again, setting off another round of crying. Albert moved even closer and said to both boys, "Let's see what else we could do. Goro, you are feeling sad, and Radwan, you are feeling sad, too." He held up a book and invited both boys to sit near him, one on one side and one on the other, but where they could see each other and the book. Albert began reading and soon both Goro and Radwan were pointing to the pictures. Later in the day, when Radwan hurt himself, Goro looked concerned and handed Radwan a toy.

Gemma, the explorer, crawled fast across the carpet. Her goal seemed clear. She had seen her favorite red ball and wanted to hold it. Lily saw her and toddled over. Albert's co-teacher was sitting near them and soon had them rolling the ball back and forth. Gemma needed encouragement to play with Lily, and Lily, who had cerebral palsy, needed the teacher to sit behind her for extra physical support.

Mobile infants' peer interactions increase significantly. Provide opportunities for them to play reciprocal turn-taking games.

The Mobile Infant Care Teacher's Decisions

Albert had introduced the clear curtain in the belief that it would be very interesting for his young movers to move through a visible, but transparent material. He adapted the environment to provide new interest. He was very satisfied with the new social game that Goro and Radwan created by being able to see each other through a transparent, but tangible material.

Albert's co-teacher knew that Gemma rarely initiates social activity with the other children and decided to use a game of rolling the ball to entice her to play with Lily. Because Lily needed to be supported between her legs, it gave Gemma the impression of playing with the adult as much as with Lily. Lily was delighted to play.

Adaptations for Special Needs. Because of her cerebral palsy, Lily sometimes needs help maintaining close contact with the other children. Albert and his co-teacher try to keep an eye on where she is in relation to the other children. Gemma is not very interested in playing with the others, and the care teachers look for opportunities to engage her in social play.

Diversity/Culture. With strong cultural backgrounds that value interdependent relationships, Goro's and Radwan's families are very happy about their emerging friendship. Gemma's family, of British background, is not sure why Albert is placing so much importance on social development at such a young age. Albert worries that he may be imposing his own cultural bias on Gemma, although he understands the research that argues for the importance of culture.

Opportunities for Mobile Infants' Social Development with Peers
Model Prosocial Behavior and Interact with Mobile Infants in Prosocial Ways. Mobile infants need secure attachments with care teachers who model prosocial behavior and develop good social relationships with children by being

responsive to their needs, comforting them when hurt, and providing a secure base for exploration.

- Be physically and emotionally available by sitting near children as they play.
- Welcome mobile infants back from their explorations with hugs, a lap, or a smile (depending on what the child needs). Make room for two children if they both need you. They may need emotional refueling (Kaplan, 1978; Mahler, 1975).

Observe and Document Mobile Infants' Peer Interactions.

Because mobile infants are quickly crawling or walking, the child experiences his or her peers in a different way. Peer interactions change. Children imitate each other's physical movements and sounds/words more often during this stage.

- Enjoy mobile infants' imitation of each other. One infant might start pounding on the table and soon several infants are joining in, making noisy music together.
- Explain to families that mobile infants can observe a peer comfort another child or hit another child and imitate the action later when they are at home. This is called *deferred imitation*.

Understand and Support Mobile Infants' Need to Communicate with Peers in Physical Conversations.

Mobile infants begin to play reciprocal games. In these types of games, peers take turns during play. One might lead and another follow when toddling around the room. Then the follower will lead and the leader will follow. Communication is primarily nonverbal, and movement is crucial. Mobile infants communicate in physical ways, taking turns in the movement conversation.

- Allow mobile infants to move with each other, for example, to chase a fly.
- Set up an environment that invites movement and reciprocal play. Hang a curtain from the ceiling for a game of "run behind the curtain" or "peek-a-boo."

Promote Prosocial Behaviors Among Peers.

Mobile infants begin to use prosocial behaviors. They may help each other, pat another child on the back, give a toy when that child is distressed, or get the teacher to help a child. As discussed earlier in this chapter, friendships emerge at 1 year of age (Howes, 1988). Two children may show a preference for each other and play games such as "I touch your nose and you touch mine" that they do not play with other children.

- Notice and name prosocial behaviors: "You are being such a good friend," "How nicely you're helping."
- Try not to step in too quickly when children approach each other. They are as likely to be prosocial, even if in a clumsy way, as they are to have a conflict, which they may be able to handle alone.
- Let children show preferences in their playmates. This is the beginning of having friendships.

Prevent Aggressive Behavior, and Encourage and Support Alternative Behavior in Positive Ways.

Mobile infants engage in more conflicts. They need support to learn alternatives to aggressive behavior.

Toddlers and twos are often prosocial; helping, comforting, and cooperating with peers.

Biting of peers may begin in this stage. Children are just learning a few words to say to their peers.

- Give choices that are developmentally appropriate to mobile infants to help reduce frustration.
    - When children engage in conflict over toys, space, or who gets to sit on the care teacher's lap:
        - Observe first to see how the children resolve the conflict (unless a child is hurt).
        - Empathize. Use words to describe the children's feelings, such as, "You look very sad with Lily sitting here."
        - Describe what is happening. For example, say, "Goro, you want the block and Gemma, you want the block."
    - Physically show children what they could do. Model words for them to use.
    - Use strategies that build relationships between the children who have the conflict. With an exaggerated shrug, say, "What should we do? I know! Let's find more blocks!"
- Set up a safe and interesting environment from which mobile infants can choose their own toys, materials, and activities when they are not eating, sleeping, or being diapered. Provide two or more of the children's favorite toys and materials.
- Based on your observations, if several children are interested in water, for example, provide many opportunities for them to explore water together. Provide individual pans, bowls, or bins placed close together. Give children water and paint brushes to use outside to "paint" the sidewalk.

Planning for Mobile Infants' Social Development

Box 8.3 provides another opportunity to use an alternate planning guide.

SOCIAL DEVELOPMENT OF TODDLERS AND TWOS

Toddlers and twos are social beings. They talk to each other with their emerging language (Katz, 2004). A child might tell a peer what to do. One child will guide another to do an activity by showing the peer how, smiling when the peer gets it right, or

Box 8.3

Individual Child Planning Guide (2) for Gemma

Child's Name: _Gemma_____ Plans for Week of (Date): _____

Person Completing the Guide: _____

Respect: Child's Emotions, Effort, Goals, Learning, and Relationships

Write an observation or use a picture or other documentation here—date all notes.

Gemma and Radwan are looking at the same toys. Gemma is interested as Radwan moves the star. More interested in being with friend than usual.

Reflect	Relate
What am I doing? **What am I feeling?** **What am I learning?**	**What will you do to support my development and learning?** • **Responsive interactions** • **Environment: Toys, materials** • **Opportunities**

prompting the other child to do something specific. Children can imitate complex actions of their peers. For example, when Sam played with play dough, he rolled his ball of dough on the table until it was stretched out. He then placed a ball of dough on the first piece of dough. Lan watched and then imitated both steps of Sam's actions.

Cooperation, prosocial development, and friendships continue to grow.

A Glimpse of Toddlers' and Twos' Social Development

Selena loves toddlers. She feels that people are naïve when they talk about the "terrible twos!" She thinks they are terrific. In just one day, she saw many acts of kindness and cooperation.

Bessie and Sam tried to comfort Chita when she took a tumble. Bessie patted Chita's arm and gave her a kiss. Sam went to Bessie's cubby and brought her a stuffed lambie to cuddle. One of the other toddlers went to get Selena.

Later, Lan was playing with the light table when Sam came up next to him. Lan was using transparent colored discs and enjoying the colors. Sam went to the supply shelf and chose tissue paper shapes, offering some to Lan. Lan, in turn, shared his discs. Within minutes, they were creating lighted, colored designs together.

Selena had recently brought large foam blocks into the room. Sam was trying to move them all from one area of the room to another in a wagon. They were large and unwieldy and did not fit into the wagon. Bessie watched him, realized what he was trying to do, and came and helped him. Sam used his words to guide her, and together they moved the blocks.

The Toddler Care Teacher's Decisions

Selena has been making small changes in the room as the children become older. She increasingly adds materials that promote the children's working together. Giant blocks, dramatic play materials, and large sheets of paper for artwork are just some of the materials she has introduced.

Selena sits back and gives the toddlers and twos time to work through small frustrations and solve problems. She also is changing the way she uses language with these children. They are increasingly able to understand and respond to words that describe the feelings and thoughts of others. This understanding of language helps the toddlers and twos play more harmoniously.

Adaptations for Special Needs. Selena is aware that Bessie is likely to have delayed social skills compared to the other children. Bessie often appears quite empathic to their feelings, but she does not have the skills to negotiate disagreements. Selena often observes the other children to see how they deal with Bessie in a conflict. They often impress her with their solutions. For example, when Bessie tried to help Sam move the blocks, he was able to give her verbal guidance.

Other times, Selena provides direction and teaches Bessie what to say. One time, Lyssa, another child in the group, took Bessie's ragdoll. Bessie cried and hit Lyssa. Selena went to Bessie and said, "You are angry at Lyssa. You want your doll back." Bessie cried into Selena's shoulder. "Tell Lyssa, 'I want my doll. Please give my doll back.' " Bessie said, "Doll. Want doll, please." With Selena there to back up Bessie's request, Lyssa returned the doll.

Diversity/Culture. All cultures value relationships and friendships. All cultures also value the ability to negotiate and settle conflicts. Some cultures, however, value the contributions of several members of a group working together; others value the accomplishment of the individual. Sam's family prefers to see him tackle and solve problems alone. They feel that it is an important aspect of his ability to learn. Although they value social skills, they do not share Selena's belief in group social processes supporting learning.

Opportunities for Toddlers' and Twos' Social Development

Understand the Importance of Imitation and Encourage It Among Peers.

Toddlers and twos imitate complex behaviors of their peers. Imitative play is likely to be spontaneous. Through imitative play, toddlers and twos communicate and increase the complexity of their communication.

- Do not interrupt imitative play. Unless the play becomes so rowdy that you are concerned that someone will get hurt, let it continue.
- Providing hats, mirrors, or streamers hanging from the ceiling to run through may stimulate imitative play.

Encourage Toddlers' and Twos' Use of Verbal or Sign Language to Communicate with Each Other. Provide practical words.

Toddlers and twos use their words with each other to communicate and to guide their peers.

- Model words that toddlers and twos can use when they are playing with each other.
- Describe what children are doing while they are doing it (parallel talk).

Promote Cooperation, Prosocial Development, and Friendships in a Variety of Ways. Cooperation, prosocial development, and friendships continue to grow.

- Encourage children to be prosocial. Give children opportunities to help each other, for example, when another child is crying or a child needs a tissue.
- Help children take the perspective of other children by talking about how another child feels.
- Model empathy, kindness, and sharing with the children.
- Set up opportunities for toddlers and twos to cooperate together—carrying heavy blocks together, or holding one end of a long tube while a peer holds the other end, or putting a large puzzle together.
- Provide art materials—crayons, nontoxic paint, markers with the caps too large for possible choking, brushes, easels, and large pieces of paper. Several children can work at an easel together or on the floor with paint and paper, watching and imitating each other.
- Long periods of time to play, both inside and outside, are very important. This gives children an opportunity to negotiate their play together.
- Appreciate times of glee.
- Read books that have prosocial themes (see Box 8.4)

> **Box 8.4**
>
> **Books for Babies:** Social Development with Peers
>
> *Big Sister, Little Sister,* LeUyen Pham. Hyperion Books (2005).
>
> *Leonardo the Terrible Monster,* Mo Willems. Hyperion Books (2005).
>
> *Little Critter* stories, Mercer Meyer. Golden Books.
>
> *Maisy* stories, Lucy Cousins. Candlewick.
>
> *Max and Ruby* books, Rosemary Wells. Grosset & Dunlap.

Observe, Document, and Facilitate Pretend Play. Play becomes more complex. You will remember that by 3 years of age, a majority of children play reciprocal, turn-taking games, and many play cooperative social pretend play (Howes, 1988). One child might pretend to be the mom, another the dad, and yet another, the dog. They are cooperating and pretending at the same time.

- Set up an interesting dramatic play area with a variety of culturally appropriate materials. Add different materials periodically to spark new interest in social pretend play.
- Join the pretend play of toddlers to help expand the ideas and provide language that is more complex. For example, if the toddlers are pretending to operate a drive-in restaurant, one of them might ask, "What do you want?" A care teacher might answer, "What is your favorite thing here? What do you like to eat?" If the answer is "Chicken nuggets," the care teacher might respond, "Do you think Mazie will like them, too?"

Conflict Has Value. Conflict has value as children learn that others have ideas that differ from their own. Toddlers and twos will say "mine" as they grasp tightly a toy that another child is trying to take. This is a normal part of development; in fact, children who say "mine" at 18 months are more likely to say "yours" at 24 months (Hay, 2006). They are learning about who owns objects and who possesses them in the moment.

- Help children on both sides of a conflict to use words to describe their feelings: "Sam wants that ball. Lan wants the ball too."
- Problem-solve with toddlers and twos. Say, "What can we do to solve this problem?" Suggest simple solutions from which children can choose.
- Use puppets to recreate a conflict and show how to resolve it.

Planning for Toddlers' and Twos' Social Development with Peers

In the following planning guide (Box 8.5), the teacher might want to focus on how to help Bessie develop more skills and strategies in negotiation. Two children are involved in this moment, but the planning should focus on Bessie.

Box 8.5

Individual Child Planning Guide (2) for Bessie

Child's Name: *Bessie*   Plans for Week of (Date):

Person Completing the Guide: _____

Respect: Child's Emotions, Effort, Goals, Learning, and Relationships

Write an observation or use a picture or other documentation here—date all notes.

Chita had been collecting balls in the play yard. Bessie followed Chita, whimpering but not asking for the balls or picking up any herself. Finally Chita turned to Bessie and handed her two of the balls.

Reflect	Relate
What am I doing?	What will you do to support my development and learning?
What am I feeling?	• Responsive interactions
What am I learning?	• Environment: Toys, materials
	• Opportunities

SUMMARY

Infants and toddlers have strong interest in other infants and toddlers. At a very early age they will smile, laugh, and try to engage each other. By the time they are 3, most children have developed many skills for playing together, cooperating, and resolving conflicts.

In the first 3 years of life, children are developing ability in the following areas:

- Interest and enjoyment of peers
- Prosocial attitudes and skills
- Play skills
- Conflict negotiation and management of aggressive feelings

These abilities develop when the families and care teachers expect social skills to develop and both model and support them. Greater mastery of both language and physical skills contribute to the increasingly complex interactions among children in the first 3 years of life.

INVENTORY OF TEACHER PRACTICES

Social Development with Peers

Basic Concepts	A	S	R	Observation/ Reflection
I provide opportunities for infants and toddlers to become interested in peers (place infants near each other, provide materials for toddlers to use together).				
I watch for opportunities to support the development of prosocial behaviors ("Touch gently" "You're such a good friend!").				
I support the development of play skills as part of social development ("Let's see if Lily wants to play with us," expand complexity of play, and include others).				
I help toddlers negotiate conflicts (give them time to sort it out, move in when needed, use feeling words, restore relationships).				
I help toddlers manage aggressive feelings with peers (stay nearby; say, "You are very angry! You can tell me, 'I'm angry'").				

A = Always, S = Sometimes, R = Rarely

REFLECTIONS

1. Suppose you are near two young toddlers. You see one reach out to the other, putting his arms around her, and then both tumble to the ground. This could be interpreted as prosocial behavior, a hug that went awry, or as aggressive behavior in one child pulling another to the floor. What would your reaction be in either situation? How could you use this moment to promote prosocial behavior?

2. What materials in a classroom or home child-care setting could encourage peers to play together?
3. It is a common experience to see two toddlers engaging in conflict over a toy. What words and actions might you use to help these children learn to negotiate such conflicts?

APPLICATIONS

1. Observe young infant, mobile infant, toddler, and two-year-old classrooms in a center using the Inventory of Teacher Practices. Interview the teacher(s) as well and discuss your observations.
2. Explore resources and research on ideas for encouraging prosocial behavior. Summarize your findings and compare and contrast them with those of a peer.
3. Document prosocial behaviors and conflict behaviors in a toddler classroom. Describe what happened before, during, and after each event. Compare your findings with those of a peer and generate conclusions about your observations.

RESOURCES

- Gillespie, L. G., & Hunter, A. (2010). "Believe, Watch, Act! Promoting prosocial behavior in infants and toddlers." Rocking and rolling: Supporting infants, toddlers, and their families. *Young Children, 65*(1), 42–43. Available at http://www. naeyc.org/files/yc/file/201001/RocknRollWeb0110.pdf
- Wittmer, D. S. (2009). *Peers in the early years. A focus on relationships.* Washington, DC: Zero to Three Press.

9

Opportunities for Learning and Thinking

After reading this chapter, you will be able to:

- RESPECT
    - Understand the foundations of learning
    - Describe what infants and toddlers learn
    - Demonstrate how to create learning opportunities for young and mobile infants, toddlers, and twos
    - Be aware of signs of possible delays or disorders
- REFLECT
    - On the individual child's learning foundations and strategies
- On how adults may support or hinder curiosity
- On your own comfort with letting toddlers take little risks or tolerate small frustrations.
- RELATE
    - Plan interactions, materials, and environments, for individual and small groups of children, to promote learning and thinking.

For infants and toddlers, everything involves learning! They are constantly using information to build new ideas about themselves, the people around them, and the objects in their world. Infants and toddlers *construct* an understanding of their world through watching, thinking, checking with trusted adults, and trying out their ideas within their current motor abilities (Bruner, 1996).

Infants and toddlers learn from familiar people and toys. They also enjoy exploring new experiences and using different strategies such as sucking, banging, throwing, looking, and trial and error. For example, each time an infant handles a ball, he or she will try old strategies (mouthing) and then often a new strategy (banging it on the floor). One day the infant might drop it, and then watch in amazement as it rolls across the floor. The next time you see the child with a ball, you might notice that he or she has remembered the previous experience as ball drops from his or her hands and rolls again.

Children construct knowledge through their interactions with the environment and others. Each infant, toddler, and 2-year-old creates mental representations of the information in the world through a sense of wonder, curiosity, exploration, and discoveries. Parents and teachers "co-construct" knowledge with the infant or toddler by listening, observing, wondering with the child, and then reflecting on the learning (New, 2000).

Infant and toddler care teachers scaffold or surround a child's learning by setting up the environment in an interesting way and being an enthusiastic, but not overwhelming, learning partner (Vygotsky, 1962). The infant or toddler care teacher observes or imitates what the baby is doing, then sensitively follows the child's lead during play. For example, if an infant seems disengaged while the teacher is singing a song, the teacher may modify the song to a livelier or quieter one or offer a different experience and see how the child responds. Infant and toddler care teachers set up an enriched environment to encourage children's problem-solving and may model a "next step" in *how* to use a toy. These responses from teachers help infants sustain the attention necessary for learning and their natural inclination for active learning.

RESPECT LEARNING AND THINKING

Infants are born with the ability and desire to learn. In the first years of life, children establish the basic processes of learning such as the ability to focus and pay attention, remember people and events, follow their curiosity, solve problems, find information, and construct knowledge. These *approaches to learning* apply to all developmental domains and can be influenced through every experience a baby encounters.

Infants and toddlers are active learners. They are interested in how to make their own bodies do new things such as rolling or bringing objects to their mouth for exploration. They are interested in the emotions, words, intentions, and actions of others. They seek out endless information about the physical world.

The Foundations of Learning

During the first 3 years of life, infants and toddlers must establish the foundations for all later learning. This foundation does not consist of knowledge of letters or numbers. It consists of a healthy brain and the basic approaches that people use for all learning. As you look at them, you will see that you are still using these skills today.

Attention. Attention is the ability to focus and concentrate. The capacity for attention evolves through a stable, responsive relationship when the adult helps the infant or toddler regulate her reactions and slowly extend quiet, alert states.

Memory. The ability to remember things that have happened previously help the world to be predictable and provide the young child with a sense of having a history, or a life that continues being. Adults help this happen by referring to things that just happened, that happened earlier in the day, and maintaining a predictable environment.

Curiosity. Infants are born curious. Keeping that curiosity alive depends on an adult being a good observer and a responsive partner.

Persistence/Mastery Motivation. Learning depends on the child's ability to manage a small amount of frustration in order to complete a goal. Adults provide the surround that helps the child regulate frustration and stay focused.

Problem-Solving. Young children's lives are filled with opportunities to solve problems: "How do I get Mommy's attention?" "How do I get back down, now that I've stood up?" Allow the child time to find a solution.

It is these approaches, which cross all domains and develop only within relationships, that make learning possible.

What Infants and Toddlers Learn

Strategies for learning are organized systems of actions and thoughts that allow the mind to make mental representations of objects and events in the world. At first, babies use reflexes to interact with the world. Then, as infants and toddlers experience information that cannot be understood fully through basic reflexive responses, they build more elaborate actions or thoughts as they construct greater knowledge.

Cause and Effect. Cause and effect explains how one action causes another to happen. For example, crying brings a caring adult, and flicking a wall switch turns on a light.

Object Permanence. Object permanence describes the concept that people and objects continue to exist even when they are out of sight.

Use of Tools. Use of tools describes using a person or an object to make something else happen, such as a mobile infant pointing for an adult to reach something or a toddler climbing on a chair to reach something on a higher shelf.

Spatial Relationships. Spatial relationships describe how objects compare in size, fit inside each other, or look bigger or smaller depending on the distance.

Young infants enjoy materials that let them create and manipulate.

Organizing Information in Categories. Categorization is the grouping of individual items because of perceived similar characteristics; for example, dogs and cats are both animals.

Ways to Communicate. Communication includes purposefully using facial expressions, sounds, gestures, words, and, eventually, pictures and print.

Numeracy and Quantity. Numeracy and quantity describe basic understandings of larger and smaller quantities, perhaps some ideas of one-to-one correspondence.

Nature and the Physical World. Understanding nature and the physical world; includes knowledge of the cycles of day and night, current seasons, weather, plants, and animals.

Cultural Expectations and Norms. Cultural expectations and norms include the rules and expectations for relationships and behavior among people in the family and culture.

Being a Person and a Member of a Relationship. The development of a sense of being oneself and what it is like to be in relationships with others.

RESPECT THEORIES OF LEARNING AND THINKING

There are two basic "camps" of thinking about how learning happens in the first 3 years of life. The nativist camp, represented by Elizabeth Spelke's Core Knowledge theory (Kinzler & Spelke, 2007, p. 90), proposes that evolution has provided people with internal systems that predispose them to pay attention to and learn about the factors in their environment that would best contribute to survival. These include Object Representation, Agents, Number, and Geometry. Object representation enables a very young infant to recognize an object because it has edges and boundaries, it moves through space in one piece, and it interacts with another object only when they are in contact. Agents, such as people, perform actions for intentional reasons. Agents cannot be inanimate. Number refers to a recognition of quantity, such as more or less, larger or smaller. Geometry is our ability to orient ourselves in space.

The other camp, the empiricists, believe that everything is learned through social and environmental interaction. Vygotsky's sociocultural theory emphasizes the importance of culture and social interaction (1978, 1987). Bruner's neoconstructionist theory promotes the idea that children build their understanding of the world through their own experiences (1996). Bandura's social learning theory focuses on imitation (1997).

Dynamic systems theory, a third alternative, looks at learning as happening as the body moves through an environment, with the limits of the body, the history of the mind, and the information of the environment all in interaction. "Clearly, cognition takes place when organisms with bodies and sensory systems are situated in structured environments, to which they bring their individual behavioral history and to which they quickly adjust" (Schoner, 2007, p. 1). Dynamic systems theory is not just a cognitive theory but an emerging theory that applies to all facets of development.

Table 9.1   Developmental Possibilities in Learning and Thinking

Young Infants	Mobile Infants	Toddlers	Twos
0–9 Months	9–18 Months	16–24 Months	24–36 Months
Young infants cry to bring an adult to comfort or feed them.	Children in this age group like toys that do something when you touch them, pull them, or bang them.	This age group understands, remembers, and anticipates the details of routines.	Twos are interested in the story and pictures in story-books.
Beginning early in this period, young infants notice that their arms or legs made something happen and will repeat the movement.	This age group points to objects, knowing you can also see them. They look in the direction you are looking when you talk about a toy.	Toddlers use realistic objects as substitutes for other objects in their pretend play.	Twos create new stories in pretend play or new structures in block building, becoming more imaginative and creative.
Young infants like to make toys do something—such as make a sound. Later in this age group, young infants may put one toy inside another.	Mobile infants like to use their mobility to explore—crawling, walking, climbing, running.	Toddlers enjoy the ease of their movement and like to use their hands to carry things around.	Begin to understand concepts such as color, size, shape, time and weight.
Young infants imitate adult expressions and gestures.	Mobile infants enjoy playing with sand, water, and dough with different kinds of play tools.	Toddlers enjoy increasingly challenging materials that suggest activities such as building, sorting, and matching shapes.	Twos may assign roles to toys and other children in pretend play; use chairs, blankets, and bookcases as substitutes for items in pretend play.

DEVELOPMENTAL POSSIBILITIES IN LEARNING AND THINKING

Table 9.1 describes the developmental possibilities in learning and thinking that may be observed in young children.

RESPECT SIGNS OF CONCERN IN LEARNING AND THINKING

For the most part, concerns about learning and thinking in the first 3 years of life stem either from biological challenges that we know make learning hard or from environmental forces that compromise a child's ability to learn.

Biological challenges include sensory impairments, Down syndrome, motor impairments, extremely low birthweight, and extreme prematurity. These issues either limit the way the child can physically interact with the world or affect the way the brain processes information. Each of these conditions would be identified very early and the child would receive early intervention services to support learning.

Of more concern to the infant care teacher or home visitor is a situation in which environmental influences limit learning. These limitations may be effects of time spent at home or in out-of-home care. Preventing children from exploring through the overuse of swings and bouncy seats, the lack of rich language being

Box 9.1

Reflect on Learning and Thinking

Approaches to Learning

- What does this young child find interesting?
- How does an infant, mobile infant, toddler, and 2-year-old use all the senses in learning about the world?
- How is each individual child able to focus and pay attention to something interesting? Is there anything that captures the attention of many children at the same time?
- How does each young child show curiosity and motivation to learn?

Thinking About and Processing Information

- How does each infant think about or process information?
- How does the toddler categorize information? Does he seem to group toys that are the same color?
- What does each infant, mobile infant, toddler, and two remember? Is it faces, voices, or maybe what an object does? How does it differ for each age group?

Concepts and Ideas About Objects and People

- What concepts or ideas does each child have while exploring an object (if I bang it, the toy will make noise) or interacting with people (if I touch my mom's nose, she will laugh)?
- What does each child know about object permanence? Is this knowledge changing over time?
- What does each toddler try to make happen with people or with materials? Does the infant make sounds to get needs met, kick feet to make a sound, bring feet to his or her mouth, or shake or bang an object to make sounds?
- How does each toddler demonstrate interest in how objects relate by size?
- How does each infant or toddler try to use the teacher/peer as a tool to reach or accomplish something?

used, and ignoring or always saying "no" may interfere with learning. Signs of these problems would be aimless wandering, aggression, or lack of interest in the people, toys, and materials in the environment.

REFLECT ON LEARNING AND THINKING

As you reflect on learning and thinking, remember that questions can guide care teachers, directors, and other professionals as they learn about individual children in the group and the group dynamics (see Box 9.1). After care teachers and/or parents document the answers in collaboration with each other, planning can occur for individual children and the group.

RELATE TO LEARNING AND THINKING

The infant and toddler care teacher *relates* to each child's current, individual interests in learning. These interests will be influenced by the child's age, temperament, personal experiences, and abilities. Age is a very strong factor because of its effect on learning within the motivational themes of security, exploration, and identity as well as the child's changing physical skills. The following sections describe learning experiences for the young infant, the mobile infant, and toddlers and twos.

THE YOUNG INFANT: BIRTH TO 9 MONTHS

The young infant strives for feelings of security and safety. The process of making the world a more predictable and understandable place involves achieving regulation of his or her reactions to the world, being able to pay attention to interesting people and experiences, using information from all the senses, and remembering things that have been seen before. The young infant relies on trusted adults to provide a sense of safety and to help him or her explore the world. Much of the young infant's learning occurs through interactions with adults during daily routines of feeding, diapering, sleep, and play.

A Glimpse of the Young Infant's Learning and Thinking

When Miriam arrives to open the classroom in the morning, she arranges materials accord-ing to her plans. She does a quick safety check and sets out the sign-in sheet for the parents. Because all care is responsive and individualized, there is no set schedule. Miriam and her co-teacher Shela document each child's day with notes and photos and use their observations to plan how to offer play materials and to think about helpful interactions. Because they have only young infants in their room, they know that each child is learning about self-reg-ulation, feeling safe and secure in relationships, how to be with other people, and how objects in the world work.

Three-month-old Adara arrives first. Her mom brought her still asleep and apologized, "I'm so sorry, Miriam. She just doesn't have her days and nights straight yet." Miriam answered, "Don't worry about it. We'll put her in her crib and I'll stay close by to comfort her when she wakes up. Anything I should know about her night?" "Well, no surprise, she was up pretty late. And she's going to be starving when she wakes up. I brought more breast milk for her."

Adara is still learning to regulate her waking/sleeping cycles in her day. For Adara, the interactions that accompany the routines of her day comprise the majority of her activities. She stares intently at Miriam's face as she talks to her about their activities together. She also plays on a floor mat, enjoying tummy time and time on her back. She is fascinated by the mirror and by watching the other children.

Four-month-old Paulo can rest on just one arm during his tummy time, using the other for reaching toys and bringing them to his mouth. He mouths toys, feels them with his fin-gers, and then studies them visually, as though comparing all the information that his dif-ferent senses give him. Batting at dangling toys from his back is also fun, but his newly acquired skill of rolling over at will is his favorite activity. Paulo is also learning about using sounds and facial expressions—especially his winning, toothless smile—as a way to engage adults and other children. Routines are still an important part of his day, and Miriam uses diapering, feeding, and comforting as opportunities for talking and closeness.

Takala is interested in Jack. Takala is crawling and Jack stares at her as though, if he watches carefully enough, his little body also will start crawling. Miriam doesn't want to rush him, but she is very encouraging when he finds himself on his hands and knees. Jack doesn't acknowledge her support. Jack and Takala are each able to sit up, Jack with some propping, Takala on her own. This frees their hands, and both spend lots of time picking up light blocks and sturdy plastic animals, mouthing them and dropping them. Takala spends much more time looking at the toys. There seems to be something missing in the quality of Jack's play.

The Young Infant Care Teacher's Decisions

Miriam understands that the babies in her care are learning all the time. They are listening to language, learning about being with other people, and learning about many things in the world. However, the most important ways she can help them learn in these first months is by helping them stay calm and alert, feel safe, and pay attention to the information that presents itself to them.

Adara's mixed-up schedule is hard on everyone, but Miriam knows that by being responsive to her needs for sleep and eating on her own schedule, she is helping

Adara make the most of her waking hours. Paulo still needs closeness and comforting, too, but he is also caught up in a new interest in the world around him. Miriam builds on his needs for security by being responsive and emotionally available to him. She has also watched Paulo's intense desire to practice his new skills of rolling and reaching, so she provides safe and interesting opportunities to him. Paulo's physical and social abilities help him learn about his own effectiveness and about the objects and people in his world.

Jack and Takala are just beginning to venture out a little on their own. Takala looks to Miriam for encouragement and interest. Takala responds as Miriam plays with them and supplies names for toys. Takala spends a lot of time examining the environment and seeming to soak up information. Miriam watches them to see what kinds of toys and materials interest them and how she can add to their learning. Both children have pets at home and show interest in animals. She makes animal sounds as they play, names the toy animals, and looks at board books with photographs of animals over and over again with them. Jack is not often interested in the play, but he frequently pushes Takala out of the way to have Miriam to himself.

Adaptations for Special Needs. Miriam has been talking with Jack's parents and the mental health consultant. Jack is very smart, but he never feels safe. It is hard for him to learn and explore when he is always watching the environment for danger. The mental health consultant has urged both Miriam and his parents to provide playtime alone with one adult. That adult needs to watch Jack's cues very carefully and respond to even the smallest signal that he may be attempting to connect with them.

Diversity/Culture. Miriam is well aware that different cultures bring different perspectives to learning as well as to other aspects of life. Takala's family is Native American, and they have explained to Miriam that they have a spiritual connection and respect for nature that they want their daughter to share. They encourage Miriam to help even these very young infants notice the changing of the seasons and the variety of life around them in the outdoors.

Opportunities for Young Infants' Learning and Thinking

Pay Attention to Attention. In the first several months, babies are learning to regulate their reactions to feelings inside their bodies and to surrounding events. As they begin to manage their reactions, with your help, they can pay attention for longer periods of time.

- Use soft colors in the room. A young baby will be drawn to bright colors and sharp contrasts. Use that interest to help the child focus on other children, toys, pictures, and you!

- Save music for times when you and a baby are swaying or dancing to the rhythms. Background music can be confusing for a baby too young to distinguish it from the more important sound of your murmuring voice.

- Think about what kinds of information the infant is processing. If arms and legs are flailing, the infant is getting a lot of information from his or her own body. If the child is also trying to watch other babies, the sheer amount of information may be overwhelming. He or she may be more comfortable watching other babies from the support of your arms.

Tune in Emotionally and Be Responsive to Each Child. Your voice, facial expressions, and movements are always interesting to a young infant. As you and an infant tune into each other, the child's ability to attend will flourish and his or her interest in people and relationships will grow.

- Hold the baby about 12–19 inches from your face when you are "conversing" or during feeding and diapering. Talk quietly to the baby about what you are doing, pausing to let the baby take a turn. He or she may coo or smile or just look intently at you to ask you to continue; or, if in need of a little break, the baby may turn the eyes away for a moment to collect him- or herself, hoping that you will wait quietly until he or she is ready to begin again.

- When a baby pokes out a trembling lower lip to cry or flashes that charming smile, he or she will watch to see your reaction. You will probably "mirror" the child's expression. Seeing that pout or smile returned on your face helps the baby learn what his or her face looks like. It shows the child that his or her own emotional experience is understood by others.

Watch for Body Awareness. Young infants are learning about their own face and body.

- Mount unbreakable mirrors on the wall just above the floor where young infants can see themselves move and make faces while playing on the floor.
- Look at board books about feelings, bodies, and things babies do.

Use Nature's Sensory Experiences. Everything is new to a young infant—light, sound, movement, texture, and color. Engage infants to notice these aspects of the world by holding them as you point out interesting things in the environment.

- Introduce the baby to "dancing sunlight" (Cryer, Harms, & Bourland, 1987, p. 170) that pours through a window with a curtain moving in the wind.
- Take the baby's hand and gently stroke it over different textures as you say words such as "hard," "soft," and "rough." Nature offers an endless variety of new experiences as babies discover leaves, grass, sand, dirt, stones, sticks, flowers, snow, and rain.

Create Sensory Experiences. Young infants use their natural curiosity and all their senses to explore. They listen, look, touch, taste, and smell.

- Offer materials that appeal to each of the senses.
- Collect empty plastic pill bottles. For the sense of smell, soak a cotton ball in vanilla, almond extract, peppermint extract, or fresh lime juice. Place one cotton ball in each bottle, seal the bottles with superglue, and punch air holes in the lid. Let the babies discover the different scents.

Provide opportunities for young infants to use all of their senses.

- Empty pill bottles can also become homemade rattles that create different sounds. Put a tablespoon of rice in one, dried beans in another, pebbles in another. Seal with superglue. Be sure it is too big for choking, over 1.25 inches in diameter and 2.25 inches deep
- Do the unusual; for example, tape a piece of contact paper to the wall and settle a sitting infant near it with some small safe toys. Soon an object will find itself on the contact paper and the baby will have a new tactile experience to discover.
- Cover an area of the floor with corrugated cardboard for crawling over.
- A collection of pieces of different textured fabric will be fascinating as the infant compares information from the sense of touch and the sense of sight.
- Fill a plastic swimming pool with crumpled tissue paper balls or plastic balls (too large to choke on) for an interesting sensory exploration.

Design Cause and Effect Experiences. Motivation to learn develops as infants "make something happen" and begin to understand cause and effect. Young infants want control over their learning. Infants clearly tell you, with engaged looks or disengaged yawning, whether they are interested in an experience. They are more interested in experiences over which they have some effect and control.

- Tie a ribbon around a baby's wrist so a movement of an arm will bring forth a display of color.
- A bell very carefully sewn into a bootie will make a sound when an infant shakes his or her foot.
- Rattles and toys that move when they are touched motivate infants to "do it again to see what happens."

Set Up Intriguing Sets of Materials. Young infants are interested in comparing and contrasting properties of objects.

- Provide objects in clusters, for example, a variety of textured teethers (Cryer, Harms, & Bourland, 1987, p. 169). Provide a small collection of noisemakers, shiny objects, or things to look through.

Talk About Things That Are Out of Sight. Object permanence experiences are everywhere an infant looks, listens, and touches. Over time, the baby begins to understand that people and objects exist even when they are out of sight.

- Your voice as you approach an infant represents your existence, even if the baby cannot see you (person permanence).
- The sounds of music under a cover, the bump of a ball showing from under a blanket, and food that disappears over the side of the highchair are all opportunities for infants to learn about object permanence.

Notice How Even Young Infants Are Using Tools. Infants develop concepts or ideas about how the world works through their interactions with interesting materials and people. Notice and provide opportunities that support tool use.

- While grasping a rattle, an infant might accidentally shake it or hit the floor with it, and the rattle immediately becomes a tool to make sound.
- A sitting infant who wriggles his or her whole body to get you to sing again is using the body as a tool.

Planning for Young Infants' Learning and Thinking

The planning guide (see Box 9.2) provides a way to be responsive to individual children while planning for an entire group. This form would be particularly useful for

Box 9.2

Individually Responsive Group Planning Guide

Name of Group: *Butterflies* _____   Week of: *March 12–16, 2012* _____

Person(s) completing this guide: _____

Respect and Reflect

The children in my group are . . .

(Summarize information from the individual planning guides)

Working on regulation/self-regulation around routines and separation

Exploring cause/effect

Enjoying using their bodies in different ways

Sometimes interested in each other

Sometimes trusting adults to respond to them and have fun with them

Learning to use sounds for communication

Relate: Plans for the Week to Meet Children's Interests and Needs

Songs/Fingerplays/Music

Stories/Books

Responsive Interactions

Environment: Toys, materials

Opportunities

Family/Cultural Experiences

Other

programs where a posted lesson plan needs to be individualized and yet protect each child's confidentiality.

For practice in planning with this form, information about Miriam's individual children is provided. The form provides space for planning actions on the care teacher's part in several areas: songs, fingerplays, and music; stories and books; responsive interactions; environment, toys, materials, and opportunities; experiences with families; and special experiences. Use the planning spaces to plan activities, materials, and interactions that would support the children's learning.

THE MOBILE INFANT: 8–18 MONTHS

The mobile infant is entranced with movement: Rolling, crawling, scooting, cruising, or toddling—if it moves him forward, it's worth doing. Movement is exciting in its own right, but it is also a marvelous tool for reaching those low shelves and cupboards that were always out of reach. The mobile infant is an explorer. Learning still involves those trusted adults and a sense of safety, but the mobile infant's own memories and growing knowledge of how things work can fill each day with discoveries.

A Glimpse of the Mobile Infant's Learning and Thinking

Albert loved the four babies in his care when they were young, but he finds them absolutely fascinating now that they are mobile and constantly exploring. They seem to be seeing the world for the first time and frequently making new mental connections. They are interested in everything and everyone. Push and pull toys are a favorite with all of these children, but each child has individual interests as well.

Gemma skipped crawling and is walking at 9 months. She climbs and slides and loves motion. She loves emptying containers of toy animals or manipulatives and tossing them around. Sometimes she just carries things from place to place, enjoying the use of both hands while she toddles around. She often checks back with Albert, meeting his eyes and grinning with joy at her own freedom. Albert knows he needs to stay within sight of Gemma so that she feels safe enough to keep moving. He constructs interesting configurations of the sturdy vinyl-covered foam climbing pieces to keep the environment interesting for her.

Radwan, at 15 months, alternates between walking and crawling to get around. He's capable at both but faster at crawling and not willing to give up his speed. Radwan is particularly interested in how things come apart and go back together. He enjoys stacking cups, giant pop beads, simple puzzles, and shape boxes. Albert appeals to Radwan's interests in both moving and in manipulatives by placing interesting toys in different places around the room so that Radwan's travels result in the discovery of favorite toys.

Lily, at 12 months, has a significant level of cerebral palsy, leaving her generally unable to move around in the environment to explore. She has always been a quiet, visual learner. Albert sees her studying pictures in books or making groupings of plastic animals or cars. Lily often looks to Albert to supply the name of something that interests her. She is also the most likely to stay near him when the group is playing outdoors. Albert finds time to sit near her and talk with her about her play.

Goro at 16 months is the oldest in the group. Albert sees a sort of planning and intention in his play. Goro will build a tower of blocks just to knock it down again. He'll dump the contents from a plastic bucket to use the bucket as a hat. He seems to balance his time between riding toys, climbing and sliding, and using toys such as Legos or puzzles that he likes to work on while sitting on Albert's lap.

Albert wanted to learn more about how the children explored object permanence. He documented how Goro hid toys in the sand and how Lily covered a picture in a book with her hand and then squealed with excitement when she uncovered it (as if she were surprised to see it). He also documented how Radwan's discovery of toys around the room was a way to check whether the objects still existed when he left them and returned. Albert shared his observations with families and asked them to notice their children's understanding of object permanence. The parents responded with interest and noticed many examples of their children's understanding of object permanence. Albert displayed photos of the children in the room and the examples from the parents on a bulletin board. Many parents commented that "seeing" examples of children's exploration of object permanence helped them understand this concept and the importance of the children's exploration and play.

The Mobile Infant Care Teacher's Decisions

The children in Albert's care show very different abilities and interests in the months surrounding their first birthdays. His planning for them is easily individualized because their interests and personalities are so distinctive.

Albert respects Gemma's desire to move but also feels that he needs to keep her aware of her surroundings and actively thinking. He finds that creating new configurations of the soft climbing materials poses interesting problem-solving experiences for Gemma. Lily is one of those quiet children who seem interested in everything. It is difficult for him to tell, sometimes, because the motor problems affect her facial expressions, her language, and her ability to manipulate materials. Albert reminds himself throughout the day to closely observe Lily and to provide a good variety of experiences for her. Recently he has noticed that she is choosing books about colors, and so Albert is creating some color matching opportunities for her. He had not thought much about the difference between physical and learning disabilities before knowing Lily. Radwan enjoys finding Albert's surprises—puzzles and manipulatives displayed in unexpected places. Radwan's interests are so diverse that Albert finds it easy to plan for him. Goro is more interested in completing a task than are the other children. He will dump an entire container of manipulatives and sit on Albert's lap, working on them for a long time. Albert plans ways to support this wonderful attention span and extend Goro's building abilities as he works.

Adaptations for Special Needs. Albert finds it very helpful to work with the physical and speech therapists. He understands that Lily is able to learn but he needs to be very thoughtful in how he presents learning opportunities. He needs to consider her interests, her physical abilities, and then figure out materials and experiences that offer her the information she wants. She is able to use a velcro mitt, so Albert created different-color felt shapes that she can pick up and manipulate. He also

This mobile infant learns about space, cause and effect, gravity, and object permanence as she plays with a toy.

brought out colorful scarves that stick to the velcro and flow as she moves. The physical therapist has shown Albert ways to bring some materials to Lily using supportive seating with a tray.

Diversity/Culture. Albert sometimes jokes that he and his small primary group of children are a mini–United Nations. He is African-American, Goro's family is Japanese, Radwan's family is Arabic, Lily's family has a French background, and Gemma's family is English. Although each of these cultures values learning, each has different expectations for learning in infancy. Goro's family believes that he is too young to think about learning, Gemma's family believes you can't start too early. Radwan's grandparents think it is silly to "plan" learning opportunities, but his parents think that Albert really understands Radwan and supports his natural intelligence. Lily's family appreciates that Albert sees beyond the disability and values Lily's ability to learn.

Opportunities for Mobile Infants' Learning and Thinking

See Movement and Exploration as Integral to Learning. Mobile infants are compelled to move and explore. They roll, crawl, cruise, toddle, walk, climb, and enjoy the new sensation of being able to carry things in their hands as they move around.

- Check the area for safety several times a day. Shelves or tables that are being used for cruising could fall over. Floors covered with toys can be hazardous if a new walker should fall. Objects that are out of reach to a crawler may be within reach to a walker.

- Provide lots of opportunities for climbing, sliding, going under, going over, pulling, pushing, and riding. (These opportunities will be described further in Chapter 11.)

Mobile Infants Enjoy Exploring All the Ways They Can Make Things Happen.

- Sand and water can be poured, touched, and held in containers. Sand can be used for burying and finding sticks, stones, or toys. Water can be used for floating and sinking.

- To encourage experimentation, offer a combination of objects in unique ways; for example, long feathers and 2-liter plastic bottles for the sitting infant. Watch how the baby experiments with different ways to systematically mix the materials

- Buttons, switches, levers, wind-up handles, and dials can be used as tools to make things happen. Battery-operated closet lights turn on and off when pressed, providing an immediate experience of cause and effect. Pop-up toys and busy boxes provide a variety of tools, but they sometimes have mechanisms that are too hard for the mobile infant who is interested in having the toy pop up. The older toddler who can work the mechanism already understands this simple cause-and-effect relationship and won't be interested in the toy. Simpler pop-up mechanisms are a better match for the mobile infant.

Acknowledge the Pretend Use of Objects. Mobile infants imitate the way they have seen adults use tools in the very beginnings of symbolic play.

- Provide toy telephones, kitchen areas, keys, and building and gardening tools for mobile infants to use in play.

- Provide dolls with clothing that is removable, bottles for feeding, beds for naps, and tubs and water for baths.

Be Creative in Offering Materials That Appear and Disappear. Mobile infants are developing a firm understanding of object permanence, the idea that people and objects exist even when they are out of sight.

- Play peek-a-boo games with mobile infants. Over these months, their new mobility may extend these games into chasing or hiding games.

- Provide opaque containers with lids for holding objects.

- Feeling boxes—sturdy boxes with holes cut for the child to reach into the box without being able to see what is inside—can be used for daily surprises. One day a soft, fuzzy fabric will be inside; another day a hard plastic ball. This provides opportunities for learning through many senses and for rich use of language.

- Drive toy cars into garages that close, or put toy farm animals away in the barn. Open the garage or barn a moment later with the child and "discover" that the toys are still there.

Devise Opportunities for Sorting into Categories. Mobile infants are organizing information by grouping, or categorizing, objects that have similar properties such as "red blocks," "stuffed animals," or "dishes."

- Offer buckets filled with plastic animals, colorful table blocks, cars, or large plastic counters that could be sorted by color, shape, size, or type (cats, dogs, birds, cows, horses).

- In looking at picture books, add categories to your conversation, such as, "There's a cow. Where are the other animals?"

Use Words Such as "In" and "Out", and "Over" and "Under" as Mobile Infants Explore Space. Mobile infants sometimes find themselves stuck in spaces that they have to back out of or cannot fit into. The question of how objects relate to each other in space is very intriguing for the infant who can move his or her body around and who can use both hands to fit cups or shapes inside each other.

- Observe the discoveries that each mobile infant is making. If one or more are exploring how to put items into containers, provide many unique containers.

Provide stacking cups, rings on a stick, and a variety of containers filled with safe and interesting objects. Muffin tins hold tennis balls differently from the way they hold slightly smaller plastic balls. Coffee cans can become simple shape boxes with just one hole cut in the top to match the shape of table blocks, ping pong balls, or the pull-off lids of frozen orange juice containers.

- Crawlers like to find little spaces such as the underside of a table. Surprise them by covering the bottom of the table with a large sheet of paper and dangling markers for drawing.

Use Routines to Provide Predictable Sequences.

Use Routines to Provide Predictable Sequences. Mobile infants are beginning to understand the sequence of the routines in their day. They may grab their jackets when it is time to go outside or crawl to the changing table when it is time for a diaper change.

- Talk to mobile infants about routines. They may show you their understanding of how meal times go and learn words that are involved in the routines.
- Different cultures may approach routines differently. Some families will expect their mobile infants to begin to develop some independence in these routines, while others will expect their children to become increasingly cooperative. Talk with families about their expectations and yours concerning routines.

Use Mathematics-Related Words.

Use Mathematics-Related Words. Although it may not be apparent, mobile infants are developing some understanding of basic math concepts such as one-to-one correspondence and larger or smaller amounts.

- Talk about one-to-one correspondence as it naturally occurs during the day. At snack time, handing out crackers, Albert might say, "Here's a cracker for Gemma, one for Lily, one for Radwan, and one for Goro. That's one, two, three, four crackers."
- As a child piles blocks or small figures, the infant care teacher could use words that describe amounts such as, "That's a *big* pile. It has *more* blocks than the *little* pile."

See Nature Through the Mobile Infant's Discovering Eyes.

See Nature Through the Mobile Infant's Discovering Eyes. The natural world is full of fascinating information for the mobile infant.

- Share a child's interest in watching a bug crawl on the ground.
- Take time to look at and talk about leaves, grass, birds, sticks, and stones.
- Let children collect items from nature and bring them into the classroom to examine over time. Talk to the children about when you collected the materials and help them remember the experience.

Planning for Mobile Infants' Learning and Thinking

Box 9.3 provides a second opportunity to practice using the *Individually Responsive Group Planning Guide.* This time you will use the information from Albert's group of mobile infants.

Box 9.3

Individually Responsive Group Planning Guide

Name of Group: _____ Week of: _____

Person(s) completing this guide: _____

Respect and Reflect

The children in my group are . . .

(Summarize information from the individual planning guides)

Moving

Playing with stacking cups, rings, activity boxes, shape boxes

Emptying and filling containers

Enjoying books

Playing with toy animals

Relate: Plans for the Week to Meet Children's Interests and Needs

Songs/Fingerplays/Music

Stories/Books

Responsive Interactions

Environment: Toys, materials

Opportunities

Family/Cultural Experiences

Other

TODDLERS AND TWOS: 16–36 MONTHS

As infants turn into toddlers, they usually bring new skills in mobility and language to their learning experiences.

A Glimpse of Toddlers' and Twos' Learning and Thinking

Selena has been caring for infants and toddlers for 30 years, since her own children were babies. She is now the primary toddler care teacher for four toddlers and twos whom she has cared for since they were young babies. She is in a room with a co-teacher and four other toddlers. Although she is the primary teacher for the four toddlers, she and her co-teacher interact with all the children.

The youngest in the group is Chita at 19 months. She is a lively child who tries hard to keep up with the others. She understands both Spanish and English, and Selena speaks both with her. Chita is still working on stable walking. She dabbles briefly in art projects or doll play but is most interested in watching her friends play. Selena knows that Chita is learning a great deal by watching but also helps her try working with new materials for a few minutes at a time.

Lan's grandparents emigrated from Vietnam, and he also is learning two languages. He is just 2 years old and likes to explore most of the materials in the classroom, but he loves being outdoors. Selena has added many natural materials to the collage box for gluing onto cardboard, increased her collection of plastic animals and insects in the block area, and found wonderful board books filled with pictures of nature. She even found a knob-handled puzzle of bugs at a garage sale.

Bessie is also 2, but very different from Lan. She enjoys stroller walks, but would otherwise prefer to stay inside. Bessie has Down syndrome, and Selena has learned a lot from the early intervention team about how to support her learning. Bessie loves holding and feeding a doll and enjoys putting rings on a stick, but is hesitant to try new materials without support. As soon as she masters something like the rings, she wants to do it over and over. Bessie genuinely enjoys the other children, and Selena uses their interests to expand Bessie's.

At 2½ Sam is a leader in the group. He uses several words together, he understands how to use the materials in the room, and he enjoys all the outdoor activities. Selena is challenged to keep him engaged and interested without making new activities too difficult for the other children. Sam loves riding toys, digging in and building with sand, and every kind of building material Selena can offer. Lately, Sam has been exploring the use of tools. He enjoys using the short fishing rod with a magnet at the end to pick up magnetic puzzle pieces. He uses one toy to push another toy around the room. Selena documented the children's use of tools and, as a result, brought in more pull toys with safe strings, some flashlights, and play spoons to feed dolls in the dramatic play area.

The Toddler Care Teacher's Decisions

Selena enjoys being able to offer a greater variety of materials to her increasingly accomplished children. For example, if the water table is holding plastic boats, she finds that each of the children has a unique way of playing with them. She finds that the children want more than one story at a sitting, and often more than one child is on her lap to hear a story at one time. Still, nothing beats quiet observation for staying on top of the children's interests.

It would be easy just to celebrate Chita's joy in movement, but observation has helped Selena to see the need to support her quiet, attentive moments. Bessie plays nicely, but needs Selena's attention to try working with new materials, especially things like shape boxes that require a combination of thinking, fine motor control, and eye-hand coordination.

Adaptations for Special Needs. Bessie needs her work with materials to be more structured and supported by Selena. However, Bessie does not like being pushed into new experiences. She can get very angry. The early intervention team suggested that Selena use a new material near Bessie and let her become curious. The early childhood special educator has helped Selena break down the learning into small steps so that she can really see which parts Bessie masters. Selena takes more structured notes when she observes Bessie so that she is really on top of her day-to-day learning.

Diversity/Culture. Chita and Lan need support for maintaining their home languages while they are learning English. Chita's Spanish is the same home language as Selena's, but trying to work with Lan in Vietnamese has been more challenging. Selena relies on Lan's family to provide her with names of toys and clothing. She has asked the local college to help her find a student who could speak Vietnamese to him. She has pictures of Vietnam on the walls but few artifacts such as cooking pots or other household items for the room.

Opportunities for Toddlers' and Twos' Learning and Thinking

Find Materials Wherein Parts Become a Whole and a Whole Can Become Parts. Parts that can be put together into a whole and whole objects that can be taken apart into pieces are a more sophisticated aspect of object permanence for toddlers and twos.

- Offer large wooden beads and reinforced strings for creating necklaces.
- Offer blocks, large Legos, and other manipulatives for building.
- Doughs and clays can be torn into pieces and remolded into a whole over and over again.
- A basket of fabric squares can be put together to create a river, cover a table, or create hats. This kind of open-ended, reusable material provides ongoing experiences in creating parts from a whole and a whole from parts.

Recognize Mathematical Concepts Throughout the Day. Mathematics may still seem like a large word for these beginning concepts, but toddlers and twos are interested in patterns, matching colors, counting, amounts, and the names of shapes.

- Do simple counting finger plays such as the following:

Three Balls

Here's a ball *(make ball with thumb and index finger)*
And here's a ball *(make ball with other thumb and index finger)*
A great big ball, I see *(put arms up and touch fingers)*
Shall we count them?
Are you ready?
One, two, three *(make all three balls in succession)*

Five Little Bees

(make fist and bring out fingers as you go or use models or finger puppets of bees)
One little bee blew and flew.
He met a friend, and that made two.
Two little bees, busy as could be—
Along came another and that made three.
Three little bees, wanted one more,

Found one soon and that made four.
Four little bees, going to the hive.
Spied their little brother, and that made five.
Five little bees working every hour—
Buzz away, bees, and find another flower.

- At snack time, ask, "Do you want one or two crackers?" Then count out the number requested.
- Point out simple geometric shapes in the environment: "This plate looks like a circle." "This block looks different, it's a triangle."
- Let children spontaneously discover matching shapes or colors and add your interest to theirs.
- Use words describing mathematical relationships such as *bigger, smaller, more, less, taller, shorter, heavy,* and *light.*
- Read books that include counting and numbers, such as the following recommended by the American Library Association:

Five Little Monkeys Jumping on the Bed, by Eileen Christelow (Clarion)
Ten, Nine, Eight, by Molly Garrett Bang (Greenwillow)

Be Ready for Materials to Be Used in New Ways—and Repeat Favorites. Toddlers and twos continue to enjoy making things happen. However, these experiences may be integrated into other areas of play.

- Toddlers and twos may enjoy mixing colors of paint with large brushes at an easel or mixing colored water in small containers with eyedroppers.
- Building in the sand may evolve into hunting for pebbles to decorate the sand building as ideas come together in more complicated ways.
- Toddlers and twos are likely to remember books, songs, and toys that they particularly like and find ways to tell you they want to repeat the experience. (See Box 9.4 for a list of books that most toddlers will like.)

Twos Pretend Play the Real Experiences in Their Lives. Offering tools for play will increase the range and complexity of pretend play for the 2-year-old.

- Car keys, a baseball cap, or dolls might lead a child to play at the things Daddy and Mommy do.
- Older children may direct play, assigning roles or actions to other children.
- Toddlers and twos may still use lots of imitation in their play, copying what they've seen adults do and copying each other.

Box 9.4

Books for Babies: Learning and Thinking

Baby Colors, Baby's World Board Books. DK Publishing (2003).

Brown Sugar Babies, Charles R. Smith, Jr. Jump at the Sun (2000).

My First Spanish Number Board Book/Mi Primer Libro de Numeros en Espanol. DK Publishing (2002).

My Very First Book of Numbers, Eric Carle. Philomel (2006).

One Red Sun: A Counting Book, Ezra Jack Keats. Viking (1999).

Peek-a-Who?, Nina Laden. Chronicle Books (2000).

A Rainbow All Around Me, Sandra Pinkney. Cartwheel (2002).

See Art as a Process, Not a Product. The process of using art materials may be interesting for longer periods of time, but toddlers and twos are not creating products yet.

- Painting can be a sensory experience of blending colors and using different parts of your body. Paint can be scented with food extracts. Sticks, stones, toy cars, blocks, sponges, and balls can all be ways to apply paint to paper. And why stop at paper? Cardboard boxes, old bedsheets, and play yard sidewalks all can provide new problems to be solved in applying paint.

- Support the experience of using art materials with comments such as, "Is that smooth or squishy?" or "Those colors are so bright together!" rather than requesting a "product" with questions such as "What is that?"

Support Problem-Solving. Sometimes you can almost watch toddlers and twos solving problems—perhaps because they often think of things to do that their bodies can't quite manage.

- Support problem-solving by staying close by and offering encouragement, but not offering solutions.

- Provide an environment that offers some challenges. Climbing up steps is easier than climbing back down. Letting two toddlers negotiate a few steps at the same time provides more learning than telling one to wait. A toddler who wants the tools that another is using with clay could be asked, "What will you do?" rather than having a teacher demand that one child surrender some of the tools.

- Offer new toys such as peg-boards and pegs without demonstrating how to use them. Let the children explore possible uses and take the information held within the materials to suggest how they might be used.

Provide opportunities for toddlers and twos to explore "cause & effect" and "the use of tools."

Box 9.5

Individually Responsive Group Planning Guide

Name of Group: _Dragonflies_   Week of: _March 12–16, 2012_

Person(s) completing this guide: _____

Respect and Reflect

The children in my group are . . .

(Summarize information from the individual planning guides)

Relate: Plans for the Week to Meet Children's Interests and Needs

Songs/Fingerplays/Music

Stories/Books

Responsive Interactions

Environment: Toys, materials

Opportunities

Family/Cultural Experiences

Other

Planning for Toddlers' and Twos' Learning and Thinking

In using the planning guide for planning for toddlers and twos (Box 9.5), review the information in this chapter about Selena's children. List what interests them and what they are doing. Use these notes to plan learning activities for these children.

SUMMARY

Infants and toddlers construct knowledge of their environment through exploration and interactions with others. They are using many approaches to learning: attention, memory, persistence/ mastery motivation, and problem-solving. They are learning basic concepts such as the following:

- Cause and effect
- Object permanence
- Use of tools
- Spatial relationships
- Categories
- Numeracy and quantity
- Communication
- The natural world
- The culture of their family and community

Infants and toddlers use increasingly sophisticated strategies as they strive to make sense of the world. Their natural curiosity motivates them to solve problems and understand how things work, including human relationships. Infant/toddler care teachers use sensitive observation and responses to plan engaging learning experiences and then support each child's explorations.

INVENTORY OF TEACHER PRACTICES

Learning and Thinking

Basic Concepts	A	S	R	Observation/ Reflection
I provide opportunities for infants and toddlers to learn about cause and effect, including being responsive to their cues.				
I support discoveries about object permanence, for example, in games like peek-a-boo.				
I provide opportunities for discoveries about using tools, including sand shovels and paintbrushes.				
I provide opportunities for discoveries about spatial relationships, such as tunnels for crawling through or cups to stack.				
I provide opportunities for discoveries about categories, including sorting colors, toy animals, and blocks.				
I provide opportunities for discoveries about numeracy and quantity.				
I provide opportunities for discoveries about nature.				
I provide opportunities for discoveries about each child's home culture.				
I observe each child carefully to determine the discoveries each child is exploring.				
I plan based on what each child or group of children is discovering.				

A = Always, S = Sometimes, R = Rarely

REFLECTIONS

1. There is a difference between teaching and supporting learning. For infants and toddlers, we describe relationships as supporting learning. How do you see your relationships supporting learning in infants and toddlers?
2. Think about something you've learned recently. How did the approaches to learning play a part?
3. How do you determine when to sit back and watch and when to step in and help as infants and toddlers come up against problems?

APPLICATIONS

1. Including a child like Lily in group care involves partnership with Early Intervention services and thoughtful planning. What would you need to consider to have her fully included in the activities?
2. The approaches to learning such as curiosity, paying attention, gathering information, solving problems, and desiring mastery cut across all domains. Observe these processes in one infant's or toddler's play. Share your observation at the next class.
3. Concepts such as cause and effect, use of tools, and spatial relationships are discovered and rediscovered throughout infancy. Create a newsletter to parents concerning what materials or activities found in the home would support these discoveries for young infants, mobile infants, and toddlers and twos.
4. Observe a program using the Inventory of Teacher Practices.

RESOURCES

- *Baby Brain Map*
  The Baby Brain Map reveals the secrets of how early care enriches development. Available at http://www.zerotothree.org
- National Scientific Council on the Developing Child. (2007). *The timing and quality of early experiences combine to shape brain architecture: Working Paper No. 5.* Retrieved from http://www.developingchild.harvard.edu

Opportunities for Language, Literacy, and Music Learning and Development

After reading this chapter, you will be able to:

- RESPECT
    - Expressive and receptive and the pragmatics of language
    - The typical pattern of language, literacy, and music learning and development
    - How to create literacy, language, and music opportunities for young and mobile infants, toddlers, and twos
    - Signs of possible delays or disorders
- REFLECT
    - On the individual child's approach to language, literacy, and music

- On how adults may support or hinder the development and learning of language, literacy, and music
- On your own comfort singing and dancing with the children
- RELATE
    - Plan interactions, materials, and environments for individual and small groups of children, to promote language, learning, and music learning and development

Box 10.1

Rules for All Languages

Although there are many languages in the world, each includes its own set of rules for the following:

- Phonology: phonemes or speech sounds or, in the case of signed language, hand shapes
- Morphology: word formation
- Syntax: sentence formation
- Semantics: word and sentence meaning
- Prosody: intonation and rhythm of speech
- Pragmatics: effective use of language (NIDCD, 2000)

Infants, mobile infants, toddlers, and twos are able and ready communicators. They communicate through movements, facial expressions, gestures, sounds, and language. Three aspects of language that care teachers need to think about when creating their curriculum for infants and toddlers are receptive language, expressive language, and communication pragmatics. Infants and toddlers learn about language and communication through interactions and early literacy and music experiences. See Box 10.1, Rules for All Languages.

Most children use speech (talk) to communicate, but younger children can also communicate by movements, facial expressions, sounds, signing, singing, or gesturing, and older children by writing. Children with communication disabilities might also use sign language, pictures, or assistive communication devices. Infants' and toddlers' ability to use language grows as they communicate with others. They understand words, use words, and learn the rules of their language.

RESPECT LANGUAGE, LITERACY, AND MUSIC LEARNING AND DEVELOPMENT

Every language is composed of a set of rules that allow people to communicate with each other (see Box 10.1). Infants and toddlers learn the rules of their language through interacting with others and literacy and music experiences.

Aspects of Language, Literacy, and Music Development

Imagine, as infants become toddlers, how their receptive language, which is remarkable at birth, develops even further. Think of the excitement of hearing infants making new sounds each day; hearing an infant say his or her first words; and listening to mobile infants, toddlers, and twos jargoning and expressing themselves with an explosion of new words. Parents and care teachers also have the satisfaction of seeing infants and toddlers learn to love books and develop an interest in the strange marks they see written. Receptive language, expressive language, the foundations of literacy development, and the love of music are part of the remarkable development of children during their first 3 years.

Receptive Language Development. Receptive language is the ability to listen to and understand language. Children can hear the differences between all the sounds spoken in their world when they are born. That is why they are called "universal language learners" (Kuhl, Tsao, & Liu, 2003). Younger infants' receptive language grows rapidly. A newborn can distinguish her mother's voice from a stranger's, and during the first few months of life, infants listen more intently to a familiar voice than to a stranger's voice. They respond to their name by 5 months, and to simple requests by

8 months of age. They are active language learners and listen intently to adults to figure out the rules of language; for example, what sounds are more likely to follow other sounds (Saffran, 2001). The number of words that 10-month-old infants can comprehend ranges from 11 to 154, and 12-month-olds can comprehend from 31 to 205 words (Fenson et al., 1994).

Expressive Language. Expressive language is the ability of children to express themselves in increasingly complex ways through sounds, movements, gestures, facial expressions, and words.

Expressive language develops in a predictable order. Communication begins with the newborn's crying. The amount of crying each day peaks at 6 weeks of age and then begins to decrease. Cooing (soft vowel sounds) can begin as early as 1 month, and by 6 months infants are adding consonant sounds such as *d*, *b*, and *m*. They engage in turn-taking conversations that consist of *ah* and later during this period of "Ma," "Da," and "Ba." By 6 months, attuned adults will hear new sounds like *ma* and *da* (consonant and vowel combinations), and by 8 months, infants are babbling sounds like *ma-ma* and *da-da*. Before 8 months, children can babble all the sounds spoken in languages across the world, but by 12 months they have begun to hear only the differences in sounds spoken in the language(s) they are hearing (de Boer & Kuhl, 2003).

Jargoning occurs when children put sequences of sounds together, but it is impossible to understand what they are saying. A child will look at an adult and repeat these sequences of sounds with sincerity and with adult intonation. The remarkable increase in the number of words that mobile infants say is described as a *language explosion* (Woodward, Markman, & Fitzsimmons, 1994). Some children will begin to put 2 or 3 words together by 18 months of age. You may hear "me go," "more milk," or "my baby." Most toddlers talk in sentences of 2 words or more, and by 3 years of age are composing at least 3-word sentences. Sentences such as "me go home," "where ball go?" and "more milk, please" sound as if toddlers are sending telegraphs with unnecessary words left out. In fact, this is called *telegraphic speech*.

Parents of young children who are learning two languages (dual language learners or DLL) during their early years may be concerned that their children will speak those languages later than other children. Most research studies of DLL infants have found that bilingual babies speak as early as monolingual babies and have as many vocabulary words, when words in both languages are counted. The latest research on DLL babies (10–12 months) has found that bilingual babies are better than monolingual babies at hearing the differences in sounds in languages that they are not learning, thus giving DLL babies a processing advantage (Petitto, Berens, Kovelman, Dubins, Jasinska, & Shalinsky, 2011) for learning new languages.

Communication Pragmatics. Communication pragmatics is the knowledge and use of conversational rules such as taking turns and using sounds, facial expressions, and words for different functions; for example, to make a statement or ask a question. By the time an infant is 2 months old, a sensitive care teacher can begin to distinguish the infant's hungry cry from a cry of pain. Infants can convey puzzlement with a furrowing of their brows, tiredness by yawning or fussing, and "I've had too much

Infants, toddlers, and twos who are read to frequently learn to love books.

stimulation" by turning away from the adult. When a baby arches her back, adults know that they missed the infant's subtle disengagement cues and now the baby is using a strong disengagement cue (Barnard & Condon, 2004) to express discomfort. Care teachers can respond to the subtle cues of discomfort before a baby cries.

Literacy Development. Literacy is the ability to communicate meaning through reading and writing; however, literacy development begins in infancy. Infants, mobile infants, toddlers, and twos learn to love books, listen to and make sounds, and comprehend language. Babies can be read to as early as they can focus on pictures that are near them. When an infant cuddles up on an adult's lap and listens to a page or more of a picture book, the infant is developing an emotional relationship with both the adult and books.

As children listen to books and look at pictures, they not only learn more about language, they learn to love the reading experience, express emotions, and learn new concepts.

Music and Fingerplays. Songs, musical instruments, and fingerplays are enjoyable ways of learning to appreciate melodies, rhythms, words, and rhymes, all of which are part of language. Infants and toddlers do not care if their teachers' voices are star quality; they appreciate the warm, loving tones of their special adults singing just to them. As children grow through these early years, they learn to appreciate different types of music, join in singing with words and hand movements, and do fingerplays with the teacher.

Wittmer and Petersen (2009) highlight the many benefits to children of singing, listening to music, making rhythms, and moving their bodies. These experiences build positive relationships between care teachers and children by providing opportunities for loving and enjoyable interactions. Singing songs together and moving to the music provides opportunities for children to experience pure joy as well as move, practice crawling, pull to stand, jump, run, experience rhythms, and feel comfortable with their bodies in space. As mobile infants and toddlers learn to move their hands to the music and sing a few words, their self-awareness increases. Songs and fingerplays improve children's receptive language and introduce new vocabulary and concepts such as "up" and "down." A transition of cleaning up toys or going outside becomes easier for mobile infants and toddlers when the teacher sings a song each time. Soon toddlers will be singing some of the song, too.

There are additional benefits to using music with infants and toddlers. Songs and fingerplays provide opportunities for symbolic play. For example, when toddlers sing, "Twinkle, Twinkle, Little Star" they use their hands to represent stars. Through the ages, lullabies and other songs have comforted and soothed babies and helped them fall asleep.

RESPECT THEORIES OF LANGUAGE, LITERACY, AND MUSIC DEVELOPMENT

Children proceed through predictable stages of language development; for example, they make soft cooing sounds (*ooh, aah*) before they begin to babble (*ma, da, ba, ga*), and they develop a vocabulary of approximately 50 single words before they begin to say two words together ("my ball"). Children who use sign language to communicate also go through predictable stages.

Infants and toddlers enjoy playing with musical instruments.

Because children are active learners, they do not just imitate what adults say (Piaget, 1952). For example, mobile infants and toddlers may overgeneralize and call anything that flies a "bird." This is because they are busy categorizing objects, people, and things. They may think that the word for anything that flies—even an airplane, a kite, or a flying squirrel—is *bird*. They add *s* and *ing* to words, so now you may hear "cats," "birds," "mouses," "mices," and "jump*ing*" (Brown, 1973). They make an error by adding the *s* to mice to make it plural (mices). They do this because they have learned a rule about adding *s* to make words plural. This error indicates that toddlers are not just imitating adults. They learn the rules as they actively process language when caring adults talk or sing with them. Soon they will learn the exceptions to those rules.

When infants and toddlers have many opportunities to talk, listen and respond to books, and listen to and participate in music activities, they are able to construct their knowledge about ways to communicate.

Vygotsky (1962) emphasized that language development is important because it influences how young children think. Vygotsky might say that when young children learn the names of shapes, they will be better able to sort the shapes by color. He also emphasized how important social interaction and culture are for infants and toddlers to learn language and use it in different ways in different environments. Research supports how important adults are for children's language development. The more words that an infant hears from responsive and sensitive adults, the more words he will speak (Hart & Risley, 1995). Parents need to use language that expands and enriches the subject; simple, direct commands limit language acquisition.

Kuhl (2011) proposes a "language magnet/neural commitment theory" of language acquisition. Infants are predisposed to attend to the sounds of language, increasingly preferring the sounds of their home language to those of foreign languages. Infants have strong computational structures for organizing information in the world around them. They use these skills to create a "map" of the sounds and patterns of language. Infants use social signals to help them choose information on which to focus. Even very young infants pay more attention to, and are more likely to imitate a human being than an animated machine. Brain circuits link perceptions and action (Meltzoff, Kuhl, Movellan & Sejnowski, 2009). This ability allows the infant to connect the sounds of language with the person who is speaking (Kuhl, 2011).

DEVELOPMENTAL POSSIBILITIES IN LANGUAGE, LITERACY, AND MUSIC

Table 10.1

Young Infants	Mobile Infants	Toddlers	Twos
0–9 Months	8–18 Months	16–24 Months	24–36 Months
Young infants can distinguish differences in sounds.	Mobile infants can understand many words before they speak them.	Toddlers understand two and three-word directions.	Twos can understand most directons when the adults use familiar language.
In the beginning of this age group, infants coo and make sounds; around 6 months, they begin babbling. They can take language turns with an adult.	Mobile infants use jargon in conversational tones. They use single words. They take language turns with an adult. Mobile infants can express many meanings and emotions with their language.	Toddlers begin to ask questions, such as "what's dat?" Toddlers say many words and begin to use two-word sentences. Toddlers express many meanings with their language—demanding, stating, asking, questioning, etc.	Two-year-olds use many two-word sentences and begin to use longer sentences, as well. Two-year-olds add "s" to words to make plurals and "ing" to words to express what they are doing at the present time—singing, playing, dancing.
Young infants like to look at pictures in books and hear the adult's voice as she or he reads.	Mobile infants like to look at pictures in a book, turn the pages of cardboard books, and point to pictures they like. They may choose one book over others.	Toddlers listen to simple stories and add information about themselves. They have favorite books that must be read over and over.	Twos listen to longer stories when an adult reads with enthusiasm. Twos have favorite books, too.
Young infants enjoy listening to songs sung to them.	Begin to do simple finger-plays, e.g., row your boat. May begin to sing a few words of a song.	May sing whole short songs. Enjoys trying to do finger-plays and moving to music.	Twos sing longer songs. They enjoy moving to music. They can make many of the motions to songs, e.g., "Wheels on the Bus."

RESPECT CONCERNS ABOUT LANGUAGE, LITERACY, AND MUSIC LEARNING AND DEVELOPMENT

Learning a language requires perceptual and cognitive abilities, including memory. Certainly, biology makes a difference in the rate of learning; however, the language environment of young children also contributes greatly to their learning. "Infants learn the forms of words by listening to the speech they hear" (Swingley, 2009). Language that is directed to infants and toddlers helps support children's language development, too; for example, when a parent says to a child, "Look, it's a blue car" (Werker, Pons, Dietrich, Kajikawa, Fais, & Amano, 2007, p. 147). Parents and teachers often use shorter sentences, emphasize words, and repeat words to help a child learn language components. Since the environment makes a difference in how children learn language, it is easy to understand that some children who aren't exposed to a rich vocabulary may be delayed in their language.

Hart and Risley (1995, 1999), after observing young children in their homes during the first 3½ years, found great differences in the amount of talk that children heard. Young children in language-rich homes (primarily professional families) often heard as many as 1000–2000 words every hour. This quantity of language was approximately 2½ times more than children in other homes (primarily lower-income families) heard. The quality and amount of talk that young children heard made a difference in their language abilities.

REFLECT ON CHILDREN'S LANGUAGE, LITERACY, LEARNING AND MUSIC DEVELOPMENT

Reflecting on children's development can start with questions about each child's development and/or the interests of the children and the discoveries they are making. For example, if a care teacher asks and documents, in collaboration with parents, "How does each child communicate that he is hungry, tired, or ready for play," the teacher learns that each child may differ due to temperament, culture, or development. Often, documenting informs both teachers and parents and leads to responsive interactions and supporting of children as they learn new ways to communicate their needs.

RELATE TO LANGUAGE, LITERACY, AND MUSIC LEARNING AND DEVELOPMENT

The infant/toddler care teacher plays an important role in each child's language development. Infants and toddlers spend so much time in group care that their opportunities for language, literacy, and music experiences depend in large part on the infant or toddler care teacher talking and singing with them.

THE YOUNG INFANT: BIRTH TO 9 MONTHS

Young infants are ready at birth to communicate with the special adults in their lives. If the child has physical or communication challenges or the adults in his life do not communicate often in turn-taking ways with the child, the child may experience

Box 10.2

Reflect on Language, Literacy, and Music Development

Communication and Language

- What sounds is each child using? Which sounds spark their interest?
- What language(s) is the child learning at home? To which language(s) is the infant most responsive?
- How does each child communicate that he or she is hungry, tired, or ready for play?
- With whom does each child like to communicate?
- How is each child progressing in language development?
- How does each child take turns in the "communication dance"?
- How do children communicate with their peers?

Literacy

- How does each child respond to being read books or shown pictures and photograph albums?
- What kind of books does each child like? Which books do children choose? Why?
- How does each child show his or her interest in books, pictures, and photograph albums?
- Are all of the children in the group enjoying books?
- What types of books are family members reading to their children? How are they chosen?
- What is each child learning through books (e.g., turning pages, pictures have meaning, or concepts about relationships)?
- How do infants and toddlers use a cozy book area?
- How is prosocial development encouraged through books?

Music and Fingerplays

- What music, songs, and fingerplays does each child enjoy?
- How do you know that children are enjoying music, a song, or fingerplays?
- When does each child begin to try to sing, move, or make gestures along with songs and fingerplays?
- How does each child respond when a favorite song from the family's culture or in their primary language is sung?
- How do infants make music?
- How does an infant tell you that the music is too loud for him or her?
- How does each baby move to music?
- What are the infants learning through music, songs, and fingerplays?
- What are the concepts (thought, ideas) that each infant or toddler is exploring in play (for example, how to put a toy in a container; how to pat hands together; how to make sounds with the voice or toys)? Can you sing about them?
- How do music, songs, and fingerplays enhance parent-child, teacher-child, and peer relationships?

delays in language. Communication through talking, listening to adults read books to them, listening to music and songs, and watching the teacher do fingerplays is a critical part of infants' brain development.

Young infants enjoy looking at the pictures in cardboard and cloth books and hearing the words that correspond with the pictures. They like to touch the pages and often want to chew a bit on the book. The goal is that infants will be grabbing a book and bringing it to you by 9 months of age because of their nourishing and rewarding reading experiences with responsive adults.

A Glimpse of the Young Infant's Language, Literacy, and Music Development

Miriam knew that a care teacher's active listening to infants' sounds leads to responsive interactions. For example, when she noticed that 3-month-old Adara was making "ah" sounds, she and the baby played a turn-taking game with the sounds, with Miriam patiently waiting for the baby to take a turn. Sometimes Miriam modeled the next step in development, saying "bah" and then waiting to see how Adara responded. Adara's language, secure attachment, and ability to self-regulate grew in this language dance as the baby intently focused on Miriam's eyes and mouth.

Miriam interacted with Paulo in much the same way, although Miriam noticed that Paulo definitely responded to "parentese," adult speech that is at a higher pitch, uses shorter words, and elongates some of the sounds, as in "Daddddy" (Thiessen, Hill, & Saffran, 2005). Paulo's ears perked up and his eyes focused right on Miriam's face when she spoke directly to him using "parentese."

Later in the day, Paulo lies on his back on the floor, his alert eyes scanning the room. Miriam's co-teacher sits on the floor with several children. Paulo kicks his foot up toward the teacher and then pulls it up to suck on his own toe. Shela uses parallel talk, talking about what Paulo is doing while he is doing it. "That's your foot. That's your toe. You're sucking on your own toe."

Jack (6 months old) and Takala (7 months old) are each saying "ma," "ba," and "da." Miriam knows that soon they will be saying "ma-ma" and "da-da," so she models these words at times.

Miriam's interest went beyond early language, and she decided to document how the babies made music. Paulo would wiggle when a teacher stopped singing as if to say, "Sing it again." Jack banged every toy in reach on the floor, table, or chair to see how it sounded. He banged two metal lids together. Sometimes he dropped two different toys on a cookie sheet taped to the floor to hear the unique sounds they made. Takala clapped her hands together and seemed to be listening to the sounds. Sometimes she crawled and pushed a musical toy ahead of herself to keep the music going.

The Young Infant Care Teacher's Decisions

After visiting one day, a friend asked Miriam why she talked so much with babies who obviously could not understand language and would not talk for months yet themselves. It is often hard for people who are not familiar with early learning and development to understand how thoroughly the foundations for language are being set in the first years of life. Miriam consciously uses language to describe what the babies are doing, what they might be feeling, and what will be happening next because she understands that this is how they begin to understand language.

Miriam looks at a book at least once a day with each child and encourages the families to look at books every day with their young infants. She sings and does fingerplays at different times throughout the day, knowing that the elements of rhythm, melody, and rhyme also are elements of language.

Adaptations for Special Needs. Miriam adapts to the abilities of each child. Each day, Miriam tries to read a story to each child; possibly two at a time, with both of them on her lap. Children enjoy these special times. With the youngest children, Miriam lies on a blanket beside them and holds the book up so they can see it. She often encourages them to touch a picture on the cardboard or cloth book.

Diversity/Culture. Miriam asked the children's parents whether they had a special song that they sang to the children, especially one in their home language or from their culture. As the children transition to sleep, Miriam sings each of them that special song from their culture.

Opportunities for Young Infants' Language, Literacy, and Music Development

Use Language with Meaning. During the first months of life, young infants listen more intently to a familiar voice than they do to a stranger's voice. Talk frequently to young infants in a responsive way (don't overstimulate) and respond to their communication attempts.

- As a primary caregiver, make a special point of talking frequently with the babies, giving them a chance to get to know your voice.
- Infants convey hunger, tiredness, fear, and frustration with their facial expressions and body. Respond to infants' communication attempts, sounds, and gestures with facial expressions and words that show you are attentively listening.
- Use the language of nurturing ("Oh, let me help you") and empathy ("Sometimes it is hard to fall asleep") for the child's experience.

Talk to Infants and Toddlers. Support infants' receptive language. With your support, it will develop rapidly.

- Point to objects as you name them.
- Play games such as "Peek-a-Boo, Where Are You" by covering your head and then peeking out.

Listen to Infants and Toddlers. Infants express themselves with coos and babbles, and by the end of the age group, some children will say a few words.

- Opportunities for young infants' language development occur in each interaction and experience that the child has with care teachers, materials, and peers. Adults support infants' expressive language development throughout the day during play, feeding, greeting, and nurturing.
- Reflect on each child's way of expressing him- or herself. You can make a poster listing all the sounds that you hear from babies in the infant room. Invite parents to add to the list with the sounds they are hearing at home.
- Use "parentese"—when adults use fewer words, use a higher pitch, elongate sounds, and speak clearly, they make language accessible to the infants.
- Encourage peer cooing and babbling by placing babies near each other.

- Name objects such as toes, nose, and rattle and actions such as wiggling, sneezing, and burping.

- Use self-talk (talk about what you are doing) and parallel talk (what the infant or others are doing). Build joint attention as both of you focus on an object or an aspect of the child's experience.

- Use sign language with children who may have delays or disabilities (when called for on their IFSPs), but also model sign language with children developing typically for several important words such as "more," "milk," or "eat" as you also speak the word. Young infants who are exposed to signs often will use sign language before they can talk.

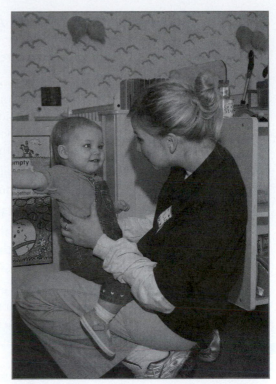

Infants can communicate with sign language or point—often before they can say any words.

Take Language Turns. Infants will engage in conversational turns beginning at approximately 2 months of age. These reciprocal interactions build relationships, language, self-regulation, and emotional competency—plus much more.

- Respond to the particular sounds that infants make. Try to respond in a way that elicits more sounds from the infant. Vary the sound a bit and see how the infant responds.

- Engage in cooing, babbling, and one-word conversations, taking language turns with the infant. Engage in a dialogue with an infant in a conversational manner by waiting for the infant to take a turn.

- Model the next step in language development and then patiently wait to see if the infant imitates or continues her previous sounds.

Use Home Languages. Support dual or multiple language learners by keeping all of their languages present.

- Infants listen carefully to and process the sounds in the languages that they hear on a regular basis, so it is important that they hear the language(s) that they will soon learn to speak.

- Audiotapes and television do not help infants learn languages. Interact with infants in responsive ways to help them learn languages.

- Encourage and support parents who speak their native language at home and/or want their children to learn two languages.

- Learn words of endearment and the names of familiar objects in the child's home language.

- Audiotape the parent reading a story in the child's home language and then play it for the child as you and the child look at a book together.

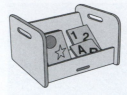

Celebrate Infants' Love of Books. Sharing books with young infants introduces them to literacy through book handling, understanding that pictures represent real things and frequently seeing print.

- Read and *relate* to infants in this age group often by rocking and reading or by lying on the floor on your back while holding the book up in the air for both you and the baby beside you to see. This is often a perfect position for engaging infants in books because babies usually need to move while you are reading or showing them pictures.
- Notice when a child engages and disengages. Stop when a baby tells you, by squirming or looking away, that he or she is tired or ready for a different activity.
- Create books with photos of the children.
- Provide books in all the spaces in the room—on the floor, by the door for parents to use when they drop off or pick up an infant, on low shelves, and by the rocking chair.
- Provide photos of familiar family, peers, and objects.
  - Create small photograph albums of their family members, group friends, pets, and familiar objects. These are fun for small hands to clasp.
  - Other photographs, placed strategically around the room, lead to teacher–infant dialogue.
  - Laminated pictures may be taped to the floor or given to the older infants in this age group so that children can carry precious pictures of their family with them as they move around the room.
  - Place an enlarged photo of an object, such as a shoe, on the wall with a real shoe nearby to encourage the child's understanding of the representational photos.
  - The ZERO TO THREE website and the National Center for Family Literacy (NCFL) provide tip sheets, activities, and research related to supporting families.

Encourage Infants' Love of Music and Fingerplays. Songs and fingerplays are key ways in which infants learn words, the rhythm of language, and the comfort and enjoyment of relationships. Infants enjoy listening to music, lullabies, and other songs. They will play with sounds with their voices and their toys. They may begin to participate in fingerplays by the end of this age period.

- Reflect on how each child responds to songs, other music, and fingerplays. As the teacher observes how children respond, he or she can offer more of what each individual child likes, as well as introduce new music and fingerplays.
- Listening to music while sitting near or on the lap of a teacher builds a child's love of different types of music and builds caring relationships.
- Sing lullabies as you rock infants to sleep.
- Give infants opportunities to make music with their sounds, shaking toys and banging them.
- Learn a variety of fingerplays and do the hand motions if waiting is required as a bottle warms.

Planning for Young Infants' Language, Literacy, and Music Development

In this chapter, you will be able to practice planning for the entire group in a way that is responsive to each child's interests and development (see Box 10.3). Use the information provided in the chapter summary about what young infants are doing and reflect on how you might plan to support their development in language, literacy, and music. Think about whether there are one or more children that may need

Box 10.3

Individually Responsive Group Planning Guide

Name of Group: *Butterflies*   Week of: *March 12–16, 2012*

Person(s) completing this guide: _____

Respect and Reflect

The children in my group are . . .

(Summarize information from the individual planning guides)

Taking turns in making sounds

Playing with different sounds

Listening to parentese

Listening to descriptions of their actions

Moving to music

Looking

Learning to use sounds for communication

Relate: Plans for the Week to Meet Children's Interests and Needs

Songs/Fingerplays/Music

Stories/Books

Responsive Interactions

Environment: Toys, materials

Opportunities

Family/Cultural Experiences

Other

additional books, for example. Are there certain songs that particular children seem to enjoy? Do you think that the young infants would enjoy hearing some new songs and fingerplays? Are there certain concepts, such as "up" and "down," that many of the children are exploring in their play? If so, emphasize those words throughout the week.

THE MOBILE INFANT: 8–18 MONTHS

Mobile infants become active participants by singing songs or moving their fingers along with much-loved fingerplays. They may sway and dance to music and enjoy making music with drums, bells, and musical toys. Favorite books become the children's friends as they are brought to the teacher so that the children can listen to them over and over again.

A Glimpse of the Mobile Infant's Language, Literacy, and Music Development

Albert had moved up from the infant room with a group of children, and now they were in a bigger room. He was glad that the children were securely attached to him. They knew they could come to him for comfort when they were tired, sad, or hurt and yet they felt safe to explore away from him as well. He also thought that his continuity of care made a difference in their language development. He knew these children well, including how they communicated, what languages they were learning, and the sounds and words that they were trying to say. He knew their families well, too, and they constantly shared their children's new language milestones.

Gemma, the 9-month-old explorer, did not have too much time for learning words right now because learning to stand and walk around large objects took precedence. Albert did not worry, though. He often used parallel talk, talking about what she was doing, without interfering with her exploration. She would also snuggle up on his lap for a story before her afternoon nap and she loved songs and fingerplays.

Albert often moved Lily so that she was in the center of the floor in the midst of the other children's play. Albert noticed that Lily listened to Radwan when he jabbered away, using sounds with the intonation of an adult. Sometimes it sounded as if he were asking a question. Goro would lean down and touch her head, saying, "Nice baby." He had just started to put two words together. Goro's mother and father spoke Japanese to him at home, so he was learning Japanese as well as English. Albert read books to Goro that had both English and Japanese words.

The Mobile Infant Care Teacher's Decisions

Language development was a special interest to Albert, so he made a point of reading articles and looking on the Internet for any new information. He had just seen new information on how the average number of words spoken to children each day maximizes language development, and he knew that he needed to talk more with the children. He watched their faces and body language, though, so that he did not overwhelm them. He waited for their responses when he talked. When they spoke with sounds or words, he made sure that he responded with interest. He also didn't interfere when a mobile infant was engrossed in experimenting with objects—turning them upside down, putting them in containers, or pushing them across the floor—except to use parallel talk, offering a few words about what they were doing, or trying to do, and how they might be feeling.

Adaptations for Special Needs. Albert's thoughtful moving of Lily so that she could watch and listen to the other children benefited Lily and the other children, too. They often brought her a toy, at first with Albert's help, but now completely on their own. Albert often models the next step in language development by saying two- or three-word sentences to Radwan and three- or four-word sentences to Goro. When Albert talks and signs with Lily, who has just begun to babble, he makes sure that he talks about what she is looking at in a book or doing at play.

Diversity/Culture. Albert knows that children are capable of learning several languages at one time, so he encourages Goro's parents to continue to speak Japanese to him at home. Goro's parents also want him to learn English, though, so Albert speaks English with him in the program, but tries to honor the home language by reading books and singing songs in Japanese. Albert knows that when he counts the number of words that Goro speaks, he should count the total number of words that Goro speaks in both English and Japanese. Soon Goro will learn to speak his Japanese words with his parents and his English words with Albert.

Opportunities for Mobile Infants' Language, Literacy, and Music Development

Talk to Mobile Infants. Receptive language continues to grow. Mobile infants can point to their nose, eyes, and other body parts when an adult asks them, "Where's your nose?" They can follow simple directions, such as "Get the ball."

- Give simple, fun directions and then wait for the child to respond.
- Play games such as "Pat-a-Cake" and "Where's Lamont?" as the child covers his or her head with a cloth.
- Observe whether children are hearing well.

Listen to Mobile Infants' Gestures. Children in this age group still use many gestures to communicate. They may raise their hands to be picked up or point to an object as if to say, "Look, a ball."

- Respond to their pointing. Say, for example, "Yes, that's a toy car," labeling the object to which they pointed. The infant is pointing to share an experience with you or a peer. Share the opportunity for a joint attention experience and the excitement of their pointing discovery. Encourage a peer to look as well.
- Respond to mobile infants' gestures, sounds, words, and jargoning with language.

Enjoy the Language Explosion. Most children rapidly learn words during this age period.

- Name items in the environment as well as their actions. Say, for example, "You're jumping" or "The ball is rolling."
- Children cannot learn the names of things and actions unless adults tell them those names, so talk with children often about categories such as birds (red cardinals, black and white penguins, and black starlings), cats (big Persian, little Siamese, fuzzy baby kittens), or different types of cheese (Cheddar, mozzarella, and Colby). Use rich, descriptive language.
- Repeat key words often. This helps mobile infants remember those words.
- Observe how many words a child has and model the next step in development for that child.

Imitate Sounds, Jabbering, or Words. Mobile infants talk more when an adult follows the child's lead and provides interesting things to talk about.

- If a mobile infant looks at a cat and says "cat," try to talk about a cat. Taking language turns help mobile infants learn the rules of conversation, such as you take a turn and then I take a turn, you talk and I listen, I listen and you talk.
- Provide a box with different items in the box each week. Talk about the items with the children. Name them, describe them, and talk about what each object does. Let children feel the item first without seeing it.

Celebrate the Literacy Explosion. There is a literacy explosion at this age, as well as a language explosion, if adults have exposed children to a variety of interesting, simple, and colorful books since they were infants.

- Provide a special area in the room with rugs, an adult couch, and comfortable children's furniture.
- Display books attractively and make them accessible to the children. Provide long periods of play time so that mobile infants can pick out books and look at them by themselves or with a peer.
- Books are not just for the book cozy corner, though. Place them around the room in strategic places. A book with pictures of blocks placed near the block area is just the right book to read to several infants who have been building with blocks.

Read Books Using Dialogic Strategies. Mobile infants enjoy books and learn more about and from books when teachers use dialogic strategies (Whitehurst et al., 1994) when reading. These strategies include encouraging children to comment on the pictures and story, asking thought questions such as "How do you think the bear feels?" and involving the child as the adult reads a picture book to him or her.

- Read to mobile infants one-on-one or in small *informal* groups. Sit on the floor or a couch and pull out a book to read. Mobile infants will come toddling over. Make room beside you and on your lap so that all the children can see the pages.

Infants, toddlers, and twos love to be read to many times a day. Strong, warm adult–child relationships grow during book reading.

Some may stay for the whole book, while others will last for a few pages. Do not expect mobile infants to sit in a circle and listen to a story.

- Involve children in the book reading. Read with enthusiasm and encourage them to comment on or point to the pictures. This helps mobile infants love books!

Choose Books with Good Messages. Mobile infants enjoy and learn about other cultures and nonsexist activities from books.

- Provide books that represent a variety of cultures, ages, and nonsexist activities. Read books that provide words in several languages.

Writing Begins When Children Make a Mark.

- Provide a creative corner where mobile infants have a chance to try toxic-free crayons on paper, fingerpaints, and large paintbrushes with paint. This builds an interest in making "a mark," which is the beginning of writing.

Use Fingerplays and Action Songs. Children of this age usually love songs with actions such as "The Eensie, Weensie Spider" or "Twinkle, Twinkle, Little Star" and will begin to say a few words from a song or fingerplay. They often move to music and enjoy making music with simple instruments or banging, shaking, dumping, and pounding.

- Props, such as finger or hand puppets, are great. Children put the puppets on their hands

---

Box 10.4

Books for Babies

All books read to young children support language and literacy development. Some books, however, can be sung as well. Bilingual books usually provide the words in two languages. Children not learning two languages will enjoy hearing the bilingual books as well.

Children's Books that Support Music Development

Bear Went Over the Mountain, John Prater, Red Fox (2002).

If You're Happy and You Know It, A. Kubler. Baby Board Books (2001).

The Itsy-Bitsy Spider, Rosemary Wells, Scholastic (1998).

Bilingual Books

Head, Shoulders, Knees and Toes (Available in English with many other languages), Annie Kubler, Child's Play (2002).

Sign and Sing Along: Itsy Bitsy Spider, Annie Kubler, Child's Play, Inc. (2005).

and move them along with a song such as, "There Was a Dear Lady Who Swallowed a Fly."

- Find stuffed animals, plastic or wood animals and people, flannel board figures, or large cutout pictures to help children represent the words in a story, song, or fingerplay. For example, point to a child to find the wooden animal in the basket as you read a story. Give each child who has gathered to hear the story a chance to find an animal represented in the book.

- Build warm relationships by relating with mobile infants through songs and fingerplays. Sing in responsive ways throughout the day by watching the infant's face and body movements. If a child arches away or kicks his or her feet, he or she may have had enough of that song. Do not take it personally—it is not your voice unless it is too loud. However, an infant may be ready to eat or sleep, and internal needs override enjoyment of the song at that moment. The goal is for infants to enjoy music and the relationships that can develop through these experiences.

- "Teachers don't have to have the best singing voices in the world to sing to infants and toddlers. Babies love to hear songs. It doesn't matter to them how a teacher sings them; children love the warm feelings that are conveyed" (Honig, 1995).

- Create a notebook or a ring of index cards with songs and fingerplays on them. Given a choice of two cards, each with a picture representing a song, mobile infants can point to a song that they want to sing.

- In response to an infant exploring the concepts of "in" and "out" with blocks in a box, you can find a song about those concepts.

Remember Age, Individual Interests, and Culture.
Each infant has language and literacy needs that are age-appropriate and individually and culturally responsive.

- Listening to music from a variety of cultures will introduce sounds that infants learning English do not hear in their language. Also, and more importantly, an appreciation for a variety of types of music will *begin* to grow.

- Play music for moods in the room. Play calm music when many babies are sleeping to set an ambience for the room for both the infants and the care teachers.

Provide Music, Songs, and Fingerplay Opportunities Throughout the Day.
Mobile infants participate in music, song, and fingerplay opportunities in all parts of the room, at any time, during transitions, and outdoors.

- Containers of toys that make music, placed together on a shelf or in a corner of the room, inspire music makers.

- Include a variety of materials (cardboard tubes, rattles) to encourage crawling and toddling infants to combine them to make music.

- Sing songs during transitions to develop routines (Honig, 1995). "It's clean-up time, it's clean-up time, time to put your toys away" is a favorite song to sing before lunch when toys are put away.

Box 10.5

Individually Responsive Group Planning Guide

Name of Group: *Mobile Infants*   Week of: *March 12–16, 2012*

Person(s) completing this guide: _____

Respect and Reflect

The children in my group are . . .

(Summarize information from the individual planning guides)

Listening to descriptions of their actions

Moving to music, singing along

Jabbering conversationally

Pointing to and naming pictures in books

Doing some fingerplay motions

Relate: Plans for the Week to Meet Children's Interests and Needs

Songs/Fingerplays/Music

Stories/Books

Responsive Interactions

Environment: Toys, materials

Opportunities

Family/Cultural Experiences

Other

Planning for Mobile Infants' Language, Literacy, and Music Development

Here is a second opportunity to plan for the group in a way that is responsive to the individual children in the group (see Box 10.5). Some notes on their interests are provided.

TODDLERS AND TWOS

It is easy to get caught up in the excitement of walking, running, and climbing that characterizes the toddler and 2-year-old period. However, the language explosion that is happening also is exciting as toddlers and twos begin to tell us about their thoughts. Toddlers need family members and care teachers to talk with them frequently, be responsive conversational partners, and provide an interesting environment that engages them.

A Glimpse of Toddlers' and Twos' Language, Literacy, and Music Development

Selena is feeling that Chita's tantrums are beginning to dominate the room. Her language skills are appropriate for her age but much lower than those of the other children. Selena believes that the tantrums are related, in part, to her language skills.

Bessie's language skills are similar to Chita's, but Selena has been working with the early intervention team to communicate using both sign language and speech. This seems to be effective for Bessie. Bessie and Chita both love stories and music, and Selena knows that these experiences will serve their language development.

Sam's language development is excellent. He is able to enjoy stories that are more complicated, and Selena takes time every day for quiet reading with Sam on her lap. Sam is most likely to organize the other children in some activity. Lately he has been taking the musical instruments from the shelf and organizing musical marches around the room. Each child takes an instrument, and they all walk around the room, playing music. Selena is delighted to see this leadership and love of music emerging.

Lan loves music. The music from his culture is very different from the songs Selena knows. Lan's mother has been sending tapes of the family singing Vietnamese songs, and Lan sometimes dances to these. Selena has been hunting for books that offer both English and Vietnamese words.

The Toddler Care Teacher's Decisions

Selena understands that Chita's tantrums will continue until Chita learns some words to say, such as "Me sad" or "Me mad." Selena acknowledges her feelings and models words for Chita to say when she is having a tantrum and when she is calm. Selena also models sign language for both Bessie and Chita. Selena reads books with faces of children expressing different emotions, and she sings songs that include words about emotions. She made "feeling faces" with paper plates and tongue depressors so that toddlers could show her a sad face or an angry face.

During playtime, which is most of the day when a child is not eating, sleeping, or being diapered, Selena invites children in the room to listen to her read stories. She sits down on the floor and shows the children the book. Lan loves these times and usually stays to hear several stories while snuggling up next to the other children. Chita does not like other children touching her, so Selena puts her on one side or on her lap with the other children by her side. Of course, other children in the room come running, too, when Selena pulls out a book. Selena is excited about books and the children respond with excitement.

Adaptations for Special Needs. Selena makes many adaptations throughout the day for each child. On some days Bessie seems irritable, so Selena is patient, kind, and affectionate with her. Chita generally does not like to be surrounded by other children, so Selena helps her stay close without others touching her. Selena adapts for this age group as well as the individual children in the group. She knows that toddlers and twos should not be required to sit in a formal group because they like to move and they learn best when they can actively experiment with their toys and other materials.

Diversity/Culture. Selena finds books with short stories for toddlers and twos as well as books with interesting faces, toys, colors, shapes, and actions in them. She always chooses books that represent a variety of different cultures. She has been introducing some books with English and Vietnamese words.

Opportunities for Toddlers' and Twos' Language, Literacy, and Music Development

Foster Toddlers' and Twos' Receptive Language. Receptive language continues to grow. Children can follow directions that are more complex. When a care teacher asks a toddler to "Please go get your coat and your shoes," the toddler may or may not respond, but most likely understands the request.

- Observe to determine whether each child understands simple and more complex directions. If not, start with a simple direction about something that you know interests the child and then progress to more complex directions. You could say, "Go get your shoes," without pointing, to see if the toddler understands and can follow through on a simple direction.

Embrace Expressive Language Growth and Pragmatic Communication Skills. This is a time of delightful growth in expressive and pragmatic communication skills.

- "Be an empathic language partner. . . . Infants and toddlers communicate when it is pleasant to communicate, when the affect or feeling of the communication is warm and loving, and when they understand that their communication attempts will get a response" (Wittmer & Petersen, 2006, p. 183).

- Continue being an enthusiastic and interactive language partner. Toddlers should enjoy communicating and using language as an effective way to communicate their needs.

- Do not correct children when they say words like "mouses" or "mices" and "deers." Rather, model the correct word by talking with them and saying the word correctly. For example, you could say, "Yes, those are mice. There is a brown mouse and a white mouse." The desire to communicate is more important than pronouncing words correctly or using correct grammar.

- Frequently talk with children about the names of objects, actions, pictures in books, and people. Be a vocabulary model who encourages children to talk and who models the enjoyment of words.

- Observe each child's language development (speech and/or signing) and responsively model the next step in development. For example, if a toddler says "Bird flying," you could say, "Yes, that bird is flying." You added *is*, which is a next step in development.

- If a child is not saying many words at this age, ask the parents to have the child's hearing checked. If the child is hearing well, then work with the family to increase the language interactions with the child at home. If delays persist, work with the family to refer the child for a free comprehensive assessment with Child Find, the early intervention office in your local school district.

- Encourage and support families of children who are learning two languages. Encourage a parent or family members to continue to speak to the child in the child's first language.

Create an Atmosphere for Enjoyment of Books. Children express their love of books by taking books to the teachers to read. Toddlers now enjoy a book with a short story, although they still may like books with one clear picture or photo on a page.

- Continue to provide board books and books that toddlers can handle easily.

- Create a warm, cozy atmosphere for reading to toddlers. Do not require all the children to sit in a group and listen. Rather, read books often during the day while sitting on the floor or in a cozy corner. Be sure to invite a child who has not heard a story for a few days or go to that child with a book. Reading to a few children at a time allows the children to see the pictures and the words and to talk about them.

- Read with emphasis, changing voices for the different characters. Show your excitement about the book. Children will pick up your enthusiasm and focus longer on a book.

- Interactive reading is key, rather than a teacher trying to read a book from start to finish. Point to the pictures and encourage children to comment on the pictures. Encourage toddlers to relate their experiences to the ones discussed in the book.

- When reading, ask thought questions, for example, "How does the bear feel?" or "What will the little bear do next?" These questions require children to think about the answer and not have just one correct answer.

- Read books with repetition and rhyme. Books such as _Brown Bear, Brown Bear_ allow children to "read" along when they are familiar with a book.

- Read books repeatedly. You may be tired of the book, but a book read often feels like an old friend to children. Children learn to predict what will happen next, become familiar with who the characters are, learn what the print looks like on each page, and can often finish a sentence for the teacher.

- As you read, point to a word and say, "That says, 'cat, c-a-t, cat.'" Do not pressure toddlers to repeat the names of the letters. Toddlers will begin to understand that the marks have meaning.

- Add books to the book area based on children's interests. Display the books so that the children can see the front cover. This makes books more inviting and helps children find books that they like.

- Books aren't just for the book area. Provide books in all the areas of the room or family child care home. A book on butterflies near a puzzle with butterflies on it encourages young children to understand that real butterflies can be represented in different ways.

Encourage Love of Music, Songs, Fingerplays, and Movement. Children's love of music, songs, and fingerplays grows when care teachers offer these opportunities each day.

- Children love repetition with songs as well as books. They will enjoy the same songs sung repeatedly during the week.

- Ask children which songs they would like to sing. Create picture cards that represent the different songs. Offer several cards to the children and let them choose.

- Sing the same transition song for clean-up time each day; for example:
  Clean up, clean up
  Everybody clean up.

- Give the children props to hold while singing a song and encourage movement.

- Observe children for their individual interests and then find a song or create a song to a familiar tune. For example, "Row, row, row your boat" could become "Find, find, find the bug."

Planning for Toddlers' and Twos' Language, Literacy, and Music Development

Box 10.6 provides an opportunity to plan for a group of toddlers and twos. This time, the form is blank. Begin by listing the interests of the group from the section "A Glimpse of Toddlers' and Twos' Language, Literacy, and Music Development." Then list ideas for planning opportunities for language, literacy, and music for the children in Selena's group.

Box 10.6

Individually Responsive Group Planning Guide

Name of Group: _Toddlers and twos_   Week of: _March 12–16, 2012_

Person(s) completing this guide: _____

Respect and Reflect

The children in my group are . . .

(Summarize information from the individual planning guides)

Relate: Plans for the Week to Meet Children's Interests and Needs

Songs/Fingerplays/Music

Stories/Books

Responsive Interactions

Environment: Toys, materials

Opportunities

Family/Cultural Experiences

Other

SUMMARY

In the first 3 years of life, children grow from attending to the sounds of their own language and familiar voices to being able to express their thoughts, feelings, and experiences in words. This impressive development occurs primarily through interaction with adults who use language with infants and toddlers in responsive, meaningful ways. These experiences often include the use of books and stories and music.

Language development is generally thought of in terms of the following:

• Receptive language

• Expressive language

• Communication pragmatics

During this age period, infants and toddlers are gaining the foundation for literacy and music skills. The qualities of literacy and music also serve language development. The infant/toddler care teacher can help build language and communication skills by being a good language partner throughout the day.

INVENTORY OF TEACHER PRACTICES

Language, Literacy, and Music Development

Basic Concepts	A	S	R	Observation/ Reflection
I talk frequently and responsively with children.				
I take language turns with children.				
I use descriptive language with children.				
I support children who are learning several languages and their families.				
I use words of affection from each child's home language.				
I use sign language when appropriate.				
I talk about what I am doing (self-talk), about what the child is doing (parallel talk), and about things the child and I are paying attention to together (shared, joint attention).				
I read to each child each day.				
I sing songs and use fingerplays throughout the day.				
I play music and sing songs from different cultures.				
I sing songs to help with transitions such as a consistent hello or good-bye song.				
I have pictures of familiar people and objects for the children to see and talk about.				
I provide developmentally appropriate and culturally relevant cloth and cardboard books in many areas of the room.				
I provide one special area of the room with a short bookshelf, the covers of the books visible, and a comfortable space for children and teachers.				
I place toys that make music together in a container on a shelf or in a corner of the room.				

A = Always, S = Sometimes, R = Rarely

REFLECTIONS

1. In what ways could you promote language during every part of the day to support language development?
2. The memory of reading books while cuddling with a beloved adult is an important one to many of us. How can a care teacher create cozy, cuddling places to read in a family child care home or center-based program?

3. Why is music important in young children's lives? Your life?
4. What elements of songs make them most popular with the infants and toddlers you observe? Do they like to hear their own names, fingerplays, repetition, or acting-out motions?

APPLICATIONS

1. Show the Inventory of Teacher Practice to a parent of a child in an early care and development program. Ask what the parent would want to add to this list.
2. Observe a program using the Inventory of Teacher Practice. Write examples for each item that you observe.

RESOURCES

- National Center on Cultural and Linguistic Responsiveness: Funded by Head Start, this website (http://eclkc.ohs.acf.hhs.gov/hslc/tta-system/cultural-linguistic) is available at the Early Childhood Learning and Knowledge Center (ECLKC). The website is filled with ideas to promote competence for dual- or multiple-language learners.
- Petitto, L. A., Berens, M. S., Kovelman, I., Dubins, M. H., Jasinska, K., & Shalinsky, M. (in press). "The "Perceptual Wedge Hypothesis" as the basis for bilingual babies' phonetic processing advantage: New insights from fNIRS brain imaging." *Brain and Language*. Retrieved on July 2, 2011 from http://www.sciencedirect.com/science/article/pii/S0093934X11001027
- Petitto, L. A., Katerelos, M., Levy, B. G., Gauna, K., Tetreault, K., & Ferraro, V. (2001). Bilingual signed and spoken language acquisition from birth: Implications for the mechanisms underlying early bilingual language acquisition. *Journal of Child Language, 28*(2), 453–496.
- Swingley, D. (2009). Contributions of infant word learning to language development. *Philosophical Transactions from the Royal Society B: Biological Sciences, 364*(1536), 3617–3632.

Opportunities for Movement and Motor Development and Learning

11

After reading this chapter, you will be able to:

- RESPECT
  - Understand the aspects of movement and motor development
  - Describe how movement develops
  - Understand how to create learning opportunities for young and mobile infants, toddlers, and twos.
  - Be aware of signs of possible delays or disorders
- REFLECT
  - On how movement and motor development are individualized

- On how adults may support or hinder movement and motor development
- On how you may affect the quality of a child's motor development
- RELATE
  - Plan interactions, materials, and environments for individual and small groups of children, to promote movement and motor development.

Movement changes almost define the stages of infancy: a cuddler, a crawler, a cruiser, a walker, a toddler. Motor development may be one of the best known, but least understood areas of development. What we do know is that most young children are motivated to move!

Nearly every change in the motor system is observable. Changes in balance, position, and ways to move all can be seen. We also use changes in the motor system to infer changes in the other systems (Adolph & Berger, 2006). Cognitive milestones such as showing surprise at novel experiences, or emotional milestones such as preferring a loved one and being afraid of strangers become apparent to adults through changes in the motor system—facial expressions, reaching out to a parent, or holding tightly to an adult care teacher. The motor system is the primary window through which we look to understand infants and toddlers.

Each change in the motor system also represents a model of how changes in developmental domains are interrelated. A new posture, such as sitting, may open a new vertical perspective on the world for the young infant. The ability to change positions or to use both hands may provide the child with a new sense of self as someone with independent capacities. A new perspective (seeing things that are higher on shelves or further away, for example), in turn, may provide new motivation for the baby to crawl or inch forward. New achievements in movement allow for new possibilities in every other domain.

Motor development used to be seen as a very natural, predictable course of development. Now, opportunities for movement, coaching and encouragement of new movements, and the physical changes in the infant's or toddler's body are all seen as factors influencing a child's motor skills.

An additional emphasis on motor development is the current concern over childhood obesity. It is uncertain as to what effect activity level or being overweight in the first 3 years of life has on later childhood and adult obesity (Deiner & Qiu, 2007; Heinzer, 2005), but it is reasonable to believe that activity patterns are set early in infancy. It may be that the first years of life set a pattern for activity level throughout life.

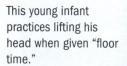

This young infant practices lifting his head when given "floor time."

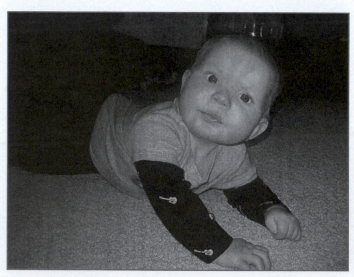

Early childhood care and education programs may either promote or inhibit activity in these early years (Story, Kaphingst, & French, 2006). Factors that influence movement include the way the environment is set up, access to the outdoors, the group size and adult-to-child ratio, and the attitude and capacity of the adults to participate in active play. The National Association for Sport and Physical Education (NASPE) has created guidelines for physical activity for children from birth to 5 years of age (NASPE, 2002).

The large muscle system is described in this chapter (the small muscle system is described in Chapter 12). The two major types of large muscle activity are discussed: movements associated with mobility, such as crawling, scooting, and walking; and movements that support a stable posture, such as balance and position shifts. Additional aspects affecting movement include perception, planning, decision making, memory, intentions, motivation, and goals (Adolph & Berger, 2006).

RESPECT MOVEMENT AND MOTOR DEVELOPMENT AND LEARNING

Infants and toddlers seem to be in motion all the time. Increasingly, researchers are examining the intentions behind the movements of even brand-new, uncoordinated newborns. We are learning about how motor development is influenced by opportunities and adult support. The abilities of infants and toddlers to move change constantly in response to growth changes in their own bodies and the opportunities and challenges of the environment.

For newborns, reflexes control much—but not all—of their motion. The newborn, who roots for mommy's nipple and closes a fist around daddy's finger by reflex, will also intentionally work hard to free his or her hands from a swaddling blanket and bring the fingers to his or her mouth. Young babies also choose to turn their heads to smell their mother's breast milk rather than that of a stranger, or to turn to the mother's face while listening to the mother's voice (Macfarlane, 1975; Sai, 2004).

Balance
Balance is how infants and toddlers manage their large head size, shifts in their body movements, and unevenness in terrain as they maintain control over their bodies.

Flexibility
Flexibility describes an infant's or toddler's ability to use the body in new ways to meet new challenges presented by the environment.

Posture
Posture is how an infant or toddler controls the body, resisting the pull of gravity.

Reaching and Kicking
Reaching and kicking quickly evolve from reflexes to intentional movements and continue to be refined over time and with opportunities to practice.

Box 11.1

Respect Developmental Possibilities in Movement and Motor Development and Learning

YOUNG INFANTS	MOBILE INFANTS	TODDLERS	TWOS
0–9 Months	8–18 Months	16–24 Months	24–36 Months
Young infants may lift their heads when held at the adult's shoulder—soon holding their heads steady and erect.	Mobile infants may first creep on their tummies and then begin to crawl on hands and knees.	Toddlers walk while carrying objects in each hand. Toddlers crouch down and pick up objects while on the move.	Twos may throw and kick a ball. Twos use push toys such as shopping carts in pretend play.
A newborn can turn her head from side to side when she is on her tummy. By 3 months (or earlier), infants may lift their head and shoulders off the ground when they are on their tummies. Turning from tummy to the back and then back to tummy often surprises a 3- to 6-month-old infant. Sitting by 6–8 months and can hold a toy in his hand.	Mobile infants pull to stand on sturdy objects and sitting people. After pulling to stand, mobile infants may cruise—stepping around something sturdy while holding on. Soon you may see a mobile infant try to stand by herself.	Toddlers are developing spatial confidence—they explore how their bodies fit into spaces. Toddlers enjoy pulling wheel toys on strings.	Twos may stand on one foot. A 2-year-old may walk upstairs by placing first one foot and then the other on a step. Depending on the size of the steps, you may see twos go up steps with one foot on each step.
An infant can hold his body still to pay attention; wiggle and move to encourage continued interaction.	Walking with help and then alone is a major accomplishment.	Toddlers can often sit on and get up from small chairs alone.	You may see twos stand and walk on tiptoes.

Increased Functionality

The baby or toddler is able to use movement to achieve personal goals with increasing skill and accuracy. This would include adapted or supported movements for infants and toddlers with motor delays and disabilities.

Mobility

Mobility is the child's ability to use the body to move from place to place.

Young children develop many skills during the early years (see Box 11.1).

RESPECT THEORIES OF MOVEMENT AND MOTOR DEVELOPMENT AND LEARNING

Dynamic systems theory is currently seen as the best explanation for motor development (Thelen & Bates, 2003). Motor development has traditionally been seen as a result of maturation of the brain and muscle systems: As the child grew older, certain motor accomplishments would follow one another naturally, universally, in about the same time frames. This view of maturation, however, did not hold up in the face of the diverse timing of skill appearance seen across cultures and the diversity of order or quality of movements. For example, cultures that promote walking consistently have infants who walk at around 9 months. Infants who are carried for the first year may not walk until well into the second year. Some children crawl before walking, others never crawl. Some have the typical hands-and-knees crawl, others combat crawl or butt crawl.

Dynamic systems theory, as described by Thelen and Bates (2003), proposes that the environment constantly invites infants and toddlers to use their bodies in new ways to accomplish new tasks. The changing weight, proportions, and control of the child's body are also a continuously changing factor. While newborns have a stepping reflex that makes them look like they are walking, this reflex disappears over the first few months. Then, around the child's first birthday, the stepping movement returns. Thelen puzzled over this until she took into account the weight of the young infant's thighs in proportion to the rest of the body. She saw that the lower legs could not support that weight. So she tried holding an infant in a tank of water to provide buoyancy and found that even infants with heavy thighs were able to step again.

Infants' body weights and proportions, postures, elastic and inertial properties of muscle, and the nature of the task and environment contribute equally to the motor outcome. Moreover, infants seemed to be exquisitely sensitive to changes in the tasks, and able to "self-assemble" new motor patterns in novel situations. (Thelen & Bates, 2003, p. 380)

RESPECT SIGNS OF CONCERN IN MOVEMENT AND MOTOR DEVELOPMENT AND LEARNING

The most basic measures of typical or delayed development are in the area of motor development. Motor development is the easiest to observe: An infant either can or cannot roll over; a toddler either can or cannot cruise. Significant delays are usually associated with either muscles that are too tight (hypertonic), restricting movement, or too loose (hypotonic), making it difficult to control movement. Cerebral palsy may produce either hypertonic or hypotonic muscles. This disorder is caused by an abnormality in, or damage to the brain in the womb, during birth, or during the first 2 years. If cerebral palsy is mild, it may not be diagnosed until the infant begins to demonstrate a weakness in a limb or on a side. If it is severe, it can affect movement, learning, hearing, seeing, and thinking. Other conditions, such as Down syndrome, cause low muscle tone, making rolling, sitting, crawling, and walking challenging and often delayed.

Motor development can be optimized through early intervention by a pediatric physical therapist. The therapist may demonstrate exercises to be repeated by the family and care teachers. She may teach the adults how to position the child to provide for the most independent use of hands. She may provide special seating furniture that supports the child's trunk. Motor delays are most likely to be identified during a well-child visit. If there are concerns, they should be checked out by a specialist. There is little to be gained by taking a "wait and see" attitude. The child may just outgrow it but may nonetheless benefit from professional intervention.

Box 11.2

Reflect on Movement and Motor Development and Learning

The following questions will help you reflect on each child's motor and movement efforts and on how well the environment supports those efforts.

Balance and Posture

- How does this infant or toddler use head, trunk, and limbs to maintain balance when on the floor, being held, or walking?
- How does balance challenge the infant or toddler in accomplishing goals?
- Is the infant or toddler able to adjust posture in ways that allow him or her to resist gravity, to accommodate for slopes, and to recover from falls? How does the child do this?

Flexibility

- How does the infant or toddler use new motor strategies to meet new challenges in the environment? For example, the child, when placed on his or her back, raises the arms above the chest to play, but when placed on his or her tummy, uses the arms as a brace to lift the head and chest.
- Can the infant or toddler use new positions to achieve new intentions? How? For example, does the infant around 7 months move into a sitting position to use both hands together with a toy?

Intentional Movements

- Does the infant or toddler turn his or her head toward a sound and then search with the eyes to locate the source of the sound?
- How does the infant "reach" with arms and legs?
- How does the infant or toddler change positions or move on purpose?

Mobility

- Does the environment provide many opportunities that invite the infants and toddlers to move?
- Is the environment safe for the child's current and emerging movement skills?
- How is the mobile infant finding ways to move around the space (rolling, crawling, commando crawling, climbing, or cruising)?
- Is the toddler exploring a variety of movements (walking, running, crouching, jumping)?

REFLECT ON MOVEMENT AND MOTOR DEVELOPMENT AND LEARNING

Notice that the questions in Box 11.2 may ask the care teacher to observe what are typically called "milestones" in development. These questions, however, ask care teachers and parents to consider "how," "when and where," and "with whom" the child maintains balance or moves, so that the answers can be used for planning rich, responsive, caring environments and interactions. It is exciting for adults to realize that an infant or toddler who has discovered that balls roll down an incline may constantly want to test what else rolls down (or doesn't roll down) inclines.

RELATE TO MOVEMENT AND MOTOR DEVELOPMENT

Infant and toddler care teachers—and families— usually take great pleasure in each new motor skill. The first time an infant sits alone, crawls, or walks is usually cause for pulling out the camera and calling the grandparents!

Changing physical skills are highly related to the developmental themes of security, exploration, and identity formation. The newborn's limited physical skills serve the child's need for security, as newborns depend on adults to hold and carry them. Simple mobility skills such as rolling and commando crawling support the mobile infant's emerging interests in exploration. The ability to move independently, use both hands to carry things while walking, climb, and jump all add to the toddler's growing sense of self as a competent person. The following sections describe how infant and toddler care teachers support movement and motor development for the young infant, the mobile infant, and toddlers and twos.

THE YOUNG INFANT: BIRTH TO 9 MONTHS

The young infant goes from depending completely on adults for support and movement to being able to lift the head, reach, roll, and sit unassisted. The closeness of being held and carried serves the young infant's needs for safety and security. These feelings are also supported as the infant begins to gain control over the head, trunk, and limbs, developing a sense of trust in his or her own abilities. Young infants also need opportunities to strengthen their necks, arms, and torsos and challenge their posture and sense of balance by having "tummy time" on the floor.

A Glimpse of the Young Infant's Movement and Motor Development and Learning

Miriam begins each day with a simple safety check of her room, including viewing it from floor level. In her small group of babies, each has very different motor abilities, and it is challenging to keep them safe while offering engaging movement activities.

Adara, at 3 months, enjoys watching her friends while stretching out on a firm mat on the floor. She can lift her head and chest while resting on her forearms and turn her head from one side to the other. She enjoys looking at a small selection of toys around her and sometimes uses one arm to reach for one. She also keeps an eye on the action when lying on her back. Sometimes she surprises herself by rolling over from her tummy to her back. Miriam keeps a close eye on Adara when she is on the floor because Adara tires from the workout she is giving herself and can suddenly need comforting.

At 4 months, Paulo is gaining accuracy with his reach and he takes great pleasure in batting at toys dangling above him. While Adara seems surprised or quietly interested in what is going on in front of her, Paulo seems to show that he can act on his curiosity and desire to explore. He can push himself up on his stomach and reach out to grab a toy and bring it to his mouth. Paulo shifts his posture back and forth and occasionally rolls over. He is not surprised, but he doesn't yet have control over rolling, either. One of the things Paulo likes to reach for is Adara, and Miriam watches to see how Adara responds. Sometimes she likes the contact, and at other times it startles her and makes her cry. Miriam manages her own discomfort to allow the two babies time to negotiate this contact.

Takala is a young but adept crawler. Miriam is concerned about her unintentionally hurting one of the other children, but it hasn't really been a problem.

Jack's body just isn't doing what he wants it to. He can lift his body off the floor, resting on hands and knees, and rock back and forth, but he cannot coordinate this movement into crawling yet. He can roll over to move around and sit with a little support. Miriam offers him interesting toys to examine from a sitting position and shows him her appreciation of his rolling. He looks at the toys but does not respond to Miriam. Still, he seems to want to crawl very badly, and Miriam just keeps assuring him that he will be crawling soon.

The Young Infant Care Teacher's Decisions

Miriam understands the importance of the rapid physical development that occurs in the first months of life. She knows that babies need opportunities, encouragement, and sometimes even a little coaching to coordinate their new movements. Her first concern is always safety, but she understands that the babies may enjoy physical contact with each other and she intervenes only when it seems that someone is unhappy or in danger.

Miriam keeps materials in the room that will invite movement. She keeps floor spaces open for rolling and crawling, graduated mats for climbing, and protected space for Adara and Paulo to be safely on the floor while watching the others. She is slowly converting her space into an area appropriate for mobile infants. She places interesting toys in spaces where Adara or Paulo will need to reach for them, adjusting their posture and balance as they do so. Miriam is a young woman who is comfortable spending time on the floor, on eye level with the children. Even as she encourages movement and motor development, though, she always keeps in mind that these are very young infants who need to be held and carried much of the time.

Miriam continues to track the children's development and sees nothing of concern in terms of motor delays. If anything, Takala seems a bit advanced in her motor skills. Miriam has become increasingly aware of the problem of childhood obesity, though, and is trying to provide many spaces for active movement. She provides the children with lots of unstructured floor time and never uses bouncy seats or swings to keep the children quiet.

Adaptations for Special Needs. The mental health consultant has explained that Jack may have two seemingly contradictory needs from the environment; however, his overall need is to feel safe. Sometimes he needs space to roll and rock on his hands and knees; at other times, however, he needs to be in a more protected space. His conflicted feelings about closeness affect his use of his body. Miriam is trying to have Jack attend to her encouragement to stay in an area that he cares about. He is more likely to be calm when left alone, but then falls into a rocking, thumb-sucking self-soothing and tunes everyone else out.

Diversity/Culture. Paulo's family is Latino by heritage. His father is proud of Paulo's ongoing achievements in movement and can't wait until he is on his feet and playing soccer. His mother is proud of him as well but doesn't like seeing babies on the floor. She disagrees with Miriam that they should even be thinking about obesity at this young age. She feels a chubby baby is healthy and well-fed. She likes Miriam but has a growing unhappiness with all the floor time. Miriam understands her concerns but is having trouble finding a middle ground of compromise.

Opportunities for Young Infants' Movement and Motor Development

Support the Developing Neck Strength. Young infants are working to strengthen their necks and hold their heads up to see the world around them.

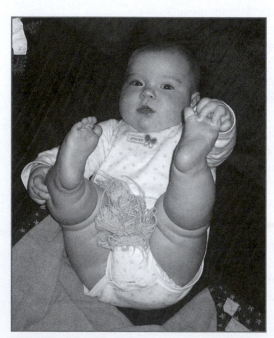

Infants learn about balance and movement as they explore their own bodies.

- Carry young infants upright against your shoulder sometimes to look at pictures, mirrors, windows, and people.

- Hold a very young baby cuddled in your arms to look at books or toys.

- Place young babies on their tummies, on the floor, near a wall-mounted mirror, with a few interesting toys to look at. Make sure the very young baby is protected from more mobile infants.

- With the baby on his or her back, slowly move an appealing toy from one side to the other to encourage the child to follow it with the eyes or by turning the head.

Exercise the Infant's Legs Through Play.
Young infants can push their feet and legs against things before they can reach accurately with their arms.

- Dangle toys where the baby can kick at them.
- Hold the baby upright in a "walking" position and let him or her push or kick against the floor.
- Do singing games that involve moving and stretching the legs in bicycle movements.

Exercise Infant's Arms Through Play.
Young infants around 4 months are gaining control of their reach and grasp.

- Dangle toys for reaching and batting.
- Play games and sing songs with babies in which you bring their hands together at midline or crossing midline, such as:

Open—shut them, open—shut them, (*stretch arms out and bring back to midline*)
Give a little clap. (*clap baby's hands together*)
Open—shut them, open—shut them, (*stretch arms out and bring back to midline*)
Lay them in your lap. (*bring baby's hands to his thighs*)
Roll them, roll them, (*roll baby's hands at midline*)
Roll them, roll them,
Roll them, just like this.
Wave them, wave them, (*wave baby's hands over baby's head*)
Wave them, wave them,
And blow a little kiss. (*blow a kiss to baby*)

Be Prepared for Rolling.
Young infants are rolling over.

- Provide safe floor space for rolling.
- Place interesting toys a little out of the baby's reach on the floor.
- Never leave babies unattended on a sofa or changing table; they could roll off.
- Protect other babies from rolling babies.
- Encourage rolling by getting on the floor with the baby at eye level.

Extend Learning by Supporting Sitting.
Young infants are sitting at around 7–8 months, freeing their hands to work together.

- Stay close by because new sitters often fall over.
- Provide lightweight, interesting toys that encourage the use of both hands together.
- Place toys beside infants in ways that promote a baby's shifting position and maintaining balance.
- Use the baby's new vertical perspective to share books, low-hung posters on the wall, and art or texture activities on low windows.
- Babies may use the sitting position for scooting across the floor.

Motivate Crawlers with the Environment. Young infants are rocking on hands and knees, may crawl on hands and knees, or pull themselves along with their arms and elbows.

- Provide many safe spaces on the floor for young infants to practice crawling.
- Provide groupings of interesting toys in places around the room that encourage the baby to use his or her new mobility to find them.
- Challenge the crawler's new skills with slight inclines or small sets of steps and platforms to invite crawling.

Planning for Young Infants' Movement and Motor Ability

If you have practiced using the planning guides in the previous chapters, it is time to add your own observations (Box 11.3). Find an opportunity to observe a young infant. Ask yourself the questions given in the reflection section to guide your observation. *Respect* what the child is currently doing in movement and motor development. Make notes or take pictures of your observations. *Reflect* on the child's current and emerging abilities. What is the child trying to do? What interactions or environmental changes might support the child in achieving motor goals? *Relate* to the child. Plan interactions, materials, and activities that would support the child. Remember, with infants, setting the environment and offering information and encouragement are good plans.

Box 11.3

Individual Child Planning Guide (1)

Child's Name: _____   Plans for Week of (Date): _____

Person Completing the Guide: _____

Respect: Child's Emotions, Effort, Goals, Learning, and Relationships
Write an observation or use a picture or other documentation here—date all notes.

Respect and Reflect	Relate
What am I doing?	**What will you do to support my learning?**
How am I feeling?	• **Responsive interactions**
What am I learning?	• **Environment: Toys, materials**
• **Emotional**	• **Opportunities**
• **Social**	
• **Cognitive**	
• **Language**	
• **Motor**	

THE MOBILE INFANT: 8–18 MONTHS

The name says it all! During this period, infants are moving with great joy and purpose. Most infants at this stage begin crawling and quickly move to pulling up to a stand, cruising around furniture, and walking. All of these new movements are more than physical accomplishments. They are part of the infant's growing interest in language, in discovering how things work, and even in the beginnings of friendships.

A Glimpse of the Mobile Infant's Moving and Developing Motor Skills

Albert's small group is naturally motivated to move and practice their new motor skills. As the children begin walking, each in his or her style and pace, Albert wants to encourage this mobility in every way. Gemma, although the youngest, loves walking and uses push and pull toys, climbing a few low steps, and climbing up and down a shallow slide. She loves the movement and has impressive postural balance—but has very little judgment about her actions.

Radwan also enjoys the push and pull toys, but he goes to the rocking horses first thing in the morning and to the riding toys when he is outside. Goro is an adept walker at 16 months and he loves the walking courses that Albert lays out with wide tape on the floor. It is a major challenge to his ability to balance.

Lily has been fitted with leg braces and introduced to the use of a walker. Albert knows that her cerebral palsy makes balance and posture challenging, but it is not impossible. He makes a point of giving her opportunities to walk with his support several times a day. He uses those moments to help her be closer to her friends. Recently he has brought some classical music CDs and some colorful gauze scarves and enticed the children to sway, swing their scarves, and dance. Lily is very engaged in this activity with her Velcro mitts and getting some good practice in correcting her balance even though she is still sitting with support.

The Mobile Infant Care Teacher's Decisions

Albert revised his classroom significantly as his young infants became mobile. Where he once had one large motor area, he now sees large motor opportunities in almost every part of his space. The mobile infants are encouraged to climb in and out of their little seats at the table. If they can, they climb up to the changing table on wide steps with rails. Push and pull toys, riding toys, and rocking toys are located in several areas. Albert uses his vinyl-covered foam climbing pieces in new configurations and different parts of the room on different days. He does not use swings, walkers, or any equipment that prevents the babies from moving.

Adaptations for Special Needs. Albert is concerned that Lily is fearful and that her lack of confidence is making it harder to attempt physical efforts. He is trying to come up with other ways to help her gain strength, balance, and confidence. The scarves and dancing seem to be working well. He is also introducing games, such as imitating, that involve various arm movements that strengthen balance. She enjoys mirroring most when Albert imitates her movements first. The physical therapist is very happy that Albert is confident enough to be creative in his support. Albert is also demonstrating that he understands Lily's other developmental needs for relationships and play. The therapist is making sure that Albert is using the braces and the walker appropriately.

A tunnel encourages mobile infants to use many of their motor skills.

Diversity/Culture. Gemma appears to have outstanding natural physical abilities. Her parents, however, believe that little girls should play quietly with dolls, and they are concerned about her activity level. They fear that she will hurt herself or be difficult to control. Albert shares the parents' concern about Gemma's lack of judgment in her climbing and running, but he appreciates her physical potential. As they discuss their differing views about gender and movement, they come upon soccer as a point of agreement. Both of Gemma's parents grew up playing soccer in English families and value the skill and coordination that they gained. Her parents donated a soccer ball to the classroom, and Albert offered to help them think about active play areas in their home on his next home visit.

Opportunities for Mobile Infants' Moving and Motor Development

Keep the Environment Safe for Cruising.
Mobile infants often use furniture to pull themselves up to a stand and then they cruise around while holding on to the furniture.

- Make sure that the environment is safe and that shelves or lightweight tables are bolted down.
- Invite cruising by placing some appealing toys on a low table or the seat of a couch.

Provide Playful Opportunities for Crawling.
Mobile infants still use crawling for speed some of the time.

- Offer large fabric tunnels for mobile infants to crawl through. The infants may need your encouragement from the opposite open end to enter and move through the tunnel.
- Create new and challenging climbing constructions with firm pillows, pads, or mattresses with washable covers.

Keep New Standers Safe and Unafraid.
Older mobile infants are able to rise to stand alone, even in an open space.

- Be nearby. Getting up is easier than getting down, and some infants may get stuck. Offer support and encouragement but help them realize that they are able to get back down alone.
- React kindly but without distress if an infant falls. For the most part, they will get up by themselves and become confident walkers. At the end of this period, games like "Ashes, ashes, we all fall down" can be a fun way of practicing falling and getting up again.

Celebrate the Accomplishment of Walking.
Older mobile infants walk for the sheer pleasure of moving in an upright position. They may try to challenge themselves by running.

- Share their joy!
- Provide safe pathways for walking.
- Play mirroring games like Follow the Leader, with the infant care teacher imitating the children as well as the children imitating the teacher. Use movements that strengthen balance and posture as well as walking.
- Provide push and pull toys for young walkers. Riding toys that require the children to "walk" them along are also good practice for alternating feet.
- Mobile infants love carrying toys or clothing in their hands as they walk. Understand that the play space may get messed up, but it's worth the new sense of ability in the little walkers.

Express Enjoyment Over the Various Efforts. Mobile infants love using their bodies in creative ways.

- Provide opportunities for dancing and singing songs that have motions.
- Provide a wide variety of balls for throwing, kicking, carrying, and putting into and taking out of containers.
- Provide small slides, tubes for crawling through, or tunnels made of blankets laid over chairs because mobile infants love to use their bodies to solve the problems of moving themselves through tight spaces.

Planning for Mobile Infants' Movement and Motor Development

Next, you have another opportunity to use a blank planning guide for your observation and planning (see Box 11.4). You practiced with this form in Chapter 8, "Opportunities for Social Development and Learning with Peers." This form asks more global questions; they are not domain related. However, because this is for practicing on

Box 11.4

Individual Child Planning Guide (2)

Child's Name: _____ Plans for Week of (Date): _____

Person Completing the Guide: _____

Respect: Child's Emotions, Effort, Goals, Learning, and Relationships
Write an observation or use a picture or other documentation here—date all notes.

Reflect	**Relate**
Date all notes:	***What will you do to support my development and learning?***
What am I doing?	• **Responsive interactions**
What am I feeling?	• **Environment: Toys, materials**
What am I learning?	• **Opportunities**

motor development, it would be good to focus your observation and planning on motor tasks with a mobile infant. Try to answer the following questions in terms of movement and motor development: What am I doing? How am I feeling? What am I learning? Think about what the mobile infant wants to continuously practice. If, for example, it is crawling, then think about how your interactions and the environment can support the child's interests. If the child is figuring out how his or her body fits into spaces, provide the child opportunities to challenge him- or herself, such as boxes to fit his or her body into.

TODDLERS AND TWOS: 16–36 MONTHS

Toddlers and twos genuinely enjoy their capacity for movement. It also serves their growing interest in friendships, learning, exploring, and their growing sense of capacity in themselves.

A Glimpse of Toddlers' and Twos' Movement and Motor Development

Chita is a true toddler. At 19 months, she was a late walker, and her gait is still wide and a little unstable. The best part of movement for her is the ability to follow other children around. Chita and Bessie, 2 years old, prefer to spend much of their time on Selena's lap. Bessie has the low muscle tone common in children with Down syndrome and is crawling. Selena, the toddler care teacher, does not engage in movement very naturally herself. Although she treasures the moments of cuddling with these two little girls, she is very aware of the importance of motivating them to engage in lots of active play during the day.

Sam's active play is increasingly becoming part of other play. He uses riding toys or wagons to move blocks from one place to another. He climbs up steps and slides down slides on his way to "put out a fire." He loves to be chased or to chase his friends. Sam and Lan have been playing mirroring games in which one child makes a motion and the other mimics him. All four children sometimes join games that involve falling into a deep pile of autumn leaves or a mound of soft snow.

The Toddler Care Teacher's Decisions

Selena knows that motivating movement is not her strength as a toddler care teacher. She has put a great deal of thought into how to use her room and materials as "another teacher." The children are able to climb onto and out of the child-size chairs at the tables for eating and play activities. A small climbing ladder is bolted to one wall. Riding toys, rocking toys, and push and pull toys are available inside and outdoors. She uses big paper for art projects that encourage large arm movements. Some days she sets up obstacle sources or balancing courses. Selena creates games that involve crouching and jumping to help the children think of new ways to use their bodies. Music, with all sorts of dancing and creative movement, always brings the children running to participate. Selena uses words to describe how the children are moving; for example, she may say to a child, "You are jumping" or "You are climbing up the ladder."

Toddlers like to challenge their motor abilities.

Adaptations for Special Needs. Selena has a lot of faith in Bessie's ability to become physically active and competent. In her long career she has seen many children with Down syndrome grow into very competent athletes. At this point, Bessie resists trying to stand, but she does want to play with the push and pull toys. The physical therapist is using her interest in these toys to support attempts at walking. Bessie's growing friendship with Chita has been very motivating for both girls to try some of the physical activities available. Bessie's muscle tone makes physical activities very difficult for her, and Selena uses her physical presence and her encouragement to keep Bessie working at movements such as climbing.

Diversity/Culture. Cultural issues have not been a major issue for Selena and her families in terms of active play. Bessie's mother sometimes expresses concern about the danger of her being hurt, and Chita's mother worries about her getting dirty. Selena listens seriously to these concerns but points out to the parents how courageous and confident these children are in their daily attempts at movement. She talks about the importance of gaining skills in movement, balance, and posture in these early years to provide a foundation for later participation in dance or sports. So far, the parents are willing to support these activities.

Opportunities for Toddlers' and Twos' Movement and Motor Development

Make Running Part of More Complex Games. Toddlers and twos enjoy incorporating running into games.

- Place different colored ribbons or crepe paper streamers around the indoor or outdoor play space. Gather a few children together and say, "Everyone run to the yellow ribbon." If they are not sure of colors, help them find the ribbons. Let each child take a yellow ribbon. If the children know the names of colors, let a child choose the next color. When they have several colored ribbons and are tired of running, play music for dancing with the ribbons.

Step Back and Let Toddlers and Twos Work on Stooping and Crouching. Toddlers and twos like to stoop and crouch.

- Point out little bugs to watch outside.
- Play games in which the children stoop or crouch or pick up small toys or colored paper shapes off the floor.
- Show the children how to jump from a crouching position.

Expand Play Areas with Movement Experiences. Toddlers and twos enjoy riding, pushing, and pulling wheel toys.

- Incorporate riding toys into the play areas of the room. Shopping carts and strollers are part of a play house area. Wagons and ride-on trucks are fun in a block area. Pretend areas might include a drive-up restaurant or a garage.

Add Dancing to Your Days. Toddlers and twos enjoy dancing to music.

- Provide a tape or CD player that the children can operate themselves for dancing.
- Spontaneously begin singing and dancing activities with one or two children, letting others join in if they are interested.

Create Areas for Going In and Out. Toddlers and twos enjoy climbing in and out of things.

- Build a tunnel of chairs and blanket or use a commercial crawling tunnel.
- Cut holes in a large cardboard box for climbing in and out of.

Notice When Peers Use Movement and Imitation in Play. Toddlers and twos like to chase, follow, and imitate in play.

- Have a fun walk in which the children imitate your different styles of walking: sideways, backwards, waving arms, slow, fast.
- Have a parade of waving streamers or pushing baby strollers.
- Let toddlers put jingle bell shakers from music sets on their ankles and march, kick, and dance.

Watch How Children Climb or Stretch to Accomplish Something. Toddlers and twos use movement to help them reach their goals.

- Set up situations where standing on tip-toes or using steps will help a toddler reach a sink or choose a book.

Box 11.5

Books for Babies: Movement

Baby Dance, Ann Taylor. Harper Collins (1999).

From Head to Toe, Eric Carle. HarperFestival (1999).

Heads, Shoulders, Knees and Toes, Annie Kubler. Marlon Creations (2002).

I Can, Helen Oxenbury. Candlewick (1995).

I Can, Can You? Marjorie Pitzer. Woodbine House (2007).

I Can Fly, Ruth Kraus. Golden Books (1951/2003).

Jamberry, Bruce Degen. HarperFestival (1994).

Box 11.6

Individually Responsive Group Planning Guide

Name of Group: _____

Week of: _____

Person(s) completing this guide: _____

Respect and Reflect

The children in my group are ...

(Summarize information from the individual planning guides)

Relate: Plans for the Week to Meet Children's Interests and Needs

Songs/Fingerplays/Music

Stories/Books

Responsive Interactions

Environment: Toys, materials

Opportunities

Family/Cultural Experiences

Other

Offer Safe Options for Jumping. Toddlers and twos are learning to jump.

- Provide safe places to jump—jumping in the middle of the floor, into a pile of leaves or firm pillows, or off of one step; all add extra interest.

Planning Guide for Toddlers' and Twos' Movement and Motor Development

This planning guide (Box 11.6) will give you an opportunity to observe a small group of toddlers and twos. Note what each child finds interesting in movement and motor development. Think about opportunities that will give children time to enjoy movement based on their interests.

SUMMARY

Nothing is more natural in infancy and the toddler months than movement. It is so natural that sometimes we don't track the important underlying foundation of movement. Infant and toddler care teachers should be observing development and learning in the areas of:

- Balance
- Flexibility

- Posture
- Reaching and kicking
- Increased functionality
- Mobility

Teachers need to constantly find a balance between encouraging infants and toddlers to practice movement and keeping them safe. Teachers should not only support the milestones of rolling, crawling, and walking, but also watch for the child's ability to adjust posture to correct for balance and to reach and kick to make things happen. Teachers should observe all the strategies that children use as they practice moving and then provide endless opportunities for them to continue developing. For example, a child who is trying to learn how to jump will possibly first put one foot down and then the other. Gradually, with many opportunities, this child will try different strategies until he or she accomplishes the goal of being a jumper.

INVENTORY OF TEACHER PRACTICES

Movement and Motor Development

Basic Concepts	A	S	R	Observation/ Reflection
I provide opportunities for infants and toddlers to practice movement throughout the day.				
I ensure that each infant has floor time every day.				
I do not use swings, bouncy chairs, or walkers that constrain children.				
I provide opportunities for infants and toddlers to challenge their balance and posture.				
I provide opportunities for infants and toddlers to use their bodies in new ways to achieve their goals.				
I provide opportunities for reaching and kicking that make things happen.				
I provide opportunities for infants and toddlers to move their bodies to the rhythm of music.				
I use language to describe what infants and toddlers are doing.				
I provide opportunities for practicing each new stage of mobility.				

A = Always, S = Sometimes, R = Rarely

REFLECTIONS

1. This chapter begins with observing that the motor system, because it is the most visible system, is our window into what interests infants and toddlers. How does motor development influence the different age groups in security, exploration, and developing a sense of self?

2. How does your own enjoyment of movement and your motor skill affect the experiences you are likely to offer infants and toddlers?
3. Sometimes, we see infants as fragile, and our protective instincts then outweigh our ability to let them practice movement. What are your own feelings about encouraging or tolerating risk?

APPLICATIONS

1. Many children with disabilities have movement and motor problems. These problems may arise because muscle tone is too loose or too tight; or sensory issues may make the child uncomfortable moving around in an environment where he or she cannot see or hear. What adaptations might you make to support motor development in a child with disabilities.
2. Describe the elements that make an environment safe for practicing new movement skills.
3. Create a list of how you could develop motor and movement skills in the art area, book area, and pretend play area.
4. Use the Inventory of Teacher Practices. Interview an infant/toddler care teacher and ask how she or he accomplishes each of the items.

RESOURCES

- *The Baby Human*
  The following video clips from motor researcher Karen Adolph's lab illustrate how infants apply the information learned in one posture/movement to another: http://www.youtube.com/watch?v=1MIyjUo-zF0&feature=relmfu http://www.youtube.com/watch?v=kBkqDqVge_c&feature=relmfu
- *An Interactive Timeline of Physical Development*
  From Parenting Counts, this timeline provides information about each milestone and includes references for the research from which the information was taken. Available at http://www.parentingcounts.org/information/timeline

Opportunities for Fine Motor Development and Learning

After reading this chapter, you will be able to:

- RESPECT
  - Understand the foundations of fine motor development and learning
  - Describe visual motor, manipulation and bilateral skills.
  - Describe developmental possibilities of fine motor
  - Be aware of signs of possible delays or disorders
- REFLECT
  - On how fine motor development affects learning and exploration
  - On how adults may support or hinder fine motor development
  - On your own comfort with letting toddlers take little risks or tolerate small frustrations
  - On cultural differences in how families encourage fine motor development
- RELATE
  - Plan interactions, materials, and environments for individuals and small groups of children, to promote fine motor development
  - Demonstrate how to create fine motor learning opportunities for young and mobile infants, toddlers, and twos

From the moment infants are born, they gaze into the eyes of their mothers and grasp tightly the fingers of their fathers or siblings. From birth to 3 years of age, the use of the fine or small muscles in the eyes, lips, tongue, hands, wrists, fingers, feet, and toes becomes stronger and more precise (Piek, 2006). Infants and toddlers learn to intentionally coordinate their eye and hand movements to reach and grasp when and where they want (visual-motor skills); explore objects by using the small muscles in their hands, fingers, and wrists (manipulation skills); and use their hands in coordination with each other (bilateral skills). By the age of 3, many toddlers also use their fine motor skills to wash their faces, brush their teeth, put on their socks and shoes, and undress themselves (self-help skills).

Infants and toddlers use their fingers, hands, and other fine muscles to learn. An infant puts his hand on an adult's face and explores cheeks, nose, and hair. The 7-month-old infant reaches out to grasp objects with an accurate aim, then waves, bangs, and tastes the object. A mobile infant picks up a toy, turns it over, manipulates all the parts, perhaps tries to bounce it, and then may end up tasting it. Toddlers use toys and materials to accomplish tasks, such as digging a hole or stringing beads.

RESPECT FINE MOTOR DEVELOPMENT

Fine motor development has three basic aspects: reaching, grasping, and manipulating objects; bilateral coordination; and self-help skills.

Reaching, Grasping, and Manipulating Objects

Infants and toddlers develop their ability to precisely and intentionally coordinate eye and hand movements as well as use their arms, hands, and fingers to hold objects, release them, and explore their properties. Young children constantly manipulate their surroundings. However, programs often have a center called the *manipulatives area.* This area has toys that children can explore using their eye/hand coordination and fine muscles.

Often there is also an area in the room called the *construction area,* especially for mobile infants, toddlers, and twos. Teachers provide blocks of all sizes and textures including wooden, foam, and vinyl; construction toys such as large Legos, wooden animals and people, cars, and trucks; and a solid floor that allows children to pile, push, and knock down stacked blocks.

Bilateral Coordination

Infants and toddlers learn to use both sides of their bodies together intentionally to manipulate and use objects. For example, by 4 months of age infants can usually clasp their hands together in the middle of their body. They also can hold an object in one hand while exploring it with the other hand. By 6 months of age an infant typically can transfer an object from one hand to the other, and by 8 months of age an infant can hold an object in each hand and excitedly bang the objects together. The ability to play pat-a-cake with a favorite adult by intentionally bringing both hands together will soon follow.

With some bilateral coordination activities, one hand will hold something steady while the other hand "operates" or explores the item. Examples of "holding" and

This toddler holds with one hand and operates with another.

"operating" include the following: (1) infants holding a container in one hand and putting blocks in the container with the other hand; (2) holding down a piece of paper with one hand and using a crayon in the other; or (3) holding a ring stack steady while putting rings on with the other hand. Other bilateral coordination activities require coordination of both sides of the body while using both hands freely. Examples of bilateral coordination with both hands used freely include the following: (1) holding beads in one hand and a string in the other, and (2) finger-painting with both hands at the same time.

Self-Help Skills

Infants and toddlers use their fine motor skills to learn to undress themselves, dress themselves, wash their faces, drink from cups, use eating utensils, and use toothbrushes to brush their teeth (to some extent).

RESPECT THEORIES OF FINE MOTOR DEVELOPMENT

The theorist and psychologist Piaget (1963) emphasized that biology influenced fine motor development. Piaget highlighted the point that infants' and toddlers' motor development advances in a predictable sequence. In the first stage of development, the sensory-motor stage, infants and toddlers learn through their senses and motor actions on the environment.

Educators have interpreted Piaget's theory to mean that children do not need lessons in how to use their developing skills. Through touching and exploring objects and people, children learn about all of their properties. They learn skills such as "reach and pull" to pull a toy by the handle to bring it closer. Then they use this schema to solve other problems, such as freeing a ball that is stuck in another toy. Play, then, is crucial to fine motor development. Infants and toddlers need time to explore, experiment with, use, and investigate toys and other materials.

Vygotsky (1978) emphasized the importance of social interaction and cultural influences. Some cultures emphasize reaching and manipulation skills while others may not. The quality of social interactions that not only provide opportunities but also support children in learning how to accomplish tasks is important. For example, a 2-year-old might be better able to learn how to put a puzzle together after an adult shares a strategy such as looking at the picture on the puzzle carefully before taking out the pieces of the puzzle one by one. The infant's or toddler's social experiences, then, influence how motor skills develop.

Relationship-based theory (Hinde, 1992), too, emphasizes that the quality of relationships influences development—including fine motor development (see Chapter 1 for more information). When a child has a warm, ongoing relationship with adults, he or she feels safe to explore the environment, manipulate objects to see how they work, experiment with how to use both sides of the body together, and begin to feed himself.

As discussed in previous chapters, Spelke and other researchers (Kinzler & Spelke, 2007; Spelke, 2000; Spelke, Phillips, & Woodward, 1995) focus on core knowledge systems. The system that is of particular interest as we think about fine motor development is the core system of object representation. This system in the brain creates principles that govern object motion. Young children learn that "objects move as connected and bounded wholes" (principle of cohesion); that "objects move on connected, unobstructed paths" (principle of continuity); and that "objects influence each others' motion when and only when they touch" (principle of contact) (Knizler & Spelke, 2007, p. 257). These principles allow infants to, for example, "predict when objects will move and where they will come to rest" (Kinzler & Spelke, 2007, p. 258).

Dynamic systems theory, on the other hand, emphasizes the role of experiences that infants need to learn how to use their fine motor skills. Some cultures provide more opportunities for children to grasp, manipulate objects, use both hands together, and feed themselves. These experiences then influence not only when and where children use their fine motor skills, but how their development proceeds.

Box 12.1 identifies the developmental possibilities in fine motor development and learning.

RESPECT SIGNS OF CONCERN IN FINE MOTOR DEVELOPMENT

Infants and toddlers who exhibit delays in fine motor skills may have challenges in coordination, planning, and/or strength. Perceptual-motor challenges include difficulty using hands and eyes together to accomplish tasks. Developmental dyspraxia includes difficulties in motor planning. Minor neurologic dysfunction (MND) also can influence children's fine motor abilities.

Cerebral palsy is a condition that can affect fine motor control. Delays and disabilities in motor control are caused by damage to the motor control centers of the developing brain. This damage may occur prenatally, during birth, and after birth until age 3. Both occupational therapy and physical therapy can help the young child develop manipulative, bilateral coordination, and self-help skills.

Box 12.1

Respect Developmental Possibilities in Fine Motor Development and Learning

YOUNG INFANTS	MOBILE INFANTS	TODDLERS	TWOS
0–9 Months	8–18 Months	16–24 Months	24–36 Months

MANIPULATIVE

Newborn infants' hands are often in a fist. Gradually they begin to use their raking grasp, then a scissors grasp, and by 9 months many are using a pincer grasp. They learn to shake, bang, hold, and let go of objects.	Can reach in a variety of ways and grasp and release objects as well. Like to shake, bang, and look at objects from different directions; put objects into containers; and dump objects out of containers. Often can turn the pages of a book, depending on the composition of the book.	Develop ability to manipulate objects in a variety of ways to make them "work" using small muscles in hands and eyes. Develop ability to cooperate with another child to accomplish a task using manipulative skills.	Continue to develop fine motor skills, e.g., thread large beads on a string. Begin to use child scissors to cut. Use fine motor skills to poke, push, and pull toys and materials, such as art materials.

BILATERAL COORDINATION

By 9 months, can sit and use both hands together. Bang objects together in the middle of the body.	Develop ability to pull to stand and walk, using both hands together while walking, stop walking to pick up objects while keeping balance.	Develop ability to use both hands together to roll playdough. Pick up heavier objects than before with both hands.	Use both hands together easily to pull a wagon that is stuck, lift heavy objects and fingerpaint.

SELF-HELP MOTIVATION AND SKILLS

By 6 months, tongue control often has developed enough to allow an adult to feed the infant with a spoon without the tongue interfering. By 9 months, many are able to pick up small pieces of safe food, such as cereal, with a pincer grasp. May be able to take off socks.	Can easily use pincer grasp to pick up food. Begins to feed self with spoon although wrist strength is developing, so they can be messy. May be able to put arm into sleeve, foot into shoe, etc.	Can fairly easily feed self with a spoon and fork or other culturally appropriate utensils, although may need help with some foods. Can pull on pants and some shirts, and pull up zippers, but have a hard time with buttons. Can begin to swish toothbrush around in mouth, but will need adult to do final brushing.	Can eat foods with a child's spoon and fork. Undresses self fairly easily. Puts on socks and shoes but sometimes not on the right feet. Can often put on easy shirts and pants. Can zip if someone starts the zipper for them. Can move toothbrush around in mouth, but will need adult to do final brushing.

If a young infant or toddler is having difficulty with fine motor tasks, the teacher should talk with the administrator of the program to follow carefully planned procedures to talk with the family about the concerns. Families then have the right to decide whether to follow up with a physician or the school district's free Child Find assessment.

REFLECT ON FINE MOTOR DEVELOPMENT AND LEARNING

One meaning of reflection is to give something serious thought and consideration. Box 12.2 provides questions that care teachers and families can observe together. Table 12.1 provides an example of a care teacher's reflection on how the infants in her room use their hands. This type of documentation helps parents and teachers see infants' motivation to learn and their skills with "new eyes."

RELATE TO FINE MOTOR DEVELOPMENT

The following sections describe fine motor (reaching and grasping, bilateral coordination, and self-help), manipulation, and construction opportunities for the young infant, the mobile infant, and toddlers and twos.

Box 12.2

Reflect on Fine Motor Development

Reaching, Grasping, and Manipulating Objects

- How does the infant reach for and grasp objects?
- What does an infant do with objects in his or her hands? Taste them, bang them on a flat surface, shake them?
- How does an infant use her fingers?
- How do infants and toddlers use their eyes and hands together?
- What do an infant's goals seem to be?
- What does an infant like to reach for and grasp with regard to adults and peers?
- How do peer relationships support young children's learning to reach, grasp, and manipulate objects?

Bilateral Coordination

- When and how does an infant or toddler use both hands together?
- When, what, and how does an infant transfer objects from one hand to another?
- When do infants and toddlers "hold and operate"?

Self-Help Skills

- What does a mobile infant do to begin to help him or herself? (Take a cloth and wash his face, for example)
- How do relationships support mobile infants' self-help attitudes and development?
- How do families and cultures differ in how they view the importance of self-help skills?

Table 12.1 Infants' Use of Their Hands

Use of Hand	Purpose
Puts hand in mouth.	Seems to be for self-comfort.
Uses hand to touch adult's face.	Exploring how face feels.
Uses hand to touch blanket.	Exploring how blanket feels.
Uses hand to grasp a rattle tightly.	In the first 3 months, this is a reflex. After that, child can intentionally grasp object.
Uses hand to touch bottle when being fed.	Exploring how bottle feels.
Uses hand to grasp adult's finger when being fed.	Seems to help her feel secure.
When sitting on the floor, uses both hands to pick up an object from the floor.	Picks up object.
Uses hand to push away spoon when being fed.	Communicates that he has had enough food and doesn't want any more.

This toddler experiments with cause and effect as he washes his hands.

THE YOUNG INFANT: BIRTH TO 9 MONTHS

Infants develop from head to toe (cephalocaudal). For example, they can control their heads before they can walk. Infants also develop strength from the center of their bodies to the outer part of their bodies (proximodistal). For example, they can control their shoulders and then their elbows before they can control their hands and fingers. Yet, even in the first 9 months of life, infants become remarkably capable at reaching, grasping, using both hands together, and manipulating objects. From 4 to 8 months they learn how to shake toys, purposefully let go of objects (which is more difficult than grasping), and bang two objects together (one in each hand). By the end of the age period, infants are often trying to pick up any item (including lint and dirt) off the floor with their thumb and forefinger. They may even begin to point.

A Glimpse of the Young Infant's Fine Motor Development

Miriam and her co-teacher have been observing and documenting how infants use their hands. They decided that they would not try to sequence the chart developmentally, but rather just to capture all the ways in which infants use their hands. A few of the examples are listed in Table 12.1.

After asking parents to add to the chart, the list became very long. Everyone was amazed at all the ways in which young infants were already using their hands to feel secure, explore the properties of objects, and communicate.

Three-month-old Adara can put her thumb in her mouth and grasp objects tightly. When being held, Adara reaches out and touches Miriam's sweater, exploring the texture with her fingers.

Four-month-old Paulo reaches out to pick up a toy and studies it with his eyes, mouth, and fingers. Batting at dangling toys when he is on his back is also fun. Paulo loves to explore Miriam's face by trying to grab her cheeks, lips, and nose.

Miriam is excited about how fast the infants in her room are developing the ability to hold on to toys and also to intentionally play the game of "I drop it and you pick it up." Miriam knows that it is difficult for infants to learn how to release objects, so she appreciates the game. She also knows that the infants are learning that out-of-sight objects still exist because they play the game over and over with a willing partner.

As Takala crawls, she stops to try to pick up every object in her path, balance on one hand, and turn the object over to inspect it. Jack isn't crawling yet, but can sit quite well. As he sits, he reaches out with his arms, hands, and fingers to pick up toys and books. Jack knows how to let go as well, so he often picks up a toy, manipulates it, and flings it down.

The Young Infant Care Teacher's Decisions

Miriam knows that infants' fine motor development and bilateral coordination improve as she interacts with the infants and because she has developmentally appropriate toys in the room. She offers a rattle to an infant who can't reach or move to toys yet. As soon as infants can sit, but not yet crawl, she places interesting items around them so that they need to move, but can grasp and manipulate toys. She also knows that as she holds infants, their fine motor skills develop as they wrap their fingers around hers or reach up to touch her face.

Adaptations for Special Needs. As Miriam observes the children, she notices what skill they are practicing. Jack is practicing his letting go and flinging as if to see how far an object will fly out of his hands, so Miriam places objects near Jack that are safe to throw. She places them just far enough away that he will need to reach if he wants a toy. Whenever she can, she plays the game of "You drop it, I'll pick it up." (Jack is very pleased and full of smiles when she does play.) For Takala, Miriam and Shela visually check the floor and environment each morning and remove any small objects that Takala could pick up and put in her mouth. Miriam knows that adapting to the children's individual needs, interests, and strengths is challenging but this actually makes her job easier because the infants are much happier and safer. Miriam also knows that when she adapts to the children's interests she gives them opportunities to practice their emerging skills, such as reaching and grasping or mouthing toys. It is exciting and makes teaching worthwhile for Miriam when she sees each day that the infants seem to be practicing new skills.

Diversity/Culture. Takala's family is Native American, and they have explained to Miriam that they have a spiritual connection and respect for nature that they want their daughter to share. Miriam asked Takala's parents if there were natural materials that they would want her to manipulate. They happily shared that they dislike plastic toys and would rather have Takala play with unpainted wooden toys. The next time Miriam had a budget to buy some toys, she bought beautiful wooden blocks. When Takala is older, her parents would like her to explore leaves, grass, and rocks and know how to handle them carefully. Miriam will make an effort to provide these natural materials to Takala.

Opportunities for Young Infants' Fine Motor Development

Provide Many Opportunities for Infants to Reach and Grasp. Reaching for objects begins with the infant seeing the object and controlling a hand movement to swipe at it (2–4 months of age). From 3 to 6 months of age, children learn to reach and intentionally grasp objects (which often go into the mouth). They use their hands and fingers like a rake to pick up objects and hold them in their palms. By 7 to 8 months they begin to use thumbs separately from the other fingers to pick up objects with a scissors grasp, and by 9 to 12 months of age they

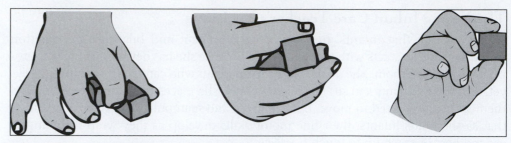

Figure 12.1   Raking, Scissors, and Pincer Grasps

can use their thumb and forefinger (pincer grasp) to pick up tiny objects (see Figure 12.1).

- In a group setting, wash rattles and teething toys after each baby uses them.
- After 3 months, offer a safe rattle, doll, teether, or other toy to the infant. Talk about the toy with the infant. Wait to see whether the infant reaches out to grasp the object.
- Lay an infant on the floor on his or her tummy. Put several toys within reach of the child's hands. By 3–4 months of age, a baby also may turn over and reach to his or her side to grasp a toy. Stay near and respond warmly when the infant looks at you.
- Observe how an infant's fine motor skills develop, from picking up a block, for example, in the palm of the hand to using the fingers to pick up the block.
- Give infants opportunities for weight bearing on their hands and arms to increase fine motor strength. Supervised tummy time during play leads to infants using their hands and arms to hold up their bodies.
- Survey the room in the morning and often during the day to remove any unsafe small objects.

Notice Infants' Ability to Release Objects; Releasing Is More Difficult Developmentally Than Grasping. By 6 months, an infant may be able to release objects. This is when the game "I drop it, you pick it up" starts. The infant is learning valuable lessons about where objects go and that they still exist when out of sight.

- Provide interesting materials—aluminum foil pie pan, flannel, cardboard, and so on—on the floor so that infants can release and drop objects to make different sounds.
- Play the game with the infant. Say, "Where did that go?" As the infant looks down, say, "There it is!" Help the infant pick it up so that the game can continue.

Support Infants' Development of Strategies. A teacher may see an infant explore objects with her or his fingers, shake toys, bang them on a surface, and

manipulate them in other ways. For example, the infant may turn a toy over and inspect it on all sides. These ways of exploring objects are called *strategiess*.

- Observe to see what strategies an infant has in her repertoire and then make toys available to enhance each strategy. When objects go into the mouth, offer the infant safe objects that have different textures. When objects are typically shaken by the infant, offer toys that make interesting noises. When an infant begins to roll objects, provide different toys that roll.

- Provide ring-stacking toys. An infant may put the rings on his or her arm or try to put the rings on the toy at around 8 to 9 months.

- Provide a rolling texture mirror (Environments, 2008) or balls of different shapes, sizes, and textures. Make these available to the crawling baby and share the infant's excitement about how he or she can make the balls roll.

Support Infants' Bilateral Development. Infants begin to use both sides of their bodies together when they hold a toy and explore it with the other hand, grasp their feet with both hands, transfer objects from one hand to the other, bang objects together, pick up toys using both hands, and clap their hands together.

- Make toys available that infants can hold easily, can transfer from one hand to the other, and that make interesting noises when banged together. Use words to describe what the infant is doing; for example, say "You are making a loud noise."

- Provide toys and board books that challenge an infant to use two hands to pick them up at around 6–9 months.

- At the end of this age period, begin to play Pat-a-Cake.
  Pat-a-cake, pat-a-cake, baker's man (*clapping hands together*),
  Bake me a cake as fast as you can,
  Roll it (*roll hands*) and pat it (*pat pretend cake*) and mark it with a B (*make a B letter in the air*),
  Put it in the oven for baby and me (*pretend to put cake in the oven*).

Notice Infants' Increasing Skills as They Crawl or Walk. When infants crawl or walk, they need to be able to see toys on a low shelf and choose the toys they want to play with. They may play with a toy for a few minutes or longer and then move on to another toy.

- In the manipulative area, arrange the toys on the shelves so that an infant can easily see each toy.

- Arrange books so that infants can see the covers of the books.

Planning for Young Infants' Fine Motor Development

Box 12.3 is a planning form that care teachers can use to plan for Jack.

Box 12.3

Individual Child Planning Guide (2)

Respect
Write an observation or use a picture, or other documentation, here—date all notes.

Jack is holding a rattle in both hands. He is looking at the rattle. Then he works to retrieve the rattle after he drops it.

Reflect	Relate
Date all notes:	What will you do to support my development and learning?
What am I doing? *Holding a rattle*	• **Responsive interactions** *Observe when you are so engaged. If you look up at an adult, the adult could say, "You have a rattle." "You are dropping and picking up the rattle."*
What am I feeling? *I am engaged*	
What am I learning? *I am learning about cause and effect, gravity, and what objects do. I am also developing my fine motor skills including reaching and grasping and bilateral skills (using both hands together).*	• **Environment: Toys, materials** • **Opportunities** *Provide other toys that you can grasp and reach. Provide materials that may be more challenging to grasp. Provide a large container that you can drop objects into.*

THE MOBILE INFANT: 8–18 MONTHS

Most mobile infants are constantly moving toward toys, handling them, trying to make them work, and then checking in with favorite teachers to show them their discoveries. As they walk, they stoop or lean down to pick up objects and explore them. They can usually reach, grasp, and release with ease and love the game of filling and dumping—learning many valuable spatial skills in the process. By 10 months of age (and possibly younger), they can adjust how they pick up an object based on what they are planning to do with it (Claxton, Keen, & McCarty, 2003). They pick up an object more slowly if they are going to put it precisely into a container, and faster if they are going to throw the object. They still struggle with picking up heavy objects, pushing large objects, and placing objects, like blocks, exactly where they want them but often they enjoy the challenge. Their bilateral coordination skills continue to improve as they use both sides of their body together in play and to feed themselves. Other self-help skills, such as undressing, may not seem as if they are helping anyone (especially if mobile infants take their diapers off), but the infants are learning how to use their fine motor skills, which eventually will allow them to feed and dress themselves.

A Glimpse of the Mobile Infants' Fine Motor Development

Albert has noticed that recently the children in his group not only are playing together more, but are very curious about each new object or toy that he brings into the room.

Because Gemma (9 months old) loves emptying containers of toy animals or manipulatives, Albert brings different containers such as shoeboxes, baskets, purses, and bags that hold different items such as laminated picture cards, cars, wooden people, balls, board books, or beanbags. Gemma spends time dumping items out of the containers and then putting the items back into different containers. Radwan is often by her side. Sometimes they play with different containers but often they are working together. They do not seem to care yet which items go back into specific containers. Albert often sits close by and both children bring him toys to hold in his lap. Each time, he shows delight and names the objects they bring him.

Because Radwan, at 15 months, is particularly interested in how things come apart and go back together, Albert and his co-teacher make sure there are ring toys, shape boxes, large Legos, and stacking cups in the manipulative area. They also have added pots, pans, baskets of velour, and vinyl fruits and vegetables (Environments, 2008) to the symbolic/dramatic play area. Radwan found them the first day they were there and stacked the pots and pans immediately.

Lily, at 12 months, loves the Peek-A-Boo Picture Board (see Figure 12.2). Albert changes the pictures under the cloth flaps frequently. Lily is happiest when Albert brings Goro over to play, too, and Albert or Goro names the pictures.

Goro, who builds a tower of blocks only to knock them down again, loves cause-and-effect toys. He enjoys the noise, too, so Albert and his co-worker found toys such as Pop-Up-Teddies for the manipulative area, rainbow baby blocks, and giant foam blocks (Environments, 2008) for the construction area.

Figure 12.2 Peek-A-Boo Picture Board

The Mobile Infant Care Teacher's Decisions

Albert knows that mobile infants must taste, touch, and test to figure out how objects and people work, so he provides many opportunities for them to do so safely. He also knows that children like motor challenges, so he provides new materials like the Peek-A-Boo Picture Board. By asking his co-teacher and collaborating with families, he tries to figure out the children's goals concerning fine motor tasks. The mobile infants have learned how to use the fine muscles in their hands to accomplish tasks. Many know that a dial needs to be turned, a doorbell pushed, a bell shaken, and an animal patted. Both Albert and the families enjoy observing the children to see how they accomplish goals that they set for themselves through fine motor skills and bilateral coordination. Albert's observation skills have changed the way he thinks about children's abilities and the way he plans for children.

Adaptations for Special Needs. Albert believes in inclusion and is happy that Lily is in his class. He knows that children learn from each other, so he tries to ask Goro or another child if he or she wants to go with him to sit by Lily when she is playing. Albert also tries to let each child struggle with a challenging toy or task. Only when Albert sees that a child is becoming upset will he ask the child whether he or she wants some help, and if the child does, Albert helps "just enough" to scaffold the child's mastery.

Diversity/Culture. Albert knows that in some families and cultures, children aren't allowed to become messy while they eat. He also knows that wrist control is just developing during this age period, so it is difficult for mobile infants to use spoons to feed themselves. He talked with the families to find out if they spoon fed their children at home or if they let them pick up pieces of food or even put their fingers into a bowl of food and eat a little while spreading much of it on their face. Based on what he discovered, he continued spoon feeding a few children while letting others feed themselves. He asked the families whether he could let the spoon-fed children partially feed themselves if they put on a used, clean shirt before eating. Most of the families were happy to compromise in this way.

Opportunities for Mobile Infants' Fine Motor and Manipulative Development

Create a Manipulative Area. A special area where children know they will find a small variety of manipulative toys encourages them to explore the materials they anticipate finding there.

- Provide interesting toys attractively displayed on low shelves.
- Sit on the floor on a camping chair to support your back or against a wall so that you are emotionally and physically available to mobile infants. Mobile infants need to explore and afterward restore their emotional energy with a caring teacher.

Increase Complexity of Toys. Mobile infants use their fine motor skills to manipulate increasingly more complex toys. Mobile infants experiment with many ways to hold and play with toys.

- Provide homemade toys such as a scarf pull (Schiller, 2005, p. 233). Fill a round oatmeal container or a coffee can with pieces of cloth or scarves tied together to make one long scarf. Make a hole in the lid and pull one end of the scarf out. Encourage the mobile infant to pull the scarf out of the container.

- Provide manipulatives such as the following:

  Balls and baskets
  Toys and containers
  Shake toys
  Stacking toys
  Large beads and string
  Two- or three-piece puzzles with knobs on them

Watch for Reaching and Grasping Motivation and Skills.

Mobile infants can reach, grasp, and use their fingers with increasing precision. By 12 months of age, a mobile infant will use his or her first finger to poke or point.

- Have fun with fingerplays. Wonderful resources include:

  The Bilingual Book of Rhymes, Songs, Stories, and Fingerplays (Gryphon House), Pam Schiller, Rafael Lara-Alecio, Beverly J. Irby

  Little Hands, Fingerplays & Action Songs: Seasonal Activities & Creative Play for 2- to 6-Year-Olds (Williamson Little Hands Series), Emily Stetson, Vicky Congdon, and Betsy Day (Illustrator)

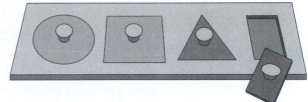

- Blow bubbles and encourage the infants to catch and pop them. Many mobile infants also like the challenge of putting a wand into a bottle and trying to blow bubbles themselves.

Entice Mobile Infants to Use Both Hands and Both Sides of Their Bodies Together.

Mobile infants can increasingly use bilateral coordination to hold and operate toys and materials.

- Encourage mobile infants to hold a book and turn the pages. Board book pages are the easiest ones to turn (see Box 12.4).

- Provide play dough. Observe how mobile infants hold play dough down with one hand and push pegs or forms into the play dough with the other hand.

- Offer fingerpainting. Observe how mobile infants might first use one finger, then two, then one hand, and soon both hands at the same time. Let them experiment and discover what happens rather than telling them what to do.

Box 12.4

> **Books for Babies:** Fine Motor Development
>
> *Baby Days: A Collection of 9 Board Books,* Little Scholastic. Cartwheel Books (2007).
>
> *Little Mouse Plays Peek-A-Boo: A Touch and Feel and Lift-the-Flap Book,* David and Noelle Carter. Intervisual Books (2003).
>
> *Open the Barn Door,* Christopher Santoro, illustrator. Random House Books for Young Readers (1993).
>
> *That's Not My Teddy—Its Paws Are Too Woolly,* Fiona Watt. Usborne Publishing Ltd. (2007).

Develop an Open-Ended Construction Area. Care teachers often create a construction area for this age group. Mobile infants use eye/hand coordination and the fine muscles in the hands to manipulate the blocks, cars and trucks, and wooden people.

- Mobile infants will need a flat space to stack blocks and lay them end-to-end on the floor.

- Observe all the ways in which mobile infants experiment with holding, carrying, placing, picking up, and laying down the objects.

- Start stacking blocks and invite the mobile infants to add to your stack.

- Understand that knocking a stack of blocks over is a learning experience as well. Mobile infants are learning about cause and effect, spatial concepts, and the properties of objects.

Make play Opportunities for Self-Help Skills. Provide children opportunities to practice self-help skills during routines. By 15 months of age many mobile infants begin to undress themselves.

- Dramatic play clothes and toys encourage children to use their fine motor skills to dress themselves, undress themselves, and handle play food, utensils, and cooking equipment.

- Encourage the children to pull off their own hat, socks, and mittens.

- Eating becomes an interesting project. Mobile infants' wrist strength is still developing, so spoon use is still messy and children often revert to using their hands.

- Use hand washing and tooth brushing as practice opportunities.

Plan from the Goals, Strategies, and Concepts of the Infants. When mobile infants are curious about an object or their own body, they have some kind of goal in mind. There is something they are trying to do or explore. Observe the children with the idea in mind that children are learning certain concepts from their toys and hands and then provide opportunities to support that learning.

- Notice, for example, whether many of the mobile infants are interested in dropping and placing objects in containers and then dumping them out. Provide different containers for them. Label what happens when objects are dumped or dropped. Observe the different strategies that children use to dump objects. Are they noticing that different objects make different sounds when dropped?

- Notice whether a child or several children are exploring the concept of space. Try offering a muffin tin and 12 tennis balls or a peg board set scaled to mobile infants' hands.

Observe the Children's Self-Help Attitudes and Skills and Document Their Learning for Children and Parents to Respect Children's Learning.

- Videotape or photograph each child as she or he attempts to put socks on or uses other self-help skills such as handwashing. Take a series of photos that can be displayed for the children and parents. Note on the documentation what goals children have and the strategies they are using.

Box 12.5

Individual Child Planning Guide

Child's Name: *Lily*   Plans for Week (Date): *May 7, 2011*

Respect: Child's Emotions, Effort, Goals, Learning, and Relationships

Picture or sample: Lily loves to open the flaps on the picture board and smiles and claps when she sees the picture under the cloth flat. She takes turns with a peer who sits by her.

What would you choose to observe?

Respect and Reflect	**Relate**
Date all notes:	**What will you do to support my development?**
What am I doing?	• **Responsive interactions**
Lifting the flap and looking at the picture.	*Lily loves it when a teacher or peer sits near here and looks at the photos with her.*
What am I feeling?	
I seem to feel happy and excited.	• **Environment: Toys, materials**
What am I learning?	• **Opportunities**
I am using my fine motor skills of reaching and grasping. I'm learning to manipulate different materials. I'm also learning new vocabulary words and that pictures are symbols for the real object or person. I am learning how to take turns with a peer when one wants to look at the pictures, too.	*Change the photos under the flap every two weeks and include a few items that Lily may not know. Try to bring in the real object, too, so that Lily can touch and play with the real object and then look at the photo.*

Provide Opportunities for Peers to Cooperate and Play Together as Well as Alone.

- Provide a cozy corner where a child can go to do a puzzle alone.
- Provide mats that children can place on the floor to define a space to work with manipulatives.

Planning for Mobile Infants' Fine Motor Development

Box 12.5 is an observation planning guide that is already filled out. What other opportunities could you offer?

TODDLERS AND TWOS: 16–36 MONTHS

Children are able to manipulate toys, real objects, and natural materials in surprisingly sophisticated ways. They make marks on paper with a sturdy crayon. They can pound and roll play dough and clay and they have figured out how to place objects (like feathers) into tall containers (like pop or soda bottles). They can begin to use a spoon to eat, although when tired or frustrated they will use what works—their hands.

A Glimpse of Toddlers' and Twos' Fine Motor Development

After Selena went to a workshop on developing children's fine motor, manipulation, and construction skills, she began to document the children's interests and how they are developing. At 9 months, Chita uses her whole hand as a fist around a crayon (supinate position) and bangs it on a piece of paper (see Figure 12.3) (Payne & Isaacs, 2005).

Lan, at 2 years of age, uses a grasp on a crayon that is more of a palm-down position in which his fingers curl around the crayon and his index finger points toward the crayon point (pronate position)(see Figure 12.4)(Payne & Isaacs, 2005). He can make more precise marks with the crayon.

Bessie also is 2 years old. With Selena's emotional support, Bessie tries to put large pegs into a pegboard, put together two-piece puzzles with knobs on the pieces, and slip large poker chips into a slot that Selena made in the plastic lid of a coffee can. Bessie also likes face puzzles that Selena makes from photos of the children in the room. Selena prints a photo on 8 × 10 paper, laminates it or covers it with clear contact paper, and then cuts it into two to four pieces.

Selena noticed that several children in her group were fascinated by light and shadows. She and her co-teacher decided that they would provide many opportunities for the children to experiment with light while developing their fine motor skills. They placed colored cellophane over the end of cardboard tubes and fastened the cellophane with rubber bands so that the children manipulate the tubes to look through them. Selena placed these tubes in the manipulative area. In the dramatic play area, they draped a blanket over a card table and provided flashlights for the children to use. They found an overhead projector and set it up in a corner of the room with a sheet on the wall. The children often played there, experimenting with light and shadows. Selena talked with the director about buying a light table that could be shared with several other classrooms. The light table came with materials that allowed the light to show through them. Selena and her co-teacher and the children all

These materials encourage children to use their eyes and hands in coordination with each other.

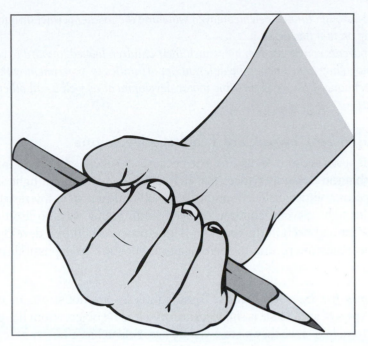

Figure 12.3   Supinate Grasp

picked up leaves, brought them inside, and examined the structure of the leaves when placed on the light table. The teachers asked families to observe what their children knew about light. Several parents commented that their children were afraid of the dark and liked a night light. So, Selena and her co-teacher provided more opportunities for the children to create and become comfortable with darkness by allowing children to take turns shutting out the lights in the room, by creating dark spaces with large boxes and blankets, and by providing

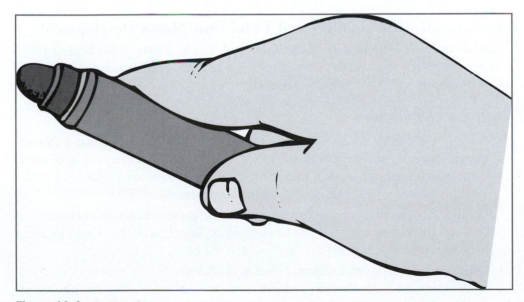

Figure 12.4   Pronate Grasp

a long crawl-through tunnel. Selena enjoyed watching the toddlers crawl through the tunnel while holding on to a flashlight.

All the parents commented on how much their children looked forward to coming to the center and how they talked about the different opportunities to experiment with light. These experiences enhanced the children's fine motor development as well as all other domains of development.

The Toddler and Twos Care Teacher's Decisions

Selena made a decision to focus on light because of several children's interests. She also knew that the new experiences that help children learn about light also support their fine motor abilities. Selena found that not all children were interested in experimenting with light. Several children enjoyed finding new ways to use the toys and equipment that had been in the room for a long time. As children develop, a familiar toy often becomes interesting to them again as they see new possibilities for what they can do with the toy.

Adaptations for Special Needs. Bessie's muscles are not strong or well coordinated. At 2 years of age, Bessie is still working on releasing objects from her grasp, a skill her friends have had since they were 1 year of age. Selena has a variety of toys that offer this experience, and she provides emotional support to help her persist through small frustrations. Selena's adaptations are responsive to Bessie's interests. She doesn't always have to offer special materials—just the *right* materials to match Bessie's interests.

Diversity/Culture. Selena knows that some of her families offer their children crayons, paper, markers, and finger painting at home, while other families are concerned about their children having such messy materials at an early age. Selena shows respect for both sets of family beliefs and concerns. However, most of the families agree that they want their children to have those experiences in the program.

Opportunities for Toddlers' and Twos' Fine Motor Development
Provide a Rich Variety of Materials. Toddlers and twos enjoy both familiar and new materials and toys to manipulate. Provide balls, pegs, construction materials—homemade and commercially produced.

Offer New Challenges.

- Offer a new experience for toddlers and twos who love to put objects into containers. Provide cardboard or plastic tubes of all sizes with different sizes of small balls, which are large enough to prevent choking. Encourage children to problem-solve about which balls fit into particular tubes.

- For toddlers and twos who enjoy cars and trucks, provide support for children as they roll the cars across the table to each other. Watch how they begin to adapt their rolling so that the other child can catch the car.

- Offer poster board with laminated photos of animals, family members, or classmates velcroed to the board. Toddlers and twos enjoy pulling the photos off the board and attaching them again. Ask, "How did you do that?" with a surprised tone of voice.

Figure 12.5   Poster Board with Laminated Photos

- For toddlers and twos who love water, offer a variety of experiences such as watering flowers with a pitcher, painting an outdoor sidewalk with a paintbrush and a bucket of water, and filling containers in the water table. Encourage them to problem-solve how to carry a small bucket of water all the way across the playground to water a flower.
- Offer flannel pieces and flannel boards while telling or reading a story to the children. Give each toddler who joins the group a flannel piece to hold and place it on the flannel board when that character appears in the story.
- Offer many opportunities for creative toddlers and twos to use art materials.
- Sing songs that engage children in fine motor and bilateral coordination activities.

Keep Interesting Building Materials in the Construction Area.

- Check the construction area: Are there blocks of all sizes and textures including wooden, foam, and vinyl; construction toys and accessories such as large Legos, wooden animals and people, cars, and trucks; and a solid floor that allows children to pile, push, and knock down stacked blocks?
- Provide larger/heavier blocks for toddlers and twos than those provided for mobile infants. Stay close to comment on the structures they build.
- Provide smaller cube blocks for toddlers and twos to line up or stack on top of each other.
- Toddlers' and twos' ability to dress and feed themselves is developing quickly.
- Toddlers and twos can help take a jacket off. If needed, pull off one sleeve and then let the toddler remove the rest of the jacket.

Box 12.6

Individually Responsive Group Planning Guide

Name of Group: _____ Week of: _____

Person(s) completing this guide: _____

Respect and Reflect

The children in my group are.... (Write about or document with brief sentences, photographs, or other means of capturing children's feeling, learning, and discovering. What interests them?)

Relate: Plans for the week to meet children's needs and interests

Songs/Fingerplays/Music

Stories/Books

Responsive Interactions

Environment: Toys, materials

Opportunities

Family/Cultural Experiences

Other

- Provide large shoes in the dramatic play area for toddlers to clomp around in, and shirts, scarves, and dress-up clothes to encourage toddlers and twos to dress and undress themselves.

- Spoons are handled more easily at this age, but children may still begin to use their hands to eat, as little hands get tired. Offer finger food as well as foods that require a spoon or fork.

- Encourage children to serve themselves with a large spoon in a bowl of apple-sauce, for example, while you hold the bowl.

- Provide small pitchers for toddlers and twos to pour their own water into a glass at the table.

Planning for Toddlers' and Twos' Fine Motor Development

Box 12.6 offers an opportunity to practice completing a group planning form. Use Selena's group to plan fine motor activities for the children for a week.

SUMMARY

Infants and toddlers rapidly learn how to coordinate their eye and hand movements to reach and grasp. They learn to use increasing precision in manipulation skills when exploring objects with the small muscles in their hands and fingers. They develop bilateral coordination skills as they hold an object with one hand and explore or operate with the other hand, pick up or manipulate objects with two hands, or use both hands freely. For example, when they hold a string in one hand and a bead in the other. They use the smaller muscles in their hands as they pick up blocks and other construction materials. By the age of 3, many toddlers also use their fine motor skills to undress themselves and put on socks, shoes, and shirts that go over the head (not button shirts). When teachers observe children carefully and respond to the children's individual and group needs, children's fine motor development, manipulation skills, and construction interests and skills develop quickly.

INVENTORY OF TEACHER PRACTICES

Fine Motor Development

Basic Concepts	A	S	R	Observation/ Reflection
Fine Motor—Reaching and Grasping				
I provide many sizes and shapes of toys.				
I provide many opportunities for children to explore and experiment with toys and materials that they can grasp, bang together, place in containers, etc.				
Fine Motor—Bilateral Coordination (use of both sides of their bodies together)				
I provide many opportunities for children to develop bilateral coordination.				
Fine Motor–Self-Help Skills				
I provide opportunities for mobile infants, toddlers, and twos to feed themselves with fingers and spoons.				
I encourage and support mobile infants, toddlers, and twos to help with undressing and dressing themselves.				
Manipulation Area				
I provide a manipulation area with a rich variety of toys and materials—puzzles, stacking rings, large beads to string, etc.				
I engage in reciprocal conversations with children in the manipulation area.				
I provide books in the manipulation area.				
Construction Area				
I provide a construction area for mobile infants, toddlers, and twos with a rich variety of toys and materials.				
I engage in reciprocal conversations with children in the construction area.				
I support teacher/child and peer relationships as children develop their fine motor, manipulation, and construction interests and skills.				

A = Always, S = Sometimes, R = Rarely

REFLECTIONS

1. What opportunities can a care teacher provide for children to use the fine muscles in their hands, fingers, and toes?
2. What opportunities could a care teacher provide to support children's bilateral coordination?
3. How could care teachers support the development of children's self-help skills while being developmentally appropriate (individually, age, and culturally)?

APPLICATIONS

1. Use the Inventory of Teacher Practices and observe in an early care and education center. Complete the inventory and discuss your observations with the teacher.
2. Interview a teacher in an early care and education program using the Inventory of Teacher Practices. Ask the teacher to reflect on how she implements the practices. Ask the teacher whether there are other practices that she or he thinks are important to use.
3. Interview two parents from different cultures. Ask them to reflect on their beliefs about self-help skills; for example, is it important that the child learn independence or interdependence (cooperation with family). Ask when they expect that children will feed or dress themselves and why.

RESOURCES

- *Developing baby's fine motor skills* by Katlyn Joy
  This is a very thorough, although accessible, article about fine motor development and activities and materials. Retrieved from http://www.thebabycorner.com/page/2501
- *Finger foods for babies*
  This article from KidsHealth.org describes how foods can safely be offered as finger foods as well as listing foods to offer. Retrieved from http://kidshealth.org/parent/pregnancy_newborn/feeding/finger_foods.html#
- Hinde, R. (1992b). Ethological and relationship approaches. In R. Vasta (Ed.), *Six theories of child development: Revised formulations and current issues* (pp. 251–285). London: JKP Press.

13

Opportunities for Creative, Symbolic/ Dramatic Play, and Sensory Development and Learning

After reading this chapter, you will be able to:

- RESPECT
  - The foundations of creativity, symbolic/dramatic play and learning, and sensory development
  - What children learn as they participate in creative, symbolic/ dramatic, and sensory play
  - Developmental possibilities
  - The behaviors of children that may indicate possible delays or disorders
- REFLECT
  - On the individual child's interests and goals during play and social interactions

- On your own comfort with creative and sensory play materials and activities
- On how culture may influence a child's, family's, and your own attitudes about creative, sensory, and symbolic/dramatic play
- RELATE
  - Plan interactions, materials, and environments for individual and small groups of children, to promote creativity, symbolic/dramatic play, and sensory play and learning,

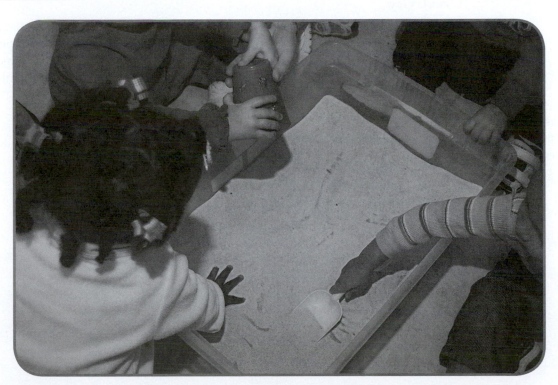

Mira, a toddler, loves to dip her hands into the water table. Lonnie, another toddler, spends hours in the creative area with play dough, crayons, and paint. Sue loves to wear hats and often holds and lovingly rocks dolls in the dramatic play area.

These children enjoy their days in creative ways while constantly learning through all their senses. Infants and toddlers are inventive. They begin to imagine, pretend, and use symbols during the first three years of life. These three areas demonstrate how infants and toddlers have wonderful ideas (Duckworth, 1987) about how the world works. Piaget, a psychologist, thought that through play children tested their guesses about how the world works, often coming to ingenious but wrong conclusions. However, through experimenting, actively exploring objects, and being surprised at the results, infants and toddlers learn as they play (Piaget, 1972).

RESPECT CREATIVITY, SYMBOLIC/DRAMATIC PLAY, AND SENSORY DEVELOPMENT AND LEARNING

When we think about young children being creative, we may also think of an area in the room in a center or in a family child care home where there are endless opportunities for children to use paint, crayons, paper, glue, scraps of material, easels, and fingerpaint. Care teachers offer these materials each day in an open-ended way to support infants and toddlers' creativity with art materials. In this chapter, we will discuss the creativity that happens everywhere in a room, family child care home, or outdoors and in the creative art area in the room.

Creativity

Young children are constantly creating things—sounds with their lips, noises with their toys, new sights by combining toys in original ways, new forms by crumpling or smoothing paper, and space by squeezing toys into a toy box. To be creative is to be imaginative, inspired, and innovative. Children may create "something" by combining

As children play, they constantly make new discoveries.

materials or ideas in ways that are brand new to them. Although creativity often results in a product (for example, a child's wonderful idea about how to quiet a crying baby doll), a person is also being creative during the process of thinking or acting. Young children may reveal creative thinking when they see the sky and describe it as a picture that continually changes, by combining several words together in new ways, or by thinking of ideas to solve a problem. There are endless opportunities for infants and toddlers to create at all times in all areas of the room.

Stages of Drawing. Just as in other domains of development, children make progress in predictable stages in their drawing and painting. More than 60 years ago, Lowenfeld (1947) observed that young children progress through the following stages: scribble (2–4 years), preschematic (4–6 years), schematic (7–9 years), dawning realism (9–11 years), and pseudorealism (11–13 years). The scribbling stage lasts from 2 to 4 years as children first make marks, then more controlled motions, then circles combined with lines, and then other shapes. Children experiment with shades of color, space, size, texture, and medium (paint, crayon, markers, etc.). At the end of the scribbling stage, children may begin to name their scribbles or part of their drawings, although the drawings may not look like what they call them. Naming and telling stories about their drawings are exciting because they represent a child's new way of thinking—the beginning of imaginative thinking and the ability to visualize in pictures (Lowenfeld, 1947; Lowenfeld & Brittain, 1987).

When infants and toddlers scribble, they do not look at a model and then try to draw it (Kellogg, 1970). Instead, they are delighting in moving their bodies and creating what seems to them to be an extension of themselves.

The preschematic stage starts in late preschool years and lasts until approximately age 7 years. During this stage children will continue experimenting with color, space, texture, strokes with a brush, and medium, but will also (at times) draw recognizable people or objects and name them (Lowenfeld, 1947). See Box 13.1 for information concerning the safety of creative arts' materials.

Symbolic and Dramatic Play

Symbolic play and dramatic play are also ways to be creative. This includes children using their bodies or objects to pretend. In imaginative or symbolic play, toddlers and 2-year-olds use symbols, such as themselves, photos, pictures, objects, and materials, to represent something real such as a telephone, a mom, cooking utensils, or an animal. Dramatic play includes children, usually toddlers, playing a role such as mom, dad, or a pet. Symbolic play and dramatic play occur in all areas of the room; for example, a toddler might suddenly drop to the floor and start meowing like a kitten.

Teachers often set up a special area in the room or home to encourage children to participate in

Box 13.1

Art and Craft Safety Guide

When teachers and families provide crayons, chalk, paint sets, colored pencils, or modeling clay or any other art materials with infants and toddlers it is recommended that parents/guardians purchase only those products labeled with the statement "Conforms to ASTM D-4236" (CPSC Document #5016) and that have no cautionary warnings on the label (U.S. Consumer Product Safety Commission, n.d.).

The U.S. Consumer Product Safety Commission (www.cpsc.gov) also maintains lists of product recalls.

symbolic play and dramatic play in depth. Often a center is created with a pretend kitchen with small-sized toy appliances, food, kitchen utensils, and telephones. Dolls, blankets, baby beds, bottles, a small bookshelf, and empty food boxes may also be in the play area. Teachers add dress-up clothes including hats, purses, shirts, scarves, and shoes to encourage mobile infants and toddlers to explore the materials. Two-year-olds are encouraged to play a role, perhaps a dog, a mom, a dad, or a cook, and objects like rocks (too large to swallow) become money, food, or medicine in children's minds. This area is often a favorite place for mobile infants and toddlers to play.

Mobile infants and toddlers grow in many areas of development while playing in the imaginative area. They grow emotionally as they feel powerful when playing with equipment, such as a pretend stove, when they are too small to touch the real one at home. They are able to express emotions such as affection, fear, sadness, and anger in a safe environment. Language grows as children not only learn the names of objects, but also describe how they are feeling, what they want a peer to do, or protest a peer entering the play. Motor development grows as children of all ages manipulate the toys, try to spread a blanket on the floor, push dolls in strollers, or handle pots and pans. Pretending and using symbols are an important part of intellectual development.

Westby (1980) created a symbolic play scale to observe and understand the stages of infants' and toddlers' development in their ability to use symbols and play roles. All infants and toddlers, including children with special needs (Casby, 2003), progress through these stages in pretend play. Westby (2000) found that from 17–19 months, children engage in autosymbolic play. They may pretend to sleep, drink from a cup, or eat from a spoon. From 19–22 months, they use objects as symbols; for example, they may use a brush on a doll's hair, feed a doll a bottle, or cover a doll with a blanket. At 24 months, children may represent daily experiences and play house, but objects must be realistic and close to life size. At 2½ years, children may represent events that are meaningful but less frequently experienced, such as doctor/sick child or store shopping. Children still need props that look like the item they are pretending to use; for example, they might use a toy apple that looks like a real apple. By age 3, children play out events of a scene in sequence—driving to the doctor, waiting in the waiting room, getting a shot, crying, and going home. A child might create a new ending; for example, instead of getting a shot from the doctor, the child's pretend dog might get the shot. Westby's scale (1980) has been helpful to teachers and other professionals who work with children with special needs, including autism, because she also identifies language development that coincides with symbolic development. Teachers who understand how children progress in symbolic play will be able to provide a variety of materials to children that will encourage this type of play.

One researcher, DeLoache (2005), has shown how difficult it is for a child to think symbolically. Her research shows that infants and toddlers often mistake a pretend object for a real object; for example, they may try to sit down in a doll's chair that is obviously (to adults) too small for them (Child Study Center, 2007).

Sensory Development

Infants and toddlers are sensory creatures who learn through sensory experiences. Infants and toddlers use their senses before they are born, and they have remarkable capabilities that they use the minute they are born. They open their eyes wide and clearly see the face of their mother from about 8–10″ away. They can smell their mother's milk, hear the voices of those who are taking care of them, and feel the touch of human skin and the blankets that swaddle them.

Infants have remarkable hearing. Researchers found that babies born prematurely between 30 to 35 weeks after conception could discriminate differences in words that were repeated with only a change in a vowel—words such as "not," "nit," and "net" (Cheour-Luhtanen, Alho, Sainio, Rinne, Reinikainen, Pohjavuori, & Renlund, 2009). Visual skills develop rapidly as well. Even at birth, infants prefer to look at faces that are right side up rather than upside down (Leo & Simon, 2009). By 10 months of age, infants looked at an object if an adult looked at it with eyes open, but not when the adult faced it with her eyes closed (Brooks & Meltzoff, 2005). They use their visual skills to understand when adults communicate interest in an object. Infants' taste and smell skills are just as remarkable.

Newborns show preferences for certain smells over others. They prefer the smell of chocolate over rotten eggs (Pomares, Schirrer, & Abadie, 2002), just as most adults do. Children's preference for certain smells also affects how they react to certain foods. Children have individual taste and food preferences early in life. There seems to be a strong-to-moderate genetic factor in young children's willingness to taste and eat foods, but this can be moderated or changed by modeling and introducing new flavors gradually (Harris, 2008).

Touch is one of the most important senses for young children. There is a growing body of evidence concerning the importance of extended skin-to-skin contact between mothers and babies immediately after birth (Vincent, 2011). This contact helps the baby regulate heartbeat and temperature. Also, appropriate touch, if it is responsive to young children's cues, promotes secure attachment. What can teachers and parents do to support sensory development? Astute teachers know that young children use their senses at all times of the day when they are playing, eating, drinking, or just being by themselves or with others. When we think about curriculum, we also think of an area in the room in a center or in a family child care home that encourages sensory exploration. This area often has a water table or tubs, a sand table or tubs, and opportunities to touch various textures and smell different scents or aromas.

RESPECT THEORIES CONCERNING CREATIVITY, SYMBOLIC/DRAMATIC PLAY, AND SENSORY DEVELOPMENT AND LEARNING

Piaget thought that creativity is an aspect of how children think through assimilation and accommodation (Ayman-Nolley, 1999). As young children create, they construct new knowledge. "The principal goal of education is to create men who are capable of doing new things, not simply of repeating what other generations have done—men who are creative, inventive and discoverers . . ." (Piaget, 1954).

Teachers cannot overestimate, however, the importance of adult support for creativity, sensory development, and imaginative play to the child's development. Vygotsky, a theorist, thought that young children learn how to imagine, pretend, and create in social interactions with important adults and peers. Adults not only set up an environment that invites sensory exploration, creativity, playing, and imagining, but also suggest different roles that young children might play, model the pretend use of objects, and participate in acting out scenarios (such as pretending to eat imaginary cookies from a plate). Vygotsky's theory (1986), called a *sociocultural theory*, emphasized that young children learn when they interact with more skilled adults and peers.

Both Piaget (1951) and Vygotsky (1986) consider play as necessary for creativity to occur. The time that teachers allow for children's play with art materials affects their creative development. Hanline, Milton, and Phelps (2007), after observing preschool children's easel drawings over three years, concluded that the amount of time that children engaged in easel painting influenced the complexity of the art product. Teachers can support children's creativity by providing interesting materials and giving children time to explore them.

Theorists emphasize the importance of imitation in young children's learning. Meltzoff (1985) found that when he demonstrated a novel way (touching his head on the toy) to activate the lights on a toy lying on a table, 14-month-olds imitated this novel way both immediately and after 24 hours. As you have probably observed, young children learn, not only through experimentation with materials, but also through their abilities to observe and imitate.

Other theorists such as Adolph and Robinson (2008), who promote dynamic systems theory, and Bronfenbrenner (2004) emphasize the role of culture and multiple levels of influence on the child and families. Creativity in some cultures may be expressed by different strategies that children devise for playing with a ball or a tin-can. In other cultures, toddlers may use their myriad plastic toys to create a train of toys. Brooker and Woodhead (2010, p. 27) describe best how children create and participate in sensory play, "Young children use every opportunity to play, with whatever resources they can find."

As you study symbolic/dramatic play of children from different cultures you may see older toddlers in the Sudan in Africa pretend to make sorghum pancakes with dirt on a can top (Katz, 2004, p. 27) and older toddlers in the United States make wheat or oat pancakes on a pretend stove in their child care center. Bornstein (2006, p. 115), as reported in Brooker and Woodhead (2010, p. 24), summarized the research in the following way, based on his summary of cross-cultural studies: "Although human societies vary in the amount and type of play, anthropological accounts attest that fully developed pretend play . . . appears to be universal". Young children in all cultures seem to try out adult roles through play.

Recent theorists called neoconstructivists (Scott, 2009) focus on brain research, perception, and how children learn. Researchers Cacchione, Möhring, and Bertin (2011) asked an interesting question that had not been explored before—can 9-month-old infants visually discriminate different artists' paintings and show preference for a particular artist? The authors then observed whether infants would habituate to one artist's painting and visually notice when a different artist's paintings were introduced. Nine-month-old infants can discriminate between Picasso's and Monet's paintings and actually prefer Picasso's, possibly because of the unusual colors and shapes.

This type of research will continue to shed light on children's ability to develop their creative, sensory, and symbolic/dramatic attitudes and skills.

RESPECT DEVELOPMENTAL AND LEARNING POSSIBILITIES IN CREATIVE, SYMBOLIC/ DRAMATIC, AND SENSORY DEVELOPMENT

The following behaviors described in Box 13.2 may occur, depending on the child's experience and culture.

Box 13.2

Developmental and Learning Possibilities in Creative, Symbolic/Dramatic, and Sensory Development

YOUNG INFANTS	MOBILE INFANTS	TODDLERS	TWOS
0–9 Months	8–18 Months	16–24 Months	24–36 Months
Create through making unique sounds with their mouth and clapping objects together to make sounds.	Can begin to make a mark with a safe crayon by banging on the paper. They create by experimenting with what different materials can do. They combine materials and objects to create.	Toddlers are constantly investigating and experimenting. They enjoy a variety of creative materials, such as finger paints, natural materials, and glue. Toddlers enjoy poking play dough and patting it into containers. Toddlers may begin to scribble with a safe marker or pencil on paper.	Twos may begin to make circles when they draw, but primarily scribble—making marks in a random way on a piece of paper. They are innovative—using and combining materials and toys in creative ways. Twos continue to enjoy a variety of art materials.
By the end of this period, the infant may begin to understand a few symbols, e.g., that the opening of a door means that mommy is home.	May understand more symbols, e.g., that a picture of a duck represents a real duck.	Toddlers engage in autosymbolic play—pretending to drink from a cup or eat with a spoon. They may start to use objects as symbols—use a brush on a doll's hair, feed a doll, or cover a doll.	Twos may represent daily experiences, such as cooking on a play stove, but objects usually must be realistic. By 2½ they may pretend to act out an event that happens less frequently—going to the doctor.
Young infants explore materials with all of their senses. They mouth, touch with their hands and feet, observe, and listen to learn. They need appropriate touch—hugs, cuddling, and holding that is responsive to their needs and communication cues.	Mobile infants are on the move, creeping, crawling, and walking. They enjoy a variety of sensory materials such as paper to crumple, light tables, natural materials, and sound boxes. They pick up small objects with their pincer grasp.	Toddlers "must" experiment to learn with all of their senses. Most toddlers enjoy sand, water, natural materials, art materials, and snow play; some children, however, may be hesitant to touch these materials. They usually "must" touch to learn. Provide safe toys and different textures to handle and walk on.	Twos continue to enjoy a variety of sensory experiences.

RESPECT SIGNS OF CONCERN IN CREATIVE, SYMBOLIC/DRAMATIC, AND SENSORY DEVELOPMENT AND LEARNING

Determining hearing and vision problems early is critically important. Researchers have found that if infants' hearing challenges are detected before 2 months of age, the outcomes for language development are significantly better (Yoshinaga-Itano & Apuzzo, 1998; Yoshinaga-Itano, Sedey, Coulter, & Mehl, 1998); but if not, children's hearing challenges are frequently discovered between 2–3 years of age, long after an optimal period for language development. The American Speech and Hearing Association (ASHA, 2009) reports that noninvasive measures should be used when infants are newborns, in order to determine hearing loss early in children's lives. Robinson (2009) reported that infants and toddlers need hearing aids (HA) or cochlear implants (CI). "CI is a small electronic device that helps hard-of-hearing children and adults sense sound. Part of it sits behind the ear and the other part is placed under the skin. A CI includes a microphone, a speech processor, a transmitter and receiver/stimulator, and an electrode array that send impulses to different regions of the auditory nerve (NIDCD, 2009)" Signs of hearing challenges in children from birth to 3 include the following:

- Does not startle at loud noises.
- Does not turn to the source of a sound from birth to 3 or 4 months of age.
- Does not say single words, such as "dada" or "mama" by 1 year of age.
- Turns head when he or she sees you but not if you only call out his or her name. This sometimes is mistaken for not paying attention or just ignoring, but could be the result of a partial or complete hearing loss.
- Seems to hear some sounds but not others. (CDC, 2011b)

Approximately 1.4 million children in the world are blind (USAID, 2009) and three times as many have serious vision challenges. Newborn screening is imperative; eye screening should be conducted at birth and at 6 to 8 weeks. To prevent blindness, cataracts must be removed by 3 months of age. Signs of vision challenges in children from birth to 3 include the following:

- Excessive tearing—this may indicate blocked tear ducts
- Red or encrusted eye lids—this could be a sign of an eye infection
- Constant eye turning—this may signal a problem with eye muscle control
- Extreme sensitivity to light—this may indicate an elevated pressure in the eye
- Appearance of a white pupil—this may indicate the presence of an eye cancer (American Optometric Association, 2012)

Infants should have their vision tested between 6 and 12 months. The American Optometric Association has a program called Project InfantSEE® in which participating doctors will provide a comprehensive infant eye assessment to children in that age range at no cost to the family (American Optometric Association, 2012).

REFLECT ON CREATIVITY, SYMBOLIC/DRAMATIC PLAY, AND SENSORY DEVELOPMENT

As care teachers together with families consider the following questions, they learn about young children's development, and are in awe at their motivation to learn, how creative they are, and how they explore with all of their senses (see Box 13.3). Young children are eager learners when given opportunities to choose in a carefully designed environment and in interactions that are responsive to both individual children and the group dynamics.

RELATE TO CREATIVE, SYMBOLIC/DRAMATIC, AND SENSORY DEVELOPMENT AND LEARNING

Infant/toddler care teachers play an important role in supporting children's creative, symbolic/dramatic, and sensory development. As teachers provide responsive interactions and create an interesting enriched environment, children develop a love of creating, pretending, using objects and materials as symbols, and exploring with all of their senses.

THE YOUNG INFANT: BIRTH TO 9 MONTHS

The young infant explores those sensory opportunities within his reach—a care teacher's face, a blanket, a peer lying next to him, the milk he drinks, and the toys he grasps—while safely near his care teacher. Within positive relationships with teachers, young infants *create* new ways each day to play with toys and communicate with others.

Box 13.3

Reflect on Creativity, Symbolic/Dramatic Play, and Sensory Development

Creative

- What objects do children combine and how do they combine them?
- How does each child explore the properties of different materials—paint, paper, fingerpaint, glue, play dough, sand, water, metal, cardboard?
- What strategies do they use to explore these materials? What surprises them? What are their goals? How are they problem-solving with the materials?
- How do children develop relationships as they experiment with creative materials?

Symbolic/Dramatic Play

- When do children begin to understand symbols, for example, a symbol for a name or a stop sign?
- When and how do children begin to use a pretend object (telephone, doll, pretend food) and play with it in an imaginative way?
- When do children begin to pretend to be someone or something other than themselves? Who or what do they pretend to be?
- How do infants and toddlers use the symbolic/dramatic play materials—dolls, baby beds, pretend kitchen appliances?

Sensory

- How do children use their sight, hearing, touch, smell, and taste to learn? Reflect on each separately and together. What are they learning?
- How do children use their senses to develop relationships?
- What are each child's interests in regard to sensory play?

A Glimpse of the Young Infant's Creative, Symbolic/Dramatic, and Sensory Development

Three-month-old Adara grasps Miriam's finger tightly as she lies on the floor. She seems to be watching how the sun reflects different colors on the wall. Her eyes turn to Miriam's face—the best sensory experience of all. Paulo, who is a few months older than Adara, shakes his rattle and then shakes it again. He is beginning to understand that he is the cause of the sound. Paulo loves the sensory feeling of putting his toes to his mouth.

Jack (6 months old) tightly holds the fur of his stuffed bunny as he puts it over his eyes to play peek-a-boo with his teacher. At times, Jack scratches or gently feels the edge of the quilt, the floor, the teacher's face, and puppets on Miriam's hands. He is seriously intent on all of these sensory experiences. He likes having his hands washed after his diapers are changed and before the teacher feeds him his favorite cereal and green beans. He solemnly anticipates the next bite of food. With his mouth open, he moves toward the spoon held by his teacher.

Takala enjoys dropping toys. She seems to listen to the sounds they make as they fall to the floor with a bang or a thump. As she moves from a sitting position to crawling, she pushes a large plastic bottle full of colored water and sparkling stars that is glued tightly shut. Sometimes she holds her favorite blanket and rubs it repeatedly on her face.

The Young Infant Care Teacher's Decisions

Miriam knows that she is the most important sensory experience for young infants but that infants are touching, tasting, smelling, looking, and listening all the time. They are learning through their senses. She lets them touch her face, her hands, and her clothing. She places them on the floor on blankets of different textures. She provides rattles and small stuffed animals for the infants to hold and feel. As she sees that they are beginning to understand that they can cause a sound, she makes sure that some of the objects they hold make different sounds when the infants shake, bang, or drop them. As she reads to one or two children, she lets the children touch the pictures in the book. She shows an infant a picture of a ball and gives the child a ball to hold to help her learn about representation.

Adaptations for Special Needs. For Jack, every moment of connection is important. Miriam uses his sense of comfort from the softness of the bunny to play a peek-a-boo game with him. He really concentrates on food, so she uses meal times as an opportunity to talk quietly to him about what he is eating and how much she likes to be with him.

Diversity/Culture. Miriam is aware that families and cultures view sensory experiences in different ways. Although Paulo's family is excited about Paulo finding his toes, they are less than enthusiastic about Paulo touching other people's faces, including their own. They value respect for another person and think that touching others (without their permission) does not show respect. As Miriam and Paulo's family discussed this issue, Miriam was able to discuss the sensory needs of infants and Paulo's parents were able to share their beliefs.

Opportunities for Young Infants' Creativity, Symbolic/Dramatic Play, and Sensory Development
Encourage Combining Materials in New Ways.

- Provide containers of different sizes and shapes: cardboard boxes, safe cans, oatmeal boxes.

- When a child begins to shake, push, or roll objects, provide water shake bottles (Miller, 1999).
- Let go of rules about keeping materials in one area.

Attend to All the Senses. In creative and sensory development, infants are learning with all their senses.

- Provide contact paper with the sticky side up. Give them safe materials, such as tissue paper, to place on the contact paper.
- Provide water shake bottles (see Box 13.4).
- Set up tubs full of safe materials of different textures (that are too large for infants to swallow)—lids, balls, small boxes.
- Create sensory books. Glue fabric of different textures on sturdy paper.
- Provide fabric squares of different textures.
- Use pill bottles to hold cotton balls soaked or rolled in different odors (vanilla, cinnamon, vinegar, etc.)

Box 13.4

Water Shake Bottles

Use safe plastic bottles and add water, oil, food coloring, beads, buttons, and other interesting materials. Tape the cap on the bottle with care so that an infant can never open the bottle. Let infants shake, rattle, and roll the bottles.

Planning for Young Infants' Creative, Sensory, and Symbolic/Dramatic Play Development

Box 13.5 offers another opportunity to add your observations. If you have the opportunity to observe a child, do so. If not, use one of Miriam's children with an expanded, if imagined, observation.

Box 13.5

Individual Child Planning Guide (2)

Child's Name: _____   Plans for Week of (Date): _____

Person(s) completing the guide: _____

Respect: Child's Emotions, Effort, Goals, Learning, and Relationships

Reflect	**Relate**
What am I doing?	**What will you do to support my development and learning?**
What am I feeling?	• **Responsive Interactions**
What am I learning?	• **Environment: Toys, materials**
	• **Opportunities**

THE MOBILE INFANT: 8–18 MONTHS

Mobile infants are learning by using all of their senses. They must touch, combine objects, create, and experiment constantly to learn about the properties of objects and about their own capabilities. Wise care teachers offer mobile infants many opportunities to move while experiencing a variety of sensory and creative materials.

A Glimpse of the Mobile Infant's Creative, Symbolic/Dramatic, and Sensory Development

Albert moved from the infant room to a larger room with a group of children. There is more room for the mobile infants to move, create, play with messy materials, and participate in imaginative play. All the children still need to touch, taste, and handle everything that they can see and hold, although they now are able to touch fragile things (like a flower) gently. The mobile infants enjoy all the opportunities that Albert provides for them to paint with all kinds of brushes and paint rollers, play with play dough, and use natural materials like feathers to create a collage. Albert also offers—on different days—all types of paint recommended by Kohl (2002) in her book First Art: Art Experiences for Toddlers and Twos*— egg paint, cornstarch vinegar paint, face paint, flour paint, fragrant paint, cold cream paint, corn syrup and food coloring paint, and many more. He makes the paint with the children and then makes it available to them. He tries to make paint available every day, but a teacher needs to be in the art area to support the children, and that isn't always possible.*

Several pans of water placed close together catch Radwan's eye. He stands beside a pan on a short table, picks up the toy giraffe in the water, and begins to wash it with a small bar of soap and a washcloth—water dripping everywhere. Radwan also likes to sit by or on a very large piece of white paper on the floor in the creative area, dip his large paintbrush into the paint, and spatter it with gusto on the paper. Albert stays close and comments as Radwan paints (without interfering with his play): "You really like to paint. What a bright red. You're coloring the paper all red." Radwan seemed to be trying to fill the white paper with paint as he holds the paintbrush with a hammer grip and paints, using the large muscles in his arms to make big blotches on the paper. Goro does not paint as often as Radwan because he gets very upset when he gets paint on his hands or clothing.

Sometimes, Goro and Radwan have fun in a small symbolic/dramatic play area. They try to put big adult-size shoes on their feet. When they try to walk with the big shoes on, Goro laughs so hard that everyone in the room begins to smile. One child leads and the other follows as they wind through the room clomping their feet. Soon, a parade of mobile toddlers is following them with gleeful laughs. Albert sits and watches, saying, "You are in a parade." Once, Goro tried to go to sleep in the doll's bed, and Goro and Radwan used baby bottles to pretend to feed the dolls.

Albert talked with Lily's parents to determine ways to help Lily participate in creative and sensory play. He also talked with the early childhood special educator (ECSE), who comes to the class on Fridays, to discuss how Albert can support Lily's development. The ECSE suggested that Albert use a supportive seat to help Lily sit at a table with the other children. In this position, Lily can play with water or sand and paint with her peers.

The Mobile Infant Care Teacher's Decisions

Albert read an article about toddler glee (Lokken 2000a, 2000b), and he is happy to see the children in his room experience glee with each other as they do symbolic/

dramatic play. Adult shoes seemed like magnets for the mobile infants' feet. They just had to put the shoes on and try to walk.

Albert observed Goro and Radwan use symbolic play that involved an object other than themselves—they fed a doll with a pretend bottle. He added more pretend materials to the symbolic/dramatic play area, such as pretend foods that represented Goro and Radwan's culture.

Albert is excited that many of the mobile infants are so enthusiastic about painting. He used to do crafts with the mobile infants (such as an egg carton caterpillar), but soon realized that (1) the infants weren't interested, (2) the products were often above their abilities to glue and paint, and (3) the end product was more his than the infants'. He read about the importance of encouraging children to create, so now he puts out the materials and observes as the children experiment with color, texture, space, lines, and the properties of different materials.

Mobile infants like to spread paint on paper on the floor with their hands and with a wide assortment of brushes. Albert knows that mobile infants try many strategies with their hands and brushes to make marks and dabs on the paper—banging, sliding, dipping, poking, and pushing. Albert often provides some words to describe what each child is doing. He tries to avoid saying, "Good boy" or "Good girl," or "That's beautiful," but rather he describes what he sees them doing or how they are feeling.

Adaptations for Special Needs. Albert knows that social interaction and participation are crucial for children with special needs. Children will imitate peers' actions when they can (Hanna & Meltzoff, 1993). Through talking with the family and the special education consultant who comes to his classroom, he is able to adapt the environment to allow Lily to be successful. He heard at a workshop: "Find a way for all children to be successful at what they want to do." Her Velcro glove can hold an adapted paint brush or a marker. She can enjoy sparkling water bottles, smelly pill containers, and different textures without adaptations.

Diversity/Culture. Albert knows that cultural sensitivity is much more than providing symbolic/dramatic play materials from diverse cultures, but he also knows that it is important for children to have their cultures represented in a center room or a family child care home. He knows that the symbolic/dramatic play area is a place where the toys and materials can represent a variety of cultures. He asks parents about their family's favorite foods and then tries to find pretend food that matches.

Opportunities for Mobile Infants' Creative, Symbolic/Dramatic, and Sensory Development

Build on Their Existing Strategies to Develop New Strategies. Mobile infants will explore crayons, paint, and other media using the strategies they have—banging, combining together, touching, tasting, smelling, throwing, bouncing, and so on.

- Offer a variety of crayons, paint, and all types of play dough to the older infants; keep children safe while using the materials; and observe their exploration and creativity.

Box 13.6

Recipe for Play Dough

Vegetable oil: 1 cup
Flour: 4 cups
Water: 1 cup
Food coloring: 1 tsp

    Mix ingredients together well. Encourage the children to mix with their hands. Knead the dough until smooth.

- Model a new strategy, such as rolling the play dough, but do not expect the mobile infant to imitate you.
- Use language to describe specifically what a child is doing—poking, squeezing, banging, and so on.

Present Creative Materials. Mobile infants are ready to paint with brushes. They usually use a hammer grip on the handles as the muscles in their hands are still developing. Their grip will become more adultlike in preschool or early elementary grades. They may start making marks with a paintbrush, but soon their hands will tire from holding a brush and they will begin to use their hands and fingers.

- Place large pieces of paper flat on the table or on the floor with an easy-to-clean surface under the paper.
- Pour the nontoxic paint from the large containers to nonspill cups or paint trays.
- Provide all types of brushes and rollers—paintbrushes, toothbrushes, bottle brushes, small paint rollers. Put several out each day and observe how children use the brushes and rollers: Which brushes or rollers are used first? Which are used the most? How do the children handle the brushes?

Use Play Dough to Experiment. Most older mobile infants like the texture of play dough and will explore the dough using all their schemas. See Box 13.6 for a recipe for play dough.

- Make a batch of nontoxic dough (see the recipe in the accompanying box) or purchase nontoxic play dough.
- Encourage mobile infants to experiment with the properties of play dough. Do not require them to make something with the play dough, but rather observe them as they squeeze, poke, and roll pieces of play dough as they explore what the material is and what they can do with it.
- Make all types of dough for mobile infants to experiment with—stretchy dough, rubbery flubbery dough, and play clay (Kohl, 2002).

Children Will Play Differently. Some mobile infants can be quite exuberant in their creative and sensory play, while others are hesitant to get wet or get paint or play dough on their hands or clothing.

- Respect family and cultural differences.
- Provide child-size aprons for children to wear when they experiment with paint.
- Start by making Jello, letting it set, placing it in baggies, and encouraging children to squeeze the bags. With this procedure, children do not get their hands wet, but they experience being creative.

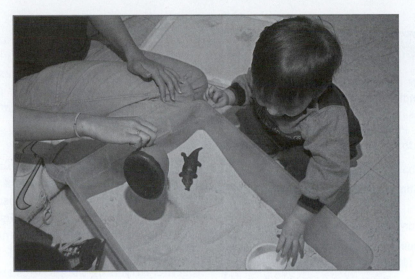

Sand, water, and other sensory materials can calm children as they learn about concepts such as space, quantity, and peer relationships.

Sand and Water Encourage Experimentation. Sand, water, and other sensory materials can calm children as they learn about the properties of the materials, experiment, and problem-solve. These materials can be therapeutic for a child who is experiencing emotional challenges.

- Miller (1999) suggests using dish tubs, baby bathtubs, or large, rectangular window boxes for water or sand play. Children can sit on the floor and easily reach into these types of containers.

- When mobile infants need their own space, provide plastic tubs—each big enough for one child to use. Set up four tubs close together to encourage social interaction while also giving each child his or her own space.

- Provide a variety of utensils, water wheels, containers, cups, funnels, plastic animals, wash cloths, and little bars of soap to encourage sensory and creative play.

- When mobile infants seem fascinated with water, support their curiosity and exploration by providing many opportunities to touch, taste, smell, listen to, and see water that is still, colored, running, dripping, or splashing over pebbles. Let them use water to wash dolls, plastic animals, toy cars, and their arms.

Provide Sensory Experiences That Contribute to Creativity, Imagination, and Problem-Solving.

- Survey the room or family child care home while asking yourself, "Are there a number of interesting textures for mobile infants to touch?"

- A piece of colored cellophane taped over the end of a cardboard tube inspires mobile infants to see the world in a new way.

- Provide unique materials with interesting textures: corrugated cardboard, velvet, contact paper with the sticky side up, and cellophane. Unique materials spark children's curiosity, create a state of puzzlement, and require children to adapt their thinking about what materials are made of or how materials can be used.

Box 13.7

Books for Babies

Infants enjoy picture books that encourage creativity, symbolic understanding, and sensory development. Provide sturdy books made of cardboard or vinyl books that are washable. Provide real objects and stuffed animals for pictures that are represented in the book.

I Hear, Helen Oxenbury. Candlewick (1995).

I Love Colors, Margaret Miller. Simon & Schuster (1999).

I See, Helen Oxenbury. Candlewick (1995).

I Touch, Helen Oxenbury. Random House Books for Young Readers (1986).

Pat the Bunny, Dorothy Kunhardt. Golden Books (1999).

The Rainbow Fish, Marcus Pfister. North-South Books (1992).

• Provide a sensory box with a sock attached to a hole in the top of the box. Cut open the closed end of the sock and glue it to the box. Add objects with different textures to the box and watch as mobile infants and toddlers put their hand in the sock with trepidation and excitement.

Books May Include a Variety of Sensory Experiences. Mobile infants enjoy teachers reading books that provide sensory experiences; for example, fuzzy tails on rabbits or textured pictures. At times, two mobile infants will sit on the floor near the book area and look at a book together, touching the pictures and laughing.

Provide Many Opportunities for Mobile Infants to Use to Pretend. Mobile infants will begin to use objects such as toy telephones to

Box 13.8

Individual Child Planning Guide (1)

Child's Name: _____   Plans for Week (Date): _____

Respect: Child's Emotions, Effort, Goals, Learning, and Relationships

Respect and Reflect	*Relate*
What am I doing?	**What will you do to support my learning?**
How am I feeling?	• **Responsive Interactions**
What am I learning?	• **Environment: Toys, materials**
• *Emotional*	• **Opportunities**
• *Social*	
• *Cognitive*	
• *Language*	
• *Motor*	

imitate how they see adults using these materials. They might pretend to talk on the telephone or use a comb on a doll's hair.

- Set up an area in the room for symbolic/dramatic play.
- Provide realistic representations of familiar objects (toy telephone, toy food, dolls).
- Create familiar scenes, such as a pretend grocery store, next to the housekeeping area to encourage children to go back-and-forth from home to store.

Planning for Mobile Infants' Creative, Symbolic/Dramatic Play, and Sensory Development

Box 13.8 provides an opportunity to practice completing a planning guide focusing on creativity. Use a real observation or one of Albert's children.

TODDLERS AND TWOS: 16–36 MONTHS

Toddlers and twos are busy creating, pretending, and using all of their senses to experience their world. Toddlers and twos awe adults with their discoveries as they experiment with materials in an enriched environment with responsive adults. Care teachers think creatively as they provide both natural materials such as sand, ribbon, and wood as well as purchased materials such as paint, crayons, paper, and sticky contact paper. When teachers give children the gift of time to explore these materials each day, children will refine and expand how they use them.

A Glimpse of the Toddler in Creative, Symbolic/Dramatic Play, and Sensory Development

Selena, the toddler teacher, knows her children well because she has been with most of the group since they were infants. Selena and her co-teacher know that Chita loves to play in water. It seems to calm Chita after she has a tantrum and often can help prevent Chita from feeling stressed. Painting and sand play also seem to calm her and she can attend to these activities for long periods of time.

Lan likes to play near other children in the symbolic/dramatic play area. He often will turn from his play and watch the other children trying on clothes, wrapping dolls in blankets, or putting "babies" to bed. Several children like to tell Lan that he is a "baby" and then they have him lie on the floor and cover him with blankets. Lan seems to enjoy this activity but Selena wonders if she should help Lan take a more active rather than a passive role during symbolic/dramatic play.

Bessie likes to play much of the time in the symbolic/dramatic play area. She wraps and rewraps dolls in baby blankets, feeds them with a pretend bottle, and puts them to bed. Sometimes she becomes distressed when other children try to play with "her" dolls and she pushes them out of the area. After being pushed out, most of the children just come back into the symbolic/dramatic play area and play with other toys. Selena tries to prevent Bessie from pushing by staying close when Bessie is with her dolls and suggesting ways for the other children to join Bessie's play.

Sam likes to try everything during play. When he is not eating or having his diaper changed, he plays with the blocks, then paints on the easel, then plays in the water, and then sits on the rug and plays with puzzles and toy cars. At times, he is drawn to the symbolic/dramatic play area, but most often, he pretends with blocks and cars. He is attracted to unique materials that Selena brings into the room and will combine them in original ways. His creative use of words often surprises both Selena and his parents.

The Toddler Care Teacher's Decisions

Selena makes sure that the water is available every day because, although all the children enjoy playing with water in a water table, Chita seems to need it to stay calm. Selena read that children not only need to trust their teacher, but also trust that certain materials such as crayons, paper, water, an easel and paint, dolls, and the symbolic/dramatic play area be available at all times.

Adaptations for Special Needs. Bessie's play tends to be less creative than that of the other children. She likes to repeat the same activity over and over. Early childhood special educators sometimes call this "perseverance," an inability to change or vary activity. Bessie's doll play, the wrapping and unwrapping of baby dolls, may be more perseverance than symbolic play. Selena isn't worried about this because Bessie's cognitive understanding is delayed, and it may take her some months before she begins real symbolic play. In the meantime, her presence in an area as busy as the play house helps Bessie have more social contact with her peers. Selena tries to coach Bessie in participating in their play.

Diversity/Culture. Selena and her co-teacher talked with Lan's family to determine whether they wanted Lan to be "passive" or if they wanted him to be a leader during peer play. To Selena's surprise, she discovered that the family thought about Lan's behavior very differently than she did. Lan's family did not consider his passive behavior with peers to be a concern and, in fact, they did not consider his behavior to be passive. Rather, they thought that his behavior represented their culture's emphasis on being cooperative and not being bossy. This information inspired Selena to ask families before assuming that she knew what they were thinking.

Opportunities for Toddlers' and Twos' Creative, Symbolic/Dramatic, and Sensory Development

Provide Opportunities for Creating and Imagining. The possibilities for creativity and imagining are endless. A creative teacher promotes creativity in children.

- Give children choices of materials.
- Encourage children to problem-solve. For example, instead of retrieving a helium balloon that is resting on the ceiling of the room, coach children about how to problem-solve getting it down. Then put away the balloon. It can be dangerous.
- Provide long periods of time and props for symbolic-dramatic play.
- Provide challenges for children—such as two toddlers moving a tire on the playground.

- Ask open-ended questions that do not have just one right answer. For example, when reading a book, ask, "What do you think the little bear will do next?"

Use Anything and Everything for Art. Toddlers enjoy experimenting with additional creative art materials. They will be less likely to try to taste materials; however, they still need close supervision.

- Provide collage materials: pieces of wood or styrofoam, stickers, labels, different types of paper, and glue.
- Provide unique materials to paint, such as bubble wrap, empty toilet paper rolls, envelopes, paper bags, or pizza box paint easels (Kohl, 2002, p. 124).
- Provide squeezing containers and fill them with paint: eyedroppers, catsup or mayonnaise squeeze bottles, glue bottles, and so on.
- Provide unique painting tools: rolling pins, curlers, wooden blocks, fabric pieces, or crunched-up aluminum foil.

Have Many Opportunities for Drawing and Painting. Toddlers will move from disordered scribbling to more controlled scribbling. Circles may appear in their drawings. A few children may name a scribble.

- Make easels, painting, and drawing materials available every day (see Box 13.9). When toddlers trust that these will be available, they will usually spend time with these materials each day—thus developing their creativity, motor, language, and thinking skills.
- Provide many scribbling materials such as crayons.
- Collect children's scribblings to create a book to take home. Add a cover and one page explaining the importance of children's scribbles for creativity, motor development, and beginning literacy (writing and representing) skills.

Pizza Box Paint Easel

Coach Children's Symbolic and Dramatic Play. Toddlers will begin to play different roles in the symbolic-dramatic area. Toddlers have had more experiences than their younger peers and they will begin to pretend to be a doctor–child, teacher–child, go grocery shopping, and so on. Teachers have an important role to play when encouraging and supporting symbolic-dramatic play.

- Set up the environment. Provide all the materials and equipment listed under the section on mobile infants. Set up a doctor's office, grocery store, and so on *beside* the home setting so that toddlers still have a secure base. Children can then go back and forth between the store, for example, and the home.
- Pretend with children.

Explore the Senses. Sensory experiences enhance emotional, social, cognitive, motor, and language development. Toddlers enjoy a variety of sensory experiences. Encourage the development of self-worth and the expression of feelings—set up experiences so that every child will be successful.

- Provide a variety of sensory experiences: water, sand, snow, dirt, bubbles.
- Use animal sounds when reading animal books. Bring objects and musical instruments that make sounds and let the children listen to them.
- Prepare different foods with the children occasionally, introducing flavors and spices.
- Check with parents before providing food such as rice, noodles, and so on in a sensory table. Many parents do not appreciate having food used as a play substance.

Encourage Peers to Share Creative and Sensory Experiences.

- Provide a water table for sand and water to allow children to play together (some children will still prefer having individual containers).
- Encourage several children to use one side of an easel together.
- Provide a long piece of white paper and encourage many of the children to paint on the paper.

Pair Peers with Shared Interests.

- Observe whether children are experimenting with, for example, gravity. Provide materials for them to think about these questions: Does water always goes down? What makes water go down? Can it go up as well (with enough force)?
- Observe whether children have a goal of using water to make marks or patterns. Provide water for them to use to paint. Provide materials for them to think about the following questions: Does water always make things wet? (Try paper, aluminum foil, and plastic.) What if you painted the sidewalk? How long will it stay wet?

Box 13.9

Individually Responsive Group Planning Guide

Name of Group: _____

Week of: _____

Person(s) completing this guide: _____

Respect and Reflect

The children in my group are . . .

(Summarize information from the individual planning guides)

Relate: Plans for the Week to Meet Children's Interests and Needs

Songs/Fingerplays/Music

Stories/Books

Responsive Interactions

Environment: Toys, materials

Opportunities

Family/Cultural Experiences

Other

Planning for Toddlers' and Twos' Creative, Symbolic/Dramatic, and Sensory Development

Box 13.9 offers another opportunity to add your observations. Use Selena's group for your planning.

SUMMARY

Infants and toddlers are naturally creative. They are resourceful and imaginative when given interesting materials with which to play and experiment. Crayons, paint, play dough, and all types of other materials are used by infants and toddlers as they experiment with color, shape, size, lines, and texture. By the end of the toddler years, they may begin to name a drawing. Naming and telling stories about their drawings is a developmental step that represents a child's new way of thinking—the beginning of symbolic and imaginative thinking and the ability to visualize in pictures (Lowenfeld, 1947).

Mobile infants and toddlers also begin to engage in symbolic and dramatic play. Mobile infants and toddlers use symbols—themselves, photos, pictures, objects, and materials—to represent something real, such as a telephone, a mom, cooking utensils, or an animal. In dramatic play, children, usually toddlers, play a role such as mom, dad, or a pet. Symbolic and dramatic play occurs in all areas of the room; however, teachers typically set up an area in the room with child-size kitchen equipment and utensils, dolls, doll beds, and dramatic play clothing.

Young children constantly learn through all their senses during all times of the day. Teachers can provide endless opportunities for infants and toddlers to explore textures and other properties of materials. Teachers can also set up a sensory area where children play with water, sand, and other media.

INVENTORY OF TEACHER PRACTICES

Creative, Symbolic/Dramatic Play and Sensory Development

Basic Concepts	A	S	R	Observation/ Reflection
I encourage open-ended experimentation with creative materials. I do not require children to make a product when using creative materials.				
I use rich, descriptive language to describe how children are using materials.				
I observe children's interests and provide opportunities for them to expand on their goals and strategies and continue investigating the properties of, for example, water or light.				
I observe the concepts that children are exploring, such as in/out, up/down, full/empty, how to initiate play with others, or how to express feelings. I provide additional opportunities for them to explore these concepts.				
I am patient and gently support children who are hesitant or who do not like to touch certain materials or textures.				
I provide creative materials that encourage children of all ages to experiment, problem-solve, and create—nontoxic paint, finger paint, glue, and crayons. I add unique natural materials—twigs, grass, and sand.				
I provide an area for symbolic/dramatic play that has many culturally relevant materials to encourage children to pretend.				
I provide a variety of sensory experiences both indoors and outdoors—sound and touch boxes, musical toys, materials with different textures. I provide an area for water and sand play.				

A = Always, S = Sometimes, R = Rarely

REFLECTIONS

1. In what ways can you support creativity during routines, during play, and in a creative arts area of the room?
2. How would you respond to a co-teacher who wants toddlers to copy pictures or create a product with art materials?
3. Reflect on what you would do as a teacher in an infant/toddler program if one child didn't want to touch any of the sensory or art materials.

APPLICATIONS

1. Talk with families to determine whether they want you to use food products such as rice and beans in a sensory table. What would be some reasons not to use food?
2. Design a creative area, a symbolic/dramatic area, and a sensory area for a toddlers and twos room in an early care and education center room. Then think about how these areas could be adapted for a family child care home.

RESOURCES

- *Creative Infant Activities*
  This LiveStrong webpage has many gentle, relationship-based ideas for creative activities—and for recognizing daily activities as creative! Available at http://www.livestrong.com/article/359313-creative-infant-activities
- *Foundation: Symbolic Play*
  The California Department of Education created a document describing the foundations of early learning and development. Their description of the foundation of symbolic play has many good ideas. It will also help you understand the progression of symbolic thought. Available at http://www.cde.ca.gov/sp/cd/re/itf09cogdevfdsym.asp

14 Opportunities for Learning About the Outdoors

After reading this chapter, you will be able to:

- RESPECT
  - The opportunities for learning about nature and the outdoors
  - What infants and toddlers learn
  - Outdoor and nature opportunities for young and mobile infants, toddlers, and twos
- REFLECT
  - On the rich variety of learning offered by nature

- On how policies may support or inhibit outdoor experiences
- On your own comfort with having infants and toddlers outdoors in your climate and community
- RELATE
  - Plan interactions, materials, and environments for individual and small groups of children, to promote a love and knowledge of nature and the outdoors

This chapter is a little different from the others in this section because it does not directly address a developmental domain. It describes a specific area of knowledge that is basic to human beings, yet our exposure to it is increasingly limited.

Nature holds an inherent fascination for infants and toddlers. Changes in weather and seasons bring new sensations and new sights. Animals, whether they are family pets, crawling bugs, butterflies, birds, or squirrels are exciting at every sighting. A young infant may be surprised by the feel of grass under her hand. A mobile infant may spend long minutes studying one blade of grass, holding it, bending it, and even tasting it. A toddler may challenge his new ability to walk on the uneven surfaces of small, grassy hills.

The outdoors offers more than a chance to learn about nature. The very openness of the air and the sky invite movement and noise, so different from the admonitions to "Use your indoor voice" or "No running inside."

Whether in an urban or rural setting, being outside also provides children with a sense of their own community. Do cars zoom by with the sounds of sirens occasionally piercing the air? Are there bird songs and the chirping of cicadas? Experiencing their own community offers infants and toddlers an emerging understanding of the world around them.

Images of babies and toddlers in the outdoors can be idyllic, perhaps drawn from adults' own memories of wondrous childhood play. How many parents and infant/toddler care teachers know that sometimes the best solution to fussiness is to move the children outside? Today, however, infants and toddlers rarely enjoy hiding in the shelter of a large bush or know the excitement of watching a thunderstorm moving closer. Today's infants and toddlers have limited access to the outdoors. One study found that children today spend less than half the time outdoors that their mothers had as children (Clements, 2004). Adults are afraid of "injury, kidnapping, ultraviolet rays, insect-borne diseases, and pollution of various sorts" (Rivkin, 2000). Play yards are often unappealing, worn, dirt surfaces with little shade and a few pieces of large muscle play equipment. Some of the basic principles of creating a play yard are described in Box 14.1.

Outdoor experiences can provide a foundation for cognitive, language, science, and social knowledge. Infants and toddlers should have the opportunity to be outdoors where they can make noise and move freely. They will learn about the patterns

Box 14.1

A Developmentally Appropriate Outdoor Play Area for Infants and Toddlers

Infants and toddlers need time outdoors every day except in the most severe weather. When outdoor areas are designed for and used only by infants and toddlers, they can offer just the right kind of challenges as well as the quiet places that babies enjoy. Here are some guidelines to consider in creating outdoor spaces for babies:

1. Above all, a play area must be safe and clean. It should be fenced, protected from traffic and casual passers-by. It must be kept free of animal droppings. Broken toys and equipment should be removed immediately.
2. Infants and toddlers need protection from wind, sun, and light rain.
3. When possible, the outdoor area should offer opportunities for learning about nature—not just plastic equipment and rubber matting. A play area should have gentle hills that young crawlers, climbers, and walkers find challenging but not overwhelming. A shallow source of water and nontoxic plants add beauty in the summer.
4. Equipment such as tables, easels, riding and pull-toys, the water table, books, and fine-motor toys can all be brought outdoors, creating a new environment that supports the children's interests each day.
5. Just as indoors, the best part of being outdoors is having a place to cuddle with a loved adult. Comfortable chairs or stiff blankets on the grass work just right.

of day and night, the seasons, weather, their community, animals, plants, water, and sand. Learning about nature, however, does not depend on wonderful outdoor spaces. Experiences with nature can occur both indoors and outdoors.

The outdoor play area for young infants should be designed to provide comfortable spaces for adults and infants to cuddle or for babies to be fed, while being protected from too much sun or wind. A smooth-surfaced porch with a clear roof can provide an outdoor space even in the rain—even allowing for children to venture out and feel the drops on their faces. Young infants should be able to watch the movement of tall grasses or leaves in the wind, watch butterflies or birds, and listen to wind chimes (Rivkin, 2000).

Mobile infants and toddlers enjoy small grassy hills, slides, places to explore, places to climb, and places to socialize. Large sand areas, covered when not in use, are inviting for building, pouring, and being with friends. Water play can come from hoses, water tables, sprinklers, or simple fountains. One idea is to build a water wall for toddlers and twos. Attach recycled plastic containers—some whole, some with a hole in the bottom, a funnel, a tube, anything that water will flow through or that will hold water—to a sturdy board. The children can use a hose or cups and a bucket to pour water into the containers and see it come out again. For some great examples, see a website called "Let the Children Play" (http://progressiveearlychildhoodeducation.blogspot.com/2011/02/planning-new-water-wall-for-water-play.html).

The ability to use the outdoors depends on more than weather. The program must have policies that support the children going outside. When parents enroll their children, they should understand that the policy, for example, is that all children go out for at least one hour twice a day. Programs should keep extra hats and warm clothing on hand for children who do not have adequate clothing. Directors and care teachers should explore with families how they feel about their children being outside. One care teacher reported that despite her program's policy of being outdoors, one parent would take the child's jacket with her when she left.

RESPECT LEARNING ABOUT NATURE AND THE OUTDOORS

As human beings we are part of the natural world. We live in the natural cycles of day and night and of the seasons of the year. We depend on plants, animals, and natural resources for our existence. Yet many young children living in urban areas have almost no exposure to the natural world. Many Americans live in dense housing without yards and lawns. Computers, televisions, and sedentary lifestyles keep people indoors. Even in childcare, it is often difficult to get the entire group ready to go outdoors at the same time, and there may be insufficient staff to split groups. The administration can make a point of having extra hands available at this time.

Children Learn About Nature

Infants and toddlers have much to learn from nature and the outdoors.

Weather and Seasons. The hour-by-hour, day-by-day changes in the air provide basic scientific information and rich language and sensory experiences.

Plants. Children respond to plants' beauty, watch how things grow, and learn that some living things are neither animals nor people.

Animals and Insects. Children learn about the huge variety of living things, how they move, and ways in which they are the same and different.

Water and Sand. Children explore the properties of liquid: pouring, spilling, building, hiding, and finding.

The Gifts of the Outdoors. Children experience feelings of serenity, countered by an invitation from the air and sky to run and make noise! There are also opportunities to learn within all of the domains. If we are even looking just at the kind of concepts we hope that infants and toddlers will learn from toys, we can see nature offering those same lessons. Cause and effect? Picking up a leaf with a ladybug and watching the ladybug fly off the now-precarious perch is real cause and effect. Mathematics? That pile of stones is *bigger*. This pail is *full* of sand. It's *heavy*. Language? "Do you feel that *gentle breeze*?"

REFLECT ON LEARNING ABOUT NATURE AND THE OUTDOORS

Reflecting on the importance of outdoor and nature experiences for infants and toddlers provides useful information on the value of these experiences for young children. Box 14.2 provides reflections that can guide care teachers' observations and documentations.

RELATE TO LEARNING ABOUT THE OUTDOORS

Being outdoors can provide a fine sense of freedom . . . One's body is no longer under need of tight control—its capabilities to shout, sing, leap, roll, stretch, and fling are unleashed. Outdoor voices are suddenly acceptable. One is more carefree. (Rivkin, 1995, p. 11)

Box 14.2

Reflect on Learning About Nature and the Outdoors

- What is this infant or toddler learning about weather and seasons?
- How does this child have opportunities to experience changes in the weather and seasons?
- How does the child experience different spaces in the outdoors?
- What vocabulary is each child learning while playing outdoors?
- How is each child developing in the emotional, social, motor, language, cognitive, and creativity domains when outside?
- How is this infant or toddler learning about plants?
- How does the child use all of his or her senses to learn about plants?
- What is each child learning about plants?
- What is this infant or toddler learning about animals? Life cycles; things that grow and things that don't?
- How does each child respond when observing birds, insects, or other animals in the outdoor environment?
- What questions do toddlers and twos ask about animals and insects?
- How does each child respond when books with photographs of animals are read to him or her?
- What is this infant or toddler learning about water and sand?
- What concepts are children exploring as they play with sand and water (object permanence, use of tools, cause and effect, being a friend, taking turns with toys, etc.)?
- How does each child play with varied materials such as containers, sieves, funnels, and toy replicas of boats, cars, animals, and people?
- Is this child experiencing the gifts of the outdoors?
- How does each child respond to outdoor experiences?
- How does this child problem solve and create with materials that are in nature or outdoors on a playground?

The infant/toddler care teacher relates to each baby's experience of nature and the outdoors. She also relates to her own experience of being outdoors with this group of children and to her own memories of being outdoors as a child.

THE YOUNG INFANT: BIRTH TO 9 MONTHS

The young infant relies on family members and the infant care teacher to safely bring him or her close to nature. Outdoor experiences for the young infant may include the routines of being fed, held, or napping. However, simply being outdoors changes these experiences. A breeze moves the leaves into changing shadows, mesmerizing young infants. The air feels different outdoors than it does indoors. The light is different. The experience may be relaxing or exciting. Either way, it still involves the infant care teacher as a companion and guide.

A Glimpse of the Young Infant's Nature Learning

Even at 3 months, Adara shows Miriam that she enjoys being outdoors. She smiles at the leaves moving overhead, perhaps out of some sense that anything that moves is alive. She kicks her legs and "talks" to the moving shadows. She calms in the warmth of the sun, protected from its harmful rays by a canopy. Miriam thought about the reflection question— How does each child respond to outdoor experiences? She then captured Adara's reactions with photographs and shared them with her family. Both Miriam and Adara's family were surprised at how a 3-month-old could respond in so many ways to outdoor experiences.

Young children enjoy going outdoors.

Paulo, at 4 months, is taking an active interest in the world around him. Miriam carries him to where he can touch the leaves on a tree. They stand for several minutes while Paulo touches the leaves and Miriam talks to him about how they feel. The leaves are fragile and tear in his grip. Miriam and Paulo rub the torn leaves in their fingers and smell the aroma. Afterwards, Paulo contentedly plays on a blanket spread on the ground, with the scent of the leaves lingering on his fingers.

Six-month-old Jack sits on a blanket where he can feel the grass. Sometimes, as he rakes his fingers through the prickly blades, he will come up with a handful of grass. He always looks surprised. Jack is also interested in the little bugs he sometimes sees moving through the grass. Miriam follows the advice of the mental health specialist and sits as close to Jack as he can comfortably manage. She talks quietly to him but finds it hard to engage him. Still, he seems more relaxed outdoors

Takala is the only crawler in the group, and Miriam keeps a close eye on her. The play yard is small, shaded by a canopy and two trees. There is a small grassy area and a flower bed filled with aromatic herbs. Takala makes a beeline for the small fountain that circulates water over rocks. The sparkle and the babbling sound of the water are entrancing. Takala laughs as she watches; like Adara, she senses that she is surrounded by life outdoors.

Everyone seems excited when a songbird lands on the fence or a butterfly passes by. Miriam knows that these babies love being outdoors. They feel the mixture of peace and freedom this space offers them compared to their indoor space.

The Young Infant Care Teacher's Decisions

Miriam lives in a gentle climate that makes the outdoors available most of the year even to young babies. However, they are in an urban area that has very limited natural outdoor space available. Her program struggles with how to create outdoor play areas that give the babies some sense of the natural world while keeping them safe.

Miriam's first responsibility is keeping the children safe. They are too young to tell her if they are too hot or too cold. She needs to watch them closely. While the children are thrilled if they spot a squirrel, she must make sure that no one gets too close. The program has a policy requiring the use of sunscreen on the children before going outdoors. Miriam also makes sure that she offers the children water while they are outdoors.

Because her children are so young and not yet moving, Miriam needs to be very thoughtful about how to engage them with nature while they are outdoors. The grass and leaves are inherently interesting. The fountain is not completely natural, but it gives the children some experience of water moving in sunlight. She has also hung wind chimes, which delight the children.

Paulo, Jack, and Takala are each able to put anything they find into their mouths. Miriam knows that she needs to watch everyone closely outdoors. Their different abilities to move also require different kinds of interaction from Miriam.

Miriam is trying to give the babies the feeling of comfort and openness that she experiences outdoors. She limits the number of toys that she brings outdoors and encourages the children to enjoy the many sensory experiences.

Adaptations for Special Needs. Miriam's group is so young that she doesn't have to be concerned about adapting any equipment. Her concern for Jack is mixed. He seems more relaxed outdoors but she wonders how he experiences the openness of the space. The mental health consultant has told Miriam that Jack, if he has not yet formed an attachment to his adoptive parents when he is older, is likely to wander away on walks. Miriam wants so much to reassure this little boy that she and his parents will be there for him.

Diversity/Culture. Paulo's family wants him kept clean and is not sure that such a young infant needs to be outdoors twice a day. Miriam has arranged to change him into clean clothes at the end of the day. Jack's parents are outdoor enthusiasts and feel that a little dirt never hurt anyone. Adara's family knows that being outdoors is very pleasurable for her but they are concerned about whether Miriam can manage all four children's needs at once. Takala's Native-American family feels very strongly that the outdoors is an important part of the curriculum and wishes that the children spent the majority of the day outdoors.

Opportunities for Young Infants' Outdoor Learning

Bring Routines Outdoors. Young infants need many opportunities to be close to their primary infant care teachers.

- Have comfortable areas outdoors where infant care teachers can hold, feed, or read to young infants. For example, use swinging benches or comfortable outdoor furniture.
- Arrange the outdoor environment to accommodate the routine care that is so much of a young infant's day: feeding, napping, and diapering.

Create a Rich Sensory Experience. Young infants use all their senses to take in information from the environment.

- Plant fragrant herbs in containers. Purchase soil for planting. Check the soil for lead content.
- Create a small fountain with babbling, sparkling water.
- Under supervision, let babies feel leaves, grass, dirt, sand, and water.
- Point out interesting sounds and sights such as a bird singing or a butterfly passing by.

Remember Outdoor Safety. Young infants need to be kept safe outdoors.

- Have a program policy requiring the use of sunscreen and protective lip balm.
- Be outdoors for limited periods of time.
- Provide shade and wind protection.
- Offer drinks frequently, as babies dehydrate quickly.
- Make sure that everything in the outdoor area is safe to ingest (nontoxic plants), no pea gravel, do a daily safety check for any hazards from people walking by (litter).
- Provide safe places for sitting and crawling infants and equipment for older infants to pull to a stand and cruise around.

Revel in Fresh Experiences. Young infants are fascinated by the wonders of nature.

- Watch sunbeams.
- Play in the sun-warmed spot on the rug.
- Listen to rain and thunder.
- Let breezes blow through the room.
- Read books about animals, plants, weather, and seasons.

Planning for Young Infants' Outdoor Learning

For this planning guide (see Box 14.3), you should observe a young infant to determine his or her interest in, and experiences with nature and outdoor learning. Note or document your observations on the top and the left side. Then fill out the planning guide with interactions and changes in the environment on the right side.

Box 14.3

Individual Child Planning Guide (1)

Child's Name: _____ Plans for Week of (Date): _____

Person(s) completing the guide: _____

Respect: Child's Emotions, Effort, Goals, Learning, and Relationships
Write an observation or use a picture or other documentation here—date all notes.

Respect and Reflect	Relate
What am I doing?	**What will you do to support my learning?**
	• **Responsive interactions**
How am I feeling?	
	• **Environment: Toys, materials**
What am I learning?	
• **Emotional**	• **Opportunities**
• **Social**	
• **Cognitive**	
• **Motor**	
• **Language**	

THE MOBILE INFANT: 8–18 MONTHS

Being outdoors is even more fun for mobile infants given their ability to move on their own. Gentle hills provide welcome challenges to the balance of the new walker or crawler. Safe places to chase or play peek-a-boo provide support for budding reciprocal interactions among peers. Sturdy garden containers invite mobile infants to pull to a stand. Sand and water offer countless occasions for pouring, spilling, and experimenting with breaking something into parts and then putting it back together into a whole. Improving vision and grasping abilities lead to discoveries about bugs and insects. Through it all, the trusted adult is nearby, offering encouragement to the little explorer while keeping him or her safe.

A Glimpse of the Mobile Infant's Learning About the Outdoors

Albert enjoys the outdoors and is ready to bundle up the babies to make sure everyone is outside for part of the day, even in cold weather. Except for the coldest days of winter, the mobile infants at least go for a wagon ride in a stroller built for four. On most days, however, these hardy babies have two opportunities each day to play outdoors. In Albert's four-season climate, however, he believes it is important to bring nature inside as well. He wants these urban children to grow up with a sense of connection to the natural world

Gemma's exceptional mobility skills and her young age (9 months) can be a dangerous combination outdoors. She can get anywhere in the play yard and will put anything into her mouth. Gemma is an easygoing baby with lots of energy. She loves making new discoveries and the outdoors presents new experiences every day. One day the wind blows the leaves across the ground. Another day a fat beetle crawls across her path. The sand feels different when it is wet than when it is dry. Albert knows that Gemma loves the feeling of openness in the play yard.

The play yard is not a huge space, but the staff has worked to make it beautiful. Because of the urban location, the play yard is in front of the building. It is surrounded by solid wood fences, with built-in polyurethane windows to allow the children to see the activity on their street. Still, the open sky and windows, the breezes, and sunlight make the experience of being outdoors very different from being indoors.

The very factors that make being outdoors appealing to Gemma make it distressing to Lily. One aspect of Lily's cerebral palsy is that it makes her extremely sensitive to different textures on her skin. A gentle breeze, sitting on grass, or the grit of sand can cause real discomfort. On the other hand, for a visual learner like Lily, the outdoors offers constant changes to watch and admire. The herbs, flowers, and tall grasses planted in garden beds always seem to be moving and changing. The butterfly garden attracts beautiful butterflies in the summer and autumn. Albert is sure to bring her positioning seat outside so she can sit comfortably and maintain her motor control. Sometimes he takes the opportunity to do Lily's exercises while they are outside on a blanket. The other children will often bring Lily a small collection of sticks or stones to play with.

Radwan goes directly to the sandbox when he goes outdoors. The first thing Albert has to do is pull the cover off the sandbox. When Radwan has satisfied his desire to dig and pour, he tests his new walking skills. The gentle, grass-covered hill is so challenging that he alternates between walking and crawling, all with a look of great concentration and determination. He enjoys using his new mobility to gather interesting artifacts for Lily's appreciation. He is just starting to use push and pull toys on the sidewalk track. At times, he prefers to sit with Lily and examine the bits of leaves, dandelions, or sticks she has collected. He enjoys looking at the nature books that Albert brings outdoors.

Goro is able to sit on a riding toy and scoot forward—or sometimes, unintentionally, backward. He will scream with excitement if a plane flies overhead or he sees a big truck through the window. Goro likes to go outdoors. He will grab his jacket and bring it to Albert as a way of asking to go outdoors or if anyone says the word "outside." Push and pull toys, the sandbox, flowing water, and finding quiet places behind flower beds provide precious moments for Goro.

Albert chose the following reflection question to observe the children in his group: How does this child problem-solve and create with materials that are in nature or outdoors on a playground? He found that Gemma had a goal of picking up every leaf that she saw and examining it; Lily tried to put the sticks and stones into a basket, although her grasp often failed her; Radwan explored object permanence as he hid toys in the sand and then later came back to find them. He also experimented with how to use a shovel to scoop sand into a bucket by trying different holds on the shovel. Goro experimented with what happened when he put his hand in the water and pulled it out again. He kept asking Albert, "What dat?" as he pointed to a bug, the water, a leaf, the grass, and Radwan. These observations helped Albert think about other materials and experiences that he could offer the children to support their interests and problem-solving abilities.

The Mobile Infant Care Teacher's Decisions

Albert sees the outdoor play yard as offering several important experiences. The children are in the fresh air and sunshine—in whatever the current weather might be, including rain or light snow. They are able to directly experience many aspects of nature in addition to weather. Grass, plants, and trees grow in the play yard. Birds, butterflies, and insects pass through. The children also have opportunities to watch some of the people and activities of their community. Planes and helicopters fly overhead, and people and their pets walk past the windows. Cars and trucks go by on the street.

Albert knows that these mobile infants are interested in exploration, especially when it involves their growing mobility skills. He works with the families to maintain an outdoor space that offers different experiences and challenges than the indoor space. Small hills challenge new walkers and crawlers. Low bushes provide spaces for hiding, although the children are still within Albert's view. Push and pull toys, low climbing structures, and simple riding toys are used both indoors and outdoors.

Adaptations. Albert thought that Lily's mobility challenges would be his greatest concern in having her enjoy the outdoors. Instead, he is learning that her sensitivity to touch is a much greater challenge. Lily doesn't want to leave the comfort of a blanket if it means touching grass or sand. With the help of Lily's early interventionist, Albert has been trying to get her used to touching different textures. If the sandbox is overwhelming, for example, a small tray with a velcroed shovel and a bowl of sand are more tolerable. Lily is also more willing to touch sticks and grasses if they are presented to her by the other children than if she has to struggle to get to them.

Diversity/Culture. The play yard has a tall fence and is kept locked when the children are indoors. However, all the families have expressed some concern about the children's safety. Urban areas sometimes bring out concerns for parents of young children.

Radwan's family in particular has been concerned about strangers on the street. They have encountered hostility in public places and are concerned about having their clearly Arab-looking child seen by strangers in the street. Albert acknowledges their concerns and has asked them to share any ideas that might make the children safer. Albert has also shown Radwan's family photos and shared stories about all that he explores and learns while being outside. Radwan's parents know that being outdoors is important and they work to contain their fears and support Radwan's enthusiasm.

Opportunities for Mobile Infants' Outdoor Learning

Tie Language to the Changing Weather. Mobile infants pay attention to changes in the weather.

- Talk about the weather as the children arrive, during outdoor time, or when looking out the window. Provide language for the weather such as *sunny and warm, windy, rain, snow, fog, cold,* and *chilly.* These authentic language experiences have real meaning as opposed to inappropriate "circle time" weather posters.
- Keep board books handy that describe weather. In reading them with a baby, talk about how the pictures are alike or different from the weather outside.

Build Memories by Noticing Changes. Mobile infants are too young to understand the concept of seasons or even remember that it used to be warm outside if it is snowy now. This brings a certain magic to the changes we all take for granted—waking to find the world white and covered with snow only to discover in a few days that the snow has melted (where did it go?) and the world seems normal again. When adults can recognize and share in this sense of wonder, they can appreciate how important it is for young children to experience it first hand.

- Look at books about seasons and talk about pictures that look like the current weather.
- Use language for the seasons as a way of enriching the language environment without expecting immediate comprehension.

Make the Most of Sensory Experiences. Mobile infants are interested in the feel, smell, and taste of plants.

- Grow nontoxic plants indoors and outdoors.
- Grow herbs in containers. (Dill, when left to flower, is attractive to butterflies.)
- Hold babies where they can touch and pull on the leaves on trees.
- Create displays of leaves, large pinecones, a branch of an evergreen with the pine needles attached, twigs and sticks, tree bark, flowers, cattails, squash, or fruits. Use objects too large to be swallowed and encourage supervised exploration.
- Provide rich language such as *smooth, prickly, pretty, soft,* or *fuzzy* to describe the objects on display. Sniff a flower or herbs with exaggeration, saying, "Smell this."

Appreciate the Many Living Things Outdoors. Mobile infants are very interested in animals and insects. They appear to understand that these are living things different from people.

- React with excitement and interest when infants spot and point to an animal or insect. Supply the name: "Oh, you see a cat!" and any additional, simple language such as, "I see that fly. It's buzzing. Do you hear that *Bzzzzzzzz*?"
- Try not to pass on your own fears—teach yourself NOT to react with fear when a child finds a spider or praying mantis. Share the child's excitement instead of showing your own discomfort.
- Provide realistic replicas of animals and bugs for play. Use language to show the mobile infant that you understand his or her interest. For example, if the mobile infant suddenly notices the eyes on the toy lamb, say, "I see that lamb's eyes. Just like my eyes (*point*) and your eyes (*point*)."
- Read and talk about the pictures in the many wonderful infant books about animals. Talk about ways we are alike and different: "The bird has eyes. Do you have eyes? Yes! The bird has wings. Do you have wings? Nooo. You have arms."

Explore Sand and Water. Mobile infants enjoy exploring the properties of sand and water.

- Outdoors, provide a sandbox kept tightly covered when not in use and a safe source of water for play.

- Indoors, have a play table available every day. Some days it may hold sand, some days water, others possibly a collection of autumn leaves or pinecones. If you notice children collecting items outside, encourage them to add their collection to the play table. Some mobile infants do better with separate containers; others enjoy the contact of playing together. Provide cups, sieves, shovels, and funnels to help the infants explore the properties of the materials.

Match the Rich Experiences to Rich Language. Mobile infants learn many concepts and new vocabulary when they are outdoors.

- Use words to describe the sensory experience of being outdoors, such as "the feel of the soft breeze" or "mmm, this daisy smells sweet."
- Name the flowers, bugs, and birds.

Share a Sense of Joy. Mobile infants are discovering the joy of being outdoors.

- Provide a safe, attractive, engaging outdoor environment for mobile infants.
- Take children outdoors at least once a day for play time or a walk, as the weather allows.
- Take time to share the experience of weather, plants, and animals with mobile infants.
- Use rich language to describe these experiences.

Planning for Mobile Infants' Outdoor Learning

For this planning guide (see Box 14.4), observe a mobile infant's experiences with, and interest in nature and outdoor learning. Respect the child's experience with

Box 14.4

Individual Child Planning Guide (2)

Child's Name: _____ Plans for Week of (Date): _____

Person(s) completing the guide: _____

Respect: Child's Emotions, Effort, Goals, Learning, and Relationships
Write an observation or use a picture or other documentation here—date all notes.

Reflect	Relate
Date all notes: What am I doing? What am I feeling? What am I learning?	What will you do to support my development and learning? • Responsive interactions • Environment: Toys, materials • Opportunities

photographs or written notes for documentation. Reflect on the child's experience by answering the following questions: What am I doing? How am I feeling? What am I learning? Finally, relate to the child's interest in nature and outdoor learning by answering the following questions: What will you do to support my development and learning? How will you adapt the environment, toys, materials, and expectations?

TODDLERS AND TWOS: 16–36 MONTHS

Toddlers and twos often are very enthusiastic about being outdoors. They are likely to grab their jackets and go to the door when the toddler care teacher announces that it is time to go outdoors. As toddlers and twos are developing a sense of their own identity, they may incorporate ideas such as "I like being outdoors" or "I'm good at digging in sand or running on hills." As toddler care teachers provide opportunities for the children to care for plants and animals, the children may also begin to have a sense of themselves as people who care for the environment.

A Glimpse of Toddlers' and Twos' Learning About the Outdoors

Selena is a gardener and treasures being able to share her love of gardening with the toddlers and twos in her care. The children are busy outdoors with their own games and discoveries but they also enjoy "working in the garden." The 2-year-olds understand something about living things starting small and growing bigger. They plant the seeds from citrus fruits and avocados indoors. In the summer, they plant carrots, green beans, pumpkins, and sunflowers in a special raised garden outdoors.

The children are making their own discoveries about weather. They play with their shadows in the sunshine. In light rain, they wear slickers and boots and use their new abilities to jump into shallow puddles. In autumn, the children pile leaves and roll in the piles. In winter, it takes more time to get the children dressed than they spend outdoors. Care teachers put this extra time to good use by helping children learn how to dress and talking about hats, mittens, and boots. The children play with snow and slide on ice while they are warm enough.

Lan is a slender child who rarely stops moving outdoors. He loves the freedom of the open space. His mother jokes about how he comes from a long line of farmers and that being outdoors is in his genes. He does love to work with Selena on the garden. He also moves from one large muscle toy to another. He likes riding toys, pulling wagons, and climbing on the structure.

Sam brings his interests in building outdoors. He likes to add leaves, seeds, sticks and stones to his sand structures. However, he will play anything if it involves the other children. He likes to chase and imitate in spontaneous games of follow-the-leader. He enjoys changes in weather and has the words to describe most of them.

Together, Sam and Lan use outdoor materials to create their own challenges. When Selena set up a wooden stair/rocking boat toy outdoors, Sam and Lan dragged a long board over and created a slide.

Bessie can enjoy examining a bug or flower for a long time. Unfortunately, when she is disturbed, or someone doesn't understand what she wants, she is likely to hit or bite.

Chita enjoys the outdoors, but the children do so many new things that she often just watches them, as though trying to learn how to be a 2-year-old. She is interested in the garden and runs outdoors to check on the flowers. She especially enjoys using a watering can on the flower garden.

The Toddler Care Teacher's Decisions

For many years, Selena was content to take the children outdoors to play with the riding toys and climbing structure. She kept pails and shovels in the sandbox. She believed that simply being outdoors had its own benefits.

In the last several years, however, she has been planning the outdoor time as thoughtfully as the indoor time. She is noting each child's interest and adding activities that might enrich their discoveries outdoors, just as she does with the indoor environment.

One day, wanting to surprise and challenge Sam and thinking about his interest in taking many pieces and building one thing, Selena collected every ball she could find in the storage cupboards and distributed them in her play yard. All the children were delighted by the surprise. Sam was challenged by how to collect the balls into one place. Eventually, he and Bessie filled a laundry basket with balls and together carried it to a patch of grass. Later, all the children got involved in trying to kick the balls—often ending up on their bottoms as they lost their balance. Pretty soon, falling down was part of the game!

Bessie's interest in caring for the dolls led Serena to set up outdoor bathtubs for dolls and a system for washing and drying the doll's clothing. Again, all the children enjoyed the activity, although it had been planned from observing one child's interests.

For Lan, her gardening partner, there is always "work" to do. They weed, water, trim, and check the plants. When there is actually a crop, everyone joins in the harvest—even if it is only one carrot per child.

Adaptations for Special Needs. Selena feels she has two ongoing challenges in adapting materials and activities to meet Bessie's needs. Bessie's low muscle tone makes physical activity challenging, so she often avoids it. Because she may be unsure of what to do with new materials, she sometimes gets stuck playing with the same materials, in the same way, over and over again.

Selena observes Bessie when she is outdoors. She reflects on how to use Bessie's interests to increase her physical activity and the diversity of her experiences. Bessie's inherent interest in nature and her dislike of crawling in grass helps her to walk more outdoors. One day, Selena hid some of the stuffed animals in the bushes or behind plants. Then she made a game of looking for them with Bessie. On other days, she and Bessie just walked around the yard checking on the garden.

Bessie's quick temper isn't that different from that of others her age. The challenge is that she doesn't seem to be learning any control over her impulses. The other children, along with being hurt, try to avoid her—further challenging her social skills. Selena supports her play with other children when she can, but she can't stay next to her all the time. It wouldn't be a good idea anyway. She does try to help the other children say a good, loud "no" to her and walk away, if she lashes out.

Riding toys are an important part of the outdoor environment. Along with learning about nature, children are encouraged to move in a different way.

Diversity/Culture. Gardening and outdoor play are not part of Sam's cultural background. His natural inclination is to bring his indoor activities outside. Selena had noticed this when he was a mobile infant and feels that she has accomplished a lot in increasing his enthusiasm for the outdoors. Bessie's family is unsure of her safety outside. The uneven ground makes it harder for her to walk than normal. They also worry about her mouthing things. Selena reassures them that are benefits in taking risks. She has a strong belief in Bessie's potential and wants to instill a sense of courage and competence now.

Opportunities for Toddlers' and Twos' Learning About the Outdoors

Use the Natural Changes in the Weather. Toddlers and twos are interested in changing weather.

- On sunny days, talk about why you are using hats, sunscreen, lip balm, and drinking water when outdoors. On cool days, talk about why everyone is wearing jackets. Talk about boots and umbrellas on rainy days, and mittens and parkas in snowy weather.

- Show the children pictures from books or posters that represent the weather. Ask, "Does it look like this outdoors today? What is our weather like today?"

- On a sunny day, help the children remember that it rained yesterday.

- On a windy day, dance with scarves to catch the wind. Watch the leaves or tree limbs dance in the wind.

- Watch for rainbows or thunder and lightning. If you can hear thunder, it's time to go inside.

Attend to Changing Seasons. Toddlers and twos may have some understanding of seasons.

- Use words to describe the current season.
- Read books about the seasons.

Plant and Grow. Toddlers and twos understand that little things grow into bigger things.

- Take seeds from fruits served at snack time and plant them.
- Plant herbs or vegetables to be harvested and eaten.
- Display flowers, leaves, squash, and pumpkins. Provide opportunities to dissect them—talk about how the inside is different from the outside; and how leaves and flowers are easy to break, while pumpkins and some squash are much harder.

Discover Animals and Insects. Toddlers and twos are interested in animals and insects.

- Sing songs and read stories about animals.
- Mimic animal sounds in stories and songs. Dance and move like animals.
- Watch for animals and insects outdoors. Examine an earthworm.
- Create a terrarium as a home for insects.
- Display found items such as bird nests, empty cocoons, or butterfly wings.
- Follow the path of a bug as it moves outdoors. Use unbreakable magnifying glasses to help children watch little bugs.

Provide Time for Sand and Water. Toddlers and twos are creative in using water and sand.

- Provide measuring cups, plastic bottles, funnels, tubing, and other materials to explore pouring and molding.
- Hide a series of objects under the sand.
- In the winter, put buckets of snow in the water table. Have mittens ready for those who want to play.

Inspire Appreciation of Beauty and Freedom. Toddlers and twos enjoy the beauty and freedom of being outdoors.

- Take children outdoors as often as possible.
- Listen well as children tell you about their discoveries outdoors.
- Let children run and make noise outdoors.
- Bring messy projects outdoors.
- Use spray water bottles or water and paint brushes outdoors to "paint" the sides of the building, sidewalks, or fences. Use food coloring in the water to spray paint snow.
- Lay on the grass and watch the clouds.

Take Books Outside and Read on a Blanket on the Ground or a Reading Bench. See Box 14.5 for a list of books that relate to nature and playing outdoors.

Planning for Toddlers' and Twos' Outdoor Learning

This final opportunity to practice planning uses the group planning guide based on the individual interests, skills, and needs of each child (see

---

Box 14.5

> ### Books for Babies
>
> *Animal Friends: A Global Celebration of Children and Animals,* Maya Ajmera, John D. Ivanko, and Global Fund for Children. Charlesbridge Publishing (2002).
>
> *Bird, Fly High,* Petr Horacek. Candlewick (2005).
>
> *The Carrot Seed,* Ruth Krauss. HarperFestival (1993).
>
> *The Flower Garden,* Eve Bunting and Kathryn Hewitt. Voyager Books (2000).
>
> *I Can Fly,* Ruth Krauss. Golden Books (2003).
>
> *Mommies Say Shhh!,* Patricia Polacco. Philomel (2007).
>
> *MOO BAA LALALA,* Sandra Boynton. Little Simon (1982).
>
> *Owl Babies,* Martin Waddell. Candlewick (2002).
>
> *Sunflower House,* Eve Bunting and Kathryn Hewitt. Voyager Books (1999).
>
> *Touch and Feel: Puppy,* DK Publishing. DK Preschool (1999).

Box 14.6

Individually Responsive Group Planning Guide

Name of Group: _____   Week of: _____
Person(s) completing this guide: _____

Respect and Reflect

The children in my group are . . .
(Summarize information from the individual planning guides)

Relate: Plans for the Week to Meet Children's Interests and Needs

Songs/Fingerplays/Music

Stories/Books

Responsive Interactions

Environment: Toys, materials

Opportunities:

Family/Cultural Experiences

Other

Box 14.6). Use the information above about Selena's group and plan nature and outdoor learning experiences for them.

SUMMARY

Infants and toddlers need time in the outdoors for fresh air, sunshine, open space, and exposure to nature. Their opportunities to learn about nature, however, exist both indoors and outdoors.

Infants and toddlers are learning emotional, social, language, cognitive, and motor skills as they play outdoors. They are also learning about:

> Weather and seasons
> Plants
> The scientific process
> Animals and insects
> Sand and water
> The gifts of nature

Infants and toddlers will follow their own curiosity in learning about nature, but infant/toddler care teachers can support their learning in many ways. By sharing their own enthusiasm, talking with children about particular aspects of weather or plants, and providing special displays indoors, the teachers promote learning. A particularly rich variety of books on nature are available for infants and toddlers because it is such a strong interest.

INVENTORY OF TEACHER PRACTICES

Nature and the Outdoors

Basic Concepts	A	S	R	Observation/ Reflection
I provide a healthy and safe outdoors environment.				
I meet infants' and toddlers' need for emotional security when they are outdoors.				
I provide opportunities for infants and toddlers to learn about weather and seasons.				
I support discoveries of plants.				
I provide opportunities for discoveries about animals and insects.				
I provide opportunities for discoveries about the joys of outdoors.				
I provide opportunities for children to move, problem-solve, and experiment with different strategies for accomplishing their own goals.				
I provide many opportunities for children to explore with all their senses.				
I use descriptive language to talk about what the children are experiencing.				

A = Always, S = Sometimes, R = Rarely

REFLECTIONS

1. What elements of being outdoors playing do you remember from your childhood? Were they positive experiences?
2. As you watch children indoors and outdoors, do you see differences in their attention or excitement? What do you think about that?
3. Parents may have many concerns about having their children outdoors. What do you find most challenging in working with families around this topic? What resolutions have you found?

APPLICATIONS

1. How can you bring nature experiences to an urban child care and education program?
2. What special efforts would you make for a child like Lily or Bessie to enjoy the outdoors fully and safely?
3. What safety concerns must you keep in mind when taking children outdoors?

RESOURCES

- *Let the Children Play*
  This website, available at http://progressiveearlychildhoodeducation.blogspot.com, has hundreds of ideas for outdoor play. This website has hundreds of ideas for outdoor play.
- *Outdoor play: Combating sedentary life styles* (by Betsy Thigpen).
  This article from Zero to Three, available at http://main.zerotothree.org/site/DocServer/outdoorplay_thigpen.pdf?docID=4881, explains the importance of outdoor play, how to provide safe outdoor experiences, and suggests many wonderful ideas for outdoor environments and adventures.

Planning Guides

Individual Child Planning Guide (1)

Child's Name: _____ Plans for Week of (Date): _____

Person(s) completing the guide: _____

Respect: Child's Emotions, Effort, Goals, Learning, and Relationships

Write an observation or use a picture or other documentation here—date all notes.

Respect and Reflect	Relate
What am I doing?	**What will you do to support my learning?**
	• Responsive interactions
How am I feeling?	
	• Environment: Toys, materials
What am I learning?	
• Emotional	**• Opportunities**
• Social	
• Cognitive	
• Language	
• Motor	

Individual Child Planning Guide (2)

Child's Name: _____ Plans for Week of (Date): _____

Person(s) completing the guide: _____

Respect: Child's Emotions, Effort, Goals, Learning, and Relationships

Write an observation or use a picture or other documentation here—date all notes

Reflect	Relate
Date all notes:	**What will you do to support my development and learning?**
What am I doing?	• **Responsive Interactions**
What am I feeling?	• **Environment: Toys, materials**
What am I learning?	• **Opportunities**

Individually Responsive Group PLanning Guide

Name of Group: _____ Week of: _____

Person(s) completing this guide: _____

Respect and Reflect

The children in my group are . . .

(Summarize information from the individual planning guides)

Relate: Plans for the Week to Meet Children's Interests and Needs

Songs/Fingerplays/Music

Stories/Books

Responsive Interactions

Environment: Toys, materials

Opportunities

Families/Cultural Experiences

Other

Group Planning for Routines

Name of Group: _____ Week of: _____

Person(s) completing this guide: _____

_____

Developing a caring community: Think about what is happening and what could happen to develop a relationship-based program for children, families, and teachers.

Routine	What is going well for the children and teachers?	What could we do to improve the experience for children, families, and teachers?
Greeting Time or Good-bye Time		
Feeding Infants and Toddler Eating Times/Oral Health		
Infant Sleep and Toddler Nap Times		
Diapering		
Toileting		
Play Times		
Outdoor Times		
Transitions		
Other Routines		
Other Routines		
Other Routines		

B Inventory of Teacher Practices

Relationships	A	S	R	Observation/ Reflection
I am aware of the many things infants and toddlers are learning. I watch them expecting to see learning happening.				
I look for the underlying processes of learning such as curiosity, attention, and a desire for mastery.				
I find ways to support the infant's or toddler's natural desire to explore and learn.				
I use my relationship with each child to encourage their learning by smiling, using words, and celebrating their accomplishments.				
I support each child's ability to pay attention by helping them manage their reactions and feelings.				
I plan for each child with regard to their family's beliefs and values.				
I reflect on the quality of my relationship with each child.				
I use the steps of respect, reflect, and relate in planning curriculum.				
A = Always, S = Sometimes, R = Rarely				

Engaging Families	A	S	R	Observation/ Reflection
I communicate daily with the family of each of the children for whom I provide primary care.				
Our program clearly communicates policies to parents.				
I provide some general information and education to families.				
I welcome families to spend time in the classroom.				
I ask families to provide photographs and tape recordings of themselves for their baby to enjoy.				
I reach out to families whose culture or race is different from mine.				
I reach out to military families on deployment.				
I reach out to families with infants and toddlers with disabilities.				
I reach out to families with mental illness or maternal depression.				
I reach out to families going through divorce and separation.				
I reach out to fathers and important males in the children's lives.				
A = Always, S = Sometimes, R = Rarely				

Responsive, Safe, and Healthy Caregiving Routines	A	S	R	Observation/ Reflection
I provide routine care in ways that are responsive to each child's cues and needs.				
I provide routine care in ways that are predictable.				
I provide routine care on-demand.				
I maintain a safe environment with daily checks of the space.				
I follow protocols for safe food handling.				
I follow protocols to prevent the spread of disease.				
I actively promote the health of the children by attending to: Well-child care Oral health Nutrition and physical fitness Reducing the risk of SIDS Reducing the risk of Shaken Baby Syndrome				
A = Always, S = Sometimes, R = Rarely				

Environments	A	S	R	Observation/ Reflection
I can identify pathways for infants learning to crawl or walk.				
There are safe areas for younger babies to play on the floor.				
When a mobile infant is driven to climb, is there a place for him to practice climbing over and over without being scolded?				
Are there spaces that invite children to be together because of plentiful or duplicate materials?				
Are there times when you say "No" because your environment isn't saying "yes"?				
A = Always, S = Sometimes, R = Rarely				

Guidance/ Realtionship Realignments	A	S	R	Observation/ Reflection
I support children's relationships with key family members and myself.				
I am responsive to individual children's uniqueness, temperament, and sensory needs.				
I show affection and comment on children's positive behavior.				
I teach and show children what to do instead of focusing on what not to do.				
I give short reasons when I ask children to do things.				
I build children's emotional vocabulary and ability to recognize and express feelings.				
I recognize that there are individual family and cultural differences in how to guide children and goals for children.				
I help children problem-solve and negotiate conflicts.				
I support children's peer relationships.				
I change the environment to respond to children's needs.				
I provide interesting and fun choices for children.				
I use "time-in" rather than "time-out."				
When children feel challenged I work collaboratively with the family to determine why and how to help the child.				
I consult with the family to refer them to community agencies for more support.				
A = Always, S = Sometimes, R = Rarely				

Observation, Documentation, Planning, and Assessment	A	S	R	Observation/ Reflection
I take time to observe each child each week.				
I find that regular observations help build my relationship with each child.				
I sometimes create specific questions for my observation. (How is Sam building with blocks?)				
I keep records of each observation (anecdotal notes, photos).				
I review the observation documentation to deepen my understanding and use as a basis for planning.				
I create individual written plans for each child (or each child within the group).				
I use a system of ongoing assessment to track each child's development.				
I regularly discuss each child's development with his or her parents.				
A = Always, S = Sometimes, R = Rarely				

Emotional Development and Attachment	A	S	R	Observation/ Reflection
I understand how young infants show me they need comfort (seek closeness, cry).				
I have many strategies to help calm a young infant (swaddling, holding upright, murmuring, rocking).				
I notice and support the ways a young or mobile infant begins to comfort himself (sucking fingers, lovey).				
I help toddlers recover from tantrums (stay nearby, say, "You were so upset!").				
I maintain a calm and pleasant attitude throughout the day.				
I understand what babies are feeling (facial expressions, body language).				
I use my face and words to tell babies I understand their feelings.				
I use my facial expressions to stay in touch with mobile infants and toddlers over a distance.				
I play games with babies imitating each other's expressions or "making happy faces, making angry faces."				
I use many words to describe feelings, read books about feelings, and sing songs about feelings.				
I respond quickly and sensitively to each young baby's cues.				
I encourage mobile infants to move and explore by letting them know I'm keeping them safe (smiling, using words, "I see you, I'm right here.").				
I have thought about my own childhood relationships and understand what made me feel safe and understood and what did not.				
A = Always, S = Sometimes, R = Rarely				

Social Development with Peers	A	S	R	Observation/ Reflection
I provide opportunities for infants and toddlers to become interested in peers (place infants near each other, provide materials for toddlers to use together).				
I watch for opportunities to support the development of prosocial behaviors ("Touch gently" "You're such a good friend!").				
I support the development of play skills as part of social development ("Let's see if Lily wants to play, with us," expand complexity of play and include others).				
I help toddlers negotiate conflicts (give them time to sort it out, move in when needed, use feeling words, restore relationships).				
I help toddlers manage aggressive feelings (stay nearby; say, "You are very angry! You can tell me, 'I'm angry'").				
A = Always, S = Sometimes, R = Rarely				

Learning and Thinking	A	S	R	Observation/ Reflection
I provide opportunities for infants and toddlers to learn about cause and effect, including being responsive to their cues.				
I support discoveries about object permanence, for example, in games like peek-a-boo.				
I provide opportunities for discoveries about using tools, including sand shovels and paintbrushes.				
I provide opportunities for discoveries about spatial relationships, such as tunnels for crawling through or cups to stack.				
I provide opportunities for discoveries about categories, including sorting colors, toy animals, and blocks.				
I provide opportunities for discoveries about numeracy and quantity.				
I provide opportunities for discoveries about nature.				
I provide opportunities for discoveries about each child's home culture.				
A = Always, S = Sometimes, R = Rarely				

Language, Literacy, and Music Development	A	S	R	Observation/ Reflection
I talk frequently and responsively with infants.				
I use words of affection from each child's home language				
I use sign language when appropriate.				
I talk about what I am doing (self-talk), about what the child is doing (parallel talk), and about things the child and I are paying attention to together (shared attention).				
I read to each child each day.				
I sing songs and use fingerplays throughout the day.				
I play music and sing songs from different cultures.				
I sing songs to help with transitions such as a consistent hello or goodbye song.				
I have pictures of familiar people and objects for the babies to see and talk about.				
I provide developmentally appropriate and culturally relevant cloth and cardboard books in many areas of the room.				
I provide one special area of the room with a short bookshelf, the covers of the books visible, and a comfortable space for children and teachers.				
Place toys that make music together in a container on a shelf or in a corner of the room.				
A = Always, S = Sometimes, R = Rarely				

Fine Motor	A	S	R	Observation/ Reflection
Fine Motor—Reaching and Grasping I provide many sizes of toys. I provide many opportunities for children to explore and experiment with toys they can grasp, bang together, place in containers, etc.				
Fine Motor-Bilateral Coordination (use of both sides of their bodies together) I provide many opportunities for children to develop bilateral coordination.				
Fine Motor—Self-Help Skills I provide opportunities for mobile infants, toddlers, and twos to feed themselves with fingers and spoons. I encourage and support mobile infants, toddlers, and twos to help with dressing themselves.				
Manipulation Area I provide a manipulation area with a rich variety of toys and materials—puzzles, stacking rings, large beads to string, etc. I engage in reciprocal conversations with children in the manipulation area. I provide books in the manipulation area.				
Construction Area I provide a construction area for mobile infants, toddlers, and twos with a rich variety of toys and materials. I engage in reciprocal conversations with children in the manipulation area. I support teacher/child and peer relationships as children develop their fine motor, manipulation, and construction interests and skills.				
A = Always, S = Sometimes, R = Rarely				

Movement and Motor Development	A	S	R	Observation/ Reflection
I provide opportunities for infants and toddlers to practice movement throughout the day.				
I ensure that each infant has floor time every day.				
I do not use swings, bouncy chairs, or walkers.				
I provide opportunities for infants and toddlers to challenge their balance and posture.				
I provide opportunities for infants and toddlers to use their bodies in new ways to achieve their goals.				
I provide opportunities for reaching and kicking that make things happen.				
I provide opportunities for infants and toddlers to move their bodies to the rhythm of music.				
I provide opportunities for practicing each new stage of mobility.				
A = Always, S = Sometimes, R = Rarely				

Creativity, Symbolic Play, Sensory Development	A	S	R	Observation Reflection
I encourage open-ended experimentation with creative materials. I do not require children to make a product when using creative materials.				
I use rich, descriptive language to describe how children are using materials.				
I observe children's interests and provide opportunities for them to expand their interest and continue investigating the properties of, for example, water or light.				
I am patient and gently support children who are hesitant or who do not like to touch certain materials or textures.				
I provide creative materials that encourage children of all ages to experiment, problem-solve, and create—nontoxic paint, fingerpaint, glue, and crayons. I add unique natural materials—twigs, grass, and sand.				
I provide a variety of sensory experiences both indoors and outdoors—sound and touch boxes, musical toys, materials with different textures. I provide an area for water and sand play.				
I provide an area for symbolic/dramatic play that has many culturally relevant materials to encourage children to pretend.				
A = Always, S = Sometimes, R = Rarely				

Nature and Outdoor Learning	A	S	R	Observation/ Reflection
I provide opportunities for infants and toddlers to learn about weather and seasons.				
I support discoveries of plants.				
I provide opportunities for discoveries of animals and insects.				
I provide opportunities for discoveries about the joys of outdoors.				
A = Always, S = Sometimes, R = Rarely				

References

Administration of Children and Families. (2003). *Child abuse and prevention treatment act*. Retrieved September 30, 2007, from http://www.acf.hhs.gov/programs/cb/lawspolicies/cblaws/capta03/capta_manual.pdf

Adolph, K., & Berger, S. (2006). Motor development. In W. Damon & R. Lerner (Series Eds.) & D. Kuhn & R. S. Siegler (Vol. Eds.), *Handbook of child psychology: Vol 2: Cognition, perception, and language* (6th ed., pp. 161–213). New York: Wiley.

Adolph, K. E. & Robinson, S. R. (2008). In defense of change processes. *Child Development, 79*, 1648–1653.

Ainsworth, M. D., Blehar, M. C., Waters, E., & Wall, S. (1978). *Patterns of attachment: A psychological study of the strange situation*. Hillsdale, NJ: Erlbaum.

American Academy of Pediatrics. (1997). Breastfeeding and the use of human milk. *Pediatrics, 100*(6), 1035–1039.

American Academy of Pediatrics. (2002). *National standards for health and safety in child care*. Lake Forest, IL: American Academy of Pediatrics.

American Academy of Pediatrics. (2005). *Diapering*. Retrieved December 13, 2006, from http://www.healthykids.us/chapters/diapering_main.htm

American Academy of Pediatrics. (2009a reaffirmed). Policy Statement: Coparent or second parent adoption by same sex couples. *Pediatrics, 109*(2), 339–340. Retrieved from: http://aappolicy.aappublications.org/cgi/content/full/pediatrics;109/2/341.pdf

American Academy of Pediatrics. (2009b reaffirmed). Technical Statement: Coparent or second parent adoption by same sex couples. *Pediatrics, 109*(2), 419–420.

American Academy of Pediatrics. (2010). Policy statement: Prevention of drowning committee on injury, violence, and poison prevention. *Pediatrics, 126*(1), 178–185.

American Association of Pediatric Dentists. (2007). *Thumb, finger, and pacifier habits*. Retrieved July 1, 2007, from http://www.aapd.org/publications/brochures/tfphabits.asp

American College of Nurse-Midwives. (n.d.). *The comprehensive benefits of breastfeeding*. Retrieved from: http://gotmom.org/The-Comprehensive-Benefits-of-Breastfeeding

American Optometric Association. (2012). *Infant vision: Birth to 24 months of age*. Retrieved from http://www.aoa.org/x9420.xml#2

American Psychological Association. (2004). *Sexual orientation, parents, & children*. Retrieved from: http://www.apa.org/about/governance/council/policy/parenting.aspx

Arnheim, R. (1972). *Toward a psychology of art*. Berkeley and Los Angeles: University of California Press.

ASL for Babies. (n.d.). Retrieved January, 2008, from http://www.aslpro.com/cgibin/aslpro/aslpro.cgi

Autism Society. (n.d.). About autism. Retrieved from http://www.autism-society.org/about-autism

Ayman-Nolley, S. (1999). A Piagetian perspective on the dialectic process of creativity. *Creativity Research Journal, 12*(4), 267–275.

Baldwin, J. M. (1975). *Thought and things: A study of the development and meaning of thought or generic logic* (Vol. III & IV). New York: Arno Press.

Bandura, A. (1986). *Social foundations of thought and action: A social cognitive theory*. Englewood Cliffs, N.J.: Prentice-Hall.

Bandura, A. (1997). *Self-efficacy: The exercise of control*. New York: Freeman.

Barnard, K., & Condon, M. (2004). *Baby cues*. Seattle, WA: NCASTAVE.

Bennett, T. (2002). *Buffering the effects of maternal depression*. Retrieved October 26, 2007, from http://www.head.startinfo.org/publications/hsbulletin73/hsb73_08.htm

Berk, L. E., & Winsler, A. (1995). *Scaffolding children's learning: Vygotsky and early childhood education*. Washington, DC: NAEYC.

Bernier, A., Carlson, S. M., and Whipple, N. (2010). From external regulation to self-regulation: Early parenting precursors of young children's executive functioning. *Child Development, 81*, 326–339.

Bodrova, E., & Leong, D. J. (2007). *Tools of the mind*. Upper Saddle River, NJ: Pearson Education.

Bogat, A. G., DeJonghe, E., Levendosky, A. A., Davidson, W. S., & von Eye, A. (2006). Trauma symptoms among infants exposed to intimate partner violence. *Child Abuse and Neglect, 30*(2), 109–125.

Bond, L. (1996). *Norm and criterion-references testing.* Retrieved November 18, 2007, from http://pareonline. net/getvn.asp?v=5&n=2

Bornstein, M. (2006) "On the significance of social relationships in the development of children's earliest symbolic play: An ecological perspective" in Göncü, A. and Gaskins, S. (eds) *Play and development. Evolutionary, sociocultural and functional perspectives,* Mahwa, NJ: Lawrence Erlbaum Associates.

Bowlby, J. (1969). *Attachment and loss: Vol. 1: Attachment.* New York: Basic Books.

Bowlby, J. (1979). *The making and breaking of affectional bonds.* London: Tavistock.

Brazelton, T. B., & Sparrow, J. (2006). *Touchpoints: Your child's emotional and behavioral development.* Cambridge, MA: Da Capo Press.

Bretherton, I. (1985). *Attachment theory: Retrospect and prospect.* Monographs of the Society for Research in Child Development, 50(1–2, Se r i a l No. 209). Oxford, UK: Blackwell.

Bretherton, I., Seligman, S., Solomon, J., Crowell, J., & McIntosh, J. (2011). "If I could tell the judge something about attachment. . . ." Perspectives on attachment theory in the family law courtroom. *Family Court Review, 49*(3) 539–548.

Brett, A., Moore, R. C., & Provenzo, J. E. (1993). *The complete playground book.* Syracuse: Syracuse University Press.

Bronfenbrenner, U. (2004). *Making human beings human: Bioecological perspectives on human development.* Thousand Oaks, CA: Sage.

Brooker, L., & Woodhead, M. (Eds.). (2010). *Culture and learning. Early childhood in focus 6.* United Kingdom: The Open University.

Brooks, R. & Meltzoff, A.N. (2005) The development of gaze following and its relation to language. *Developmental Science, 8*(6), 535–543.

Brown, R. (1973). *A first language: The early stages.* London: George Allen & Unwin.

Brownell, C. A., & Kopp, C. B. (2007). *Socioemotional development in the toddler years. Transitions and transformations.* New York: The Guilford Press.

Brownell, C. A., Ramani, G. B., & Zerwas, S. (2006). Becoming a social partner with peers: Cooperation and social understanding in one- and two-year-olds. *Child Development, 77*(4), 803–821.

Bruner, J. (1990). *Acts of meaning.* Cambridge, MA: Harvard University Press.

Bruner, J. (1996). What we have learned about early learning. *European Early Childhood Education Research Journal, 4*(1), 5–16.

Bruner, J. (1996a). *The culture of education.* Cambridge, MA: Harvard University Press.

Burwick, A., & Bellotti, J. (2005). *Creating paths to father involvement: Lessons from Early Head Start. Issue brief.* Retrieved October 24, 2007, from http:// www.mathematica-mpr.com/publications/pdfs/ creatingpaths.pdf

Cacchione, T., Möhring, W., & Bertin, E. (2011). What is it about Picasso? Infants' categorical and discriminatory abilities in the visual arts. *Psychology of Aesthetics, Creativity, and the Arts,* no pagination specified.

Carlson, E. A., & Sroufe, L. A. (1995). Contribution of attachment theory to developmental psychopathology. In D. Cicchetti & D. Cohen (Eds.), *Developmental psychopathology: Vol. 1. Theory and methods* (pp. 581–617). Oxford, UK: Wiley.

Carvajal, F., & Iglesia, J. (2002). Face-to-face emotion interaction studies in Down syndrome infants. *International Journal of Behavioral Development, 26*(2), 104–112.

Casby, M. W. (2003). The development of play in infants, toddlers, and young children. *Communication Disorders Quarterly, 24,* 175–183.

Centers for Disease Control and Prevention (CDC). (2007). *Recommended immunizations for babies.* Retrieved November 25, 2007, from http://www.cdc.gov/ vaccines/spec-grps/infants/downloads/rec-iz-babies.pdf

Centers for Disease Control and Prevention (CDC). (2011a). *Hearing loss in children.* Retrieved from http:// www.cdc.gov/ncbddd/hearingloss/facts.html

Centers for Disease Control and Prevention (CDC). (2011b). *Sudden unexpected infant death and sudden infant death syndrome.* Retrieved from http://www.cdc. gov/sids

Cheour-Luhtanen, M., Alho, K., Sainio, K., Rinne, T., Reinikainen, K., Pohjavuori, M., & Renlund, M. (1996). The ontogenetically earliest discriminative response of the human brain. *Psychophysiology, 33:* 478–481.

ChildHelp. (n.d.) *Definitions of child abuse.* Retrieved from http://www.childhelp.org/page/-/pdfs/Child-Abuse-Definitions.pdf

Child Study Center. (2007). *Research projects.* Retrieved July 12, 2008, from http://www.faculty.virginia.edu/ childstudycenter/researchprojects.html

Civitas. (n.d.). *Building Blocks: A child care professional's review of the basic standards that guide your practice.* Retrieved December 17, 2006, from http://nrc.uchsc. edu/RESOURCES/BuildingBlocks.pdf

Claxton, L. J., Keen, R., & McCarty, M. E. (2003). Evidence of motor planning in infant reaching behavior. *American Psychological Society, 14*(4), 354–356.

Clements, R. (2004) An investigation of the state of outdoor play. *Contemporary Issues in Early Childhood, 5*(1), 68–80.

Courage, M. L., & Richards, J. E. (2008) Attention. In Marshall Haith & Janette Benson (Eds.), *Encyclopedia of early childhood development*. New York: Elsevier.

Cryer, D., Harms, T., & Bourland, B. (1987). *Active learning for infants*. Columbus, OH: Pearson-Dale Seymour Publications.

Curtis, D., & Carter, M. (2000). *The art of awareness: How observation can transform your teaching*. St. Paul, MN: Redleaf Press.

Curtis, D., & Carter, M. (2003). *Designs for living and learning: Transforming early childhood environments*. St. Paul, MN: Redleaf Press.

Dale, L. P., O'Hara, E. A., Keen, J., & Porges, S. W. (2011). Infant regulatory disorders: temperamental, physiological, and behavioral features. *Journal of Developmental Behavioral Pediatrics, 32*(3), 216–224.

de Boer, B., & Kuhl, P. (2003). *Investigating the role of infant-directed speech with a computer model*. Retrieved from http://ilabs.washington.edu/kuhl/pdf/deBoer_Kuhl_2003.pdf

Deiner, P., & Qiu, W. (2007). Embedding physical activity and nutrition in early care and education programs. *ZERO TO THREE Bulletin, 28*(1) 13–17.

DeLoache, J. S. (2005, August). Mindful of symbols. *Scientific American, 36*, 72–77.

Dichtelmiller, M., & Ensler, L. (2004, January). *Infant/toddler assessment: One program's experience*. Retrieved November 18, 2007, from http://www.journal.naeyc.org/btj/200401/dichtel.asp

Duckworth, E. (1987). *The having of wonderful ideas and other essays on teaching and learning*. New York: Teachers College Press.

Eckerman, C. O., & Didow, S. M. (1996). Nonverbal imitation and toddlers' mastery of verbal means of achieving coordinated action. *Developmental Psychology, 32*, 141–152.

Eckerman, C. O., & Peterman, K. (2001). Peers and infant social/communicative development. In G. Bremner & A. Fogel (Eds.), *Blackwell handbook of infant development* (pp. 326–350). Oxford: Blackwell.

EHSNRC. (1996). *Developmental screening, assessment, and evaluation: Key elements for individualizing curricula in Early Head Start programs*. Washington, DC: Early Head Start National Resource Center.

Eisenberg, N., & Fabes, R. A. (1998). Prosocial development. In W. Damon (Series Ed.) & G. Harris. (2008). Development of taste and food preferences in children. *Current Opinions in Clinical Nutrition and Metabolic Care, 11*(3), 315–319.

Emde, R. N., & Clymen, R. B. (1997). "We hold these truths to be self-evident": The origins of moral motives in individual activity and shared experience." In S. W. J. D. Noshpitz (Series Ed.), & S. Greenspan & J. Osofsky (Vol. Eds.), *Handbook of child and adolescent psychiatry: Vol. I. Infants and preschoolers: Development and syndromes* (320–339). New York: Wiley.

Environments. (2008). www.environments.com, 1-800-EI-CHILD.

EQ Initiative. (2007). *Spoiling. Expanding quality in infant/toddler care*. Colorado Department of Education.

Erikson, E. (1950). *Childhood and society*. New York: Norton.

Erikson, E. H. (1963). *Childhood and society*. New York: Norton.

Fagot, B. I. (1997). Attachment, parenting, and peer interactions of toddler children. *Developmental Psychology, 33*(3), 489–499.

Fenson, L., Dale, P., Reznick, S., Bates, E., Thal, D., & Pethick, S. (1994). Variability in early communicative development. *Monograph of the Society for Research in Child Development, 242*(59).

Forman, G., & Hall, E. (2005). *Social clay*. Retrieved September 15, 2007, from www.videatives.com/content-new/store/product_info.php?products_id=77

Gandini, L. (2001). Reggio Emilia: Experiencing life in an infant-toddler center. In L. Gandini & C. P. Edwards (Eds.), *Bambini. The Italian approach to infant/toddler care* (pp. 49–54). New York: Teachers College Press.

Gandini, L., & Goldhaber, J. (2001). Two reflections about documentation. In L. Gandini & C. Edwards (Eds.), *Bambini: The Italian approach to infant/toddler care* (pp. 124–145). New York: Teacher's College Press.

Gesell, A., Halverson, H. M., & Amatruda, C. S. (1940) *The first five years of life: A guide to the study of the preschool child, from the Yale clinic of child development*. New York: Harper's.

Great Start DC. (2011). Preparing our infant and toddler professional workforce for the 21st century. Retrieved from http://greatstartdc.org/gstart2011/wp-content/uploads/2011/04/Great-Start-DC-Infant-and-Toddler-Workforce-Action-Plan-Full-Report.pdf

Greene, A. (2007). *Separation anxiety and object permanence*. Retrieved November 10, 2007, from http://www.drgreene.com

Greenman, J. (2003). *What do they do?* Retrieved October 30, 2007, from http://www.brighthorizons.com/site/pages/What_DoTHEYDorr.pdf

Greenman, J. (2004). The experience of space, the pleasure of place. *Child Care Information Exchange*, 34–37.

Gunnar, M. R., & Cheatham, C. L. (2003). Brain and behavior interface: Stress and the developing brain. *Infant Mental Health Journal*, 24: 195–211.

Hanline, M. F., Milton, S., & Phelps, P. C. (2007). Influence of disability, gender, and time engaged on the developmental level of children's art work: Findings from three years of observation. *Journal of Early Intervention, 29*(2), 141–154.

Hanna, E., & Meltzoff, A. N. (1993). Peer imitation by toddlers in laboratory, home, and day-care contexts: Implications for social learning and memory. *Developmental Psychology 29*, 701–710.

Harms, T., Cryer, D., & Clifford, R. M. (2006). *Infant/toddler environment rating scale—Revised*. New York: Teachers College Press.

Harris, G. (2008). Development of taste and food preferences in children. *Current Opinion in Clinical Nutrition and Metabolic Care, 11*(3), 315–319.

Hart, B., & Risley, T. (1995). *Meaningful differences in everyday lives*. Baltimore: Brookes.

Hart, B., & Risley, T. (1999). *The social world of children learning to talk*. Baltimore: Brookes.

Hartup, W. W. (1996). The company they keep: Friendships and their developmental significance. *Child Development, 67*, 1–13.

Hastings, P. D., Utendale, W. T., & Sullivan, C. (2007). The socialization of prosocial development. In J. E. Grusec & P. D. Hastings (Eds.) *Handbook of socialization: Theory and research*. Guilford: New York.

Hay, D. F. (2006). Yours and mine: Toddlers' talk about possessions with familiar peers. *The British Psychological Society, 24*, 39–52.

Hay, D. F., & Cook, K. V. (2007). The transformation of prosocial behavior from infancy to childhood. In C. A. Brownell & C. B. Kopp (Eds.), *Socioemotional development in the toddler years* (pp. 100–131). Transitions and transformations. New York: Guilford Press.

Hay, D. F., Payne, A., & Chadwick, A. (2004). Peer relations in childhood. *Journal of Child Psychology and Psychiatry, 45*, 84–108

Heinzer, M. (2005). Obesity in infancy: Questions, more questions, and few answers. *Newborn and Infant Nursing Review, 5*(4), 194–202.

Hertenstein, M. J. (2011). The communicative functions of touch in adulthood. In M. Hertenstein & S. Weiss (Eds.), *The handbook of touch: Neuroscience, behavioral, and applied perspectives*. New York: Springer Publications.

High/Scope. (n.d.). *Infant-Toddler COR*. Retrieved November 18, 2007, from http://www.highscope.org/Content.asp?ContentId=85

Hinde, R. (1992a). Ethological and relationship approaches. In R. Vasta, *Six theories of child development: Revised formulations and current issues* (pp. 251–285). London: JKP Press.

Hinde, R. (1992b). Ethological and relationship approaches. In R. Vasta (Ed.), *Six theories of child development: Revised formulations and current issues* (pp. 251–285). London: JKP Press.

Honig, A. (1995). Singing with infants and toddlers. *Young Children, 52*(5), 72.

Honig, A. S. (2002). *Secure relationships. Nurturing infant/toddler attachment in early care settings*. Washington, DC: NAEYC.

Honig, A. S. (2007). *Exploring nature with your baby*. Retrieved October 27, 2007, from http://content.scholastic.com/browse/article.jsp?id=1049

Hossain, Z., Field, T., Pickens, J., & Gonzalez, J. (1995). Infants of "depressed" mothers interact better with their nondepressed fathers. *Infant Mental Health Journal, 15*, 348–357.

Howes, C. (1988). Peer interaction in young children. *Monographs of the Society for Research in Child Development* (serial no. 217), 53(1).

Howes, C., & Hamilton, C. E. (1992). Children's relationships with caregivers: Mothers and childcare teachers. *Child Development, 63*, 859–866.

Howes, C. (2009). Friendship in early childhood. In K. H. Rubin, W. M. Bukowski, & B. Laursen (Eds.). *Handbook of peer interactions, relationships, and groups* (pp. 180–194). New York: Guilford Press.

Howes, C., & Phillipsen, L. (1998). Continuity in children's relationships with peers. *Social Development, 7*(3), 340–349.

Hu, H., Téllez-Rojo, M. M., Bellinger, D., Smith, D., Ettinger, A. S., Lamadrid-Figueroa, H., Schwartz, J., Schnaas, L., Mercado-García, A., & Hernández-Avila, M. (2006). Fetal lead exposure at each stage of pregnancy as a predictor of infant mental development. *Environmental Health Perspectives, 114*(11), 1730–1735.

Ilari, B., & Johnson-Green, E. (2002). Music for young children. *ZERO TO THREE, 23*(1), 49–52.

Iverson, J. M., & Wozniak, R. H. (2007). Variation in vocal-motor development in infant siblings of children with autism. *Journal of Autism and Developmental Disorders, 37*, 158–170.

Izard, C., & Malateste, C. (1987). Perspectives on emotional development I: Differential emotions theory of early emotional development. In J. D. Osofsky, *Handbook of infant development* (2nd ed., pp. 494–554). New York: Wiley.

Jablon, J., Dombro, A., & Dichtelmiller, M. (1999). *The power of observation*. Washington, DC: Teaching Strategies.

Johnson, S. P. (2010). How infants learn about the visual world. *Cognitive Science, 34*, 1158–1184.

Kaplan, L. J. (1978). *Oneness & separateness: From infant to individual*. New York: Simon & Schuster.

Karruppaswamey, N., & Myers-Walls, J. (n.d.). *Providers talking with parents about divorce*. Retrieved October 25, 2007, from http://www.ces.purdue.edu/providerparent/Parent-Provider%20Relationships/ProvidersTalking.htme

Katz, J. R. (2004). Building peer relationships in talk: Toddlers' peer conversations in childcare. *Discourse Studies, 6*(3), 329–347.

Katz, J., & Snow, C. (2000). Language development in early childhood: The role of social interaction in different care environments. In D. Cryer & T. Harms (Eds.), *Infants and toddlers in out-of-home care* (pp. 49–86). Baltimore, MD: Paul H. Brookes.

Kellogg, R. (1970). *Analyzing children's art*. Palo Alto, CA: Mayfield.

Kinzler, K. D., & Spelke, E. S. (2007). Core systems in human cognition. *Progress in Brain Research, 164*, 257–264.

Klein, H. A. (1991). Temperament and childhood group care adjustment: A cross-cultural comparison. *Early Childhood Research Quarterly, 6*(2), 211–224.

Klinnert, M. D., Emde, R. N., Butterfield, P., & Campos, J. J. (1986). Social referencing: The infant's use of emotional signals from a friendly adult with mother present. *Developmental Psychology, 22*(1), 427–432.

Kohl, M. F. (2002). *First art: Art experiences for toddlers and twos*. New York: Gryphon House.

Kohnstamm, G. A. (1989). Temperament in childhood: Cross-cultural and sex differences. In G. A. Kohnstamm, J. E. Bates, & M. K. Rothbart (Eds.), *Temperament in childhood* (pp. 483–508). New York: Wiley.

Kuhl, P. K. (2011). Who's talking? *Science, 333*, 529.

Kuhl, P. K., Tsao, F., & Liu, H. (2003). Foreign-language experience in infancy: Effects of short-term exposure and social interaction on phonetic learning. *Proceedings of the National Academy of Sciences, 100*, pp. 9096–9101. Washington, DC: National Academy Press.

Kupetz, B., & Green, E. (1997). Sharing books with infants and toddlers: Facing the challenges. *Young Children, 52*(2), 22–27.

Lally, J. (1995). The impact of child care policies and practices on infant/toddler identity formation. *Young Children, 51*(1), 58–67.

Lally, J. (2000, March). *Infants have their own curriculum: A responsive approach to curriculum planning for infants and toddlers*. Retrieved March 5, 2008, from http://www.headstartinfo.org/publications/hsbulletin67/hsb67_03.htm

Lally, J. R., Griffin, A., Fenichel, E., Segal, M., Szanton, E., & Weissbourd, B. (2003). *Caring for infants and toddlers in groups*. Washington, DC: ZERO TO THREE Press.

LeDoux, J. (2000). Emotion circuits in the brain. *Annual Review of Neuroscience, 23*, 155–184.

Leo, I., & Simon, F. (2009). Newborns' mooney-face perception. *Infancy, 14*(6), 641–653.

Lieberman, A. F. (1993). *The emotional life of the toddler*. New York: Free Press.

Lindavist, G. (2003). Vygotsky's theory of creativity. *Creative Research Journal, 15*(2 & 3), 245–251.

Lokken, G. (2000a). The playful quality of the toddling style. *International Journal of Qualitative Education, 13*(5), 531–542.

Lokken, G. (2000b). Tracing the social style of toddler peers. *Scandinavian Journal of Educational Research, 44*(2), 163–176.

Losonczy, M. (2004). Infants' emotional expressions in response to social and non-social stimuli. *International Social Science Review, 79*(3/4), 124–136.

Lourdes, D., O'Hara, E. A., Keen, J. & Porges, S. W. (2011) Infant regulatory disorders: Temperamental, physiological, and behavioral features. *Journal of Developmental & Behavioral Pediatrics, 32*(3), 216–224. Retrieved from http://journals.lww.com/jrnldbp/Abstract/2011/04000/Infant_Regulatory_Disorders__Temperamental.7.aspx

Lowenfeld, V. (1947). *Creative and mental growth*. New York: Macmillan.

Lowenfeld, V. (1964). *Creative and mental growth* (4th ed.). New York: Macmillan.

Lowenfeld, V., & Brittain, W. L. (1987). *Creative and mental growth*. New York: Macmillan.

Macfarlane, A. (1975). Olfaction in the development of social preferences in the human neonate. *Ciba Foundation Symposium* (pp. 103–117).

Mahler, M. S. (1975). *The psychological birth of the infant*. New York: Basic Books.

Mahler, M., Pine, F., & Bergman, A. (1975). *The psychological birth of the human infant*. New York: Basic Books.

Main, M. (1983). Exploration, play and cognitive functioning as related to infant-mother attachment. *Infant Behavior and Development, 6*, 167–174.

Main, M., Kaplan, N., & Cassidy, J. (1985). Security in infancy, childhood, and adulthood: A move to the level of representation. In I. Bretherton & E. Waters (Eds.) *Growing points of attachment theory and research.* Monographs of the Society for Research in Child Development, vol. *50*(1–2), serial no. 209. Chicago: University of Chicago Press, pp. 66–104.

Malchiodi, C. A. (Ed.). (2008). *Creative interventions with traumatized children.* Oxford: Guilford.

Mann, M., Pearl, P., & Behle, B. (2004). Effects of parent education on knowledge and attitudes. *Adolescence, 39*(154), 355–360.

Marrs, J., Trumbley, S. & Malik, G. (2011) Early childhood dental caries: Dental caries overview. *Pediatric Nursing, 37*(1), 9–15. Retrieved from http://www.medscape.com/viewarticle/740461

Mayo Clinic. (2006). *Introducing solid foods: What you need to know.* Retrieved December 26, 2006, from http://www.mayoclinic.com/health/healthy-baby/PR00029

Mayseless, O., & Scher, A. (2000). Mother's attachment concerns regarding spouse and infant's temperament as modulators of maternal separation anxiety. *The Journal of Child Psychology and Psychiatry and Allied Disciplines, 41*, 917–925.

McElwain, N. L., Cox, M. J., Burchinal, M. R., & Macfie, J. (2003). Differentiating among insecure mother-infant attachment classifications: A focus on child-friend interaction and exploration during solitary play at 36 months. *Attachment & Human Development, 5*(2), 136–164.

MedlinePlus. (2011). Reactive attachment disorder of infancy or early childhood. Retrieved from http://www.nlm.nih.gov/medlineplus/ency/article/001547.htm

Meisels, S., Dombro, A., Marsden, D., Weston, D., & Jewkes, A. (2003). *The ounce scale.* New York: Pearson Early Learning.

Meltzoff, A. (1985). Immediate and deferred imitation in fourteen- and twenty-four-month-old infants. *Child Development, 56*, 62–72.

Meltzoff, A. N., Kuhl, P. K., Movellan, J., & Sejnowski, T. J. (2009). Foundations for a New Science of Learning. *Science, 325*, 284–288.

Miller, K. (1999) *Simple Steps.* New York: Gryphon House.

NASPE. (2002). Active start: A statement of physical activity guidelines for children birth to five years. Retrieved July 28, 2007, from http://www.aahperd.org/NASPE/template.cfm?template=ns_active.html

National Association for the Education of Young Children. (2011). Code of Ethical Conduct and Statement of Commitment. Retrieved from http://www.naeyc.org/positionstatements/ethical_conduct

National Association for the Education of Young Children. (n.d.). *Toilet learning for toddlers.* Retrieved November 25, 2007, from http://www.naeyc.org/ece/1998/17.asp

National Center for Family Literacy Web site. Accessed March 9, 2008, at http://www.famlit.org

National Center for Health Statistics. (2009). *Teen births.* Retrieved from http://www.cdc.gov/nchs/fastats/teenbrth.htm

National Center for Learning Disabilities. (2010). *What is executive function?* Retrieved from http://www.ncld.org/ld-basics/ld-aamp-executive-functioning/basic-effacts/what-is-executive-function

National Infant Toddler Childcare Initiative. (2010). Infant/toddler early learning guidelines fact sheet. Retrieved from main.zerotothree.org/site/DocServer/Infant-Toddler_Early_Learning_Guidelines_Factsheet.pdf

National Institute of Child Health and Development (NICHD). (2006). *Safe sleep for your baby: Ten ways to reduce the risk of sudden infant death syndrome* (SIDS). Retrieved from http://www.nichd.nih.gov/publications/pubs/safesleepgen.cfm

National Resource Center for Health and Safety in Child Care and Early Education. (n.d.). *Healthy kids, healthy care: Parents as partners in promoting healthy and safe child care.* Retrieved December 5, 2006, from http://www.healthykids.us/chapters/toys_2.htm

National Scientific Council on the Developing Child. (2004). *Children's emotional development is built into the architecture of their brains.* Working Paper #2. Retrieved from http://developingchild.harvard.edu

National Scientific Council on the Developing Child. (2007). *The timing and quality of early experiences combine to shape brain architecture.* Working paper No. 5. Retrieved from http://developingchild.harvard.edu

New, R. (2000). *Reggio Emilia: Catalyst for change and conversation.* ERIC Digest. Retrieved July 2, 2007, from ERIC Clearinghouse on Elementary and Early Childhood Education: http://www.ericdigests.org/2001-3/reggio.htm

NICHD Early Child Care Research Network. (1999). Chronicity of maternal depressive symptoms, maternal sensitivity, and child functioning at 36 months. *Developmental Psychology, 35*(5), 1297–1310.

NICHD Early Child Care Research Network. (2006). Infant-mother attachment classification: Risk and protection to changing maternal caregiving quality. *Developmental Psychology, 42*(1), 38–58.

NIDCD. (2000). *Speech and language development milestones.* Retrieved December 11, 2007, from http://www.nidcd.nih.gov/health/voice/speechandlanguage.asp

Office of Head Start. (2005). *Head Start Program Instruction (ACYF-PI-HS-05-03).* Retrieved January 25, 2007, from www.acf.hhs.gov/programs/hsb/policy/pi2005/acyfpihs_05_03.html

Onunaku, N. (2005). *Improving maternal and infant mental health: Focus on maternal depression.* Los Angeles, CA: National Center for Infant and Early Childhood Health Policy at UCLA.

Osofsky, J. D. (1995). Children who witness domestic violence: The invisible victims. *Social Policy Report, 9*(3), 1–16.

Panksepp, J. (2000). Developing mechanisms of self-regulation. *Development and Psychopathology, 12*(3), 427–442.

Papoušek, M. (2011). Resilience, strengths, and regulatory capacities: Hidden resources in developmental disorders of infant mental health. *Infant Mental Health Journal: Special Issue: WAIMH 11th World Congress, Yokohama, Japan, Akachan ni Kanpai (Celebrating the Baby: Baby, Family, and Culture), 32*(1), 29–46.

Park, R. D., & Welsh, M. (1998). Social relationships & academic success. *Thrust for Educational Leadership, 28*(1), 32–34.

Payne, V. G., & Isaacs, L. D. (2005). *Human motor development: A lifespan approach.* 6th ed. Boston: McGraw-Hill.

Petitto, L. A., Berens, M. S., Kovelman, I., Dubins, M. H., Jasinska, K., & Shalinsky, M. (2011). The "Perceptual Wedge Hypothesis" as the basis for bilingual babies' phonetic processing advantage: New insights from fNIRS brain imaging. *Brain Language, 121*(2), 130–143. Retrieved from http://www.ncbi.nlm.nih.gov/pubmed/21724244

Phillips, D., & Crowell, N. (1994). *Cultural diversity and early education.* Retrieved October 26, 2007, from http://www.nap.edu/readingroom/books/earlyed/index.html

Phinney, J. S., & Baldelomar, O. A. (2011). Identity development in multiple cultural contexts. In Lene Arnett Jensen (Ed.), *Bridging cultural and developmental approaches to psychology: New syntheses in research and policy* (pp. 161–186). New York: Oxford University Press.

Piaget, J. (1951). *Play, dreams, and imitation in childhood.* New York: Norton.

Piaget, J. P. (1952). *The origins of intelligence in children.* New York: International Universities Press.

Piaget, J. (1954). *The construction of reality in the child.* New York: Basic Books.

Piaget, J. (1963). *The origins of intelligence in children.* New York: W. W. Norton.

Piaget, J. (1972). *To understand is to invent.* New York: Viking.

Piek, J. P. (2006). *Infant motor development.* Champaign, IL: Human Kinetics. *Play with a Purpose Catalog.* Development and Learning Products for Young Children (2008). Available at http://www.pwaponline.com or 1-888-330-1826.

Pomares, C. G., Schirrer, J., & Abadie, V. (2002). Analysis of the olfactory capacity of healthy children before language acquisition. *Journal of Developmental and Behavioral Pediatrics, 23*(4), 203–207.

Pubmed. (2009). *Cerebral palsy.* Retrieved from http://www.ncbi.nlm.nih.gov/pubmedhealth/PMH0001734

Raikes, H. (1993). Relationship duration in infant care: Time with a high-ability teacher and infant-teacher attachment. *Early Childhood Research Quarterly, 8,* 309–325.

Ramamoorthy, S., & Myers-Walls, J. (2006). *Talking to parents about problems in development.* Retrieved October 24, 2007, from http://www.ces.purdue.edu/providerparent/Parent-ChildcareProvider%20Relationships/TalkingAboutDev.htm

Rivkin, M. (1995). *The great outdoors: Restoring children's right to play outside.* Washington, DC: National Association for the Education of Young Children.

Rivkin, M. (2000, December). *Outdoor experiences for young children.* Retrieved October 31, 2007, from http://www.ericdigests.org/2001-3/children.htm

Rothbart, M. (2007). *Temperament, development, and personality. Current directions in psychological science, 16*(4), 207–212.

Rothbart, M. K., Derryberry, D., & Hershey, K. (2000). Stability of temperament in childhood: Laboratory infant assessment to parent report at seven years. In V. J. Molfese & D. L. Molfese (Eds.), *Temperament and personality development across the life span* (pp. 85–119). Hillsdale, NJ: Erlbaum.

Rubin, K. (2002). *The friendship factor.* New York: Penguin Books.

Rubin, K. H., & Coplan, R. J. (2004). Paying attention to and not neglecting social withdrawal and social isolation. *Merrill-Palmer Quarterly, 50,* 506–534.

Ryalls, B. O., Gul, R. E., & Ryalls, K. R. (2000). Infant imitation of peer and adult models: Evidence for a peer model advantage. *Merrill-Palmer Quarterly, 46*, 188–202.

Saffran, J. (2001). Words in a sea of sounds: The output of infant statistical learning. *Cognition, 81*(2), 149–169.

Sai, F. (2004). The role of the mother's voice in developing mother's face preference: Evidence for intermodal perception at birth. *Infant and Child Development, 14*(1), 29–50.

Sanchez, S. (1999). *Issues of language and culture impacting the early care of young Latino children.* Retrieved November 24, 2007, from http://www.nccic.org/pubs/sanchez99.html

Schiller, P. (2005). *The complete resource book for infants. Over 700 experiences for children from birth to 18 months.* Beltsville, MD: Gryphon House.

Scholastic Parents. (2007). *9 parent-tested ways to ease separation.* Retrieved November 17, 2007, from http://content.scholastic.com/browse/article.jsp?id=1368

Schöner, G. (2007). Development as change of system dynamics: Stability, instability, and emergence. In J. P. Spencer, M. S. C. Thomas, & J. L. McClelland (Eds.), *Toward a new grand theory of development? Connectionism and dynamic systems theory re-considered.* Oxford University Press: New York, NY:

Scott, K. A. (2009). Language outcomes of school-aged internationally adopted children: A systematic review of the literature. *Topics in Language Disorders, 29*, 65–81.

Sheese, B. E., Rothbart, M. K., Posner, M. I., White, L. K., & Fraundorf, S. H. (2008). Executive attention and self-regulation in infancy. *Infant Behavior and Development, 31*(3), 501–510.

Sheppard, M. (1994). Social support and maternal depression: A review and application of findings. *British Journal of Social Work, 24,* 287–310.

Shonkoff, J., & Phillips, D. (2000). *From neurons to neighborhoods.* Washington, DC: National Academy Press.

Siegel, D. (1999). *The developing mind: How relationships and the brain interact to shape who we are.* New York: Guilford.

Singer, D. G., & Revenson, T. A. (1996). *A Piaget primer: How a child thinks* (rev. ed.). New York: Plume/Penguin.

Spelke, E. (2000, November). Core knowledge. *American Psychologist,* 1233–1243.

Spelke, E., & Kinzler, K. (2007). Core knowledge. *Developmental Science, 10*(1), 89–96.

Spelke, E. S., Phillips, A. T., & Woodward, A. L. (1995). Infants' knowledge of object motion and human action. In D. Sperber, D. Premack, & A. Premack (Eds.), *Causal cognition: A multidisciplinary debate.* Oxford: Oxford University Press.

Story, M., Kaphingst, K., & French, S. (2006). The role of child care settings in obesity prevention. *The Future of Children, 16*(1), 143–168.

Swingley, D. (2009). Contributions of infant word learning to language development. *Philosophical Transactions of the Royal Society B, 364,* 3617–3622.

Tantrums. (2006). Retrieved November 15, 2007, from http://www.babycenter.com/0 tantrums 11569 bc

Teaching Strategies. (2006). *The creative curriculum for infants, toddlers & twos.* Washington, DC: Teaching Strategies.

Thelen, E., & Bates, E. (2003). Connectionism and dynamic systems: Are they really different? *Developmental Science 6*(4), 378–391.

Thiessen, E., Hill, E., & Saffran, J. (2005). Infant-directed speech facilitates word segmentation. *Infancy, 7*(1), 53–71.

Thomas, A., & Chess, S. (1977). *Temperament and development.* New York: Bruner-Mazel.

Torelli, L. (2002). Enhancing development through classroom design in Early Head Start. *The Magazine of the Head Start Association.* Retrieved July 9, 2008, from http://www.spacesforchildren.com/enhanc.html

Tremblay, R. E., & Nagin, D. S. (2005). The developmental origins of physical aggression in humans. In R. E. Tremblay, W. W. Hartup, & J. Archer (Eds.), *Developmental origins of aggression.* New York: Guilford.

Tremblay R. E., Nagin, D. S., Séguin, J. R., Zoccolillo, M., Zelazo, P. D., Boivin, M., Pérusse, D., & Japel, C. (2004). Physical aggression during early childhood: Trajectories and predictors. *Pediatrics, 114*(1), 43–50.

Trevarthen, C. (2001). Intrinsic motives for companionship in understanding: Their origin, development, and significance for infant mental health. *Infant Mental Health Journal, 22*(1–2), 95–131.

United States Agency for International Development (USAID). (2009). *USAID blindness program assists one million children in 23 countries.* Retrieved from http://www.usaid.gov/news-information/press-releases/usaid-blindness-program-assists-one-million-children-23-countries

United States Consumer Product Safety Commission. (n.d.) *Art and craft safety guide.* Retrieved from http://www.cpsc.gov/CPSCPUB/PUBS/5015.pdf

University of Illinois Extension. (2008). *Providing child care for the teen parent: A caregiver's guide*. Retrieved March 4, 2008, from http://www.urbanext.uiuc.edu/teencare/01.html

Vincent, S. (2011). Skin-to-skin contact. Part one: Just an hour of your time . . . *The Practising Midwife, 14*(5) 40–41.

VORT. (2004). *Hawaii early learning profile. (HELP® birth to 3)*. Palo Alto: VORT.

Vygotsky, L. S. (1962). *Thought and language*. Cambridge, MA: MIT Press.

Vygotsky, L. S. (1978). *Mind in society: The development of higher psychological processes*. Cambridge, MA: Harvard University Press.

Vygotsky, L. (1986). *Thought and language*. Cambridge, MA: MIT Press.

Vygotsky, L. (1987). *The collected works of L. S. Vygotsky. Volume 1: Problems of general psychology*. New York: Springer Publishing.

Warren, Z., Veenstra-VanderWeele, J., Stone, W., Bruzek, J. L., Nahmias, A. S., & Foss-Feig, J. H. (2011) A systematic review of early intensive intervention for autism spectrum disorders. *Pediatrics, 127*(5), 1303–1311.

Waters, E., & Cummings, E. M. (2000). A secure base from which to explore relationships. *Child Development, 71*, 164–172.

Waters, E., Hamilton, C., & Weinfield, N. (2000). The stability of attachment security from infancy to adolescence. *Child Development, 71*, 678–683.

Werker, J. F., Pons, F., Dietrich, C., Kajikawa, S., Fais, L., & Amano, S. (2007). Infant-directed speech supports phonetic category learning in English and Japanese. *Cognition, 103*(1), 147–162.

Westby, C. E. (1980). Assessment of cognitive and language abilities through play. *Language, speech, and hearing services in schools, 11*, 154–168.

Westby, C. E. (2000). A scale for assessing development of children's play. In K. Gitlin-Weiner, A. Sandgund, & C. Schaefer (Eds.), *Play diagnosis and assessment* (pp. 15–57). New York: Wiley.

WestEd. (1995). *The program for infant/toddler caregivers. Trainer's manual, module I: Social-emotional growth and socialization* (p. 21). Sacramento, CA: California Department of Education.

Whaley, K., & Rubenstein, T. (1994). How toddlers "do" friendship: A descriptive analysis of naturally occurring friendships in a group childcare setting. *Journal of Social and Personal Relationships, 11*, 383–400.

Whitehurst, G. J., Arnold, D. S., Epstein, J. N., Angell, A. L., Smith, M., & Fischel, J. E. (1994). A picture book reading intervention in day care and home for children from low-income families. *Developmental Psychology, 30*(5), 679–689.

Williamson, G., & Anzalone, M. (2001). *Sensory integration and self-regulation in infants and toddlers: Helping very young children interact with their environment*. Washington, DC: ZERO TO THREE.

Wittmer, D. S. (2009). *A focus on peers in the early years*. Washington, DC: ZERO TO THREE Press.

Wittmer, D. S., & Petersen, S. H. (2006). *Infant and toddler development and responsive program planning: A relationship-based approach*. Upper Saddle River, NJ: Pearson.

womenshealth.gov. (2011). Breastfeeding. Retrieved from http://www.womenshealth.gov/breastfeeding/why-breastfeeding-is-important

Wong, V., Hui, L. H., Lee, W. C., Leung, L. S., Ho, P. K., Lau, W. L., Fung, C. W., & Chung, B. (2004). A modified screening tool for autism. *Pediatrics, 114*(2), 166–176.

Woodward, A. L. (2009). Infants' grasp of others' intentions. *Current Directions in Psychological Science, 18*, 53–57.

Woodward, A. L., Markman, E. M., & Fitzsimmons, C. M. (1994). Rapid word learning in 13- and 18-month-olds. *Developmental Psychology, 30*(4), 553–556.

Yoshinaga-Itano, C., and Apuzzo, M. L. (1998). Identification of hearing loss after age 18 months is not early enough. *American Annals of the Deaf, 143*, 380–387

Yoshinaga-Itano, C., Sedey, A. L., Coulter, D. K., & Mehl, A. L. (1998) Language of early- and later-identified children with hearing loss. *Pediatrics, 102*(5), 1161–1171.

ZERO TO THREE website. Accessed March 9, 2008, at http:zerotothree.org.

Zwaigenbauma, L., Bryson, L., Rogers, T., Roberts, W., Brian, J., & Szatmari, P. (2005) Behavioral manifestations of autism in the first year of life. *International Journal of Developmental Neuroscience, 23*, 143–152. Retrieved from http://radlab.ucsd.edu/Zwaigenbaum.pdf

Index